# Handbook of Crisis Counseling, Intervention, and Prevention in the Schools

*Second Edition*

# Handbook of Crisis Counseling, Intervention, and Prevention in the Schools

*Second Edition*

Edited by

**Jonathan Sandoval**
*University of California, Davis*

LEA
2002

LAWRENCE ERLBAUM ASSOCIATES, PUBLISHERS
Mahwah, New Jersey London

Lawrence Erlbaum Associates, Inc., Publishers
10 Industrial Avenue
Mahwah, New Jersey 07430

Cover design by Kathryn Houghtaling Lacey

**Library of Congress Cataloging-in-Publication Data**

Handbook of crisis counseling, intervention, and prevention in the schools / edited by Jonathan Sandoval. —2nd ed.
p. cm.
Rev. ed. of: Crisis counseling, intervention, and prevention in the schools. 1988.
Includes bibliographical references and index.
ISBN 0-8058-3615-2 (cloth : alk. paper)— ISBN 0-8058-3616-0 (pbk. : alk. paper)
1. School psychology—United States. 2. Crisis intervention (Mental health services)—United States. 3. Mental health counseling—United States. I. Sandoval, Jonathan. II. Crisis counseling, intervention, and prevention in the schools.

LB1027.55 .C74 2001
371.7'13—dc21

2001031552

Books published by Lawrence Erlbaum Associates are printed on acid-free paper, and their bindings are chosen for strength and durability.

Printed in the United States of America
10 9 8 7 6 5 4 3 2 1

# Contents

# Preface to the Second Edition

The first edition of this book filled a gap in the preparation and education of many school-based professionals. It not only became assigned reading in various graduate programs but enjoyed success among several school-based practitioners: school psychologists, school counselors, school social workers, school nurses, and administrative staff. Events since the early 1990s have led to an even greater appreciation of the school as a place where traumatic events may occur and, consequently, of the need for information of this type. In addition, policymakers in schools have begun to realize how much learning is effected by the conditions that children face in their homes and neighborhoods. Children need support for their learning in the form of crisis intervention and prevention.

This edition updates the original edition and introduces five new chapters: diversity in crisis intervention, bullying, violence and disaster, rape and sexual assault, and eating disorders. While covering new ground, the central message of these chapters remains the same: School guidance personnel can do much to reduce children's stress and to facilitate their coping and healthy development. Along with the chapters contributors, I feel confident that this book provides the kind of information and inspiration that is needed to reach these goals.


## ACKNOWLEDGMENTS

I wish to thank Carla Lacy for her support in the preparation of the manuscript for the book and Davis students Lisa Krause, who provided library research, and Joanna Abbott, Jennifer Grimes, Tim Larrabee, and Dorine Waidtlow, who helped in reviewing chapters. I also wish to acknowledge the support of Lane Akers at Lawrence Erlbaum Associates for seeing this project through to completion.

*Jonathan Sandoval*

# PART I

# GENERAL PRINCIPLES OF CRISIS COUNSELING AND PREVENTION

CHAPTER

# 1

# Conceptualizations and General Principles of Crisis Counseling, Intervention, and Prevention

Jonathan Sandoval
University of California, Davis

Perhaps the feature of a crisis that is most dramatic to witness is the effect on individuals. Children in crisis suddenly function with greatly diminished capacity in meeting everyday demands. Students whom others have seen only behaving competently and efficiently suddenly become disorganized, depressed, hyperactive, confused, or hysterical (Pynoos, 1994). Customary problem-solving activities and resources seem to evaporate. Individuals who are in what Caplan (1964) termed a state of psychological disequilibrium often behave irrationally and withdrawn from normal contacts. They cannot be helped using usual counseling or teaching techniques. Nevertheless, children in crisis are usually also in school. School psychologists and other guidance personnel must be able to support teachers, parents, and the children themselves during periods of crisis for children. In addition, school personnel must be forward thinking and anticipate that crises will occur in children's lives. They must be prepared to act and find ways to help children master the challenges of crises when they occur.

## A HISTORY OF CRISIS INTERVENTION THEORY

The earliest work on crisis intervention is usually attributed to Lindemann (1944) and his studies of the aftermath of the Coconut Grove nightclub fire. This disaster, which occurred in Boston in the late 1930s, took a large toll of human life. For the first time, a social scientist conducted systematic observations of the reactions of victims and their families to a natural disaster, although others, including Freud, noted the traumatic impacts of war on combatants (Saigh & Bremner, 1999). The Coconut Grove study, plus Lindemann's efforts in opening a mental health agency in Wellesley, Massachusetts, formed the basis of his ideas about crisis and crisis intervention which linked observations of social transitions and reactions to traumatic events.

Erikson (1962) contributed the next major milestone in crisis intervention theory with the 1950 publication of *Childhood and Society*. Erikson's theory revolves around the notion of specific crises characterizing each developmental stage of an individual's life. His contribution was the notion of crisis as a normal developmental phenomenon and that intervention which leads to a balanced resolution at the time of a crisis would prevent later problems in emotional development and maturation.

The third early pioneer was Gerald Caplan whose formulations about the primary prevention of emotional disorders and mental health consultation led to the notion of an entirely new field of preventative psychiatry (Caplan, 1961, 1964). Caplan's data came from early work with Peace Corps volunteers, with parents reacting to premature birth, and with families coping with the affliction of tuberculosis. His (and others' associated with the Harvard School of Public Health) adoption of ideas from public health and the application of them to mental health settings had an enormous influence that led to the blossoming of crisis intervention centers throughout the country.

Caplan's work came at a time when there was a great push on the part of the federal government for community mental health agencies and at a time of great social unrest in our country. The 1960s brought unprecedented illegal use of psychoactive drugs on the part of adolescents and young adults. These forces, particularly drug abuse, led to the creation in the community and on college campuses of crisis counseling agencies, often nontraditional in nature, which could deal with the problems of alienated youth, especially drug overdose (Beers & Foreman, 1976). During this time, the use of telephone crisis lines also became widespread, spurred on by a growing interest in suicide prevention services (Golan, 1978).

The late 1970s and early 1980s saw the burgeoning of great interest in brief psychotherapy (e.g., Bellak & Small, 1978; Davanloo, 1978). This trend emerged as a result of cuts in mental health funding and of new techniques and procedures for dealing rapidly with mental health problems. Mental health workers began to appreciate that as much benefit could be gained in six to eight sessions as had earlier taken years.

Another recent trend has been an interest in stress and its impact on physical and mental health. Theorists such as Hans Selye (1974) and Adolph

Meyer (cited in Moos & Schaefer, 1986) noted how a variety of environmental events may have broader effects than previously believed. Physical events may have emotional sequelae and vice versa. Normal life events such as graduation from school, birth of a child, marriage, not to mention unpleasant events such as job failure, a death in the family, or divorce may foreshadow the development of symptoms and disease. Moreover, stressful events are additive or perhaps multiplicative in their action, in that the more events with which the individual must cope, the more likely an illness response will develop (Moos & Schaefer, 1986).

During the 1980s and 1990s the focus shifted to more extreme forms of crisis intervention. In succeeding revisions of the American Psychicatric Association's Diagnostic and Statistical Manual, the concept of posttraumatic stress disorder (PTSD) came to be refined and identified in children and youth (Saigh & Bremner, 1999). The definitions of PTSD have focused more attention on this phenomenon and more study of therapeutic techniques to amelorate the effects. Also in the last decade, there have been a number of school-based acts of terrorism and violence that have been widely publicized and discussed in the popular media. Perhaps the most dramatic example was the murderous attack on Colombine High School in Littleton, Colorado. These events have led to legislation outlawing the posession of certain types of weapons, and increased attention to the causes and prevention of violence in youth. Although crisis theory has had a relatively brief history, sufficient research findings and clinical observations exist for school psychologists and other school mental health workers to apply the ideas and techniques to the school setting, and crisis response teams exist in many school districts (Brock, Sandoval, & Lewis, 2001).

## DEFINITIONS AND DISTINCTIONS

The term *crisis* is used generically to stand for both the event and the reaction. It is useful to make a distinction, however. Klein and Lindemann (1961) offered the following definition:

> An emotionally hazardous situation (or emotional hazard) refers to any sudden alteration in the field of social forces within which the individual exists, such that the individual's expectations of himself and his relationships with others undergo change. Major categories of hazards include: (1) a loss or threatened loss of significant relationship; (2) the introduction of one or more new individuals into social orbit; (3) transitions in social status and role relationships as a consequence of such factors as (a) maturation, (e.g., entry into adolescence), (b) achievement of a new social role (e.g., marriage), or (c) horizontal or vertical social mobility (e.g., job promotion). (p. 284)

Klein and Lindemann use the term *hazard* to capture the notion that many individuals are able to pass through such alterations with little difficulty or with a minimum amount of stress. Others, however, find themselves immobilized or damaged by the hazard. Natural disasters and acts of terrorism would be included in their definition of hazard.

Klein and Lindemann (1961) reserved the term *crisis* "for the acute and often prolonged disturbance that may occur in an individual or social orbit as a result of an emotional hazard" (p. 284). Emotional hazards faced by school children include losses in significant relationships associated with the death of a parent; parental divorce and remarriage; death of a sibling or the loss of a parent to illness; maturational challenges such as the beginning of puberty; and transitions such as those accompanying movement into new schools, or new educational programs. Nonpromotion is a hazard, but so is promotion to a new grade with its separation from a known, possibly favored teacher and the adjustment to change and an unknown, new teacher. Disasters typically bring about these same disruptions as they often result in loss of life or of status, such as becoming homeless. Some children will navigate these hazards with little or no ill effect. Others will develop crisis reactions and come to the attention of school psychologists and other school personnel.

Caplan (1964) offered a general view of an emotional crisis as a "psychological disequilibrium in a person who confronts a hazardous circumstance that for him constitutes an important problem which he can, for the time being, neither escape nor solve with his customary problem solving resources" (p. 53). Caplan viewed a crisis as being a period when the individual is temporarily out of balance. This state of of disequilibrium provides an opportunity for psychological growth as well as a danger of psychological deterioration. Although there are great risks that may occur to the future mental well-being of an individual who passes through a crisis, there is also an opportunity for an individual to change. It is an old but traditional cliché to point out that the Chinese character for crisis includes ideographs related to the concept of danger as well as the concept of opportunity. The primary goal in helping an individual who is undergoing a crisis is to intervene in such a way as to use the situation to enhance personal growth, or at least to restore the individual to a previous level of functioning. The goal is not to reorganize completely the individual's major dimensions of personality, but to restore the individual to creative problem solving. Of course by successfully resolving a crisis an individual will most likely acquire new coping skills that will lead to improved functioning in new situations, but that is only a desired, possible outcome, not the sole objective of the process.

Because failure to cope is at the heart of a crisis, and the promotion of coping is an overall objective of crisis intervention, it is useful to consider what normal coping entails. Moos and Billings (1984) identified a taxonomy of coping skills organized into three domains, each with three skills. The first is *appraisal-focused* coping. The three skills in this domain enable the individual to find meaning and to understand the crisis, that is, to apprehend it in a productive manner. They are (a) logical analysis and mental preparation, (b) cognitive redefinition, and (c) cognitive avoidance or denial. Thus, in first becoming aware of a hazardous event, a child may think it through rationally, step by step, and prepare for what will probably happen next, may re-frame the hazard in a variety of ways, or may keep all or part of it at a distance, mentally, until he or she is ready to deal with it.

The second domain is *problem-focused* coping. The three skills in this domain enable the individual to confront the reality brought about by the crisis. These are (a) seeking information and support, (b) taking problem-solving action, and (c) identifying alternative rewards. This last skill involves changing activities and relationships so there may be substitutions for the sources of satisfaction lost by the hazardous event.

The third domain is *emotion-focused* coping. Here, the three skills enable the child to manage the feelings generated by the crisis and to maintain affective equilibrium. The three skills are (a) affective regulation, (b) emotional discharge, and (c) resigned acceptance. These skills allow one to maintain control of emotions, or to vent them in a way that brings relief. Many situations cannot be controlled, however, and resigned acceptance may lead to avoidance and withdrawal as a way to protect the self. As we see later in the chapter, and in this book, much of crisis intervention is directed at stimulating one or more of these coping skills, or even teaching them depending on the individual and the type of hazard he or she is attempting to negotiate.

There has been a great deal of interest in the concept of *resilience*, or the personal and situational factors that enable some children to overcome difficult situations or events (Werner, 1989). Children who are able to negotiate hazardous situations without a crisis response may be characterized as having good social competence, good problem-solving skills, a degree of autonomy, and a strong sense of purpose and the future (Bernard, 1992). They also come from supportive family and school environments with high expectations and encouragement of participation in meaninful activities. Some children will be vulnerable to hazardous events and transitions, and others will not.

## TYPES OF CRISES

Although there are a number of ways that the crises may be defined and outlined (cf. Aguilera, 1988; Smith, 1990), most authorities distinguish between developmental crises and situational crises. Developmental crises occur when an individual moves from one developmental stage to another. Situational crises, however, are incidents that are unexpected and accidental. Perhaps the most useful taxonomy has been developed by Baldwin (1978; Burgess & Baldwin, 1981). Baldwin emphasized in his taxonomy the impact on the individual rather than the nature of the hazard.

## Dispositional Crises

Baldwin (1978) called his first class of crises dispositional crises. These crises are "distress resulting from a problematic situation in which the therapist responds to the client in ways peripheral to a therapeutic role; the intervention is not primarily directed at the emotional level" (p. 540). In a dispositional crisis an individual typically lacks both information and the encouragement to go about solving a problem in an unusual way. The school psychologist who helps a pupil learn about a local program for overweight teenagers might be dealing with such a crisis. In general, the major counseling strategy with these pupils is to provide information, particularly information that would be difficult for the child or adolescent to obtain on his or her own. If the client is capable of doing most of the "research," the counselor merely points the way. The act of obtaining the information on one's own builds self-confidence and increases the chance of the information being believed. Another specific strategy is to rule out possible hidden, serious emotional implications of the seemingly innocent request for information. The counselor must be sure the current problem is not an offshoot of another, more serious situation. The school psychologist should also consider referring the client on. Another expert may provide either information that is more comprehensive or more authoritative than is available at the school. If the real reason for the request is to discuss a more serious problem outside of the scope of solution in the school, a referral for long-term therapeutic intervention may be required.

## Anticipated Life Transitions

Baldwin's (1978) second category subsumes crises of anticipated life transitions. These are crises "that reflect anticipated but usually normative, life transitions over which the client may or may not have substantial control" (p. 542). Common transitions for children are entering school, moving from grade to grade, moving to another school, or moving from a self-contained special education classroom to a mainstreamed one. The birth of a sibling or pregnancy in a teenager also fit this category in as much as they are transitions from one status (only child or adolescent) to another (sibling or mother).

One approach to dealing with crises related to life transitions is to provide information about what is about to occur in the person's life. As a preventative technique, I discuss anticipatory guidance in another major section, but a child in the middle of a transition also needs to know what is likely to occur next and what the normal experiences and emotions are for those going through such a transition. This kind of normative information can be provided by school personnel.

An alternative is to let peers supply the information. Another strategy is to establish support groups consisting of a number of children facing the same transition. If the group functions well, it may facilitate the expression of feeling and the acquisition of productive coping mechanisms as members share experiences and join in mutual problem solving. Even young children can do productive group problem solving through devices such as a Magic Circle, or other structured approaches to classroom discussions of children's self-identified conflicts and problems (Jones, 1968).

## Traumatic Stress

A third class of crises result from traumatic events. These are "emotional crises precipitated by externally-imposed stressors or situations that are unexpected and uncontrolled, and that are emotionally overwhelming" (Baldwin, 1978, p. 543). Young (1998) noted six types of traumatic hazards: severe illness or injury; violent or unexpected death; threatened death or injury; acts of war; natural disasters; and man-made industrial disasters. Traumatic events for children in school include the sudden death of a family member, catastrophic illness, hospitalization, parental disablement, parental divorce, physical abuse, pregnancy, sexual assault, and academic failure. Often, the pupil facing one or more of these events is emotionally overwhelmed and unable to bring into play previously learned coping strategies.

The counselor's first goal is to help the child understand the impact of what has occurred. Because of the suddenness of occurrence, the counselee probably has not had time to think through all of the impacts of what has happened. Exploration of the event and the attendant feelings will get the child to gain needed perspective and overcome defensive reactions. Traditional nondirective helping interviews (Benjamin, 1981) can accomplish this task and can stimulate appraisal-focused coping (Moos & Billings, 1984). Another goal for helping in this kind of crisis is to mobilize any existing coping mechanisms the child may have. If the individual has characteristic ways of dealing with stress in other situations, the counselor can remind the child of these, be they appraisal-, problem-, or emotion-focused, and facilitate the transfer of the old skills to the new crisis (Brenner, 1984).

If the counselee is not coping at all, it may be possible to provide the pupil with new coping mechanisms. Brenner (1984) referred to the process as teaching new coping strategies, and believes the new technique will be more easily learned if it is close to the child's initial reaction.

> For example, Joshua's teacher helped him substitute sublimination for impulsive acting out as a coping technique after his mother deserted him. Josh's first impulse was to express his anger by running around the classroom, pushing furniture and people out of his way. His teacher helped him to think of several vigorous physical activities which would not be destructive but which would still serve to release his pent-up emotions. (p. 173)

Another way of helping victims of traumatic crisis is to relieve them of other, unrelated stressors (Brenner, 1984). A child whose parents are divorcing may be relieved of certain expectations at school if those expectations are adding to the child's sense of being overwhelmed. If, however, the child is using school work in a sublimation strategy, it might be wiser to search for other potential stress sources that need to be eliminated.

### Maturational–Developmental Crises

Crises in this fourth category result "from attempts to deal with an interpersonal situation reflecting a struggle with a deeper (but usually circumscribed) issue that has not been resolved adaptively in the past and that represents an attempt to gain emotional maturity" (Baldwin, 1978, p. 544). Focal issues for this class of crises include dependency, value conflicts, sexual identity, capacity for emotional intimacy, responses to authority, and attaining reasonable self-discipline. All of these issues may erupt in schoolchildren but are more visible during adolescence.

These crises are different from others in that they usually occur as another episode in a pattern of relationship problems that have similar dynamics. In secondary schools, the attainment of sexual maturity by young people precipitates a number of these crises, as does adolescence in general. Struggles with parents and teachers often develop to the point of crisis in this class. A special case of such a crisis is the discovery in adolescence of a homosexual orientation (Ross-Reynolds & Hardy, 1985; chap. 14, this volume).

Once again, the counselor can be of help with clients in this kind of crisis by facilitating the exploration of thoughts and feelings. In this instance, however, the hope is to identify issues underlying the crisis. This strategy will be particularly attractive to dynamically oriented counselors. What thoughts and feelings does the client have about significant others and the self? What value conflicts are be experienced and what are their origins? What themes and conflicts appear to be unresolved? Are these issues related to trust, acceptance and control of aggression, attitudes toward learning, separation, accepting limits from others, and so on?

Next, the counselor works to support the individual in crisis to redefine relationships and develop adaptive interpersonal skills. Because most of these crises involve creating new ways of acting with other people in the student's social environment, helping them learn new prosocial strategies is effective. Strategies for making friends may be taught directly (Stocking, Arezzo, & Leavitt, 1980) but providing models to observe (or even read about, e.g., Fassler, 1978) is also beneficial.

## Crises Reflecting Psychopathology

Baldwin (1978) described the fifth category: "These are emotional crises in which a preexisting psychopathology has been instrumental in precipitating the crisis or in which psychopathology significantly impairs or complicates adaptive resolution" (p. 546). The problems of a child hallucinating in school or a severely depressed adolescent might well achieve crisis proportions. Eating disorders may come to the attention of teachers. These kinds of crises, although present in the school, are rarely the kind that special services practitioners are trained for and thus usually result in a referral to outside community resources. School personnel do have a role in preventing a worsening of the child's adjustment by keeping him or her functioning academically as well as possible.

In addition, the special services personnel may assist teachers and administrators to appreciate that the child has problems that cannot be resolved in school yet can be managed in a reasonable way in the classroom. Generally, with children experiencing this kind of crisis, it is wise not to respond to the underlying problem. This in-depth treatment is a task for professionals.

What can be done is to support the child's attempts to respond to the stressful situation as adaptively as possible. Whatever the child is doing in school that is appropriate and productive can be acknowledged and encouraged. At the same time, the counselor can search for ways to reduce stress, especially by eliminating any stressors that may be pushing the child beyond his or her capacity to cope.

In addition, the counselor must look for ways to support other school staff and even parents who will also undergo trauma in dealing with a psychopathological child. Consultation skills and techniques are particularly valuable in this respect.

## Psychiatric Emergencies

This sixth class consists of "crisis situations in which general functioning has been severely impaired and the individual rendered incompetent or unable to assume personal responsibility" (Baldwin, 1978, p. 547). Examples include acutely suicidal children, alcohol intoxification, drug overdoses, reactions to hallucinogenic drugs, acute psychoses, and uncontrollable anger. These are all "classic" crises of the type where the individual is often dangerous to him or herself or others.

The counselor's efforts in this type of crisis are directed at assessing the danger by attempting to learn the physical or psychiatric condition of the pupil. Facts must be gathered to clarify the situation so that action may be taken quickly and appropriately. Much of this information may need to be determined from persons other than the child.

The first principle in psychiatric crises is to intervene quickly so as to reduce danger. The school professional must be willing to mobilize all medical or psychiatric resources necessary and thus must be familiar with state law and local community agencies. Prior to the need for such information, school practitioners should familiarize themselves with community resources. Not only must they know about existing agencies, they must learn the detail of what services are offered and they must know the key personnel to contact (Sandoval, 1985a). Learning which pupils to refer to outside experts takes a novice a long time because of the need to follow up on referral cases, and the difficulty in evaluating one's own competence. School practitioners must routinely review their cases with supervisors and peers. In the review, not only does counselor knowledge and skill need to be examined but so, too, does counselor objectivity.

## CRISIS COUNSELING AND INTERVENTION

### Crisis Counseling Goals

One approach to considering the goals for work with children in crisis is to consider tasks the children must accomplish if they are to manage the crisis situation successfully and emerge intact. Moos and Schaefer (1986) identified five major adaptive tasks as follows.

1. Establish the meaning and understand the personal significance of the situation. The child must come to view the event personally. He or she must realize all of the short- and long-term ramifications of what has occurred and to assign it a meaning. This meaning will undoubtedly be limited by the child's cognitive and emotional development.

2. Confront reality and respond to the requirements of the external situation. The child must marshal resources in able to continue or in the conventional social roles remaining. The victim still must go to school, play in the neighborhood, and be part of a family in spite of the crisis.

3. Sustain relationships with family members and friends as well as with other individuals who may be helpful in resolving the crisis and its aftermath. The child, particularly, must depend on others for assistance in dealing with the crisis situation. The child must keep lines of communication open to parents and friends and look to them for support. Where adult authorities are involved, such as other school personnel, or medical or social agency helpers, the child must be able to cooperate and use the assistance rendered.

4. Preserve a reasonable emotional balance by managing upsetting feelings aroused by the situation. The powerful emotions stemming from a crisis must be mastered. Through a combination of appropriate expression and the use of strategies to manage or block the full impact of the event, children can achieve a sense of hope that will enable them to continue functioning.

5. Preserve a satisfactory self-image and achieve a sense of competence and mastery. The child must search for new roles in which to be competent or to return to old arenas where he or she has been successful in the past in order to achieve a sense of competence. Because many crises threaten a sense of self, the individual must work particularly hard to find compensating ways to feel good about the self.

## Generic Counseling Principles

Given that crisis counseling is different from usual school counseling and has the aforementioned goals, it is useful to indicate a general strategy for helping people in a crisis situation. What follows is a generic model taken from the work of Lindemann (1944), Caplan (1964), and Rusk (1971) and others (see Golan, 1978; Roberts, 2000, or Slaikeu, 1990 for an exhaustive model). An individual counselor will change and adapt these techniques depending on the type of crisis, the age of student, and the specifics of the type of crisis. Although I have outlined the principles in the general order that they are applied in a crisis, they are not necessarily sequential in practice.

In working with a pupil in crisis:

1. Begin counseling immediately. By definition, a crisis is a time when a child is in danger of becoming extremely impaired emotionally. The longer the pupil remains in a hazardous situation and is unable to take action, the more difficult it will be to facilitate coping and a return to equilibrium (Nader & Pynoos, 1993). When a person remains in a state of confusion without any kind of human support, anxiety and pain are sure to result.

2. Be concerned and competent. The pupil will need a certain amount of reassurance during a crisis situation. The more the counselor can present him or herself as a model of competent problem solving and demonstrate the process of taking in information, choosing between alternatives, and tak-

ing action, the more the child will be able to begin to function appropriately. This higher functioning will come about both from a sense of safety and security and from observeing a clear model. The counselor does not call attention to his or her competence but keeps it in the background as the counseling goes on.

3. Listen to the facts of the situation. Before proceeding, the counselor must carefully gather information about the events leading up to the crisis, eliciting as many details as possible. Not only will solutions come from these facts, but concrete knowledge of the situation will also put into perspective the pupil's behavior—Is this child behaving rationally or irrationally? Such a determination allows the counselor to judge the severity of the crisis and to proceed accordingly.

4. Reflect the individual 's feelings. The counselor should explicitly focus the discussion on the pupil's affective experience and encourage its appropriate expression. The objective here is not only to create empathetic understanding, but also to legitimize affect. The child must learn that feelings can be discussed and are an important part of problem solving. By reflecting feelings the counselor also "primes the pump" in that it gives the counselee a way to begin and continue exploration of what occurred. Reflecting feelings is an important strategy to make psychological contact (Slaikeu, 1990). Koocher and Pollin (1994) identified eight fears associated with a medical crisis that must be expressed and dealt with: Fear of loss of control, loss of self-image, depencency, stigma, abandonment, isolation, death, and expressing anger.

5. Help the child realize that the crisis event has occurred. Do not accept the child's defensiveness or let the mechanisms of denial or other defensives operate and prolong the crisis situation unnecessarily. Some denial may actually be coping, in that it gives the child a chance to be desensitized to what has occurred. Prolonged or complete denial may not lead to coping. Encourage the pupil to explore the crisis events without becoming overwhelmed. By asking appropriate well-timed questions, the counselor can control the pace of exploration. Roberts (2000) suggested questioning to determine previous coping methods and dangerousness or leathality.

6. Do not encourage or support blaming. This strategy also is a way of avoiding the pupil's defensiveness and of encouraging coping. If one can put blame aside, and focus on what has occurred, the child may more quickly move on. Dwelling on being a victim leaves one in a passive position rather than moving on to an active role. The focus should be shifted to self-esteem issues and internal strengths rather than remaining oriented toward external causation and guilt.

7. Do not give false reassurance. The counselor should always remain truthful and realistic, even though it is tempting to offer unrealistic comfort. The individual in crisis will always suffer anxiety, depression, or tension, and

the counselor must acknowledge that the discomfort will probably continue for some time. At the same time, it is possible to provide some sense of hope and expectation that the person will ultimately overcome the crisis. The counselor should be clear that there will always be scars and tenderness resulting from a crisis. Nevertheless, the child or adolescent will be able to get on with his or her life eventually, and may even develop new strengths.

8. Recognize the primacy of taking action. The individual will need real assistance in accomplishing everyday tasks during the time of crisis. Every crisis counseling interview should have as an ultimate outcome some action that the client is able to take. Restoring the client to the position of actor rather than victim is critical to success, because taking effective action helps to restore a sense of self.

## Generic Crisis Intervention Principles

In addition to interviewing the child or *counseling*, the counselor also must take action or *intervene*, with or without the participation of the person in crisis. These interventions may be within or outside of the counseling setting. With younger children, particularly, it will be expeditious to make changes in the environment, in the classroom, or at home to reduce stress.

1. Facilitate the re-establishment of a social support network. If possible, get the child to accept some help from others. It is usually possible to find either a group of peers or family members who can provide emotional support and temporary physical assistance during the crisis. In this way the pupil's energies may be devoted to coping with the crisis. If family is not available, there are often community resources available and the counselor should be knowledgeable about them (Sandoval, 1985a).

2. Engage in focused problem solving. Once the counselor has been able to formulate an accurate, comprehensive statement about the counselee's perception of the situation, identifying all of the sources of concern, it will be possible to begin the process of exploring potential strategies to improve or resolve the emotionally hazardous situation. Jointly, the counselor and pupil review the strategies explored and select one for trial. The outcome should be an action plan (Roberts, 2000). This is much like the problem solving that occurs in other kinds of counseling but must be preceded by the steps previously mentioned. Moving too quickly to problem solving is a common mistake of novices (Egan, 1994). However effective the problem solution is, the very process of turning attention to the future, away from the past, is beneficial in and of itself. Some solutions may involve actions by others such as teachers or school administrators. To the extent necessary, the counselor may act as an intermediary communicating with authorities on the child's behalf.

3. Focus on self-concept. Any action strategies must be implemented in the context of what the client thinks it is possible for him or her to accomplish. The crisis situation often leads to a dimunition in self-esteem and the acceptance of blame for the crisis. With an emphasis on how the person did cope well given the situation so far and how the person has arrived at a strategy for moving forward, there can be a restoration of the damaged view of the self. Counselors can emphasize what positive there is in the situation, even if it seems relatively minor. Even the victim of a sexual assault can be congratulated for at least surviving physically.

4. Encourage self-reliance. During the process of crisis counseling, the counselee will have temporarily become dependent on the counselor for direct advice, for stimulating action, and for supplying hope. This is a temporary situation and before the crisis intervention interviews are over, the counselor must spend some time planning ways to restore the individual to self-reliance and self-confidence. Typically in counseling this is done by the counselor consciously moving into a position of equal with the counselee, sharing the responsibility and authority. Although earlier the counselor has taken charge, eventually he or she must return to a more democratic stance. Techniques such as onedownsmanship, where the counselor acknowledges the pupil's contribution to problem solving while minimizing the counselor's own contribution (Caplan, 1970), permit the counselee to leave the crisis intervention with a sense of accomplishment. Helping individuals to find alternative rewards and sources of satisfaction (i.e., using problem-focused coping, is most helpful).

Although these principles may generally apply to all crisis counseling and intervention, it is important to realize that there are specific techniques that are appropriate to a given kind of crisis. Table 1.1 lists goals and general intervention techniques that seem most appropriate for each of Baldwin's crisis types. Other chapters in this volume contain a number of specific ideas for particular crises. Slaiku's (1990) concept of psychological first aid is explored in chapter 12 on traumatic events.

## The Counselor in Crisis

Not much has been written explicitly about the counselor's feelings and adaptive behavior at a time of crisis. However it is clear that disaster workers such as fire fighters are adversely affected by responding to a crisis (Everly, Lating, & Mitchell, 2000, Mitchell, 1986, 1987). Those responding to airline disasters seem to have a particularly difficult time, but all emergency workers are subject to the same reactions as the victims of the crisis. They too will exhibit symptoms of stress. Responses are individual and may

TABLE 1.1
General Principles: Counseling Goal Interventions Particularly Relevant to Baldwin's Six Classes of Emotional Crisis

| *Crisis Type* | *Goals* | *General Intervention* |
|---|---|---|
| 1. Dispositional crises | Confront reality | • Provide information—educate<br>• Rule out hidden, serious emotional implications<br>• Refer to expert |
| 2. Anticipated life transitions | Confront reality | • Anticipatory guidance<br>• Provide support groups |
| 3. Traumatic stress | Establish meaning | • Help client understand the impact of what has occurred |
| | Preserve emotional balance | • Mobilize existing coping mechanisms |
| | Preserve self-image | • Provide new coping mechanisms |
| 4. Maturational/developmental crises | Sustain relationships | • Identify underlying issues<br>• Support client in redefining relationships and developing adaptive interpersonal responses |
| 5. Crisis reflecting psychopathology | Preserve self-image | • Support attempts to respond to stressful situation as adaptively as possible |
| | Confront reality | • Find ways to reduce stress<br>• Refer to experts<br>• Do not respond to underlying problems |
| 6. Psychiatric emergencies | Preserve self-image | • Intervene quickly to reduce danger |
| | Establish meaning | • Assess medical or psychiatric condition<br>• Clarify situation<br>• Mobilize all medical or psychiatric resources necessary |

not be apparent to an observer or supervisor. Often witnessing the aftermath of traumatic event can recall a crisis workers own past experience of trauma and loss (e.g., Carroll, 1998). Training and supervision permits the avoidance or diminution of countertransference while serving as a helper during a crisis.

In a sense, then, a crisis in a child is also a time of crisis for the counselor. Because the event may have come up suddenly and unexpectedly and because the child's problem may be quite serious, the counselor is likely to experience heightened anxiety and momentary disorganization. A number of principles for the counselor's behavior may also be identified.

1. Remove distractors and other stressors acting on you. Set aside your other duties and roles. Order your priorities and realize your limit. Give as much time as you can to the crisis and put off what is not urgent.

2. Avoid impulsive action. You must act quickly but you should also take time to plan in a time of crisis. Gather your thoughts and think through the possibilities prior to seeing the affective parties in a crisis situation.

3. Delegate authority. The medical response to a crisis is the triage process. Not only are the most important risks to the patient assessed and identified but also roles are assigned to various medical personnel. In the schools there is the ideal of the multidisciplinary team, and with effort it can be a reality. In times of crisis, by delegating authority among school psychologists, counselors, social workers, school nurses, administrators, and teachers, there will be a minimum of duplication of effort and a greater likelihood that professionals will be tackling those tasks they can do best.

4. Model calmness in a way consonant with your personality. Although Carl Rogers (1957), for example, argued that the counselor should always be genuine and honest with the client, there are times when such openness may not be in the best interest of the client. If the counselor is overly upset and angry about the child's predicament and acts it out in front of the client, it may have the effect of getting in the way of emotion-focused coping.

5. Be prepared. The Scout motto is still valuable. The more one is informed about the particular crisis the child is experiencing, the easier will be the process of working with him or her. One aim of this book is to provide school psychologists and other school personnel with the knowledge base to begin to work with the common crises they will encounter. Be prepared has another meaning, however, and that is to anticipate that various crises will occur and to expend some energy into planning and executing prevention programs that will keep hazardous situations from developing into crises for large numbers of children.

6. Seek supervion and debriefing. Poland and McCormick (1999) suggested that the crisis caregivers may help themselves and others cope in the aftermath of a crisis by knowing oneself and respecting one's limitations; by asking for special support from your family; by taking care of oneself physically, by supporting other members of that team; by using humor; by recognizing that you, yourself, will be impacted by the crisis; and by talking to others. The goal of a debriefing is to detect burnout among crisis workers and move toward an individualized stress management intervention when it is detected. The debriefing itself can provide emotion-focused coping, in that it permits the expression of ideas and emotions in a psychologically safe environment.

## PREVENTION PROGRAMS

Many of the early pioneers in crisis intervention (e.g., Caplan, 1961; Klein & Lindemann, 1961) came from a background in public health and stressed the prevention of crises. At least five general strategies have been used in the schools to prevent various kinds of crises from occurring. They are educational workshops, anticipatory guidance, screening, consultation, and research (Sandoval, 1985b).

### Educational Workshops and Programs

An educational workshop is a short intensive course of study on a topic that generates feelings and emotions. As a result, workshops emphasize student participation and discussion. It is preventive to the extent that the topic of the workshop is intended to forestall future mental health problems. A number of programs exist for children under the general heading of psychological education. Programs such as classroom meetings, Magic Circle, and others (Miller, 1976) help children express their feelings about what is occurring in the social environment of the classroom, and attempts to free them from the anxiety that may occur from crises that may develop in the classroom. Others have pointed out the value of a psychologist's role in all curriculum designs (e.g., Jones, 1968), because so many school subjects can bring up unpleasant emotions. Specific curriculum materials have been developed on topics such as death, dying, suicide, and illness as is pointed out in later chapters in this book.

### Anticipatory Guidance

The second technique, anticipatory guidance, also has a variant called emotional innoculation. Offering anticipatory guidance consists of orienting a student intellectually to events that are likely to occur in the future and helping him or her prepare effective coping strategies. Emotional innoculation puts the emphasis on future feelings rather than on the cognitive. Events in question are ones that experience has shown are difficult for individuals to cope with and may influence educational performance. Examples of anticipatory guidance are programs that are designed to help children adjust to new institutional settings, or programs that inform students as to what can be expected, both intellectually and emotionally, when a new sibling is born.

### Screening Programs

A third preventive technique involves setting up procedures to identify children who are vulnerable to particular hazardous situations so that they might receive special assistance at the appropriate time. Screening programs consist of designing means (usually questionnaires, rating scales, or group tests) to determine who is at a high risk of not coping. The follow-up intervention might be anticipatory guidance, a workshop, a special remediation program, or preventive counseling.

Screening has been particularly effective in identifying children who are at risk of educational failure but it is conceivable that screening could be designed to identify children who are also at risk for other kinds of crises. An example would be an effort to learn which families, in the near future, plan to enlarge their numbers so that children might be identified for workshops designed to facilitate the adjustment to a new sibling.

### Consultation

Serving as a consultant is another important way that school psychologists and other special services personnel can act preventively in crises. Consultation is defined as one professional helping a second professional be more effective in his or her job (Caplan, 1970). In this context, a consultant is defined as a special services worker collaborating with teachers, administrators, or parents to help them deal more effectively with the child or teacher in crisis. By working with teachers, and possibly with parents, a mental health professional can help these key adults support children when they become involved in a crisis situation and be sensitive to the various emotional needs a child may have during times of crisis.

### Research

Doing research is not usually conceived of as a preventive activity. Nevertheless, the more that is known about a phenomenon through research, the better able we are to predict and control that phenomenon. The more we understand about crises, the more effective we will be in creating workshops, educational curriculum, anticipatory guidance programs, screening programs, and consultation interventions. Evaluative and case study research on crises and crises intervention programs are within the capability of the school psychologist and should be thought of as important preventive activities.

## DEVELOPMENTAL ISSUES IN CRISIS COUNSELING

A number of texts on counseling, even texts focusing solely on counseling children, ignore an important point. A child of 5 and an adolescent of 16 have radically different faculties for dealing with information and reacting to events. Differences in cognitive, social, and emotional development mean that they will respond differently to hazards and will need to be counseled differently should they develop a crisis reaction. The same event, the death of a parent, for example, may be a crisis for a preschooler as well as a high-school senior, but each will react and cope with the event differently. Counseling with younger children often involves the use of nonverbal materials, many more directive leads in order to elicit and reflect feelings, and a focus on concrete concerns as well as fantasy.

Traditional talk therapists such as nondirective counseling capitalize on a client's capacity for rational thought and high level of moral development and are more likely to be effective with adolescents. With adolescents, the school psychologist can also acknowledge and use the age-appropriate crisis of establishing an identity.

In reviewing the generic crisis counseling principles just outlined, it seems reasonable to expect that younger children would have a greater difficulty acknowledging a crisis, and would be more prone to use immature defenses such as denial and projection to avoid coping with a crisis. In contrast, an adolescent might use more advanced defenses such as rationalization and intellectualization. In counseling children, more time might be spent on exploring reactions and feelings to the crisis situation and establishing support systems that engage in lengthy problem solving. With older adolescents, then, it may be possible to focus much more on establishing reasonable expectations and avoiding false reassurance, as well as spending more time on focused problem-solving activities.

## CONCLUSION

School psychologists have a powerful role to play in helping children cope with and regain equilibrium after a crisis response to a hazardous situation. Adding together exemplars of Baldwin's six classes of crisis yields a large number of events that occur in the school-age population and that undoubtedly interfere with the effective learning of children in schools. The techniques and theories of crisis counseling have a relatively short history of being applied and evaluated. Much of what is done with a child in crisis depends on what kind of crisis it is, the age of the child, the time available to the counselor, and the counselor's skills. To be efficient, group interventions that are preventative in nature may be necessary to cope with the strong need for crisis counseling in the schools. The next two sections of this book deal with crisis counseling and intervention in particular kinds of situations. School psychologists and others in the schools can have an enormous impact on the mental health of children if they are aware of and act immediately in helping students develop positive coping responses in times of crisis. Children may regain equilibrium, not lose precious time away from learning to emotional disorganization, and possibly even develop successful new coping strategies as a result of successfully passing through a crisis. They will be able to face emotional hazards throughout their lifetimes with a greater degree of confidence and success. If we are successful in developing our crisis counseling and intervention skills, and in implementing prevention programs, future children surely must benefit.

## REFERENCES

Aguilera, D. C. (1998). *Crisis intervention: Theory and methodology* (8th ed.). St. Louis, MO: Mosby.

Baldwin, B. A. (1978). A paradigm for the classification of emotional crises: Implications for crisis intervention. *American Journal of Orthopsychiatry, 48*, 538–551.

Beers, T. M., Jr., & Foreman, M. E. (1976). Intervention patterns in crisis intervention. *Journal of Counseling Psychology, 23*, 87–91.

Bellak, L., & Small, L. (1978). *Emergency psychotherapy and briefpsychotherapy* (2nd ed.). New York: Grune & Stratton.

Benjamin, A. (1981). *The helping interview* (3rd ed.). Boston: Houghton Mifflin.

Bernard, B. (1992). Fostering resiliency in kids: Protective factors in the family, school, and community. *Prevention Forum, 12*(3), 1–16.

Brenner, A. (1984). *Helping children cope with stress*. Lexington, MA: D. C. Heath.

Brock, S. E., Sandoval, J., & Lewis, S. (2001). *Preparing for crises in the schools* (2nd ed.). New York: Wiley.

Burgess, A. W., & Baldwin, B. A. (1981). *Crisis intervention theory and practice*. Englewood Cliffs, NJ: Prentice Hall.

Caplan, G. (1961). *An approach to community mental health*. New York: Grune & Stratton.

Caplan, G. (1964). *Principles of preventative psychiatry*. New York: Basic Books.

Caplan, G. (1970). *Theory and practice of mental health consultation*. New York: Basic Books.

Carroll, S. (1998). Crisis and counter-transference; Caretaking the caretaker. *National Association of School Psychologists Communique, 27*(3), 28–29.

Davanloo, H. (1978). *Basic principles and techniques in short-term dynamic psychotherapy*. New York: Spectrum.

Egan, G. (1994). *The skilled helper* (5th ed.). Pacific Grove, Ca: Brooks/Cole.

Erikson, E. (1962). *Childhood and society* (2nd ed.). New York: Norton.

Everly, G. S., Lating, J. M., & Mitchell, J. T. (2000). Innovations in group crisis intervention. In A. R. Roberts (Ed.), *Crisis intervention handbook: Assessment, treatment and research* (pp. 77–94). New York: Oxford University Press.

Fassler, J. (1978). *Helping children cope*. New York: The Free Press.

Golan, N. (1978). *Treatment in crisis situations*. New York: The Free Press.

Jones, R. M. (1968). *Fantasy and feeling in education*. New York: New York University Press.

Klein, D. C., & Lindemann, E. (1961). Preventive intervention in individual and family crisis situations. In G. Caplan (Ed.), *Prevention of mental disorders in children* (pp. 283–306). New York: Basic Books.

Koocher, G. P., & Pollin, I. (1994). Medical crisis counseling: A new service delivery model. *Journal of Clinical Psychology in Medical Setting, 1*, 291–299.

Lindemann, E. (1944). Symptomatology and management of acute grief. *American Journal of Psychiatry, 101*, 141–148.

Miller, J. P. (1976). *Humanizing the classroom*. New York: Praeger.

Mitchell, J. T. (1986, September–October). Critical incident stress management. *Response!*, pp. 24–25.

Mitchell, J. T. (1987). Effective stress control at major incidents. *Maryland Fire and Rescue Bulletin*, pp. 3, 6.

Moos, R., & Billings, A. (1984). Conceptualizing and measuring coping resources and processes. In L. Goldberger & S. Breznitz (Eds.), *Handbook of stress: Theoretical and clinical aspects* (pp. 109–145). New York: Macmillan.

Moos, R. H., & Schaefer, J. A. (1986). Life transitions and crises. A conceptual overview. In R. H. Moos & J. A. Schaefer (Eds.), *Coping with life crises. An integrated approach* (pp. 3–28). New York: Plenum.

Nader, K., & Pynoos, R. (1993). School disaster: Planning and initial interventions. Handbook of post-disaster interventions. *Journal of Social Behavior and Personality, 8*, 299–320.

Poland, S., & McCormick, J. S. (1999). *Coping with crisis: Lessons learned.* Longmont, CO: Sopris West.

Pynoos, R. S. (1994). *Traumatic stress and developmental psychopathology in children and adolescents*. Lutherville, MD: Sidran Press.

Roberts, A. R. (2000). An overview of crisis theory and crisis intervention. In A. R. Roberts (Ed.), *Crisis intervention handbook: Assessment, treatment and research* (pp. 3–30). New York: Oxford University Press.

Rogers, C. R. (1957). The necessary and sufficient conditions of therapeutic personality change. *Journal of Consulting Psychology, 21*, 95–103.

Ross-Reynolds, G., & Hardy, B. S. (1985). Crisis counseling for disparate adolescent sexual dilemmas: Pregnancy and homosexuality. *School Psychology Review, 14*, 300–312.

Rusk, T. N. (1971). Opportunity and technique in crisis psychiatry. *Comprehensive Psychiatry, 12*, 249–263.

Saigh, P. A., & Bremner, J. D. (1999). The history of posttraumatic stress disorder. In P. A. Saigh & J. D. Bremner (Eds.), *Posttraumatic stress disorder: A comprehensive text* (pp. 1–17). Boston: Allyn & Bacon.

Sandoval, J. (1985a). Notes on teaching school psychologists about community resources and agencies. *Trainers' Forum, 5*(2), 1–4.

Sandoval, J. (Ed.). (1985b). Mini-series on crisis counseling in the schools. *School Psychology Review, 14*, 255–324.

Selye, H. (1974). *Stress without distress.* New York: The New American Library.

Slaikeu, K. A. (1990). *Crisis intervention: A handbook for practice and research* (2nd ed.). Needham Heights, MA: Allyn & Bacon.

Smith, L. L. (1990). Crisis intervention: Theory and practice. In J. E. Mezzich & B. Zimmer (Eds.), *Emergency psychiatry* (pp. 305–331). Madison, CT: International University Press.

Stocking, S. H., Arezzo, D., & Leavitt, S. (1980). *Helping kids make friends.* Niles, IL: Argus Communications.

Werner, E. (1989). High-risk children in young adulthood: A longitudinal study from birth to 32 years. *American Journal of Orthopsychiatry, 59*, 72–81,

Young, M. A. (1998). *The community crisis response team training manual* (2nd ed.). Washington, DC: National Organization for Victim Assistance.

CHAPTER

# 2

# Preparing for the School Crisis Response

Stephen E. Brock
Lodi Unified School District, Lodi, CA

Despite the best of school crisis prevention efforts, it needs to be recognized that crisis events and their consequences cannot be completely avoided. For example, it is impossible to prevent natural disasters such as hurricanes, tornadoes, earthquakes, and floods. Also, whereas much can be done to prevent school violence, it seems unlikely that we can protect our schools from all acts of random violence. Thus, it is critical for schools to be prepared to respond to crisis situations (Brock, Sandoval, & Lewis, 2001).

The importance of school crisis response preparedness cannot be understated. Although it is next to impossible to prepare for all contingencies, crisis response measures place schools in the best possible position to respond to traumatic circumstances. The need for this preparedness is reinforced by the fact that the school crisis response is multifaceted. As illustrated in Fig. 2.1, the crisis response may include a number of different activities. Response plans help to ensure that none of these activities are overlooked in the often chaotic times following a crisis. Crisis response plans also help to ensure that there is very little delay in the provision of crisis services. The need for an immediate response is especially important when it comes to the provision of crisis intervention (also known as psychological first aid). The effectiveness of these services has been suggested to increase directly as a function of the intervention's proximity in both time and place to the crisis (Slaikeu, 1990).

In the pages that follow, this chapter reviews activities that the author's experiences have found to be important to school crisis response preparedness. They include obtaining necessary crisis response background knowledge, developing crisis response teams, and establishing crisis response planning and procedural guidelines. These activities have previously been documented in detail elsewhere (Brock, Sandoval, & Lewis, 1996; Brock et al., 2001). For additional information regarding these activities the reader may consult these publications.

## OBTAINING BACKGROUND KNOWLEDGE

A prerequisite to school crisis response preparedness is to obtain necessary background knowledge. Specifically it is important for the crisis response planner to have an understanding of what the crisis response involves and what situations may require its use. Also, it is critical to know the defining characteristics of the person in crisis and to understand how to provide crisis intervention services. This section reviews four specific educational activities that the author has found to be productive.

### Literature Review

The most basic, yet perhaps the most important, strategy for obtaining crisis response background knowledge is to review the available literature. Journal articles are often a valuable source of information. The author's review of this literature has found several recent articles that do an excellent job of describing the school crisis response. These articles include Adams (1996), Cornell and Sheras (1998), Mathers (1996), and Nye (1997).

In addition to journal articles, there is a growing library of school crisis response books. The first edition of the current volume, for example, was one of the first books devoted specifically to the school crisis response. In addition to the current volulme, other books that provide a comprehensive review of the school crisis response are Brock et al. (2001), Fairchild (1997), Johnson (1993), Petersen and Straub (1992), Pitcher and Poland (1992), and Poland and McCormick (1999).

### Training Programs

A powerful complement to the school crisis response literature review is participation in crisis intervention and response training programs. These programs are especially helpful in the development of crisis intervention skills. Examples of specific programs the author has found to be helpful include *Critical Incident Stress Management* (Mitchell & Everly, 1996), *Suicide Intervention Workshop* (Ramsay, Tanney, Tierney, & Lang, 1996), and *National Community Crisis Response Team Regional Training Institute* (Young, 1998).

The following paragraphs provide brief descriptions of each of these programs.

The two-day Basic *Critical Incident Stress Management* (CISM) course prepares participants to provide crisis intervention services. Topics covered include pre-incident education, defusings, demobilizations, and crisis intervention team development. Special emphasis is placed on the development of *CISM*. The two-day *Advanced CISM* course continues this preparation. Topics covered include posttrauma syndromes and special (or difficult) crisis intervention issues.

The two-day *Suicide Intervention Workshop* is a superior learning experience that helps to develop the basic confidence and competencies needed to assist a person at risk of suicidal behavior until the danger of injury has passed or until additional resources are mobilized. It is one of the best workshops of its type that the author has attended. Learning modules explore participant attitudes toward suicide, provide knowledge about suicide risk assessment, and train participants in a suicide intervention model.

In the author's opinion, the five-day *National Community Crisis Response Training* provides the most comprehensive training in crisis intervention currently available. Topics covered during Day one include acute and chronic stress reactions. Day two reviews the topic of death and dying. Day three introduces participants to a model of individual and group crisis intervention. Days four and five provide further review and practice of crisis intervention skills. This is an ideal training for an entire local team to attend together and can help to ensure a common level of crisis intervention skill.

## Internet Resources

Another resource for obtaining background knowledge that has become increasingly valuable is the Internet. Recently there has been significant growth in the number of web sites of interest to school crisis response planners. A specific site I have found to be helpful is the *National Center for PTSD* (www.dartmouth.edu/dms/ptsd). This Center, and its web site, are programs of the U.S. Department of Veteran Affairs. It provides information on a broad range of research and training programs. A helpful document found within this site is "Information About PTSD." Also, found on its "Fact Sheets" page are the following: "PTSD in Children," "Survivors of Natural Disasters," and "PTSD and the Family." With Acrobat™ Reader (free viewing software) viewers can download a PDF file titled "Disaster Mental Health Services: A Guidebook for Clinicians and Administrators." This document, which is in the public domain, addresses the reactions of survivors; how to help survivors, helpers and organizations; and mental health team and program development. Again, via Acrobat™ Reader, PDF files for the *PTSD Research Quarterly* can be viewed.

Also, helpful is the *U.S. Department of Education's* web site (www.ed.gov). From the Department's home page, viewers can connect to the "School Safety Resources and Statistics" page. Here the document "Early Warning, Timely Response: A Guide to Safe Schools" can be accessed. A similar resource, the *School Violence Virtual Library* (www.uncg.edu/edu/ericcass/violence/index.htm), is produced by the ERIC Counseling and Student Services Clearing house. This web site includes pages for students, parents, and practitioners. Topics include "Punishment and Intervention," "School Environment," "Security Measures," "Avoiding Violence," "Dealing with Violent Children," "Crisis Intervention," and "Media Impact."

Finally, in the author's opinion, one of the best web sites for crisis response planners is operated by the *Federal Emergency Management Agency* (www.fema.gov). Available in both English and Spanish, it contains a variety of resources that parents and students will also find helpful. By accessing this site's Virtual Library and Electronic Reading Room viewers can browse *FEMA for Kids*, which contains disaster preparedness activities, curriculums, and games for children. It also includes resources for adults such as a mental health checklist and a discussion of how to help child victims. With Acrobat™ Reader (free viewing software) viewers can download a PDF file titled "How to Help Children After a Disaster: A Guidebook for Teachers." The *Preparedness, Training and Exercise* room includes an emergency preparedness checklist and a disaster supply kit list. It also includes suggestions for how to prepare for and respond to a variety of specific crisis events (e.g., nuclear disaster, hazardous materials, wildfires, hurricanes, landslides, mud flows, floods and flash floods, fire, extreme heat, earthquakes, thunderstorms and lightening, tornadoes, tsunamis, volcanoes, and terrorism). Again, by using Acrobat™ Reader viewers can download a PDF file titled "Disaster Preparedness Coloring Book." This document includes coloring activities for children and "Action Steps for Adults" on helping children respond to and prepare for a variety of disasters. For additional review of internet web sites of interest to the school crisis response planner the reader may consult Brock et al. (2001).

## Informal Training Options

In addition to the formal resources mentioned earlier there are a variety of other less formal strategies for acquiring knowledge about the school crisis response. Perhaps the most valuable of these strategies is to consult with other schools or school districts that have already developed a crisis response plan. There currently exist a number of excellent school crisis response models. Rather than reinventing the wheel, crisis response planners may find it beneficial to discuss the school crisis response with their colleagues in other schools. Professional conferences and workshops are often a place to find information about local crisis response planning. Also, in some instances it may be helpful to employ school crisis response specialists to act as consultant and/or to provide local crisis response training opportunities. Local, state, or national professional associations, as well as schools of educational psychology, may prove helpful in identifying these specialists.

## BUILDING CRISIS RESPONSE TEAMS

After having begun to acquire the knowledge necessary to prepare for the school crisis response, response planners will be in a position to begin team building efforts. Although each of the team building activities discussed in this section are essential to the comprehensive school crisis response, obtaining administrative support is a prerequisite to system-wide crisis preparedness. Thus, whereas all of the activities described in this section may occur simultaneously, this action is described first. Other team building activities discussed in this section include defining crisis intervention roles and responsibilities, and teams.

### Obtaining Administrative Support

If the crisis response planning effort is a "top-down" effort (i.e., it is initiated by school administration), then this step will be relatively straightforward. It will require administration to be aware of the factors important in the initiation and implementation of any school change effort.[1] On the other hand, if the crisis response planning effort is a "bottom-up" effort, then obtaining administrative support will be more involved.

When crisis response planning is initiated by nonadministrative personnel, the author recommends as a first step the formation of a Crisis Response Planning Committee (CRPC). This committee should be representative of the district or the school(s) within which the planning is to take place. CRPC efforts should focus on obtaining and disseminating the knowledge needed to undertake crisis response planning, and then begin to develop a rough outline of a crisis preparedness procedure. At this point the committee will find itself in a position to approach school or district administration regarding the desire to institutionalize crisis response planning.

The author's experience suggests that it may not be surprising to find some administrations cool to this type of planning. There are many competing demands placed on today's schools. This fact combined with the un-

[1]For information on the initiation and implementation of school change efforts the reader is referred to Fullan (1991).

pleasant feeling generated by considering traumatic circumstances, may understandably generate resistance to crisis planning. The author's advice in such a situation is to not let this resistance get in the way of planning. As with any school change effort, timing is critical to the initiation of school crisis response preparedness. There will come a time in the life of every school and school district when it is more receptive to crisis preparedness. Unfortunately, this is often immediately after a significant crisis event.

## Defining Crisis Response Roles and Responsibilities

An essential crisis response team building activity is to define specific crisis response roles. The author recommends that individuals be identified as responsible for each of the crisis response components indicated in Fig. 2.1. Specific team roles are briefly discussed in the following paragraphs.

The *School Crisis Response Coordinator* should be an administrator or administrative designee (Pitcher & Poland, 1992; Purvis, Porter, Authement, & Boren, 1991). It would clearly be beneficial for the coordinator to have an awareness of the objectives, methods, and limitations of crisis intervention in the schools. Planning responsibilities would include coordinating the de-

FIG. 2.1. This figure is designed to help illustrate the variety of activities that comprise the school crisis response.

velopment of crisis response plans, and reviewing these plans with school staff members at least annually. Crisis intervention duties would include declaring that a crisis situation exists (Cornell & Sheras, 1998), making a determination regarding the level of crisis response required, and overseeing all initial crisis response activities.

The *Crisis Intervention Coordinator* should have a clear understanding of the objectives, methods, and limitations of school crisis intervention (Pitcher & Poland, 1992). Typically, an individual with a background in school social work, psychology, or counseling would be assigned to this position. The crisis intervention coordinator would have several planning responsibilities. These would include the development of psychological triage and crisis intervention referral procedures, the development of psychological first aid resources, and the identification of community mental health referral sources. Immediately following a crisis event the crisis intervention coordinator's responsibilities would include identifying psychological trauma victims, ensuring the provision of psychological first aid, and identifying those who may need professional mental health interventions.

The *Emergency Medical and Health Coordinator* is typically a school nurse. Specific preparedness responsibilities would include providing first-aid training (e.g., CPR), ensuring that medical first aid materials and equipment are available, and establishing communication links with local doctors, hospitals, and emergency medical personnel. In some cases the medical liaison's secondary prevention responsibilities may include participation in, or management of, the medical triage of crisis victims (Young, 2000). In most cases, however, this will be done by emergency medical personnel (e.g., paramedics). In these instances the medical liaison would facilitate communication between paramedics and the crisis response team. Once immediate medical needs are taken care of, the medical liaison would facilitate communication between hospitals, doctors, and other medical personnel and the crisis response team. Additionally, the medical liaison would assist in communicating to parents and staff the medical conditions of those who were injured.

The *Security and Safety Coordinator* is typically a school administrator. In some cases a school or a school district may have its own security personnel who will fill this role. Ideally this person will have ongoing contacts with local police or sheriff's departments. Planning activities would include general safety planning, the development of plans designed to ensure student safety following a crisis (e.g., staff identification, bomb threat procedures, student evacuation procedures, and so forth), and working with law enforcement to ensure that they are familiar with school crisis response team procedures (Cornell & Sheras, 1998). During a crisis response this individual would implement safety and security procedures and facilitate communication between local law enforcement and the school.

The *Media Management Coordinator* is responsible for establishing procedures for working with broadcast and print journalists. In districts that have a media spokesperson, this individual will naturally fill this role. Immediately following a crisis, the Media Management Coordinator would be responsible for the dissemination of crisis facts (Nye, 1997) and for ensuring that the media is able to assist and not hinder the response.

The *Debriefing and Evaluation Facilitator* is an administrator or school mental health professional who has the responsibility for evaluating the preparation of the crisis response team and the effectiveness of their actions. Following a crisis response, this individual determines what has worked, and what needs to be improved. Another important role is monitoring and facilitating the mental health of crisis workers themselves.

It is recommended that more than one individual be designated to fill each of these roles. This is designed to account for the possible physical or psychological unavailability of crisis response team members (e.g., due to illness, injury, or psychological traumatization stemming from the crisis event). A summary of specific crisis planning and crisis response responsibilities for each of the crisis response team roles are provided in Table 2.1.

## Defining Crisis Response Teams

In addition to identifying individual crisis response roles and responsibilities, crisis response planning should also identify institutional roles and responsibilities. As conceptualized by the author, doing so involves the delineation of crisis response "levels." Specifically, it is recommended that a school crisis response plan include the identification of multiple hierarchical teams.

Arguably, the most important, yet also the most basic, crisis response team is the *school site-level team*. This team should be composed of school site personnel, with individuals designated to fill each crisis response team role listed earlier. The author's experiences have found that well-prepared school resources are typically able to independently manage most crisis situations. The importance of the school level response is highlighted by the fact that it can be very reassuring to students and parents to see familiar school staff members responding to a crisis situation. On the other hand, it can increase perceptions of threat and danger if the crisis response team is composed of individuals not identified as being a part of the school community. Such a response will communicate that the crisis event was so severe that school resources are unable to manage the crisis. Of course, it needs to be recognized that some crisis events are so severe that they will overwhelm available school site-level crisis response resources and this is when a having multiple hierarchical crisis response teams becomes essential.

If school site-level resources are unable or insufficient to independently manage a crisis situation, then assistance from a *school district-level crisis re-*

TABLE 2.1
School Crisis Response Team Roles and Responsibilities

| *Role* | *Crisis Planning Responsibilities* | *Crisis Response Responsibilities* |
|---|---|---|
| Crisis Response Coordinator | • Initiating and supervising all crisis planning activities.<br>• Reviewing crisis response plans at least annually. | • Declaring that a crisis situation exists.<br>• Supervising all crisis response activities.<br>• Requesting district-level crisis response assistance if needed. |
| Crisis Intervention Coordinator | • Ensuring that psychological first aid resources are available.<br>• Developing psychological triage and referral procedures.<br>• Identifying mental health resources to be used in times of crisis. | • Identifying psychological trauma victims.<br>• Supervising the provision of psychological first aid to trauma victims.<br>• Identifying those in need of professional mental health assistance. |
| Emergency Medical and Health Coordinator | • Ensuring that medical first aid resources are available.<br>• Establishing communication links with emergency response personnel (e.g., paramedics). | • When needed, supervising the initial provision of medical first aid to trauma victims.<br>• Acting as a liaison between emergency response personnel and the school.<br>• Monitoring the status of seriously injured (hospitalized) crisis victims. |
| Security and Safety Coordinator | • Ensuring that school safety/security plans are developed (including staff identification, evacuation, danger signal, bomb threat, and traffic management procedures).<br>• Establishing communication links with local law enforcement. | • Implementing school safety/security procedures (including traffic management, and student/parent reunification).<br>• Acting as a liaison between law enforcement personnel and the school. |
| Media Management Coordinator | • Developing press release templates.<br>• Establish procedures and/or rules for working with the media during crises.<br>• Establishing communication links with local media. | • Helping to determine what crisis information will be shared.<br>• Preparing announcements and press releases.<br>• Acting as a liaison between the media and the school |
| Debriefing and Evaluation Facilitator | • Ensuring that critical incident stress debriefing resources can be made available to crisis response team personnel. | • Provide debriefing to all personnel involved in the crisis response.<br>• Help to evaluate crisis response effectiveness. |

*sponse team* should be made available. It is important to note that involvement of district-level resources in a school crisis response should not be viewed as excusing site-level teams from the crisis response. No one will know a school's population better than those individuals who work there regularly. Thus, site-level personnel will be critical to the successful implementation of any district-level crisis response.

The author recommends that the district-level team should be similar in structure to school site-level teams. However, on this team district-level personnel will typically fill most of the crisis response roles. Also, it is expected that district-level team members will have greater school crisis response expertise than their site-level counterparts. Thus, although the school site-level response is suggested to be preferable, consultation with the district-level team should be encouraged and welcomed. In addition, because of their typically greater expertise, a district-level team may play an important role in providing the training and supervision needed to develop effective school site-level teams.

Although it would be used infrequently, a *regional-level crisis response team*, is also recommended. The author's experiences have found this level of crisis response to be critical following mass disasters (e.g., the Stockton school yard shooting which left 5 students dead and 30 wounded). The establishment of such a team can be facilitated by having local school districts enter into mutual aid agreements with each other. These agreements allow districts to share emergency response resources and might be considered an insurance policy. A policy that a school district purchases by agreeing to send its own trained staff to other school districts following mass disasters (Brock, 1998).

A regional-level team should be similar in structure to the school site-level team. Although a regional-level crisis response will be a very infrequent occurrence, this team may take on important crisis response planning responsibilities. Given that it is likely that this team will have access to the most highly trained local crisis responders, it is in a strong position to offer regional crisis response training programs.

## Developing Crisis Response Planning Guidelines

As conceptualized by the author, the development of crisis response planning guidelines should include both procedures for designating specific individuals to fill the specific crisis response roles (Table 2.1) and the completion of several specific crisis preparedness tasks. Both of these activities are now discussed.

***Designating Crisis Response Responsibilities.*** Once crisis response roles and responsibilities have been developed, this procedure will be relatively straightforward. Planning guidelines will simply need to document which individuals have been designated to fill specific roles. As was previously mentioned, alternates will need to be identified to address the contingency of a crisis response team member being unavailable. Additionally, it will be important to ensure that the listing of individuals filling crisis response team roles is updated at least annually. Doing so accounts for the fact that personnel may move or decide they no long wish to be a part of the crisis response team.

***Complete Crisis Preparedness Tasks.*** In addition to the preparedness activities specified in Table 2.1, crisis response planning guidelines also need to specify the completion of tasks that the response team will need to complete cooperatively. These tasks are described in Table 2.2.

### Developing Crisis Response Procedural Guidelines

In addition to the preparedness tasks just described, it is critical for school crisis response teams to develop crisis response procedural guidelines. These guidelines, which help to ensure that important crisis response tasks are not left undone, include the following activities.

***Assess the Crisis Situation.*** The first task to be completed following a crisis event, is for the response team to assess the crisis situation. This involves determining the crisis facts and estimating the potential school impact. This information needs to be made immediately available to district office personnel and all crisis response team members. It can be used to decide on the level of crisis response required (e.g., school site-level vs. district-level). Information sources helpful in obtaining crisis facts includes law enforcement, medical personnel, and the families of crisis victims.

***Disseminate Crisis Information.*** After having gathered the available crisis facts, decisions need to be made about what information is to be shared with staff and students, and how this will be done. Sharing such information is often critical to a school crisis response as crisis rumors are often more frightening than are crisis facts. It is recommended that crisis facts be disseminated in as normal and natural an environment as possible. For example, announcements sharing crisis facts can be read by teachers to their student in the classroom. Intercom announcements and all school assemblies should be avoided. Additionally, when making decisions about what information to share with a school, it may be appropriate to avoid mentioning particularly horrific or grisly details of the traumatic circumstance. If such details are not publicly available and speculated upon, then there will be no reason to discuss them. This recommendation stems from the observation that individuals can become traumatized after learning about the vic-

TABLE 2.2
Crisis Preparedness Tasks Completed Cooperatively by the Crisis Response Team

*Identify crisis intervention locations.* Locations need to be identified as places where crisis intervention can be provided following a crisis. In doing so, attention needs to be given to the fact that some interventions will be individual while others will be group Also, it needs to be kept in mind that following major crises large numbers of parents may arrive simultaneously to retrieve their children. Thus, common parent waiting areas (within which parents can be provided crisis information and crisis intervention) need to be identified.

*Designate specific phone lines to be used for specific reasons.* Following a crisis available phone lines can be quickly overwhelmed. Thus, specific lines to be used for specific purposes should be identified. The establishment and maintenance of "hidden phone lines" is very important. These lines, which should not be available to the public, are the ones to be used by staff for emergency communications. Making sure that cellular phones are available is also helpful.

*Designatef a crisis response team base of operations.* A central location from which the crisis response team will operate needs to be identified. The chosen location should be equipped with computers, telephones, paper, pens, telephone directories, emergency power, and portable two-way radios. Many times this will be the school office. As a part of this preparedness activity, procedures need to be established for identifying and monitoring the additional crisis response personnel utilized as part of a regional- and/or district-level response. Sign-in procedures need to be established so that school administration is always aware of who is on site at a given time. Procedures for getting messages to crisis response team members and support staff need to be developed.

*Establishing a phone tree among all classified, certified, and administrative staff.* A phone tree is a method for ensuring quick, effective communication of crisis situation facts during nonschool hours. Such a system is especially important given the observation that crises may be better resolved if staff members are informed of an incident before students (Purvis, Porter, Authement, & Boren, 1991).

*Establish a crisis response "toolbox."* During the initial phases of a crisis response it is often hard for people to consider details. Thus, it is recommended that a "toolbox" be created. This toolbox should centrally house all of the documents and materials developed by team members as part of their crisis preparedness activities (e.g., psychological triage or risk screening materials; a list of mental health referral resources; preparedness statements; evaluation, bomb threat, and traffic management procedures; medical first aid materials; etc.). Other materials recommended for inclusion in the toolbox include a school map, a set of school keys, a schedule of all classes, and a list of all students enrolled in the school (Thompson, 1995).

*Note.* Adapted from Brock et al. (2001).

timization of a relative or close associate (American Psychiatric Association, 1994). However, no matter how horrific the crisis facts, if students have questions about them, it will generally be appropriate to answer them in as honest and direct a fashion as is possible.

***Identify Crisis Victims.*** As the crisis facts become apparent, crisis response personnel will begin to be able to identify both the physical and the psychological victims of the crisis event. Arguably, the most important factor in determining degree of psychological trauma is proximity to the crisis event (Pynoos et al., 1987). However, familiarity with crisis victims is also an antecedent of psychic trauma (Milgram, Toubiana, Klingman, Raviv, & Goldstein, 1988). It is essential that the crisis response procedural guidelines specify a procedure for identifying and keeping track of crisis victims. Parent, teacher, and student referral procedures need to be implemented to help ensure that no trauma victim slips through the cracks.

***Provide Crisis Intervention Services.*** As psychological trauma victims are identified, decisions need to be made regarding the provision of crisis intervention services. When there are large numbers of psychological trauma victims, a psychological triage will need to be conducted. Use of triage will help response teams make crisis intervention treatment priority decisions. It will be important to carefully document all crisis interventions. A question that needs to be addressed is whether individual trauma victims require professional mental health intervention. The presence of any degree of lethality (i.e., suicidal or homicidal thinking) or an inability to cope with the traumatizing circumstances independently are the most frequent reasons for making professional mental health counseling referrals.

***Debrief and Evaluate the Crisis Response.*** Finally, it is essential that crisis response procedural guidelines include activities designed to care for the caregivers. Following a crisis response, all crisis team members will need to be offered critical incident stress debriefing. Additionally, it will be important for the team to evaluate the effectiveness of the response. No two crises are alike. Thus, given the proper reflective thought, all crises are potential crisis response learning experiences.

## CONCLUDING COMMENTS

In concluding this chapter it is important to acknowledge that the best of plans are useless if they are allowed to sit on a shelf collecting dust. Readiness checks and drills are important if preparedness and response procedures are to remain effective over time. One strategy for ensuring the viability of these procedures is to develop and adopt a school district crisis response policy. Ideally, such policy mandates school personnel to undertake crisis preparedness activities.

## REFERENCES

Adams, C. M. (1996). Adolescent suicide: One school's response. *Journal of Secondary Gifted Education, 7,* 410–417.

American Psychiatric Association. (1994). *Diagnostic and statistical manual of mental disorders* (4th ed.). Washington, DC: Author.

Brock, S. E. (1998, November). School crisis intervention mutual aid: A county-level response plan. *Communiqué, 27,* 4–5.

Brock, S. E., Sandoval, J., & Lewis, S. (1996). *Preparing for crises in the schools: A manual for building school crisis response teams*. New York: Wiley.

Brock, S. E., Sandoval, J., & Lewis, S. (2001). *Preparing for crises in the schools: A manual for building school crisis response teams* (2nd ed.). New York: Wiley.

Cornell, D. G., & Sheras, P. L. (1998). Common errors in school crisis response: Learning from our mistakes. *Psychology in the Schools, 35*, 297–307.

Fairchild, T. N. (Ed.). (1997). *Crisis intervention strategies for school-based helpers* (2nd ed.). Springfield, IL: Charles C. Thomas.

Fullan, M. G. (1991). *The new meaning of educational change*. New York: Teachers College Press.

Johnson, K. (1993). *School crisis management: A hands-on guide to training crisis response teams*. Alameda, CA: Hunter House.

Mathers, K. (1996). Never again would we be the same: The Oklahoma City bombing. *NASSP Bulletin, 80*, 38–43.

Milgram, N. A., Toubiana, Y. H., Klingman, A., Raviv, A., & Goldstein, R. (1988). Situational exposure and personal loss in children's acute and chronic stress reactions to a school bus disaster. *Journal of Traumatic Stress, 1*, 339–352.

Mitchell, J. T., & Everly, G. S. (1996). *Critical incident stress management: The basic course workbook*. Ellicot City, MD: International Critical Incident Stress Foundation.

Nye, K. P. (1997). He's got a gun! *American School Board Journal, 18*, 43–45.

Petersen, S., & Straub, R. L. (1992). *School crisis survival guide: Management techniques and materials for counselors and administrators*. West Nyack, NY: Center for Applied Research in Education.

Pitcher, G., & Poland, S. (1992). *Crisis intervention in the schools*. New York: Guilford Press.

Poland, S., & McCormick, J. (1999). *Coping with crisis: A complete and comprehensive guide to school crisis intervention*. Longmont, CO: Sopris West.

Purvis, J. R., Porter, R. L., Authement, C. C., & Boren, L. C. (1991). Crisis intervention teams in the schools. *Psychology in the Schools, 28*, 331–339.

Pynoos, R. S., Frederick, C., Nader, K., Steinberg, A., Eth, S., Nune, F., & Fairbanks, L. (1987). Life threat and post traumatic stress in school-age children. *Archives of General Psychiatry, 44*, 1057–1063.

Ramsay, R. F., Tanney, B. L., Tierney, R. J., & Lang, W. A. (1996). *Suicide intervention workshop*. Calgary, AB: LivingWorks Education.

Slaikeu, K. A. (1990). *Crisis intervention: A handbook for practice and research* (2nd ed.). Newton, MA: Allyn & Bacon.

Thompson, R. A. (1995). Being prepared for suicide or sudden death in schools: Strategies to restore equilibrium. *Journal of Mental Health Counseling, 17*, 264–277.

Young, M. A. (1998). *The community crisis response team training manual* (2nd ed.). Washington, DC: National Organization for Victim Assistance.

Young, M. A. (2000, January/February). Addressing trauma and violence in our schools. *Psychology Teacher Network, 10*(1), 5–7, 11.

CHAPTER

# 3

# Culture, Diversity, and Crisis

Jonathan Sandoval
University of California, Davis

At present, many of those responding to a hazardous event will come from White, middle class, English monolingual, North American backgrounds. They will tend to draw on their experiences with a similar clientele, and operate from values based in Western European culture. At the same time, many of those traumatized will come from a wide diversity of backgrounds and there is great potential for a lack of connection between the helper and the clients. Ideally a crisis response team would be made up of helpers from all cultures represented in the school, but this will not often be possible. Crises come at unpredictable times and the diversity of many schools is so great, it would be impossible at a moment's notice to have trained personnel available so as to match helper with client.

More rapidly than any other institution, our schools are going through tremendous changes to accommodate new populations. In most regions, the children and the families they serve are becoming increasingly diverse. Since 1985, the number of children entering school without full English proficiency has grown by about 70%. One school-age child in seven speaks a language other than English at home (Garcia, 1995). Ethnic minority students comprise 70% to 96% of the students in 15 of the nation's largest school districts (Kellogg, 1988). Much of this diversity comes from immigration from Mexico and Central America, and from economically depressed or war-torn areas of the world such as Eastern Europe. There a numerous ways that culture must be taken into account if a crisis worker is to successfully engage with the parents and families of the children in today's schools. This chapter outlines many of the most important cultural considerations to keep in mind. Other relevant resources on working with culturally diverse families are Cartledge and Johnson, 1997; Castillo, 1997; Congress, 2000; McGoldrick, Giordano, & Pearce, 1996.

## Competencies of the Multicultural Counselor

Sue and his colleagues have outlined the competencies needed for effective multicultural counseling (Sue et al., 1998). They list three general dimensions: Counselor awareness of own Assumptions, Values and Biases; Understanding the Worldview of the Culturally Different Client; and Developing appropriate Intervention Strategies and Techniques. Under each of these dimensions they indicate a set of Attitudes and Beliefs, Knowledge, and Skills. They believe that "Becoming multiculturally competent means the ability to free one's personal and professional development from the unquestioned socialization of our society and profession (Sue et al., 1998, p. 37). But it also means acquiring the skills outlined. In addition, "Multiculturally competent counselors also consider factors such as the impact of the sociopolitical system on people of color in the United States, have knowledge and information about particular cultural groups, and are able to generate a wide range of appropriate verbal/nonverbal responses to client needs" (Pope-Davis & Dings, 1995, p. 288). The process of gaining the multicultural counseling competencies involves study, prolonged exposure to other cultures, self-examination, and supervision. The first step is often making counselors aware that they do have a set of culturally determined attitudes and beliefs.

## Attitudes and Beliefs From the Dominant Culture

One simple definition of culture is the shared language, ideas, beliefs, values, and behavioral norms of a group of individuals with a group identity. Culture regulates how individuals interact with one another and provides a structure for organization to occur. Culture is not a static phenomenon, however, it is constantly evolving. Children come from a culture, but are early on exposed to the school culture, which is often closely related to the dominant culture. Children can be bicultural or even tricultural, when one considers that there may be a separate adolescent culture.

Most crisis workers come from the dominant culture or have assimilated to it. Because assimilation is so powerful, members of the dominant culture are often unaware that their values and attitudes are not universal and shared across all people. As a result, there is utility in making the values and attitudes of the dominant culture explicit. If the helper comes from a nondominant culture, it will be equally important for this professional to acknowledge the cultural "baggage" he or she brings to work. The dominant culture of the United States is derived from the White Anglo-Saxon Protestant tradition (Spring, 2000). The core values of this tradition include mutual respect, individual rights, tolerance of differences, respect for the rule of law, democracy, and individual achievement. These values are expressed in connection with schooling, work, family, social organization, property, and the environment. The core values of other cultures may or may not contrast.

The dominant culture in the United States, for example, values independence and individuality. Competition is healthy. Achievement reflects individual effort. We value self-expression, although not great displays of emotion. The culture advocates democratic family relationships. Family ties are loose, and the parents, alone, are responsible for their children. There is a belief that individuals can change and control events and that nature can be dominated. Religion is distinct from other parts of our culture. Punctuality is important and it is reasonable to plan for the future.

In contrast, the Latino culture values interpersonal relationships and loyalty to the extended family. Dignity and honor are highly respected. Group cooperation is more important than individual achievement. Extremes of emotion may be expressed. Many relations are hierarchical, rather than democratic. There is a strong belief that events are controlled by fate (God) rather than humans, and religion is integrated into everyday life. Time is flexible and extendable.

The cultural differences between groups are not trivial and can easily lead to miss-communication. In addition, cultural differences have important implications for crisis intervention and crisis prevention. For example, in assisting Latino children to mediate a hazardous event, religious beliefs will be much more important to consider in this group than in members of the dominant culture, and the social context of actions planned will be critical to success.

After crisis workers have come to acknowledge the values and attitudes embedded in their own culture, and have recognized the legitimacy of alternative cultural stances, the challenge becomes, "How can helpers with a particular (dominant) worldview learn to work with members of a different culture?" Counselors are typically taught to suspend their value judgments in working with others, but are not often prepared to work with others with truly different concepts of how the world operates. What it takes to do this work is the acquisition of new understandings and skills to work with the diversity in schools. I turn to these skill in a later section of this chapter, but first I review some of the stressors and resources available to culturally diverse families during times of crisis.

## STRESS AND COPING DURING TIMES OF CRISIS

Extra stressors are present in the lives of immigrant and many other culturally diverse groups, including poverty, discrimination, and need for assimilation. Many migrating families have already experienced crisis events in their home country, such as torture, rape, and loss of home and family. As a result, these children and their families may be particularly vulnerable when school related crises occur.

Many culturally diverse groups are at the bottom of the economic pyramid in this country. Immigrant fathers may have difficulty in finding jobs in this county that are at the same income and status level as at home (Congress, 2000). Thus poverty will be a factor in how they respond and are able to cope when a crisis occurs. Lack of family resources, for example, not having the funds to properly bury a deceased family member, exacerbates trauma (Lewis, 1970).

Another stressor is changed gender roles. Women may find it easier to find work than do men, and the culture in the United States supports different kinds of freedoms than elsewhere. Traditional roles may reverse causing tensions that may result in substance abuse and domestic violence (Congress, 2000).

There may be another role reversal in immigrant homes—that between children and adults. Children often learn English faster than their parents and become the family's contacts with the outside world. They become the family spokesperson. They often become more competent in English than in their home language, further alienating them from their parents and their culture. As a consequence of their time in school and in the neighborhood, they also become more quickly acculturated, and are willing to spend less time in traditional roles such as providing child care for younger siblings (Congress, 2000). Intergenerational conflicts around schooling and achievement are also common.

Additional stressors for immigrants include legal difficulties related to immigration status, and divided families, with some members remaining in the homeland. For many culturally diverse families, poor health is also a stressor, in part, because of lack of access to health care. Infant mortality is greater, maternal death rates are higher, and life expectancies for many groups are much lower than for White Americans.

Immigrants from war ravaged countries may also have experienced terrorism and violence or have witnessed atrocities. These stressors leave a legacy that may take generations to resolve (Danieli, 1988).

The effects of cumulative stress or unresolved issues related to grief or previous trauma make individuals from culturally diverse backgrounds more at risk for Post Traumatic Stress Disorder (PTSD). On the other hand, those from nondominant cultures do have some important resources for coping with traumatic events and life changes.

Families represent a greater source of social support in many cultures. The notion of family is often extended beyond the biological, and more people are available to provide support in a time of crisis. For example, urban Black families may have multiple resources available to crisis victims as the extended family may reach deeply into the community (Stack, 1974). Another strength can be religion. The Black church is a powerful source of support for Black women in particular (Congress, 2000). Finally, because of the higher incidence of crisis in diverse communities, coping strategies may already have developed that can be reactivated to help negotiate the current crisis. In crisis intervention, it is always important to build on strengths and to avoid a deficit model in dealing with others.

## IMPLICATIONS OF DIVERSITY FOR PREVENTION

### Work With Communities

A first step in prevention is to begin working with different diverse communities. Within these communities school-based professionals should identify and establish relationships with influential leaders and attempt to find cultural mentors that can help staff understand traditions, values, and attitudes they will encounter among families. These leaders can also be used in times of crisis to build the necessary bridges between the school and families. Potential translators for use in an emergency can also be identified.

With the assistance of community members, school personnel can also identify families who are already vulnerable, so that referrals to outside agencies may be facilitated. Establishing a full-service school is an helpful approach to building more resilient families.

### Provide Information in Home Languages

Communications from the school to the home about crisis preparedness or about resources in the aftermath of a traumatic event should be available in languages other than English. The issue of translation is covered later in the chapter, but materials providing anticipatory guidance for developmental crises, or lists of resources in times of traumatic crises, for example, can be developed in many languages and distributed at appropriate times.

### Address Social Issues

Although outside of the purview of the school, responsible helping professionals can work as citizens to advocate for social justice and equity. By joining with others to promote employment opportunities, access to mental and physical health care, and educational opportunities for families at or below the poverty line, school professionals can contribute to better capacity in diverse communities to negotiate hazardous events successfully.

## CULTURE AND THE REACTION TO TRAUMATIC EVENTS

Traumatic events often result crisis reactions that show themselves in a number of symptoms such as fear, confusion, emotional numbing, and disordered sleep. The specific symptoms of a crisis response may have a specific cultural manifestation. At the same time, ordinary, culturally appropriate coping may seem dysfunctional to western eyes.

For example, many individuals from Asian cultures are more likely to develop somatic complaints in response to crisis. Another example of cultural patterns influencing responses is that fears and nightmares may have a focus on spirits and ghosts.

Sometimes a reaction to a traumatic event will be culturally appropriate but will seem to western eyes to be a breakdown of ordinary coping. Extreme outward expression of grief by wailing and crying followed by self-mutilation and threats of suicide following the death of a loved one may be normal coping behavior expected of a survivor in a particular culture. Klingman (1986) offered the example of a medical staff considering sedating a grieving person when the perceived extreme response was actually a normal one for a person from a Middle Eastern culture. A cultural informant or mentor from the school community will be very useful in indicating what normal reactions to various traumatic events are for a particular culture.

On the other hand, what appears to be confusion and poor coping may simply be the result of a lack of understanding of English, rather than a crisis reaction. Confusion may simply be a lack of comprehension for language or cultural reasons.

The reverse may also be the case: A naïve crisis worker might, incorrectly attribute confusion and disorientation that are crisis related, to cultural differences or language problems. Sometimes resisting stereotypes can also lead to difficulty.

## IMPLICATIONS OF DIVERSITY FOR CRISIS COUNSELING

The first chapter of this volume outlined a number of generic crisis counseling and crisis intervention principles. As general principles, they must be modified for individuals, as there will be wide variation within a cultural group. In addition, the general principles might be modified to take cultural differences into account. In the following section, I elaborate on some of these crisis counseling principles with respect to cultural issues. Later, I elaborate on crisis intervention.

## Be Concerned and Competent

It is true that the crisis counselor must be seen as a potential resource. Nevertheless, how one comes to be seen as concerned and competent has cultural dynamics.

***Social Status.*** Social status refers to a person's position in a social order based on such factors as gender, age, economic position, educational accomplishment, and so on. Each culture may give status to particular individuals. Asian cultures, for example, defer to age; other cultures may defer to the female head of the family. In working with families during times of crisis, the crisis intervener's status may vary from group to group. The age of the crisis counselor may be an advantage in one group but not another. Insofar as possible, it would be helpful to match counselors to clients so that the counselor has high status with respect to the culture. Insofar as crisis intervention is more directive than other forms of counseling, a high-status helper will be more effective than a low-status one.

By the same token, when working with a family or community during a crisis it will be important to direct communication and get cooperation from high-status individuals in that group. In working with a migrant Mexican-American family, for example, communications might first be directed to the father, acknowledging his status.

***Dress.*** Many cultures have expectations for what is considered appropriate or modest dress. In much of the world, men are expected to wear suits and women to wear dresses. Modesty may involve covering the head or other parts of the body. Crisis responders should attempt to dress conservatively and professionally, as such an appearance will help inspire confidence as well as show respect. A professional dressed in blue jeans, for example, might quickly loose credibility with Southeast Asian clients.

## Listen to the Facts of the Situation

In making psychological contact, attention should be given to a number of factors to improve communication. Getting people to tell their story requires establishing rapport and using good, culturally appropriate listening skills. The counselor should attend to communication styles, sociolinguistic issues, and nonverbal communication.

***Communication Styles.*** Styles of communication can range from the assertive and voluble to the quiet and indirect. Arabic families, for example, have an assertive style (Wilson, 1996). Often shouting is used for effect. An initial "no" may mean "yes" unless the *no* is repeated several times. To be persuasive, it is appropriate to show emotion, repeat points, and pound the table. It is usual to talk around the subject before coming to the point.

In contrast, in Asian cultures there is a subtle use of language and emotions (Li & Liu, 1993). Members of this group value harmony and avoid confrontation and argument. A third person may act as a mediator to facilitate communication between persons in conflict. Individuals seldom express emotions. In contrast to the dominant culture that values directness, Asian and many other cultures prefer to come to the point of a conversation in an indirect manner. More patience in listening may be required with individuals from these cultures than with individuals from the dominant culture.

***Sociolinguistic Issues.*** In order not to violate an important cultural convention, it is usually safe to observe good diplomatic protocol. In approaching individuals, they should be greeted appropriately (e.g., "Hello") and the helper should introduce him or herself. Politeness is paramount, and the helper should ask permission to speak and to do things for the individual in crisis. Saying "please" and "thank you" is important, as is acknowledging limitations and weaknesses that spring from a lack of cultural or linguistic knowledge, and apologizing quickly when an error or gaff has been committed. Often it will be appropriate to apologize in advance when the helper is uncertain about discussing a sensitive area. Special care should be taken in asking questions. In many cultures asking direct questions is considered rude. Asking indirect questions (Benjamin, 1981) may yield a better response.

***Nonverbal Communication.*** Attention to nonverbal communication is also important during a time of crisis. A number of dimensions including eye contact and proximity can be very different between members of different cultures (Hall, 1959). Because these behaviors are subtle, counselors may easily miss them.

Counselors are often advised to make good *eye contact* with clients. In our dominant culture, we traditionally make direct eye contact to indicate we are attending to the client and then allow our gaze to drift during conversation. In contrast, in Middle Eastern culture, sustained eye contact is the norm. In contrast, in Asian and Native American groups, to show respect and deference to elders, direct eye contact is avoided. A child from such a culture may well be paying attention, even though he or she does not return eye contact.

In conversation, dominant culture members prefer *space between discussants*—up to 5 feet. In contrast, both Hispanic and Arabic conversationalists will gravitate to a shorter proximity, perhaps 2 feet, between discussants. Crisis workers must not misinterpret violations of "personal space" when clients end up closer than accustomed.

Some cultures use more *gestures* while speaking than do others. The eastern Mediterranean cultures are particularly known for gesticulating as they speak. Smiling, giggling, and laughing may be particularly misleading. In Asian culture, these all may denote suppression of emotion rather than insensitivity. The same smile in a traditional Vietnamese person may mean happiness or sorrow, agreement or disagreement, embarrassment or confidence, comprehension or confusion. A smiling person from these cultures should not be assumed to be unaffected by trauma.

The dominant culture views *touching* as appropriate following a traumatic event as acceptable, although not appropriate in many other contexts. Children in this tradition would be comforted by being held when upset. Nevertheless, physical contact should be initiated with great care. Hugging, patting, or embracing between a helper and a client may be viewed as inappropriate in some cultures (e.g., Hmong), although seen as appropriate in others (e.g., Hispanic). Cultures often have strong traditions regarding the appropriateness of physical contact. In the dominant culture, physical contact between males is rare. In contrast, within Asian cultures (Li & Liu, 1993, March) touching is acceptable between members of the same gender, and shaking hands is more acceptable than hugging. In a number of cultures (e.g., among the Hmong), it is inappropriate for strangers to touch a child on the head. African Americans may consider the act of touching an African American child's head by a White American, extremely racist.

## Reflect the Individual's Feelings

Crisis workers should be aware that expression of emotions is a highly important dimension of culture. Typically, following most other intervention models, persons in crisis are encouraged to express their feelings about the traumatic event that happened to them. Crisis counselors encourage those in crisis to surface and share their feelings, which are reflected back and summarized by the counselor. Asian cultures traditionally suppress emotions (Li & Liu, 1993, March) and may feel further stress when pressured by crisis counselors to focus on their feelings. Value may be placed on maintenance of dignity, inner and emotional strength. Thus, emotions may be suppressed to maintain dignity.

In contrast, crisis counselors may become concerned or uncomfortable with the other extreme. African American families often show very intense, demonstrative expressions of their feelings in public, which may be perceived by Western culture as unrestrained and crass (Willis, 1992).

### Help the Child Realize That the Crisis Event Has Occurred

In many cultures, denial is seen as an acceptable coping strategy rather than as a defense. In many Hispanic families, the adult reaction to a crisis event may be a decision to protect and not tell the children of the crisis event (Bellatin, personal communication, March 1995). Family secrets may be kept, and nobody asks or talks about such issues as illness, death, sexual abuse, or suicide. Crisis workers should be aware that children coming from a cultural background with this belief may not have the opportunity to tell their crisis story at home. In the Asian culture, denial and guilt may be part of the cultural values where human suffering is seen as part of the natural order (Li & Liu, 1993).

## IMPLICATIONS OF DIVERSITY FOR CRISIS INTERVENTION

In intervening on behalf of a child or family in the aftermath of a traumatic event, the school mental health worker must also take culture into consideration. There are culturally acceptable ways of accomplishing each of the following tasks.

### Facilitate the Re-Establishment of a Social Support Network

Social support in many cultures comes from the family and from religious practices and traditions. Religion is a particularly powerful form of support.

***Religion.*** A religious tradition and the spirituality that goes with it is of enormous help during a time of crisis. Within a religion are usually rituals associated with many of the crises people encounter, particularly the loss of death. Knowledge of the grieving process and traditions of various cultures is indispensable to crisis workers.

Religious worldviews that emphasize mystery about life and the role of fate or luck, permit believers to make sense of traumatic events and find meaning. Facilitating culturally relevant healing rituals such as an exorcism or a cleansing ceremony to take place is very helpful following a crisis incident. Relaxation of strict separation between church and state in schools may facilitate a speedier and more positive crisis resolution.

On the other hand, religious injunctions and traditions can also precipitate a crisis when an event takes on added dimensions because of strong taboos. A suicide or a sexual assault may be a clear crisis in almost any culture, but have even more serious consequences in religions where these events bring extra shame to a family or cause children to be unmarriageable.

According to Lee and Armstrong (1995), all cultural groups have traditional attitudes about behavior defined as abnormal when it is outside of the culturally defined boundary of optimal psychological functioning. In many cultures when individuals enter a crisis state, they turn to others who are acknowledged within their communities as possessing special insight and helping skills. The anthropological term *shaman* is used to cover people called medicine man or woman, witch, witch doctor, sorcerer, or traditional healer. Within the shamanic tradition, there is an emphasis on a holistic approach, nonordinary reality and emphasis on the psychospiritual realm of personality (Lee & Armstrong, 1995). Although many of the shaman's practices and beliefs may be considered primitive and unsophisticated to Western eyes, these traditional methods have served to give comfort to the victims of crises for millennia.

If a child is from a shamanic culture, it may be useful to locate a traditional healer or shaman from the community and consult with them as appropriate. Richardson (1991) recommended that after exploring with a client his or her worldview, determining that the child's belief system includes traditional beliefs, and determining that the client or the family could benefit from the services of a traditional healer, it will be appropriate to elicit the aid of the shaman. Folk healers may be difficult to identify, as they are not known outside their community, but the family or others in the community can help to locate them. The Western crisis counselor should be available to participate, if invited, in ceremonial activities or practices that will help the client cope. In preparing for crises it is valuable to have a referral system in place that includes traditional healers.

In most religions some days, weeks, and even months have a special significance for both coping with crisis events and for intervening in a crisis. We must be aware of appropriate holidays where the focus may be on coping with a crisis and support the use of this tool. For example, for families of Mexican heritage, the Day of the Dead (following the Western Halloween) is a time to remember departed, and come to view death as a both a normal part of life and as a blessing.

***Food.*** During times of crisis, food has often been an important solace, and meals are a time of social interaction. In many cultures, friends and neighbors provide food to those who are grieving following a death. Additional social activity can be stimulated through the preparation of meals. Social routines around food can re-connect victims to social support.

## Engage in Focused Problem Solving

Helping individuals in crisis consider courses of action that will assist them improve or resolve an emotionally hazardous situation often is at the heart of counseling. Counseling may be done individually or in groups, and in or outside of the context of the school.

***Attitudes Toward Counseling.*** The acceptability of counseling as an aid to problem solving is culturally determined. Particular attention should be paid to how mental illness and the specific crisis event is perceived by the culture of the client. For example, within the Arabic culture, the mentally ill are likely to be maintained within the family. Feelings of guilt may lead to overprotection, denial, or isolation, resulting in rejection of a long-term therapeutic program (Wilson, 1996). In the Hispanic culture, having mental problems related to a crisis may be perceived as being "crazy," which is considered very shameful and something to be hidden from others. In the Asian culture, where it may be viewed negatively to single out an individual as different, seeking help for a mental health problem might be perceived as bringing shame to the family (Morrow, 1988, November/December). Strategies other than individual counseling may be more acceptable. If individual work is necessary, because of the focus on physical health, public health services may be viewed as more acceptable than mental health services outside of a medical setting.

***Group Work.*** Group intervention may be particularly appropriate for working with linguistically and culturally diverse students or their parents in crisis (Esquivel, 1998). Esquivel argued that group interventions are effective because they are consistent with a common aspects of many cultures: A collective orientation and an emphasis on family and group values. Since migration, poverty, and intergenerational conflict may disrupt many family resources; the group serves as a substitute for family in emphasizing cooperation, cohesiveness, and interdependence among group members. A number of group techniques have been devised to be culturally relevant. Some notable examples are Cuento therapy, using folk tales; Hero–Heroine Modeling using biographical information; and Unitas, an intervention using older peers to recreate family (Esquivel, 1998). Although not specifically developed for crisis intervention, these techniques may be used or adapted for traumatic situations.

Support groups, in the form of school-based "Neighborhood Club" have also been used to help poor children cope and problem solve following chronic exposure to urban violence (Ceballo, 2000). Support groups have the advantage of giving members a common ground on which to interact.

Group work in the form of family therapy is another proven valuable option (McGoldrick et al., 1996). Issues of family conflict and acculturation can be resolved as well as problem solving accomplished in this setting. Typically this would take place via referral.

## LANGUAGE ISSUES

At this point, I address a particularly difficult issue with respect to cross-cultural crisis counseling and intervention: Language. Language is one of the most important manifestations of culture. If possible, crisis interveners should speak the same language as their client. Sue et al. (1998) stated,

> Culturally skilled counselors take responsibility for interacting in the language requested by the client; this may mean appropriate referral to outside resources. A serious problem arises when the linguistic skills of the counselor do not match the language of the client. This being the case, counselors should (a) seek a translator with cultural knowledge and appropriate professional background or (b) refer to a knowledgeable and competent bilingual counselor. (p. 41)

Because crises occur suddenly and without warning, it may be difficult to find a linguistic match between helpers and clients. Clearly, it would be best for crisis intervention with non-English speakers to be done by a psychologist who has demonstrated proficiency in the child's first language. The availability of trained speakers of some languages, such as Spanish, may be sufficient, but given the large number of languages spoken in the United States, it will not be possible to match every non-English speaker to a proficient helper of the native tongue. In this instance, there is little choice but to turn to work with interpreters.

***Working With Interpreters.*** It is a simple fact that many important cultural concepts cannot be satisfactorily translated from one language to another. Literal translation does not work because meaning is inextricably bound with cultural values and worldview.

Before working with an interpreter, the crisis counselor must learn about the dynamics of the interpretation process. Some of these dynamics include: how to establish rapport with participants, how to anticipate the loss of information inherent in the interpretation procedure, how to use the authority position of the professional, how to use appropriate nonverbal communication, what method and techniques of interpretation are available, how to obtain accurate translations, and how to discourage personal evaluations by the translator (Figueroa, Sandoval, & Merino, 1984).

The next task is to identify a potential translator (Sandoval & Duran, 1998). In the school setting, there may be teacher aides, or noncertificated staff members such as community liaisons who may be available. Parents and community members may also serve. The best-educated native speaker is often the best candidate to serve as an interpreter, as he or she will be able to learn what is needed quickly. In addition to the linguistic competence of the potential interpreter, the individual's personality will have to be taken into account. The emphasis should be on someone who will be able to establish rapport with the individual being counseled. McIvor (1994) argued, "although helpful, it is not essential that they (interpreters) have knowledge of mental health issues, but it is essential that they have a particular knowledge of the political and cultural background from which the survivor comes. It is often ignored that the interpreter should be socially, ethnically and politically acceptable to the survivor" (p. 268). A final point to be explored in selection is the dialect of the language spoken by the potential interpreter. A well-educated person may have class and dialect differences from the child. Newcomers to the United States may speak unusual dialects that other speakers of the language may have difficulty comprehending. It is very important to verify the dialect match between the children in the school and the interpreter.

The third task is to prepare the interpreter. If translators are inexperienced, it will be necessary to educate the individuals in the techniques of translating in crisis context. Interpreters must learn ethical concepts, particularly the importance of keeping information confidential, how not to elaborate responses or questions inappropriately, how to deal with physical gestures and other kinesthetic information, and how to establish and maintain rapport. The psychologist will be using the interpreter as a proxy and should feel confident that good professional practice will be followed. If there is time, interpreters should also be schooled in the elements of psychological first aide (Brock, Lewis, & Sandoval, 2001).

## IMPLEMENTING CULTURALLY SENSITIVE CRISIS INTERVENTION

In conclusion, when faced with an individual who is recognizably from a culture different from the crisis worker, some modification in approach should be considered. However, there is sufficient cultural diversity present in our population for the counselor to view every child and family through a cultural lens. It is reasonable to assume at the onset of any encounter that the individual will come from a unique culture or subculture, even if it is the "culture" of the family of origin. Some assessment has to be made to establish how to work best with the client.

## Examine Fit of Individual and Cultural Norms

A first step will be to learn the extent to which the client has become acculturated to the dominant culture. Informants can assist in this and careful interviewing can also detect an individual's worldview.

## Consider What Culturally Relevant External Resources Are Available to the Person in Crisis

The second step is to examine resources and strengths. Prime resources in many cultures are the clergy, but others who can help are an influential neighborhood leader or politician. In non-Western (and Western) cultures the family is an important system of support during times of crisis and they must be mobilized, recognizing that definitions of "family" differ considerably.

## Determine the Client's Capacity to Use the Resources

Not all individuals in crisis will be able to use either conventional resources or culturally provided resources. Attitudes toward seeing help and sources of help should be examined and taken into account.

## Make Appropriate Referrals

As the first, and perhaps only person on the scene, do what you can to be helpful. Attend to physical needs, offer appropriate reassurance and anticipatory guidance, and help those in a crisis state to take positive action to facilitate coping. As soon as possible, however, facilitate an appropriate referral to a culturally appropriate helper, and follow up to determine that a connection has been made.

A crisis is a time when the normal world is radically disrupted. But crises are not so unusual that humankind have not been able to develop ways of dealing with them. As crisis interveners, the best we can do is to be facilitators of processes that have been institutionalized in culture to help individuals cope. We must honor and respect the culturally based mechanisms available to comfort and heal those affected by traumatic events.

The relationship of culture to crisis is manifold. It may help to determine what incident is perceived as a crisis event, and it will impact how an individual deals with a crisis event. Moreover it may dictate appropriate ways of helping an individual during a crisis reaction.

But it must be remembered that individuals also have a personality and that a personality may be consistent or inconsistent with the culture from which the person comes. As a result, one cannot presume that an individual will share all of the ideas, beliefs, values, and norms of the group with which he or she identifies. Individual and regional variation is always great within a particular culture. In addition, an individual may identify with more than one group, such as someone who considers herself gay, African American, and Buddhist. In approaching someone with multiple identities, it may be very difficult to predict which values and behaviors will be manifest. The safest stance will be to be aware of the shared worldview of different cultures so they may be recognized and used, but to proceed with caution to avoid stereotyping and making unwarranted assumptions.

## ACKNOWLEDGMENTS

Sharon Lewis and Malu Antunez de Bellatin have been helpful "cultural informants" during the writing of this chapter.

## REFERENCES

Alexander, C. M., & Sussman, L. (1995). Creative approaches to multicultural counseling. In J. G. Ponterotto, J. M. Casas, L. A. Suzuki, & C. M. Alexander (Eds.), *Handbook of multicultural counseling* (pp. 375–384). Thousand Oaks, CA: Sage.

Benjamin, A. (1981). *The helping interview* (3rd ed.). Boston: Houghton Mifflin

Brock, S. E., Sandoval, J., & Lewis, S. (2001). *Preparing for crises in the schools* (2nd ed.). New York: Wiley.

Cartledge, G., & Johnson, C. T. (1997). School violence and cultural sensitivity. In A. P. Goldstein & J. C. Conoley (Eds.), *School violence intervention: A practical handbook* (pp. 391–425). New York: Guilford Press.

Castillo, R. J. (1997). *Culture and mental illness: A client-centered approach.* Pacific Grove, CA: Brooks/Cole.

Ceballo, R. (2000). The neighborhood club: A supportive intervention group for children exposed to urban violence. *American Journal of Orthopsychiatry, 70,* 401–407.

Congress, E. P. (2000). Crisis intervention with culturally diverse families. In A. R. Roberts (Ed.), *Crisis intervention handbook: assessment, treatment and research* (pp. 430–448). New York: Oxford University Press.

Danieli, Y. (1988). Treating survivors and children of survivors of the Nazi Holocaust. In F. M. Ochberg (Ed.), *Post-traumatic therapy and victims of violence* (pp. 278–294). New York: Brunner/Mazel.

Esquivel, G. B. (1998). Group interventions with culturally and linguistically diverse students. In K. C. Stoiber & T. R. Kratochwill (Eds.), *Handbook of group intervention for children and families* (pp. 252–267). Boston: Allyn & Bacon.

Figueroa, R. A., Sandoval, J., & Merino, B. (1984). School psychology with limited-English-proficient (LEP) children: New competencies. *Journal of School Psychology, 22,* 121–143.

Garcia, E. E. (Ed.). (1995). *Meeting the challenge of linguistic and cultural diversity in early childhood education.* New York: Teachers College Press.

Hall, E. T. (1959). *The silent language.* Greenwich, CT: Fawcett.

Kellogg, J. B. (1988). Forces of change. *Phi Delta Kappan, 70,* 199–204.

Klingman, A. (1986). School community in disaster: Planning for intervention. *Journal of Community Psychology, 16,* 205–216.

Lee, C. C., & Armstrong, K. L. (1995). Indigenous models of mental health intervention. In J. G. Ponterotto, J. M. Casas, L. A. Suzuki, & C. M. Alexander (Eds.), *Handbook of multicultural counseling* (pp. 441–456). Thousand Oaks, CA: Sage.

Lewis, O. (1970). *A death in the Sanchez family*. New York: Vintage.

Li, C., & Liu, T. C. (1993). How to work effectively with Asian-American families. *NASP Communiqué, 21*(6), 23–26.

McGoldrick, M., Giordano, J., & Pearce, J. K. (1996). (Eds.). *Ethnicity and family therapy* (2nd ed.). New York: Guilford Press.

McIvor, R. J. (1994). Making the most of interpreters. *British Journal of Psychiatry, 165*, 268.

Morrow, R. D. (1988). Cultural differences . . . Be aware!" *CASP Today, 38*(3), 4–5.

Pope-Davis, D. B., & Dings, J. G. (1995). The assessment of multicultural counseling competencies. In J. G. Ponterotto, J. M. Casas, L. A. Suzuki, & C. M. Alexander (Eds.), *Handbook of multicultural counseling* (pp. 287–311). Thousand Oaks, CA: Sage.

Richardson, B. L. (1991). Utilizing the resources of the African American church: Strategies for counseling professionals, In C. C. Lee & B. L. Richardson (Eds.), *Multicultural issues in counseling: New approaches to diversity* (pp. 65–75). Alexandria, VA: American Counseling Association.

Sandoval, J., & Duran, R. P. (1998). Language. In J. Sandoval, C. L. Frisby, K. F. Geisinger, J. D. Scheueneman, & J. R. Grenier (Eds.), *Test interpretation and diversity* (pp. 181–211). Washington, DC: American Psychological Association.

Spring, J. (2000). *The intersection of cultures* (2nd ed.). Boston: McGraw-Hill.

Stack, C. (1974). *All our kin: Strategies for survival in a black community*. New York: Harper.

Sue, D. W., Carter, R. T., Casas, J. M., Fouad, N. A., Ivey, A. E., Jensen, M., LaFromboise, T., Manese, J. E., Ponterotto, J. G., & Vazquez-Nutall, E. (1998). *Multicultural counseling competencies*. Thousand Oaks, CA: Sage.

Willis, W. (1992). Families with African American roots. In E. W. Lynch & M. J. Hanson (Eds.), *Developing cross cultural competence: A guide for working with young children and their families* (pp. 121–150). Baltimore: Paul H. Brookes.

Wilson, M. (1996). Arabic speakers: Language and culture, here and abroad. *Topics in Language Disorders, 16*(4), 65–80.

# PART II

# CRISIS THROUGHOUT CHILDHOOD AND ADOLESCENCE BUT PARTICULARLY COMMON IN THE ELEMENTARY SCHOOL

CHAPTER

# 4

# School and Learning: School Entry, School Failure, and the Discovery of Learning Disabilities

Colette L. Ingraham
San Diego State University

Performance in school can be affected by a wide range of crises. When one is experiencing a life crisis, it can influence the ability to concentrate, think, remember, relate to others, and maintain one's psychological balance and feelings of well-being. In this respect, when a child is experiencing a crisis at home, in the community, or at school, school achievement needs to be understood within a broader context than what takes place in the classroom. Students who are experiencing a crisis need additional support to help them cope with the crisis and to reduce lasting effects on their learning at school.

Some crises are directly related to what happens in school. This chapter identifies three common school-related crises and describes students who are at risk of each crisis. The first section discusses who is at risk of crises associated with school entry, perceived academic failure, and learning disabilities. The second section describes several strategies for intervention and prevention of crises in school learning.

## WHO IS AT RISK?

Three types of crises that impact student learning are the sources of numerous referrals to school professionals. The competent professional who understands the dynamics associated with each type of crisis is better able to provide rapid, effective intervention.

## School Entry

Entry to school involves a wide range of new experiences for any child. The adjustment from home or preschool to school includes learning a whole set of new skills, rules, expectancies, and so on. Classroom rules may differ from the rules of the home, and the methods and consistency with which rules are enforced may also be different. Social interaction takes place with new adults, peers, and perhaps new languages and cultures, and with a much larger number of similar-aged persons than previously experienced. There are expectations for learning concepts, fine motor movements, sharing, demonstration of knowledge, and so on that may represent new patterns of behavior. In fact, everything about school may be new and unfamiliar.

Most children are able to make all of the adjustments needed to adapt to entrance to school. But for some, school entry becomes a crisis sometimes called *school refusal* (or *school phobia* in earlier literature). Gordon and Young (1976) defined *school phobia* as "a partial or total inability to attend school" (p. 783). Unlike the truant, the authors explain, the school phobic child stays at home with the parents and is absent for consecutive days or weeks at a time. The incidence of school refusal or school phobia is relatively low (King, Ollendick, & Tonge, 1995), ranging from 3 to 17 cases per thousand school-age children per year (Gordon & Young, 1976). Johnson (1979) cited several studies in which school phobics account for less than 8% of the cases seen in psychiatric clinics. Referrals for school refusal or school phobia are most common around the age of 11 (Last & Perrin, 1993), but they are also frequent for ages 5–6 and 13–14 (Smith, 1970, as cited in King et al., 1995), and ages 7–8 (Johnson, 1979). School refusal is seen among children of a variety of cultures. For example, there is concern about the rising incidence of school refusal in Japan (Iwamoto & Yoshida, 1997). Last and Perrin (1993) reported that among children seen at one clinic specializing in anxiety disorders, 53.6% of the White and 30% of the African-American clients demonstrated clinical characteristics of school refusal. In the study, the mean age at intake was 12.6 (*SD* 3.5) and 11.6 (*SD* 3.8) for the White and African-American groups, respectively, and for both races, the rate of school refusal was higher in the low-SES group as compared to the high-SES group.

The use of the term *school phobia* has been challenged as an inappropriate classification for school refusal and avoidance behaviors because it does not meet the criteria of a psychological phobia and it does not encompass the full range of behaviors seen with school refusal (Kearney, Eisen, & Silverman, 1995; Paige, 1997). *School refusal*, a term used more frequently in more recent literature (Evans, 2000; King et al., 1995; Paige, 1997), refers to "children who are frequently absent and/or attend school under duress or following tantrums or noncompliance" (Paige, 1997, p. 342.) The prevalence of school refusal is thought to be relatively low, but estimates vary greatly because of differences in the definition and diagnostic criteria of school refusal (Evans, 2000; Kearney, 1995; King et al., 1995; Paige, 1997).

The etiology of school refusal continues to generate controversy (Atkinson, Quarrington, & Cyr, 1985; Evans, 2000; Gordon & Young, 1976; Johnson, 1979; King et al., 1995). Some theorists contend that school phobia or school refusal are more accurately described as a manifestation of separation anxiety from the mother than as a fear of school, but others maintain that separation anxiety does not attend to other school-related factors or avoidance behaviors (Pilkington & Piersel, 1991). Others describe the school phobic child as having an overinflated feeling of importance in the family (Leventhal & Sills, 1964) and preferring the security of home to the ambiguities and newness of the school environment. Evans (2000) noted that recent efforts have focused on a functional classification of three refusal subtypes, according to the variables that work to maintain school refusal: anxiety, avoidance, and malingering. Correct identification of the subtype is critical to developing the appropriate intervention. Kearney and Silverman (1993) developed a scale to assess the maintaining variables of school refusal behaviors, including positive and negative reinforcement. Earlier, Atkinson et al. (1985) identified a classification scheme for school refusal to characterize the various types of etiologies and descriptions of school refusal. This scheme suggests a complex phenomenon and considers several variables: extensiveness of disturbance, mode and age of onset, fear sources, and gender. Another perspective hypothesizes that, in some cases, the child who is reluctant to attend school may be displaying symptoms of an idiosyncratic defense mechanism that attempts to protect an inaccurate self-concept (Ingraham, 1988a). According to this view, the self-concept is threatened by the realities, competition, and uncertainty of the school environment. Staying home with a supportive adult protects the child's feeling of self-worth and self-efficacy by limiting the incoming information about the child's abilities and comparison with other children that are typical at school. Silverman and Ginsburg (1995) summarized three different reasons children refuse to go to school, each leading to different intervention options:

> Fear of a specific stimulus in the school setting (which could suggest the presence of a specific phobia); problems with separation from loved ones (which could suggest the presence of separation anxiety disorder); or fear of a certain social situation, such as speaking in class (which could suggest the presence of social phobia). (pp. 161–162)

Gordon and Young (1976), Johnson (1979), and King et al. (1995), reviewed numerous intervention studies that report varying degrees of success in treating the child who refuses to attend school. Brief intervention approaches such as behavior modification, relaxation training, systematic desensitization, and similar techniques appear to be successful for treating school refusal in children and providing rapid re-entry into school. In some cases, pharmacotherapy is used in combination with other treatments of school-refusing children, especially when the child is diagnosed with a *DSM-IV* disorder such as separation anxiety or major depression (King et al., 1995). The need for long-term psychotherapy is still being debated in the literature.

Whatever the etiology of school refusal, once the child is attending school regularly, the crisis counselor can work with the teacher and parent to increase the child's comfort and self-confidence at school by developing successful interpersonal and intrapersonal experiences within the school setting. Gradually building the child's self-esteem and self-efficacy as a student, building an accurate self-perception, and increasing feelings of belonging with the class are important to overcome any previously internalized negative self-image. Interventions may include group participation; responsibilities such as monitor, partner, or tutor; and pairing the student with peers for achievement tasks. The goals of follow-up interventions may include increasing the child's sense of self-efficacy in the school environment and maintaining feelings of self-worth, while modifying the accuracy of the child's self-image, if needed, so that it includes the newly experienced successes at school. This type of follow-up is designed to promote continued positive mental health and information processing once the behavioral symptoms of school attendance have been addressed.

## Perceived Academic Failure

Many populations are at risk of academic failure and a host of systemic issues have been proposed to promote educational equity and success (Barona & Garcia, 1990; Durlak, 1997; McWhirter, McWhirter, McWhirter, & McWhirter, 1998; Slavin, Karweitt, & Madden, 1989). There may be large groups of students who are failing to meet school performance standards or who leave school before completion. Based on a compilation of several sources, Durlak (1997) reported that, "One out of three children experiences significant problems in learning to read and up to 18% of high school seniors read at least 4 years below grade level; the annual high school dropout rate is 25%" (p. 55). The incidence of school leavers is much higher in some communities and among some ethnic groups. McWhirter et al. (1998) offered a host of indicators for identifying the potential to drop out of school, including higher than average risk rates among students with learning disabilities, as well as those who are intellectually gifted, gay and lesbian, or ethnic minority.

When there are groups of populations of students failing in school, systemic interventions are needed to address the concerns. Careful assessment of the situation involves an examination of the curriculum, instructional approaches, school climate, expectations for performance, dropout rates, and so forth as a means to fully understand the factors that may be related to the rates of failure. School professionals should look for patterns of referrals as a way to identify groups of students who may be at risk of school failure and to develop effective systemic interventions (Ingraham & Bursztyn, 1999).

Sometimes individual students are identified as failing. Each year, school psychologists, counselors, and student study teams or intervention assistance teams receive countless referrals for students who have been identified by someone as failing in school. When the reasons for school failure relate to the curriculum, instruction, or other systemic factors, the intervention should address those concerns. When perceived academic failure relates to a specific student, then one of the first issues that arises is *who* perceives the situation as an academic failure? The teacher, parent, or student may perceive the student as failing in school, and it is important to clarify in whose eyes the student is failing. In many cases, an indirect method of services such as consultation is an effective way to address the concern. When the adults in the students' lives are concerned about the students' progress in school, school professionals should begin with consultation to determine the nature and basis of the concern. At the individual level of intervention, tutoring, individualized instruction, or other academic interventions may be appropriate, as described later in this chapter. In situations where numbers of individuals with similar failure patterns are identified, systemic interventions should be explored as a more appropriate means of prevention and intervention of school failure.

When a *parent* raises the concern, a parent–teacher conference is recommended to explore the similarities or differences in the adult perceptions of the situation and ideas for intervention. Parents may be keenly attuned to their child's school performance and feelings about school and can be source of early identification of students who are experience difficulty in school. In some cases, parents may hold unrealistic expectations for student performance. A conference can include sharing of information about the student's progress, observations of the student at home and school, and discussion of the expectation for progress, all of which can help determine the course of action to take. Parents and educators can develop powerful partnerships to support student learning (Ammon, 1999; Lynch & Hansen, 1998).

When the *teacher* perceives the student as failing, consultation with the teacher may be the first step. Through consultation, one can learn the origins of the teacher's concern, including the definition, duration, pervasiveness, and evidence of the student's school performance. Depending on the consultant's assessment of the problem situation, a variety of consultation approaches may be used to work with the teacher to increase the student's academic success (e.g., Caplan & Caplan, 1993; Conoley & Conoley,

1992; Erchul & Martens, 1997; Gutkin & Curtis, 1990; Ingraham, 2000; Rosenfield & Gravois, 1996). Classroom observations and collaborative study of student work samples can lead to many successful instructional interventions (see Henning-Stout, 1994). The consultant can use an ecological problem-solving approach (Conoley & Conoley, 1992) to consider factors associated with the curriculum or classroom environment, as well as psychological factors associated with learning, such as those reflected in the learner-centered principles (American Psychological Association, 1993).

In cases where the student's academic work has been problematic over time, a consultant can work with the teacher to assess the problem and develop interventions (see Ames, 1992; Harmin, 1994; McCombs & Pope, 1994; Rosenfield & Gravois, 1996). A referral to the school's intervention assistance team may be made if the interventions developed through this individual consultation do not improve the student's learning. In cases where the student's performance has suddenly dropped, the consultant or counselor can explore any potential changes in the student's life that may account for a rapid decline, such as a major change within the home or family, potential abuse or substance abuse, trauma, and so on. Depending on the nature of the crisis, other chapters of this book or Webb (1991) might be appropriate guides for the crisis counselor.

There are some cases of perceived academic failure where the individual's psychological approach to learning is part of the issue. In such cases, direct intervention with the *student* may be needed. Students who experience performance anxiety, fear of failure, fear of success, or a perceived crisis related to their school performance may need direct and immediate attention by a responsible adult. In these cases, the adult's intervention can be informed by an understanding of some of the psychological processes that can occur when a student is in crisis over a self-perceived failure. Perceptions of academic failure vary from person to person and can occur at any point during one's schooling. Additionally, the antecedents and consequences of perceived failure for any individual vary greatly. The psychological factors associated with the student's perception of academic failure are the focus of the reminder of this section.

From the student's perspective, a crisis associated with a perceived academic failure may be any event that relates to the student's feelings of worth that the individual interprets as a failure in school (Ingraham, 1988a). The number of students who experience some form of perceived academic failure each day is great. Every day some students experience their first low grade on an assignment, some are placed in the slowest reading group, some are sent home with notes of reprimand, some are detained for misconduct or unfinished work, and some received failing grades. Depending on the student's perception, any of these experiences could be interpreted as an academic failure, and for some, a psychological crisis. For one student, a "B" grade on a project may lead to feelings of success and pride, but for another student who may be accustomed to grades of "A" or who was anticipating this project to earn a grade of "A," the "B" grade could lead to devastation and crisis. The impact of any of these experiences on the student's feelings of self-esteem, self-worth, and coping and defending strategies determines the extent to which the experience may result in a crisis situation for the student.

Since 1975, several psychological theories have emerged that help identify groups of students that are susceptible to perceived academic failure. Theories of self-efficacy (see review in Zimmerman, 2000), self-worth (Covington, 1992), school-related attribution (Weiner, 1986), and achievement goals theory (Ames, 1992) all suggest that students who do not feel a sense of personal control, responsibility for achievement, and mastery, are at risk of negative self-perception and school failure. Some have demonstrated that self-esteem is most threatened when the student receives negative feedback about self in an area of self-concept that is highly valued by the individual (Harter, 1993; Ingraham, 1986). Students who base their self-worth on their success in the classroom may be more likely to experience crisis related to perceived academic failure, compared with students who do not care much about school performance because their social life (or other area of interest) is the basis for their self-worth.

Some patterns of attribution, cognition, and learning predispose students to diminished feelings of worth in the face of perceived failure. Among students who base at least some of their self-esteem on their success in school, school failure may be particularly distressing when the failure is attributed to stable internal causes such as low ability (Covington, 1992) or to the student as a person, rather than the process of what the student did (Kamins & Dweck, 1999). Although some students can develop effective learning and thinking approaches on their own (Winnie, 1997), students with a history of academic failure are likely to have lower self-concepts of ability, lower expectancies for future success, fewer problem-solving strategies, and feelings of helplessness (Covington, 1992; Pintrich & Schunk, 1996; Stipek, 1993.) Among high-achieving students, girls reported more frequent use of self-regulated learning strategies and higher mastery goals than boys (Ablard & Lipshultz, 1998), suggesting that the gender patterns may be linked with achievement levels.

Students with ineffective coping strategies may also be candidates for crisis in the face of school failure. Goleman (1995) illustrated the importance of emotional learning and the high costs of what he called emotional illiteracy. Covington (1992), Ingraham (1985), and Licht (1983), among others, have highlighted the importance of knowing the right problem-solving strategy for the problem at hand. Students who continue to use ineffective strategies increase feelings of frustration and may eventually reduce school effort. Some have reported that students with learning disabilities (Cullen & Boersma, 1982; Licht, 1983) may not have effective problem-solving strategies in their repertoire of coping resources for school tasks, or they may attribute their successes and failures to external rather than internal causes (Pintrich, Anderman, & Klobucar, 1994). In addition, students' overall mood and level of self-esteem can influence the way they think about a specific negative event (Sanna, Turley-Ames, & Meier, 1999). Finally, students who experience test anxiety are at risk of crises related to school failure. Huberty (1997) noted that performance or test anxiety is far more common than many professionals realize and that it can affect many areas of one's life, including cognition, learning, and social development. Johnson (1981) noted that the prevalence of test anxiety is estimated to be as high as 30% of school-age children.

In addition to certain students who are at risk of school failure, as previously described, there are also identifiable developmental transitions that are predictive of populations at risk of school failure. The concurrence of cognitive, social, and emotional developmental transitions, coupled with environmental changes at school, creates times of developmental crisis. For example, students in Grades 3 and 4 are typically expected to concentrate longer, remember more, and demonstrate more academic skills than students in earlier grades. These increased performance expectations occur at the same time that students are cognitively more aware of how they compare with peers, and, with the emergence of cognitive decentration, they may be more aware of how others perceive their abilities. Poor achievement, coupled with the alarm of parents, teachers, or even chiding peers, can lead to crisis at this age due to the clear feedback that the student is not performing well. The student who is not doing well in school may begin forming cognitive–affective patterns that are not conducive to effective information processing or a negative self-evaluation that may lead to feelings of helplessness and decreased motivation to try.

Given the potential for self-doubt in the classroom, the simultaneous change from the primary playground to the upper grade playground at recess may further contribute to the child's insecurity. Now the fourth grader may be playing with older students, sometimes with new games and social rules for conduct, thus increasing the unfamiliarity and potential threat to self-esteem. It is no surprise that students are often referred for difficulties with academics, self-esteem, peer relations, frequent absences, and so forth around this age. The frequency of referrals for school refusal at this age is also not surprising, given the cognitive–affective dynamics taking place. Whenever the student is in transition from one developmental phase to another, especially when developmental transitions are accompanied by changes in the school environment, expectations, and social groupings, self-esteem may be more vulnerable to crisis with any perceived academic failure.

## Students With Disabilities and School Crises

When a student is initially diagnosed as having a specific learning disability or evidence of developmental delay, for some people, there is relief in the discovery of some "reason" for the frustrations and difficulties in school. For others, however, the initial diagnosis may be perceived as a crisis. Harry (1992) studied the different ways families respond to the initial diagnosis of learning disability or mental retardation. She reported some poignant accounts of families who thought the school personnel made an incorrect diagnosis or were trying to show that their child was crazy. Sometimes the parent or student expresses feelings of denial, guilt, or depression at the time of diagnosis. For some, placement into a special education program may be perceived as a failure or crisis, whereas for others, it may be a welcomed opportunity for assistance.

The individualized educational program (IEP) team can provide useful assistance as the diagnostic information is shared with parent and student, helping to support both during this critical time. Families need information about the findings of the IEP team, communicated in terms that are clear and culturally familiar (Harry, 1992; Lynch & Hansen, 1998). For example, educators should be aware that the Spanish term *bien educado* means well-mannered, not well-educated in terms of school achievement. Once the student is placed in special education programs, careful monitoring of the student's attitudes, behavior, and achievement is also important in order to provide early intervention when needed, before the student experiences a crisis. There are many reasons to support inclusion of students with disabilities in general education programs (Villa & Thousand, 1995), including the finding that inclusion leads to greater self-esteem and affective responses that support success in school (Falvey, Givner, & Kimm, 1995).

Students with learning disabilities represent a special population that is at risk of school failure and potential school-related crises. There are several ways in which students with disabilities are particularly vulnerable to crises in school. According to present classifications, the most prevalent types of disabilities involve disabilities with learning and/or development. Students with developmental delays are at risk of failure at school both socially and academically because they may not be as intellectually agile as their peers, both on the playground and in class. Academically, the student may have difficulty learning at the same rate as agemates, and unless special instruction or curriculum is provided, the student may be subject to academic frustration and failure.

Students with learning disabilities, by definition, have difficulty in one of the basic psychological processes, frequently in the area of auditory or visual information processing. A student with a learning disability may experience difficulty following directions, comprehending information, remembering, or articulating thoughts. Many of these areas of difficulty are exactly the types of skills needed to succeed in the typical educational program. These are also the same skills that are needed to use logical information-processing and problem-solving strategies in solving nonacademic, social or personal problems. Consequently, the student with a learning disability also may be handicapped in the use of strategies to cope with crisis. Difficulties with making a plan, sustaining concentration, and ignoring distractions, are common in many students with learning disabilities. The ability to contain emotional frustration over a failure, to put a failure into proper perspective, and to continue experimenting with alternate strategies may be very difficult for the student with disabilities.

The self-esteem and self-confidence of students with learning disabilities may be threatened by feelings of being different from peers and by difficulties with social interaction. Students with learning disabilities often have difficulty in social judgment, in understanding cause–effect relationships, in inhibiting inappropriate behavior, and in articulating their thoughts to others. Problems in anticipating events and in self-expression can interfere with satisfying peer relations and social behaviors. Gresham (1997) concluded that, "students with mild disabilities have poorer social skills than 75% to 90% of their nondisabled peers . . ." (p. 42). Gresham (1997) summarized the research on assessment and intervention for students needing to develop improved social skills. He also provided some valuable ways to conceptualize the principles and objectives of social skills training.

Adjusting to transitions, new environments, new teachers or routines, and new social groupings may be especially problematic for students with disabilities. Unless students have good coping strategies, positive self-esteem, and high self-confidence, students with disabilities may be vulnerable to self-esteem threats associated with uncertain or unfamiliar educational experiences. Students with disabilities may benefit from extra support during times of change and transition in order to prevent experiences of crisis. Because these students are commonly identified for special education services, it is relatively easy to anticipate and plan ways to ease the transitions for students with disabilities. Educators can carefully plan any transitions or changes in the educational program so that students are prepared in advance of the changes. Anticipatory guidance, role play, buddy systems, and similar techniques can provide needed support.

In addition to interventions within the school and classroom, some of the most important preventive interventions for students with disabilities involve working with the families of the students. Fish (1995) described several approaches for supporting families in adjusting to a student with a disability and empowering the family to be a strong support system for the student's success. These approaches begin with a family-centered perspective that includes the family, rather that just the child, as the focus of support and intervention. Fish also summarized the best practices for working with parents of children with disabilities, including educational–information sharing, advocacy, support, facilitation of healthy family functioning, and individualized services to the student and family that attend to the family's uniqueness and sociocultural background.

## INTERVENTION FOR SCHOOL-RELATED CRISES

Effective intervention for students experiencing a crisis involves attention to the student's ecology, potential support system, and the student's own psychological cognitive–affective processes. Within the psychological domain, attention to self-concept, self-esteem, and patterns of information processing is especially important. School professionals can use knowledge about the cognitive–affective processes associated with a crisis reaction to provide intervention services that go beyond the traditional crisis intervention strategies of calming affect and restoring stability in functioning. School professionals can also teach students effective coping strategies, thereby supporting students in recovering from the immediate crisis and developing skills for mastery over future situations.

### The First Two Levels of a Crisis Intervention Response

Crisis intervention for problems with school learning involves two levels. First, the crisis counselor provides emotional support and structuring during the initial steps in crisis intervention (see chap. 1). Here the goals are to calm the individual and provide emotional and physical safety. The first-level approaches for crisis with school learning resemble other types of crisis counseling. This crisis counselor's assessment of the individual's psychological resources, functioning, and coping capacity is useful in planning the appropriate second-level intervention. Some students will be ready to begin problem solving shortly after crisis counseling begins, whereas other students may have experienced devastation that leads to immobilization and pervasive feelings of self-doubt and helplessness. The types of goals appropriate for second-level intervention will depend on the nature of the crisis, the developmental level of the student, and the crisis counselor's assessment of the student's cognitive–affective processing.

For students who are experiencing a debilitating reaction to a school-related crisis, the early goals of the intervention involve carefully rebuilding the student's sense of self efficacy and mastery (Ingraham, 1988b). The first tasks should involve small goals with reasonable opportunities for success, outcomes that are clearly attributable to the student's own efforts, and a noncompetitive setting. Initially, this sense of mastery and satisfaction can come from simple accomplishments such as organizing one's supply case or backpack, feeding the class animals, or collecting student assignments for a teacher. The purpose of these initial tasks is to take some action that breaks the anxiety/depression/immobilization cycle while producing some visible form of accomplishment. Simple, tangible accomplishments offer concrete proof of one's efforts and symbolize mastery and order over one's environment. If the student is ready for tasks in the academic realm, intervention might include planning a schedule to complete the night's homework assignment, or dividing the book report assignment into manageable pieces and deciding what to do first. The level of complexity of the task and the amount of independent effort involved will depend on two factors: (a) the crisis counselor's assessment of the amount of coping resources available in the student's repertoire at the time of the crisis, and (b) the perceived magnitude of the failure that resulted in the crisis.

Once the student overcomes the initial emotional reaction to the crisis, other strategies can be used to redirect the cognitive–affective processing into constructive patterns. For example, attribution retraining is useful for students who show dysfunctional information-processing characteristics such as learned helplessness. The goal of the training is to reinforce students for attributing the causes to controllable internal attributions such as effort. When the student fails, the student is encouraged to think that it was due to insufficient effort rather than inability or external causes. Specific and focused interventions can be very successful at improving students' academic self-concept and developing more effective attributional patterns (Craven, Marsh, & Debus, 1991). Not surprisingly, high self-efficacy, self-confidence, and self-esteem are considered important individual characteristics of resilient children and youth (Doll & Lyon, 1998).

The literature includes some specific suggestions for the types of reinforcements and classroom strategies that are most effective for students with different attributional patterns. Educators can use interactional approaches to meet the needs of some students and self-directed learning for others. Children who tend to attribute failure to internal causes such as low ability—the most common attributional pattern for children who have a history of failure—benefit from programs that use social reinforcement or tutoring (Bugental, Whalen, & Henker, 1977; Cullen & Boersma, 1982; Johnson, 1981; Licht, 1983) as opposed to programs that rely on self-instruction. Children in regular or special education who attribute achievement internally and who have high levels of perceived control, on the other hand, achieve better with reward systems and classroom structures that use self-talk or self-controlling motivational approaches (Ames, 1992; Bugental et al., 1977; Covington, 1992). Once again, the crisis counselor's assessment of the attributional patterns of the student are key to selecting the most effective type of reinforcement during recovery from the crisis.

Instruction in problem solving is another strategy that is effective after the student has emotionally recovered from the immediate crisis. The DECIDE model of problem solving was developed specifically for at-risk children and adolescents. "DECIDE stands for the steps to be taken: (a) define the problem, (b) examine variables, (c) consider alternatives, (d) isolate a plan, (e) do action steps, and (f) evaluate effects," (McWhirter et al., 1998, p. 227). The crisis counselor can link the problem-solving process with the student's attributions about the outcomes of problem solving as a way to mediate constructive cognitive–affective processes. These strategies teach students to identify which strategies are working and to take credit for their successes, thereby building accuracy of self-concept of ability and feelings of mastery.

The modification of self-concept and self-confidence requires meaningful reinforcement and repeated experience, especially in the initial phases of overcoming a crisis. Approaches that offer sustained interaction between the helping adult and the student are needed to rebuild constructive cognitive–affective patterns. Attribution retraining, problem solving and cognitive restructuring are only three recommended approaches for intervention with children who have experienced failure in school. More information about these and other approaches is available in Henker, Whalen, and Hinshaw (1980) and Licht (1983). A new and innovative approach for the reconstruction of meaning is to use narrative counseling techniques to support the development of problem-solving skills. Narrative counseling originated in the social constructionist and family systems perspectives. It is proposed as a tool to transform the practice of school counseling and work with difficult cases for conflict resolution in schools (Winslade & Monk, 1999).

Interventions at the classroom level are also important to consider. When classroom environments are based on principles of mastery learning (Ames, 1992; Covington, 1992; McCombs & Pope, 1994), cooperative learning (Johnson, Johnson, & Holubec, 1994; Slavin, Karweit, & Wasik, 1994), or supporting the development of emotional intelligence (Goleman, 1994), a classroom climate may develop that serves to reduce or prevent school failure and individual psychological crises in learning. Wilson (1995) discussed ways that teachers' groupings of students and the types of feedback they provide students can influence the students' self-concept development.

Whatever approach the crisis counselor uses in the second level of intervention, the underlying counseling goals are similar. At the individual level, the student is encouraged to modify self-concept to match reality, to gain broader perspective on the situation, and to plan steps to cope with the previous crisis. As the student regains access to coping strategies (and possibly learns new ways to handle situations), the counselor helps articulate what the coping strategies are and how the student is developing mastery over his or her feelings, thoughts, and behaviors. This metacognitive process helps the student conceptualize the coping strategies that were useful and develops internal attributions for their successful use. Finally, the counselor helps the student transfer effective coping strategies from other areas of life to the problematic situation. The counselor can seek the involvement of different members of the student's ecology, such as parents, teachers, and peers, in developing a support system to sustain the new learning. At the family, classroom, or systems level, the goal is to develop environments and support systems to sustain healthy development and learning and promote resilience in the face of crises. Here, approaches such as consultation, collaboration, parent education, and inservices can be used to empower key adults to support healthy student functioning.

Steve's case is an example of a frequent type of school crisis. His IEP team is moving him from a self-contained special day class to a regular fifth-grade class with support from the Resource Teacher. He is afraid of the change because he has grown accustomed to the special class, and he feels unsure of how he will survive most of the day with 30 other students in his new class. He remembers, with terror and embarrassment, his experiences in school before his placement into a special class in the second grade. During the second level of intervention, the counselor helps Steve focus on the coping skills he already has, helping him realize how to apply these to the fearful transition. The counselor might ask questions such as:

> What are the rules in your current special class? How did you learn the rules of your class?
>
> What happens when you do something right? How did you learn what the teacher expects of you? What can you do if you need help?

The counselor directs Steve's attention to his knowledge of rules, expectations, and his clues for learning these. Then the counselor helps Steve anticipate what to expect in the new class and how to use his coping strategies to adjust more smoothly. Finally, it is important for Steve to have a very concrete awareness of the resources and strategies to assist him in the new class if he needs help or feels panic. Rehearsing strategies for getting help, regaining his composure, and using tools such as lists or written reminders will assist him during the transition period. The crisis counselor also consults with Steve's receiving teacher and parents about ways to make Steve's transition smoother. Together, they develop a transition plan that gradually introduces Steve into the new classroom environment, beginning with one period a day, then one day a week, and increasing as Steve is ready for greater inclusion in the regular class. In addition, they identify a student in the new class who will act as a buddy to Steve both in the classroom and during breaks. Steve is introduced to the peer before the move to the new class. Steve's parents and teachers are watching for ways to reinforce Steve's successful adaptation to his new class.

## PREVENTION OF SCHOOL CRISES AND EARLY INTERVENTION

Many types of school-related crises can be reduced through prevention programs, anticipatory guidance, and well-timed intervention. The following five guidelines are central to planning effective prevention and early intervention services for children at risk of crises associated with school.

### *1. Intervene Early in the Child's Development*

The development of emotional patterns that lead to success in life begins very early (Goleman, 1994), and student feelings of self-worth are often tied to the success or failure experiences of students in school (Covington, 1992). There appears to be a critical age in the child's development when lasting attitudes and patterns of processing information are formed. Comparison of developmental theories and numerous developmental studies suggest that around the age of 10, children are susceptible to some of the dysfunctional self-perception and attribution patterns that perpetuate school failure (Ingraham, 1988b). Once patterns of low self-esteem, lack of internal success attributions, or overly defensive protection of self-esteem set in, they are increasingly difficult to modify. Prevention activities in the second and third grade might teach students coping skills and productive information-processing patterns, prior to the critical cognitive–affective transition that takes place around age 10. Programs that support the development of healthy emotional and cognitive patterns (e.g., APA, 1993; Ames, 1992; Ammon, 1999; Covington, 1992; Durlak, 1997; Goleman, 1994) can begin at the preschool level or earlier.

### *2. Support the Use of Effective School-Wide Instructional Practices*

Three key elements of the curriculum and instructional process may help prevent school-related crises: (a) curriculum that is relevant and connected to students' life experiences, (b) instructional approaches that build on the learning styles and previous experiences of the students, and (c) opportunities to become reflective and resourceful learners. Educational approaches that use reflective thinking, ongoing evaluation of one's work, and curriculum that is integrally connected to the students' life experiences can create vibrant classrooms that foster educational success, self-understanding, and effective psychological functioning (Paris & Ayres, 1994). Instructional approaches that support learners in developing an understanding of their own thoughts, approaches, problem-solving abilities, and self-perception can prevent some school-related crises. Learner-centered principles (APA, 1993) were developed by the American Psychological Association in an effort to disseminate much of the current science about learning and psychological functioning. Several resources can support the school's development of innovative and meaningful learning opportunities for students at the classroom or systems level (e.g., Harmin, 1994; Mangieri & Block, 1994; McCombs & Pope 1994; Paris & Ayres, 1994; Wilson, 1995.)

Some have proposed that too much emphasis in society is placed on the self and that we should teach and support greater levels of interconnectedness. Hwang (1995) introduced the notion of "other-esteem" to include, "respect, acceptance, caring, valuing and promoting of others who may think, feel and act differently from us" (p. 15). Programs that foster other-esteem include attention to teaching tolerance and appreciation of multiculturalism. It is conceivable that a school's instructional approaches could include attention to both self-esteem and other-esteem, thus promoting a healthy balance between individual development and interconnectedness and cooperation. Such an approach would probably be more culturally inclusive, as well.

### *3. Develop School-Wide Prevention Programs*

An effective prevention program has several components (Adelman & Taylor, 2000; Cowan et al., 1996; McWhirter et al., 1998; Slavin, Karweit, & Wasik, 1994). Two aspects of prevention programs are significant, those that promote resilience and those that prevent or reduce risk factors (Doll & Lyon, 1998). It is important for the philosophy and actions of the school staff and community to communicate the worth of each student, regardless of their level of achievement (Paris & Ayres, 1994). Students need an opportunity to develop their self-concept in a variety of areas—academic, social, physical, and other domains. Specific performance feedback about what parts are done well, what needs improvement, and suggestions for how to improve helps students to develop an accurate self-concept and to identify strategies for improvement. Academic material at the appropriate level for each student is important for success to be within reach, thereby reducing feelings of frustration, avoidance, and failure. Teachers need support and information to help them plan instructional activities within the levels of functioning of their students and in providing feedback in ways that support the development of constructive cognitive–affective processes. When the school has a positive climate for learning and development, prevention programs then can focus on students at risk of difficulty within the positive school environment. For example, the Primary Mental Health Project (Cowan et al., 1996) has evolved since the 1970s as a program designed to promote emotional wellness among children in schools. It provides intervention and support for students who are often overlooked in traditional intervention efforts.

The major emphasis of a program designed to prevent school crises is one that supports the development of effective learning strategies, accurate and comprehensive self-esteem, problem solving, and coping skills. Students need to develop and practice coping strategies (e.g., Goleman, 1994), problem solving and decision making (McWhirter et al., 1998; Shure, 1992). Another important component in a school-wide prevention program is specific instruction and practice in seeking support when needed. The first step is to teach students how to know when they need help. Then students need to know how to seek help in appropriate ways. Help seeking that is necessary, focused on specific content features, and targeted at appropriate help providers is considered most adaptive (Newman & Schwager, 1995). The school curriculum can offer students instruction and practice in analyzing, searching for causes of events, determining all the steps involved in a task, and making use of problem-solving strategies and a variety of thinking skills. This includes practice in planning and carrying out multistep solutions. Additionally, students can be taught skills in conflict resolution (Johnson & Johnson, 1995; Lane & McWhirter, 1992) and peer helping (Jundall, 1995; McWhirter et al., 1998), two strategies for reducing school problems and building the self-esteem of those who are helpers. Recent research with seventh graders indicates that students with positive self-regard, especially self-perceived peer social competence, were less vulnerable to victimization than those with low self-regard (Egan & Perry, 1998). They concluded that, "poor self-concept may play a central role in a vicious cycle that perpetuates and solidifies a child's status as a victim of peer abuse" (p. 299).

A school climate of cooperation is also valuable in supporting student academic and psychological success. Stevens and Slavin (1995) documented increased achievement in reading, language, and math among elementary students in the project's cooperative schools, compared with students in traditional schools. Of particular significance, both gifted and academically handicapped students in the cooperative schools also outperformed their respective peers in traditional programs. A cooperative school climate also helps in reducing violence and conflicts (Johnson & Johnson, 1995). The Comer model (Comer, 1996) is built on participatory community involvement that improves the school climate and the success for all students.

Good prevention and intervention programs in school are strengthened when parents and teachers are involved and educated in issues that can affect their children's development and success. Workshops, inservices, articles in the school newsletter, and informational fliers for parents (e.g., see Capuzzi & Gross, 1989; National Association of School Psychologists, 1992) can provide parents and teachers with information about a wide range of issues that can affect the lives of students, with valuable suggestions for how to respond in ways that support students. Preservice and inservice programs for teachers and other educators can support the development of meaningful home–school partnerships to increase the involvement of parents in their chidren's education (Ammon, 1999). Attention to the potential cultural diversity between families and school personnel is particularly important in building successful home–school bridges (Brown, 1997; Edens, 1997; Ingraham & Meyers, 2000; Lynch & Hansen, 1998; Rogers et al., 1999).

Some excellent resources are available to support the development of prevention programs for a variety of risk factors and to support resilience (e.g., Barona & Garcia, 1990; Capuzzi & Gross, 1989; Cowan et al., 1996; Durlak, 1997; Johnson & Johnson, 1995; Lewis, Sugai, & Colvin, 1998; McWhirter et al., 1998; Paris & Ayres, 1994; Slavin, Karweitt, & Madden, 1989; Slavin, Karweit, & Wasik, 1994.). An examination of many of the recent media and curriculum catalogues reveals a wide variety of books, films, software programs, and materials that can be used for school-wide prevention programs.

### *4. Plan Early Intervention for At-Risk Populations*

Through planning, early interventions can be developed for individuals and groups of students likely to become at risk of school difficulties. Anticipatory guidance prior to major transitions, developmental crises, and other predictable times of difficulty is a cost-effective and advisable intervention strategy. Groups of students who are identified as at risk of school crises, such as students changing schools, students failing classes, or students showing early signs of dysfunctional cognitive–affective processing are obvious targets for early intervention. When students are going to experience a major change in their educational experience or placement, careful. planning for the transition can reduce the prevalence of crises. At the individual level, teachers and parents can be on alert for early signs of negative cognitive–affective patterns and can seek early intervention. Students who make statements such as "I can never do anything right," "Why should I even try—I won't get it anyway," "I have to get a 'B' or I might as well have failed" could be identified for early intervention programs. Statements like these show perceptions of low self-efficacy, low self-concept of ability, or unrealistic expectations for performance.

### *5. Use Consultation and Intervention Assistance Teams*

Consultation, an indirect form of services delivered by an individual or team, can be used to develop early interventions before situations escalate to a crisis level. When teachers and parents have access to professionals trained in consultation service delivery, they can seek appropriate help regarding their concerns about students. Consultation can help identify and intervene with factors related to the current crisis and can support the consultee in generalizing newly learned problem-solving strategies to future situations. At the individual level, consultation can help identify factors contributing to the current problem situation and it can support the teacher or parent in developing effective interventions (Caplan & Caplan, 1993; Conoley & Conoley, 1992; Erchul & Martens, 1997; Gutkin & Curtis, 1990; Ingraham, 2000.) Consultation teams (e.g., Rosenfield & Gravois, 1996) can generate ideas for interventions and draw upon the expertise of a variety of school professional. Consultation may provide a more cost-effective method of intervention in school-related crises than direct services such as individual counseling. Moreover, it may more effectively intervene on contextual variables, such as the curriculum or teacher–student relationship, that may be part of the problem situation.

## SUMMARY

Many school-related crises can be prevented or reduced in intensity through early intervention. With an ecological approach to working with the student's family, teachers, and peers, support systems can be mobilized to offer the most effective types of interventions to foster student success in school. In general, prevention of school-related crises is enhanced when schools involve parents and teachers as partners in promoting learning, development, and resilience. Learning goals for each student should include the development of self-worth and self-efficacy, skills in problem solving and conflict resolution, and strategies for positive learning and social interaction. From a cognitive–affective perspective, goals for individuals should include: (a) development of an accurate, well-articulated, and diversified self-concept, and (b) information-processing patterns that allow the student to assess the causes of school success and failure and to modify strategies based on achievement feedback. Students who know how to seek out performance information are better prepared to solve problems and reduce anxiety associated with the unknown, new situations, and changes in routine. Students who have an array of personal resources and coping strategies at hand are more resilient. Students who know when they need help and how to seek assistance are better equipped to solve problems and prevent crises.

School professionals who are knowledgeable about the dynamics of healthy and dysfunctional cognitive–affective processes are in a better position to intervene at both individual and systems levels. At the individual level, school-related crises are often integrally associated with perceived threats to self-esteem and self-worth. The crisis counselor who understands the relationship of crisis with self-esteem and information processing is prepared to carefully assess the dynamics of the crisis and plan effective interventions. At the classroom, school, or systems level, the context for learning and the school climate can have a significant impact of the prevalence and intensity of school-related crises. The prevalence of crises with school learning can be greatly reduced with prevention and early intervention. Durlak (1997) estimated that prevention programs have reduced the incidence of school failure by 26%–90%, depending on the specific study and measured outcomes. He emphasized the need to develop prevention programs with multiple levels of intervention (individual, groups, schools).

## REFERENCES


Ablard, K. E., & Lipshultz, R. E. (1998). Self-regulated learning in high-achieving students: Relations to advanced reasoning, achievement goals, and gender. *Journal of Educational Psychology, 90*, 94–101.

Adelman, H. S., & Taylor, L. (2000). Moving prevention from the fringes into the fabric of school improvement. *Journal of Educational and Psychological Consultation, 11*(1), 7–36.

American Psychological Association (1993). *Learner-centered psychological principles: Guidelines for school redesign and reform.* Washington DC: Presidential Task Force on Psychology in Education, American Psychological Association.

Ames, C. (1992). Classroom goals, structures, and student motivation. *Journal of Educational Psychology, 84*, 261–271.

Ammon, M. A. (Ed.). (1999). *Joining hands: Preparing teachers to make meaningful home-school connections.* Sacramento, CA: California Department of Education, Commission on Teacher Credentialing.

Atkinson, L., Quarrington, B., & Cyr, J. (1985). School refusal: The heterogeneity of a concept. *American Journal of Orthopsychiatry, 55*, 83–101.

Barona, A., & Garcia, E. E. (Eds.). (1990). *Children at risk: Poverty, minority status, and other issues in educational equity.* Washington, DC: National Association of School Psychologists.

Brown, D. (1997). Implications of cultural values for cross-cultural consultation with families. *Journal of Counseling & Development, 76*, 29–35.

Bugental, D. B., Whalen, C. K., & Henker, B. (1977). Causal attributions of hyperactive children and motivational assumptions of the two behavior-change approaches: Evidence for an interactionist position. *Child Development, 48*, 874–884.

Caplan, G., & Caplan, R. B. (1993). *Mental health consultation and collaboration.* San Francisco: Jossey-Bass.

Capuzzi, D., & Gross, D. R. (1989). *Youth at risk: A resource for counselors, teachers and parents.* Alexandria, VA: American Counseling Association.

Comer, J. (Ed.). (1996). *Rallying the whole village: The Comer Process for reforming education.* New York: Teachers College Press.

Conoley, J. C., & Conoley, C. W. (1992). *School consultation: Practice and training* (2nd ed.). Boston: Allyn & Bacon.

Covington, M. V. (1992). *Making the grade.* New York: Cambridge University Press.

Cowan, E. L., Hightower, A D., Pedro-Carroll, J. L., Work, W. C., Wyman, W. C., & Haffey, W. G. (1996). *School-based prevention for children at risk: The primary mental health project.* Washington DC: American Psychological Association.

Craven, R. G., Marsh, H. W., & Debus, R. L. (1991). Effects of internally focused feedback on enhancement of academic self-concept. *Journal of Educational Psychology, 83*, 17–27.

Cullen, J. L., & Boersma, F. (1982). The influence of coping strategies on the manifestation of learned helplessness. *Contemporary Educational Psychology, 7*, 346–356.

Doll, B., & Lyon, M. A. (Eds.). (1998). Resilience applied: The promise and pitfalls of school-based resilience programs mini-series in *School Psychology Review, 27*(3).

Durlak, J. A. (1997). *Successful prevention programs for children and adolescents*. New York: Plenum.

Edens, J. H. (1997). Home visitation programs with ethnic minority families: Cultural issues in parent consultation. *Journal of Educational and Psychological Consultation, 8*, 373–383.

Egan, S. K., & Perry, D. G. (1998). Does low self-regard invite victimization? *Developmental Psychology, 34*, 299–309.

Erchul, W. P., & Martens, B. R. (1997). *School consultation: Conceptual and empirical bases of practice*. New York: Plenum.

Evans, L. D. (2000). Functional school refusal subtypes: Anxiety, avoidance, and malingering. *Psychology in the Schools, 37*, 183–191.

Falvey, M. A., Givner, C. C., & Kimm, C. (1995). What is an inclusive school? In R. A. Villa & J. S. Thousand (Eds.), *Creating an inclusive school* (pp. 1–12). Alexandria, VA: Association for Supervision and Curriculum Development.

Fish, M. (1995). Best practices in working with parents of children with disabilities. In A. Thomas & J. Grimes. *Best practices in school psychology, III* (pp. 1061–1070). Washington DC: National Association of School Psychologists.

Goleman, D. (1995). *Emotional intelligence: Why it can matter more than IQ*. New York: Batman.

Gordon, D. A., & Young, R. D. (1976). School phobia: A discussion of etiology, treatment, and evaluation. *Psychological Reports, 39*, 783–804.

Gresham, F. M. (1997). Social skills. In G. G. Bear, K. M. Minke, & A. Thomas (Eds.), *Children's needs II: Development, problems and alternatives* (pp. 39–50). Bethesda, MD: National Association of School Psychologists.

Gutkin, T. B., & Curtis, M. J. (1990). School-based consultation: Theory, techniques and research. In C. R. Reynolds & T. B. Gutkin (Eds.), *The handbook of school psychology* (2nd ed., pp. 577–611). New York: Wiley.

Harmin, M. (1994). *Inspiring active learning: A handbook for teachers*. Alexandria, VA: Association for Supervision and Curriculum Development.

Harry, B. (1992). Making sense of disability: Low-income, Puetro Rican parents; theories of the problem, *Exceptional Children, 59*, 27–40.

Harter, S. (1993). Causes and consequences of low self-esteem in children and adolescents. In R. F. Baumeister (Ed.), *Self-esteem: The puzzle of low self-regard* (pp. 87–116). New York: Plenum.

Henker, B., Whalen, C. K., & Hinshaw, S. P. (1980). The attributional contexts of cognitive strategies. *Exceptional Education Quarterly, 1*(2), 17–30.

Henning-Stout, M. (1994). *Responsive assessment: A new way of thinking about learning*. San Francisco, Jossey Bass.

Huberty, T. J. (1997). Anxiety. In G. G. Bear, K. M. Minke, & A. Thomas (Eds.), *Children's needs II: Development, problems and alternatives* (pp. 305–314). Bethesda, MD: National Association of School Psychologists.

Hwang, P. O. (1995). *Other-esteem: A creative response to a society obsessed with promoting the self.* San Diego: Black Forrest.

Ingraham, C. L. (1985). Cognitive-affective dynamics of crisis intervention for school entry, school transition and school failure. *School Psychology Review, 14*, 266–279.

Ingraham, C. L. (1986). Dimensions of self-concept and valuation and their relationship with self-esteem, effort and grades: A cross-sectional analysis. Doctoral dissertation, University of California, Berkeley, 1985. *Dissertation Abstracts International, 47*, 837A.

Ingraham, C. L. (1988a). School-related crises. In J. Sandoval (Ed.), *Crisis counseling, intervention, and prevention in the schools* (pp. 35–49). Hillsdale, NJ: Lawrence Erlbaum Associates.

Ingraham, C. L. (1988b). Self-esteem, crisis and school performance. In J. Sandoval (Ed.), *Crisis counseling, intervention, and prevention in the schools* (pp. 21–33). Hillsdale, NJ: Lawrence Erlbaum Associates.

Ingraham, C. L. (2000). Consultation through a multicultural lens: Multicultural and cross-cultural consultation in schools. *School Psychology Review, 29*, 320–343.

Ingraham, C. L., & Bursztyn, A. (1999, August). Systems interventions: Psychologists' roles in shaping school culture, educational policy, and institutional advocacy. In M. Henning-Stout (Chair), *Cross-cultural school psychology—Advances in the field*. Symposium at the annual meeting of the American Psychological Association, Boston.

Ingraham, C. L., & Meyers, J. (Guest Eds.). (2000). Multicultural and cross-cultural consultation: Cultural diversity issues in school consultation, special issue of *School Psychology Review, 29*, 311–470.

Iwamoto, S., & Yoshida, K. (1997). School refusal in Japan: The recent dramatic increase in incidence is a cause for concern. *Social Behavior & Personality, 25*, 325–319.

Johnson, D. S. (1981). Naturally acquired learned helplessness: The relationship of school failure to achievement behavior, attribution, and self-concept. *Journal of Educational Psychology, 73*(2), 174–180.

Johnson, S. B. (1979). Children's fears in the classroom. *School Psychology Digest, 8*, 382–396.

Johnson, D. W., Johnson, R. T. (1995). *Reducing school violence through conflict resolution*. Alexandria, VA: Association for Supervision and Curriculum Development.

Johnson, D. W., Johnson, R., & Holubec, E. (1994). *Cooperative learning in the classroom*. Alexandria, VA: Association for Supervision and Curriculum Development.

Jundall, J. A. (1995). *Peer programs: An in-depth look at peer helping*. Bristol, PA: Accelerated Development.

Kamins, M. L., & Dweck, C. S. (1999). Person versus process praise and criticism implications for contingent self-worth and coping. *Developmental Psychology, 35*, 835–847.

Kearney, C. A. (1995). School refusal behavior. In A. R. Eisen, C. A. Kearney, & C. E. Schafer (Eds.), *Clinical handbook of anxiety disorders in children and adolescents* (pp. 19–52). Northvale, NJ: Jason Aronson.

Kearney, C. A., Eisen, A. R., Silverman, W. R. (1995). The legend and myth of school phobia. *School Psychology Quarterly, 10*, 65–85.

Kearney, C. A., & Silverman, W. K. (1993). Measuring the function of school refusal behavior: The school refusal assessment scale. *Journal of Clinical and Child Psychology, 22*, 85–96.

King, N. J., Ollendick, T. H., & Tonge, B. J. (1995). *School refusal: Assessment and treatment*. Boston: Allyn & Bacon.

Lane, P. S., & McWhirter, J. J. (1992). A peer mediation model: Conflict resolution for elementary and middle school children. *Elementary School Guidance and Counseling, 27*, 15–24.

Last, C. G., & Perrin, S. (1993). Anxiety disorders in African-American and White children. *Journal of Abnormal Child Psychology, 21*, 153–164.

Leventhal, T., & Sills, M. (1964). Self-image in school phobia. *American Journal of Onhopsychiatry, 34*, 685–695.

Lewis, T. J., Sugai, G., & Colvin, G. (1998). Reducing problem behavior through a school-wide system of effective behavior support: Investigation of a school-wide social skills training program and contextual interventions, *School Psychology Review, 27*, 446–459.

Licht, B. G. (1983). Cognitive-motivational factors that contribute to the achievement of learning disabled children. *Journal of Learning Disabilities, 16*, 483–490.

Lynch, E. W., & Hanson, N. J. (Eds.). (1998). *Developing cross-cultural competence: A guide for working with children and their families* (2nd ed.). Baltimore, MD: Paul H. Brookes.

Mangieri, J. N., & Block, C. C. (Eds.). (1994). *Creating powerful thinking in teachers and students: Diverse perspectives*. Fort Worth, TX: Hartcourt Brace.

McCombs, B. L., & Pope, J. E. (1994). *Motivating hard to reach students*. Washington DC: American Psychological Association.

McWhirter, J. J., McWhirter, B. T., McWhirter, A. M., & McWhirter, E. H. (1998). *At-risk youth: A comprehensive response* (2nd ed.). Pacific Grove, CA: Brooks Cole.

National Association of School Psychologists. (1992). *Helping children grow up in the 90's: A resource book for parents and teachers*. Silver Spring, MD: National Association of School Psychologists.

Newman, R. S., & Schwager, M. T. (1995). Students' help seeking during problem solving: Effects of grade, goal, and prior achievement. *American Educational Research Journal, 32*, 352–376.

Paige, L. Z. (1997). School phobia, school refusal, and school avoidance. In G. G. Bear, K. M. Minke, & A. Thomas (Eds.), *Children's needs II: Development, problems and alternatives* (pp. 339–347). Bethesda, MD: National Association of School Psychologists.

Paris, S. G., & Ayres, L. R. (1994). *Becoming reflective students and teachers with portfolios and authentic assessment*. Washington DC: American Psychological Association.

Pilkington, C. L., & Piersel, W. C. (1991). School phobia: A critical analysis of separation anxiety theory and an alternative conceptualization. *Psychology in the Schools, 29*, 382–393.

Pintrich, P. R., Anderman, E. M., & Klobucar, C. (1994). Intraindividual differences in motivation and cognition in students with and without learning disabilities. *Journal of Learning Disabilities, 27*, 360–370.

Pintrich, P. R., & Schunk, D. H. (1996). *Motivation in education: Theory, research, and applications*. Englewood Cliffs, NJ: Merrill/Prentice Hall.

Rogers, M. R., Ingraham, C. L., Bursztyn, A., Cajigas-Segredo, N., Esquivel, G., Hess, R., Lopez, E C., & Nahari, S. G. (1999). Providing psychological services to racially, ethnically, culturally, and linguistically diverse individuals in the schools: Recommendations for practice. *School Psychology International Journal, 20*, 243–264.

Rosenfield, S. A., & Gravois, T. A. (1996). *Instructional consultation teams: Collaborating for change*. New York: Guilford Press.

Sanna, L. J., Turley-Ames, K. J., & Meier, S. (1999). Mood, self-esteem, and simulated alternatives thought-provoking affective influences on counterfactual direction. *Journal of Personality and Social Psychology, 76*, 543–558.

Shure, M. B. (1992). *I can problem solve (ICPS): An interpersonal cognitive problem-solving program*. Champaign, IL: Research Press.

Silverman, W. K., & Ginsburg, G. (1995). Specific phobias and generalized anxiety disorder. In J. S. March (Ed.), *Anxiety disorders in children and adolescence* (pp. 151–180). New York: Guilford Press.

Slavin, R. E., Karweit, N. L., & Madden, N. A. (Eds.). (1989). *Effective programs for students at risk*. Boston: Allyn & Bacon.

Slavin, R. E., Karweit, N. L., & Wasik, B. A. (Eds.). (1994). *Preventing early school failure: Research, policy and practice*. Boston: Allyn & Bacon.

Stevens, R. J., & Slavin, R. E. (1995). Effects of a cooperative learning approach in reading and writing on academically handicapped and nonhandicapped students. *Elementary School Journal*, January, 241–262.

Stipek, D. J. (1993). *Motivation to learn: From theory to practice* (2nd ed.). Needham, MA: Allyn & Bacon.

Villa, R. A., & Thousand, J. S. (Eds.). (1995). *Creating an inclusive school*. Alexandria, VA: Association for Supervision and Curriculum Development.

Webb, N. B. (Ed.). (1991). *Play therapy with children in crisis: A casebook for practitioners*. New York: Guilford Press.

Weiner, B. (1986). *An attributional theory of achievement and emotion*. New York: Springer-Verlag.

Wilson, M. (1995). Best practices in systems influences on children's self-concept. In A. Thomas & J. Grimes (Eds.), *Best practices in school psychology, III* (pp. 359–368). Washington DC: National Association of School Psychologists.

Winnie, P. H. (1997). Experimenting to bootstrap self-regulated learning. *Journal of Educational Psychology, 89*, 397–410.

Winslade, J., & Monk, G. (1999). *Narrative counseling in schools: Powerful & brief.* Thousand Oaks, CA: Corwin, Sage.

Zimmerman, B. J. (2000). Self-efficacy: An essential motive to learn. *Contemporary Educational Psychology, 25*, 82–91.

CHAPTER

# 5

# Divorce: Crisis Intervention and Prevention With Children of Divorce and Remarriage

Andrew M. Lamden
Private practice, Marin County, CA

Mariam J. King
Center for the Family in Transition

Ruth K. Goldman
San Francisco State University

Although statistics indicate that the rate of divorce in the United States has leveled off in the past 6 years, a large number of families continue to experience divorce each year (Shaw, Emery, & Tuer, 1993; Norton & Miller, 1992). In fact, divorce and marital separation are second only to death of a parent as stressful events for youngsters (Coddington, 1972). Given that approximately 2% of children living in the United States are faced with parental divorce each year (Emery & Forehand, 1996) and the speculation that 25% of children experience a parental breakup by age 14 (Baydar, 1988), it is crucial to understand the impact that divorce has on children. The need to develop and implement effective means of addressing these difficulties continues to be the focus of researchers and mental health clinicians who work with large numbers of children. Researchers have investigated how crisis intervention techniques can best be adapted to ameliorate the negative, long-term effects of familial disruption on youngsters (Goldman & King, 1985; Kalter, Pickar, & Lesowitz, 1984; Pedro-Carroll & Cowen, 1985; Stolberg & Cullen, 1983; Wallerstein & Kelly, 1980). However, most divorce-related child research conducted over the past decade has led to a better understanding of how parental conflict and parenting styles, within marriage or divorce, affect children. In fact, many recent studies have found that the adjustment problems of children of divorce can in part be accounted for by the experiences of these children within marriages that later end in divorce. (Buehler et al., 1998; Kelly, 2000; Cummings & Davies, 1994; McNeal & Amato, 1998). Clearly, this new information has important implications for intervention and treatment.

This chapter reviews some of the earlier and more current divorce research. Efforts at adapting a spectrum of preventive mental health techniques, including those of crisis intervention, to fit the unique aspects of marital crises as they affect children and school systems, will be the focus. The central program described here attempts to treat children and families at different stages of resolution to the marital crisis—the newly separated or divorced family, the remarried family, and the chronically embattled divorced family. Other recently developed programs are briefly described.

## The School and Divorce

During times of familial disruption or conflict, school can offer children nurturance and continuity as well as a place where age-appropriate developmental tasks can be pursued:

> One 7-year-old whose parents had recently divorced was having nightmares. In his dollhouse play he showed a little boy awake at night while everyone else slept. The boy runs around the house from room to room. "I dream that the house is falling apart, but sometimes I have good dreams. I dream that I'm in school and I'm making things."

For this child, the school environment was a supportive one in which he could develop and be less hindered by his preoccupations at home.

Our interest in working in the schools is rooted in the belief that an individual's capacity to cope with familial change and the resulting stress is partially dependent on the quality of support and guidance available from extrafamilial organizations in which that person functions (Peterson, Leigh, & Day, 1984; Stolberg & Cullen, 1983). The single most important formal institution providing such support outside the home is the school (Drake, 1981; Drake & Shellenberger, 1981; Kelly & Wallerstein, 1979). Because the school as a system is confronted with large numbers of families attempting to cope with the transitions brought about by divorce, strategies for intervention must be designed to address the needs not only of the individual student so affected, but also those of the classroom teacher and the school as a whole. In this chapter, we describe programmatic efforts designed to accommodate the organizational structure of the school to the structure of the postdivorce family. Schools, however, are faced with problems in their ability to offer support to students from these families. In addition to dealing with anxiety and depression in the students, many of these youngsters develop learning and behavioral problems secondary to the stress of the familial disruption.

## THE HAZARD OF DIVORCE FOR CHILDREN

Divorce, separation, and remarriage are processes that introduce rapid, multiple structural changes and require adaptation of all family members. Anxiety experienced at this time increases a child's need for a stable "holding environment" (Winnicott, 1971), while the nature of these familial changes temporarily undermines the capacity to parent (Wallerstein & Kelly, 1980), leaving the child vulnerable to even greater anxiety and depression. Because the changes required are of such great magnitude, it is likely that the family system will have difficulty providing nurturance, sustaining intimacy, and containing anxiety. For some families, this failure is transitory, with the family structure restabilizing 2 to 3 years postseparation. For others, there is a permanent familial disequilibrium, resulting in what Hunter and Schuman (1980) described as the "chronically reconstituting family."

Unlike other stressful events, such as a death in the family, the announcement of a divorce does not rally the support of the community. In fact, the members of the divorcing family may find themselves excluded from the social–familial network that provides support in other crisis situations. The media and public often view divorced families and mental health professionals as seriously flawed structures and environments, whereas the married or intact family has generally been considered to be a more positive and nurturing environment for children.

However, recently researchers have pointed out that marital conflict is a more important predictor of child adjustment than is divorce itself or post-divorce conflict (Buehler et al., 1998; Kline et al., 1991). Several large longitudinal studies found that as many as half of the behavioral and academic problems of children coming from marriages whose parent later divorced were observed 4 to 12 years prior to the separation. The symptoms of these children currently in intact families were similar to those reported in children with divorced parents: conduct disorders, antisocial behaviors, difficulty with peers and authority figures, depression, and academic and achievement problems (Cherlin et al., 1991; Elliot & Richards, 1991). Regardless of parents' marital status, high marital conflict experienced during childhood has been linked to increased depression and other psychological disorders in young adults (Amato & Keith, 1991; Zill, Morrison, & Coiro, 1993).

Numerous writers have described the behavioral changes and disruption in the child's ability to learn associated with the stress of parental separation and divorce (Hetherington, Bridges, & Insabella, 1998; Guidubaldi, 1984; Wallerstein & Kelly, 1980). Divorce has been associated with lowered academic performance and achievement test scores, although the differences between divorced and children with never divorced parents are modest (McLanahan & Sandefur, 1994).

Teachers report an increase in restlessness, aggression toward peers, tendency to daydream, and inability to concentrate following a divorce or separation. Of note is that children with divorced parents have poorer school attendance, watch more TV, do less homework, and have less parental supervision of their schoolwork: patterns that are primarily attributable to family disruption (McLanahan, 1999). A national survey study found that high levels of marital and family discord prior to divorce accounted for much of the link between parental divorce and measures of educational attainment (Furstenberg & Teitler, 1994). However, other research points as well to the reduced resources and lowered parental monitoring postdivorce as important factors influencing achievement (McLanahan & Sandefur, 1994). Important to note, moreover, is that when fathers are involved with the child's school and schoolwork after separation, there is less decline in academic functioning. Children with involved fathers get better grades, are less likely to get suspended or expelled, and appear to like school better (Nord, Brimhall, & West, 1997).

For adolescents a marked increase in absenteeism and tardiness is often present in children of divorce (Goldman, 1981). Children with divorced parents are also less likely to earn a college degree, in part because parental aspirations for educational attainment increase for adolescents in never divorced families but decrease for adolescents in divorced homes (McLanahan, 1999).

Recent studies report smaller differences between the adjustment and achievement problems when comparing children of divorce and children in never divorced families. However, aspects of the divorce experience clearly increase the risk for many children, particularly for those in high conflict situations as their parents separated and divorce (Emery, 1999; Hetherington, 1999; McLanahan, 1999).

The pioneering and most comprehensive of the studies was conducted over a period of 10 years by Wallerstein and Kelly. The results of this research in which 60 families with 131 children from Northern California for 10 years, (many of the families continue to be followed beyond the 25-year mark) continues to yield a rich source of clinical and conceptual material (Wallerstein, 1983, 1984; Wallerstein & Kelly, 1980). Five years postdivorce, Wallerstein and Kelly noted that approximately one third of the children in their study were faring well and considered themselves happy. Approximately one third were doing reasonably well and were able to pursue academic goals, and the remaining continued to be at least moderately depressed. Various factors including age of the child, gender, family dynamics, and resources available for support, have enormous impact on how children cope with divorce.

## Risk Factors Linked to Parental Conflict Style

Research clearly indicates that the intensity and frequency of parent conflict postdivorce, the style of conflict, its manner of resolution, and the presence of buffers to ameliorate the effects of high conflict are the most important predictors of child adjustment (Kelly, 1994). In older children and adolescents, *severity* of conflict had the largest and most consistent impact on adjustment. Intense conflict leads to more externalizing (disobedience, aggression, delinquency) and internalizing (depression, anxiety, poor self-esteem) symptoms in both boys and girls, when compared to children experiencing low-intensity conflict. Buehler et al. (1998) found that overtly hostile conflict styles (e.g., physical and verbal affect, and behaviors such as slapping, screaming, contempt, or derision), were more strongly associated with externalizing and internalizing behaviors in children of all ages than either covert conflict styles or frequency of conflict. In addition, severe marital conflict that focuses on the child is more predictive of child behavior problems than is frequency of marital conflict or conflict that is not child centered. Children who are the focus of conflict express more self-blame, shame, and fear of being drawn into the conflict (Grych & Fincham, 1993).

Current studies indicate that *frequency* of parental conflict, one of the earliest and most common measures used in marital research, has been demonstrated repeatedly to play a role in adjustment, in that high-frequency conflict is linked to more negative effects on children (Johnston, 1995).

Researchers have also studied the manner in which mothers and fathers are affected by marital conflict and divorce. Mothers in high-conflict marriages tend to be less warm and empathic toward their children, more rejecting, more erratic and harsh in discipline, and use more guilt and anxiety-inducing disciplinary techniques, compared to mothers in low-conflict marriages. These more negative parenting behaviors are also associated with poorer social awareness and social withdrawal in the child (Belsky, Youngblade, Rovine, & Volling, 1991; Cummings & Davies, 1994; Fincham, Grych, & Osborne, 1994; Harrist & Ainslie, 1998; Kline et al., 1991).

Fathers in high-conflict marriages withdraw more from the parenting role and from their children compared to fathers in low-conflict marriages, and tend to remain less active postdivorce. It is generally accepted that mothers are the holders of the father–child relationship, both during marriage and after divorce, and that mother's attitudes toward fathers' parenting role affects the extent of fathers' parenting more so than his own attitude (Doherty, 1998; Pleck, 1997). Angry mothers may exclude fathers in order to preserve power and control, during and after the marriage or divorce. Thus, for the child in the high-conflict marriage, the consequence may be not only less father involvement, but more negative interactions with, and feelings of rejection by the father as well.

## Risk Factors Linked to Gender

In numerous studies over the past three decades, children with divorced parents have been reported to be more aggressive, impulsive, and to engage in more antisocial behaviors, when compared to matched samples of children with never divorced parents (Kelly, 1994). Although some earlier studies reported that boys from divorced families had more externalizing problems than did girls, others have not. In a more recent, nationally representative sample of 618 married and divorced–never remarried families assessed at two points in time, no gender differences could be linked to divorce (Vandewater & Lansford, 1998). Rather, in the overall population boys had significantly more externalizing behaviors than did girls, regardless of family structure. Of significance is that the study also did not support earlier reports that depression and anxiety were more common for girls than boys as a result of divorce. Hetherington (1999) pointed to the complexity of the gender–age adjustment issue, in that adjustment and achievement in boys and girls after divorce were found to vary by age, time since divorce, type of parenting, and type and extent of parental conflict.

## Risk Factors Linked to Age

Research findings regarding the risk factors correlated with the child's age at the time of divorce and the length of time spent in the divorced household are contradictory. The work of Hetherington, Cox, and Cox (1978) suggested that more detrimental effects are associated with children of younger ages, a finding supported by Kurdek and Berg (1983), who reported that older children have fewer adjustment problems.

The Guidubaldi study (Guidubaldi, Perry, Cleminshaw, & McLoughlin, 1983) indicated that older girls adjust better to divorce than younger girls do, with the reverse being true for boys. This finding is further supported by a 2-year follow-up in which fifth-grade girls from divorced families were most indistinguishable from those in intact homes, whereas fifth-grade boys show an increase in problems over those presented in first grade (Guidubaldi, 1984). However, in families with extreme and continuing high conflict after divorce, children with more frequent transitions, and shared access, more emotional and behavioral problems existed, particularly among girls, than did children in sole custody situations (Johnston, 1995).

## Risk Factors Linked to Parental Adjustment and Environment

Closure or resolution of the divorce happens at both the level of the family as a whole and at the individual level. Wallerstein (1983) conceptualized the child's resolution of the divorce as a series of developmental tasks. These tasks follow a particular time sequence beginning with the critical events of the parental separation and culminating in young adulthood. However, persistent, intense marital discord and marital dissatisfaction, including discipline, parent–child aggression, and affective responses, pervasively undermine the quality of parenting (Fincham et al., 1994), and have a negative impact on the child's ability to successfully master the important developmental tasks associated with divorce resolution.

Kurdek and Berg (1983) identified parent-related factors that influence positive adjustment following marital breakup. They found that children's divorce adjustment is significantly related to "their mothers' use of social support systems, to their mothers' own divorce adjustment, to low maternal stress levels, and to low interpersonal conflict" (p. 58). The quality of the interaction with the noncustodial parent figured significantly, whereas the frequency and regularity of the visits were not significantly related to good adjustment. After divorce, there is no buffering effect provided by the nonresidential parent when the child experiences erratic, hostile, or depressed parenting in the custodial residence. However, buffers have been identified in research that help protect children in high-conflict marriages, including a good relationship with at least one parent or caregiver, parental warmth, the support of siblings, and for adolescents, having good self-esteem and peer support (Emery, 1999; Neighbors, Forehand, & McVicar, 1993). A positive school environment can also provide a crucial buffer when the child's home and family life is increasingly chaotic. When some of these buffering factors are present at the time of divorce, adjustment is improved.

# COMMON AGE-SPECIFIC REACTIONS TO DIVORCE

## Preschoolers–Kindergartners

In Wallerstein and Kelly's (1980) initial study, which focused on postseparation reactions, they noted that 2- and 3-year-olds regressed in their behaviors. These toddlers, struggling with issues of mastery, often lost recently acquired toilet-training skills and showed signs of separation anxiety, such as clinging behavior, or the converse of reaching out too quickly to strangers. Children between 3;9 and 4;9 years frequently displayed bewilderment, irritability, aggressive behavior, and self-blame (Gardner, 1976; Hetherington, 1979).

Although Wallerstein and Kelly have addressed themselves primarily to the affective component in divorce-related responses, Neal (1983) extended their work into the cognitive domain. He found that the youngest group (3- to 6-year olds) understands parental divorce entirely from an egocentric perspective. They link feelings of attachment to physical closeness, and therefore when one parent moves away from the child, the syllogistic assumption is that the child did something wrong to cause this physical distance. Misconceptions about the reasons for the marital break-up occur frequently. Furthermore, feelings of loss and sadness, fears of abandonment, deprivation, yearning for the noncustodial parent, and confusion about the divorce create frequent conflicts for children at this age.

## Latency-Age Children

Wallerstein and Kelly (1980) reported that early elementary school-aged children (ages 7 to 8) appeared sad, were observed to be deeply grieving, and experienced feelings of split loyalty, fantasies of responsibility and reconciliation. Despite their greater understanding of the divorce, they seemed unable to lessen their suffering. By contrast, older latency-aged children (9 to 10 years), although experiencing feelings of loneliness, shame, intense anger, rejection, and helplessness, along with continued loyalty conflicts, appeared more able to utilize adult interventions.

Kurdek and Berg (1983) reported that 9- to 12-year-olds could adjust to the divorce better if they experienced an internal locus of control and if they had good interpersonal understanding. Favorable adjustment was positively related to children's perceptions that factors were under their control and that they understood issues in terms of psychological feelings and relationships rather than along concrete dimensions.

## Adolescents

A recent large-scale study reported that when conflict was low after divorce, adolescents in joint physical custody were better adjusted, but not in high-conflict postdivorce situations (Maccoby & Mnookin, 1992). Springer and Wallerstein (1983) examined the responses to divorce of a nonclinical population of young adolescents, age 12 to 14. They described five hallmarks of these young peoples' reactions to the marital rupture: (a) keen ability to attend to parental relationships and burgeoning ability to judge each parent and his or her behavior as individual; (b) a deep sense of loss of the intact family and loss of hope for what that family might have been; (c) profound concern that overt parental conflicts will become public, leading the adolescent to experience shame and embarrassment; (d) increased rivalry with siblings accompanied by an increased dependency on the intact sibling subsystem; and (e) an ability to maintain distance from the parental discord by sporting a "cool" stance, use of sarcasm and humor, and use of extrafamilial sources of interest and support. In those cases where the adolescent was not able to maintain distance, there was a strong alliance or identification with one parent. These young people were more easily drawn into loyalty conflicts that impaired their normal development.

## CONCEPTUALIZING A COMPREHENSIVE MODEL OF PREVENTION

Earlier crisis intervention studies have helped us understand emotional responses to loss (Caplan, 1981). Lindemann's (1944) pioneering work was aimed at reducing the traumatic effects of catastrophic loss when individuals were the victims of natural disasters. Bowlby (1980, 1982); Ainsworth (1969); and Mahler, Pine, and Bergman (1975) studied the impact of attachment, separation, and loss on the child. Special attention was given to the young child's attempt to master the temporary or permanent loss of the primary care-taking figure at particular developmental phases.

Children experiencing the crisis of divorce frequently must deal with ongoing or repeated experiences of loss coupled with feelings of rejection. In many cases, the decision to divorce is preceded by one or more parental separations involving the departure of one parent from the existing family (Bloom, Asher, & White, 1978). The child faces the additional complexity of knowing that the parental decision to separate and divorce was made by choice, which at some level is experienced by the youngster as a rejection. Typically, the youngster is also expected to develop relationships with subsequent parent substitutes and newly acquired siblings. Competition for attention, affection, and feelings of isolation are frequent occurrences.

Although many writers have described efforts at treating children of divorce in groups, little was previously written that conceptualizes the activity group as part of an overall preventive approach to children as members of schools and communities (Drake, 1981). As the realization becomes clearer that the "typical" American family is no longer the "norm," the need for organizational changes to accommodate the multiplicity of actual family structures also becomes clearer. Although a direct counseling service with students represents one way of helping them cope with stress, a broader preventive perspective is necessary. The original concept for helping children cope with divorce through group intervention was developed in conjunction with the School Services Program of the Center for the Family in Transition (Wallerstein & Kelly, 1980). A school-based intervention incorporating activity groups for children of divorced families, along with ongoing teacher training and consultation, plus parent involvement, was designed. Through collaboration with administrators and faculty, the group interventions became an avenue for helping to create system changes for families in transition at both the school and family level. Over the subsequent years to the present, recent researchers, educators, and mental health professionals have further developed and implemented divorce-related groups (Pedro-Carroll, Sutton, & Wyman, 1999; Roseby & Johnston, 1997).

## Effective Administrative Changes

At the administrative level many educators and administrators have been encouraged to look critically at their policies toward nonresidential parents. Issues including the re-design of registration forms to include both parents, and the establishment of policies encouraging issuance of duplicate report cards, parent–teacher conferences, and school calendars, have been addressed and implemented within many schools. Due to limitations in time and economic resources, these changes have taken place slowly and with more effort than one would expect. For example, administrators continue to develop guidelines for faculty members faced with the complexities of conducting parent–teacher conferences with parents who do not reside together. As Ricci (1979) pointed out, children continue to need both parents. The refusal of social institutions such as the schools to open up avenues that encourage responsible relationships on the part of both parents with their children only serves to weaken family ties in the postdivorce family. It is through administrative consultation aimed at effecting such changes that school psychologists and counselors can best apply a model of primary prevention in their schools.

## Working With Teachers

In a preventive intervention, it is clear that one cannot work effectively within a system by offering service to one segment without understanding the nature of the impact on the related segments, and without developing plans to address the impact. It is only by helping teachers acquire greater understanding of a child's classroom behavior as a response to this disruption, and by developing more effective strategies for aiding a student's learning, despite the disruption, that one is able to support individual or group work with the child.

The following serves as an illustration of how collaborative efforts with teachers led to a better understanding of a child's school performance, increased empathy for the youngster, and enhanced the possibility of reaching the student educationally through the use of alternative strategies:

> A frustrated teacher complained of the immature quality of one girl's illustration for an essay, using it as an example of the generally poor quality of the student's work. The clinician was able to reframe the "immaturity" in this particular illustration of a house and a bunny rabbit in a sunny field by talking about this 12-year-old's desperate need for mothering and comfort, which were triggered by the assigned topic, "Those were the Good Ol' Days." When seen in light of a longing for the pre-divorce family, this child's "immature" work was less frustrating to the teacher.

In-service training for teachers has been used to educate them about children's reactions to marital crisis. We have found that Wallerstein's (1983) conceptualization of the child's resolution of the divorce as a *series of developmental tasks* is a useful educational concept. Elucidating common age-specific postdivorce behaviors and how these might be seen in the classroom is equally important. Vignettes and case presentations are used as a way of helping groups of teachers think about how they cope with troublesome classroom behavior, and how they deal with nonresidential parents. For example, one often-voiced complaint on the part of teachers is the difficulty in handling the anger of the latency-age boy, which often surfaces as "acting up" in class and refusing to do school work. In several cases where these youngsters' nonresidential fathers were invited by the teacher to discuss the problem and become an active part of the teacher–parent team, the children's troublesome behavior lessened.

## INDIVIDUAL COUNSELING INTERVENTIONS

### General Considerations

References are drawn primarily from the seminal work of Wallerstein and Kelly, which remains the richest source of clinical data regarding age-specific risk and postdivorce interventions. More recent work by Roseby and Johnston (1997) and Pedro-Carroll et al. (1999) elaborated on Wallerstein's ideas and provide detailed examples of school interventions. In their article on brief interventions, Kelly and Wallerstein (1977) described the divorce-specific assessment (particularly useful to school psychologists). They evaluated the following factors: (a) each child's overall developmental achievements; (b) each child's unique responses to, and experiences with, the divorce; and (c) the support systems available to each child. In particular, they were concerned with how the child understood the meaning of the divorce.

In formulating school-based interventions for children with familial disruptions, the following must be considered: (a) a youngster may be experiencing a chronic and highly stressful series of events lasting in some cases for the entirety of the youngster's school years; (b) a youngster may be experiencing a set of indirectly related transitions such as loss of home, change in neighborhood or school, and so on, increasing the stress of the actual familial disruption; (c) a youngster may simultaneously lose the support of extrafamilial figures and be particularly needy of nurturance from empathic adults with whom he or she spends time; and (d) a youngster's capacity to cope with stress is dependent on his or her sex, age, developmental temperament, and problem-solving skills.

### Interventions With Preschoolers

Wallerstein and Kelly (1980) suggested that interventions with preschoolers, who do not have a history of emotional difficulties, should focus primarily on the parents. The central intent should be to help parents communicate more effectively with their preschooler and better understand the causes of the child's distress. Frequently, preventive interventions involve stabilizing aspects of both the care-taking situation and visits with the noncustodial parent.

### Interventions With Young Elementary School Children

Interventions for this age group need to take cognizance of the child's realistic understanding of the basis for the divorce. Just as children of this age generally have difficulty in talking about issues involving strong feelings, they have considerable trouble in talking about their parents' divorce. Wallerstein and Kelly (1980) found it necessary to develop an indirect technique for discussing the multiple and complex feelings that arose from the marital disruption. For example, the therapist would recount what such an experience was like for other youngsters of the same age, while specifically utilizing familial information unique to this child's situation in order to help the child express the painful feelings. Thus, the "divorce monologue" was born. Similar storytelling approaches utilizing fantasy, displacement, and projection are described by Kalter et al. (1984) and by Roseby and Johnston (1997).

## GROUP INTERVENTIONS

Research in crisis theory and its application has shown that individuals who receive cognitive guidance and emotional support for coping with a stressful situation have a reduced risk for developing mental and physical illnesses. The use of group techniques in meeting the needs of individuals in stressful situations has proven successful. Often, in fact, children who have lived with conflict show a marked preference for group over individual treatment. In a group, they can reduce some of the shame about their family situation and find out that they are "not the only one" (Roseby & Johnston, 1997), thus, normalizing the divorce experience.

Beginning with the work of Cantor (1977, 1979), time-limited counseling groups have been used to help students whose parents recently were separated or divorced and who showed signs of behavioral disruptions. Typically, these groups are offered to older elementary school students of both genders. Content centers on a child's confusion concerning the reasons for the divorce, loyalty conflicts, visitation issues, problems with stepparents and siblings, and so on. Children report that sharing reactions to typical divorce-related issues offers them support and comfort. When postgroup interviews are held, group members uniformly indicate that the groups were of help to them.

Roseby and Johnston (1997), and Pedro-Carroll et al. (1999) described successful school-based group intervention programs. A 2-year follow-up of a school-based group for young children of divorce reports significant decrease in postdivorce anxiety, and overall improvement in coping (Pedro-Carroll et al., 1999). Stolberg and Cullen (1983) and Stolberg and Garrison (1985) described groups that are part of a multimodel prevention program designed to facilitate postdivorce adjustment of mothers and children. Their 12-session children's groups were structured to include weekly meetings of 1 hour each with small groups of students ages 7 to 13. Participants were from families who were within 33 months of parental separation. Relaxation, impulse and anger control techniques, and communication skills were taught through methods that included modeling and role playing. Outcome data indicated that the child participants attained better self-concepts at the end of 12 sessions. At the 5-month follow-up, child participants also were found to have improved social skills.

Pedro-Carroll (1985), Pedro-Carroll and Cowen (1985) and Pedro-Carroll et al. (1999) reported on children's school groups in which they used a variation of Stolberg and Cullen's (1983) strategies for teaching effective coping skills to children in the postdivorce family. Their 10-week-long groups included students from fourth to sixth grade, with widely varying lengths of time from the parental divorce. In the first three sessions, the main goal is to build support for children by giving them opportunities to share common feelings related to the parental divorce and to help clarify common misconceptions about divorce. This process is accomplished by the use of filmstrips on parent–child reactions to marital dissolution and discussions of feelings common to children in the divorcing family. Sessions 4 through 9 attempt to help children learn social problem-solving skills. Using role playing and discussion, leaders emphasize defining problems, thinking of ways to solve problems or recognizing that a problem cannot be solved by the child alone, and recognizing consequences of behavior.

With the acquisition of better coping skills, children feel less out of control and the tendency to act out is decreased as the sense of mastery increases. Sessions 10 and 11 are spent focusing on understanding the causes of anger and helping youngsters to express anger appropriately. The final sessions are used to help children arrive at more differentiated views of the family through discussion of various family forms, and to terminate the group. The participants reported an increased sense of mastery as well as a decreased sense of isolation and confusion. Positive effects of the group intervention were seen both clinically and statistically.

## Setting Up the Group

This section discusses issues involved in conducting direct group interventions on the school site with elementary and junior high school students. Our experience has come from working as outside consultants in suburban public school systems in California.

***Group Structure.*** Groups met once weekly for 50–75 minutes over a 6- to 12-week period. Variation in duration and number of group sessions was dictated by the vagaries of the school calendar. Our preference is for a 1-hour weekly meeting, over a 10-week period. This is the general consensus of the length of session and number of weeks in the literature referred to previously.

***Group Heterogeneity.*** Groups have included children from families in which the initial disruption ranged from 10 years to 3 months prior to the start of the group intervention. Those children with greater distance from the initial familial disruption helped those children for whom the divorce and resulting trauma were more recent. This is a finding confirmed by Kalter and his colleagues (Kalter, Schaefer, Lesowitz, Alpern, & Pickar, 1988). In some groups, not all of the children had experienced the loss of the intact family as a result of divorce. Children were also included whose parents, although never married, did live together and co-parent, subsequently terminating their living arrangements. As in most of the group interventions described in the literature, our groups were primarily mixed gender groups, with five to eight children in each. Less than five children is too few because the loss of a member due to absenteeism is a common phenomenon and more than eight children does not allow enough time for the discussion of individual concerns. Establishing same-gender groups for young adolescents has some advantages over mixed-gender groups. Because parental dating and sexuality are especially important concerns at this age, single-gender groups allow these young people to discuss their perceptions of parental sexuality without the burden of concurrently feeling strong heterosexual pulls toward others in the group.

***Confidentiality.*** Confidentiality, always an important issue in treatment, assumes a magnitude not easily grasped until one actually works in the school setting. Group members have a history with one another before the group starts, as do their parents and teachers. Addressing the issue of confidentiality with all concerned is vital. The extension of the group over a period of 10 to 12 weeks helps surmount the greater resistances to disclosure caused by the fact that children see and know one another in a context other than the group setting. An example of such a problem was experienced when two young adolescents who were boyfriend and girlfriend were asked to be in the same group. Although they initially complied, their difficulty in discussing the recent divorce of their parents in front of one another was insurmountable, and eventually both left the group. Letting students know prior to the group who the participants may be is a prudent move that gives children and leaders time to assess the previously established interpersonal relationships among children. Although this raises a new question of confidentiality, on balance this seems minor in comparison with selecting a compatible group.

***Pregroup Interviews.*** Considerable attention was given to differentiating longstanding psychopathology from reactive responses to the familial change. The group leader conducted individual interviews with each child participant lasting between 1 and 2 hours. Wallerstein's (1983) conceptualization of the child's resolution of divorce as a series of developmental tasks, the Kinetic Family Drawing (K-F-D), the Coopersmith Scale of Self-Esteem (Coopersmith, 1967), along with the divorce-specific assessment technique (Wallerstein & Kelly, 1980), were utilized to gain the necessary diagnostic information for structuring group interventions.

***Postgroup Interviews.*** An individual interview was carried out within 1 month of the final group session. Its purpose was to evaluate the child's subjective response to the group, to offer an opportunity to discuss specific family and school problems in greater depth, and to offer the child an opportunity to request the group leader's help in dealing with significant adults in his or her life. In some cases this resulted in family sessions or conferences among school personnel, child, and parents in order to address problems that the child had reported. The vast majority of participants (95%) expressed enthusiasm over group participation, and stated that the peer support they had gained was critical to them.

***Follow-up Interviews.*** In those schools where we have worked on-site for a period of years, we have employed a follow-up with the students, their parents, and faculty participants. These interviews take place approximately 9 to 10 months after the initial group intervention. The extent of the follow-up varies with information provided either by faculty or through our own observations regarding youngsters at risk. Depending on the students' postdivorce adjustment, a variety of interventions are instituted, ranging from special class placement and referrals for psychological treatment to consultation and collaboration with parents and faculty and administration.

## Assessing Referrals to the Group and Determining Group Content

Although the literature just reviewed describes excellent school-based group interventions, writers have not sufficiently demonstrated how such interventions address either the child's particular family situation or the stage of resolution the child has reached. Most of the programs that have been described in the literature accept children into groups with widely varying time from divorce. However, this heterogeneity may result in groups where the crisis of coping with the actual divorce is not the primary need of the participant. Inclusion of children with many years distance from the marital rupture may shift the focus of the group from one of a crisis intervention to a model characterized by the tenets of tertiary prevention. Thus, the demands for collateral work with parents and teachers increase. In the group itself, issues involving adjustment to the postdivorce family and "working through" loss, disappointment, and anger rather than coping with crisis come to the fore.

How such a group may facilitate working through can be seen in the following example:

> One group participant was a child whose father had recently returned from a vacation announcing he had remarried while away. Not only was the child not invited to the wedding, he was not even told of plans for the marriage. During a group meeting when this child happened to be absent, the group planned a picnic. Knowing the child's struggle with feelings of being left out and powerless, the group leader met with the child individually to let him know of the proposed plan. During this meeting the group leader commented on the similarity between the two circumstances and the child was able to acknowledge his feelings.

Because of the probable mandate to provide treatment for students exhibiting problems at school, and due to the constraints of time placed on the school psychologist or counselor, it is not likely that these professionals will be able to offer group interventions to an entire school population.

In screening students referred to groups and determining the actual content of group sessions, the following should be considered:

We have found that those participants who had experienced a familial change within 2 years of participation benefited most from the group. They were able to use the group to lessen confusion, increase coping skills, and gain emotional support. Children with longstanding difficulties and no recent familial change benefited less from the standardized group format. However, when individualized group sessions were combined with collateral work with parents and teachers to meet specific needs of children in the latter group, more benefit accrued. By using historical information gained in individual interviews, group sessions that differed significantly from group to group could be constructed. Group activities were "tailor-made" to address specific issues in the youngsters' histories. For example: In one group of students with great disparity in length of time from initial marital separation, the common themes of all sessions related to parental remarriage. Sibling rivalry and problems of having to share with stepparents were addressed through interpreting the competition among group members for attention from the leader and their response to including a new member in the group. In another group with several children from remarried families, family trees were constructed. Over half of the participants "discovered" that their grandparents had been divorced. The feelings that they might have in common with their parents as "children of divorce" became the focus of discussion.

Some group activities lend themselves particularly well to being used with many different groups while retaining their individual nature. For instance, "Dear Abby" letters can be written by the group leader prior to meeting posing problems from the lives of the particular group members. These can then be answered as part of a group activity. Journals can be used in many ways during a group to give a sense of privacy and individuality. For example, sketch books in which youngsters can write to the group leader between sessions and receive answers confidentially can give a sense of continuity to the group, "holding" youngsters between sessions. In an early group session in which the idea of the journal is introduced, a Polaroid picture taken of each child and incorporated as a front-piece. During the final session, after discussing how children can use their peer group for support, group Polaroid photos added to the journal give children a concrete group remembrance to leave with.

### Parent Participation

A school administrator or pupil personnel employee made initial contact with the custodial parent, and almost without exception consent was given for the child's participation in a group. Following this, a letter detailing group goals and logistics was sent along with a written consent form. The custodial parent was then engaged in face-to-face contact with the group leader either (a) in an individual pregroup interview, (b) a one-time evening meeting for parents of all participating children with individual postgroup interviews, or (c) a series of four evening group meetings designed to parallel the children's group. The choice of format evolved during the 5 years of our work in the schools and is based on availability of clinical time and the perceived needs of the parents and school. All parents were requested to complete a questionnaire on their child that asked for school history, previous psychotherapy, description of current custody arrangements, and their view of the child's strengths and weaknesses. Parents were told that the information would be kept confidential and would not become part of the child's school record. Included in the questionnaire was a request to contact the child's noncustodial parent. Because research clearly indicates that children who have continued stable contact with both parents generally fare better in the postdivorce family, we believe that inclusion of the noncustodial parent in school-related activities is crucial to good postdivorce adjustment.

We found that in most families in which both parents still resided in the same geographic area, permission to contact the noncustodial parent was readily given. Parent group meetings were less specifically child-focused than individual consultations with parents. Group participants used the meetings primarily to relieve a myriad of divorce related feelings including, anger, guilt, shame, and worry. However, these psychoeducational parent groups can also be used to provide both information about the effects of family conflict in general and then translate these general issues into more specific problems of individual children (Roseby & Johnston, 1997).

## Teacher Participation

Consistent involvement of teachers is an important facet of creating successful prevention models for the school system. Although direct work with families, either in group or individual interventions must be carried out by a person with professional mental health training, it is the teacher who will have the greatest cumulative effect on the largest number of students and therefore must be a central collaborator in this process. Of major importance as well are administrators who make policy determinations regarding how the needs of single parent and remarried families will be incorporated in their schools. Our intervention thus has included a strong emphasis on consultation to teachers regarding the child participants in our groups. After discussing their referral suggestions, each classroom teacher was asked to fill out two written evaluations at the beginning and end of the group. These evaluations helped teachers focus their attention on students in a behavior-specific way. During the course of the group, the leader was available for weekly consultations with the teachers of participating youngsters. In many instances such consultations took the form of a 5-minute check-in. In some cases, the group leader facilitated conjoint conferences among teachers, parents, and students in an effort to enhance communication about a student's school progress.

The cumulative effect of such consultative efforts has been considerable. At the secondary prevention level, the classroom teachers involved in this approach have come away with an informed stance vis-à-vis these families. This is reflected in their more thoughtful approach to including nonresidential parents in academic planning, in their sensitivity to the language with which they describe nonintact families, and in the development of skills to recognize what may be a reactive depression to the family change.

## CONCLUSION

Given the prevalence of divorce in the United States, coupled with the clear evidence that many youngsters have resultant learning problems, school personnel must become prepared to engage in prevention strategies with this population. Evidence has mounted sufficiently to indicate that the school may well be the single most comprehensive continuing resource for children during the divorce crisis. This places the school psychologist or counselor in a unique position to intervene broadly at the systems level and develop appropriately varied and comprehensive programs to meet this community need. Examples of preventive school-based programs that address the multiple and frequently chronic stressors affecting the lives of children and adolescents experiencing divorce were described. The need to assess each youngster's respective resolution of the divorce and accommodation to the postdivorce family as critical elements in planning on-site, time-limited psychoeducation groups was also highlighted. Further, given the nature of the stressor and the resultant family disequilibrium, often continuing beyond a 2- or 3-year period, the school becomes a primary (if not exclusive) source of ongoing support and guidance for youngsters. Educators and mental health professionals are able to provide short-term group interventions for students in the larger context of teacher, administrator, and parent collaboration. The effectiveness of this model lies in ongoing, but brief contacts with identified children at risk, their families, and school personnel, as required.

## ACKNOWLEDGMENT

The first author would like to thank Mariam J. King, Ruth K. Goldman, and Susan Zegans for their contributions to the chapter in the first edition of this book.

## REFERENCES

Ainsworth, M. (1969). Object relations, dependency and attachment: A theoretical review of the infant mother relationship. *Child Development, 40*, 969–1025.

Amato, P. R., & Keith, B. (1991). Parental divorce and adult well-being: A meta-analysis. *Journal of Marriage and Family, 53*, 43–58.

Belsky, J., Youngblade, L., Rovine, M., & Volling, B. (1991). Patterns of marital change and parent–child interaction. *Journal of Marriage and Family, 53*, 487–498.

Bloom, B. L., Asher, S. J., & White, S. W. (1978). Marital disruption as a stressor: A review and analysis. *Psychological Bulletin, 85*, 867–894.

Bowlby, J. (1980). *Attachment and loss. Vol. 3: Loss, sadness and depression.* New York: Basic Books.

Bowlby, J. (1982). Attachment and loss: Retrospect and prospect. *American Journal of Orthopsychiatry, 52*, 664–678.

Buehler, C., Krishnakumar, A., Stone, G., Anthony, C., Pemberton, S., Gerard, J., & Barber, B. (1998). Interparental conflict styles and youth problem behaviors: A two-sample replication study. *Journal of Marriage and the Family 60*, 119–132.

Cantor, D. W. (1977). School-based groups for children of divorce. *Journal of Divorce, 1*, 183–187.

Cantor, D. W. (1979). Divorce: A view from the children. *Journal of Divorce, 2*, 357–361.

Caplan, G. (1981). Mastery of stress: Psychosocial aspects. *American Journal of Psychiatry, 138*, 413–420.

Cherlin, A., Furstenberg, F., Chase-Lansdale, L., Kiernan, K., Robins, P., Morrison, D., & Teitler, J. (1991). Longitudinal studies of divorce on children in Great Britain and the United States. *Science, 252*, 1386–1389.

Coddington, R. D. (1972). The significance of life events as etiologic factors in the diseases of children—II. A study of a normal population. *Journal of Psychometric Research, 16*, 205–213.

Coopersmith, S. (1967). *The antecedents of self esteem*. San Francisco: Freeman.

Cummings, E. M., & Davies, P. T. (1994). The impact of parents on their children: An emotional security perspective. In R. Vesta (Ed.), *Annals of child development* (Vol. 10, pp. 167–208). Bristol, PA: Jessica Kingsley Publishers.

Doherty, W. J. (1998). Responsible fathering: An overview and conceptual framework. *Journal of Marriage and the Family, 60*, 277–292.

Drake, E. A. (1981). Helping children cope with divorce: The role of the school. In I. R. Stuart & L. E. Abt (Eds.), *Children of separation and divorce: Management and treatment* (pp. 147–172). New York: Van Nostrand Reinhold.

Drake, E. A., & Shellenberger, S. (1981). Children of separation and divorce: A review of school programs and implications for the psychologist. *School Psychology Review, 10*, 54–61.

Emery, R. (1999). *Marriage, divorce, and children's adjustment* (2nd edition). Thousand Oaks, CA: Sage.

Emery, R. E., & Forehand, R. (1996). Parental divorce and children's well-being: A focus on resilience. In R. J. Haggerty & L. R. Sherrod (Eds.), *Stress, risk, and resilience in children and adolescents: Processes, mechanisms, and interventions* (pp. 64–99). New York: Cambridge University Press.

Fincham, F. D., Grych, J. H., & Osborne, L. N. (1994). Does marital conflict cause child maladjustment? Directions and challenges for longitudinal research. *Journal of Family Psychology, 8*, 128–140.

Furstenberg, F. F., & Teitler, J. O. (1994). Reconsidering the effects of marital disruption: What happens to children of divorce in early adulthood? *Journal of Family Issues, 15*, 173–190.

Gardner, R. (1976). *Psychotherapy with children of divorce.* New York: Jason Aronson.

Goldman, R. K. (1981). *Teachers look at children of divorce in the classroom.* Corte Madera, CA: Center for the Family in Transition.

Goldman, R. K., & King, M. J. (1985). Counseling children of divorce. *School Psychology Review, 14*, 278–290.

Grych, J., & Fincham, F. (1993). Children's appraisal of marital conflict: Initial investigations of the cognitive-contextual framework. *Child Development, 64*, 215–230.

Guidubaldi, J. (1984). *Differences in children's divorce adjustment across grade level and gender: A report from the NASP-Kent State Nationwide Project.* Kent, OH: Kent State University.

Guidubaldi, J., Perry, J. D., Cleminshaw, H. K., & McLoughlin, C. S. (1983). The impact of parental divorce on children; report of a nationwide NASP study. *School Psychology Review 12*, 300–323.

Harrist, A. W., & Ainslie, R. C. (1998). Marital discord and child behavior problems: Parent-child relationship quality and child interpersonal awareness as mediators. *Journal of Family Issues, 19*, 140–163.

Hetherington, E. M. (1979). Divorce: A child's perspective. *American Psychologist, 34*, 851–858.

Hetherington, E. M. (Ed.). (1999). *Coping with divorce, single parenting, and remarriage: A risk and resiliency perspective.* Mahwah, NJ: Lawrence Erlbaum Associates.

Hetherington, E. M., Bridges, M., & Insabella, G. M. (1998). What matters? What does not? Five perspectives on the association between marital transitions and children's adjustment. *American Psychologist, 53*, 167–184.

Hetherington, E. M., Cox, M., & Cox, R. (1978). Play and social interaction in children following divorce. *Journal of Social Issues, 35*, 26–49.

Hunter, J. E., & Schuman, N. (1980). Chronic reconstitution as a family style. *Social Work, 26*, 446–451.

Johnston, J. R. (1995). Children's adjustment in sole custody compared to joint custody families and principles for custody decision making. *Family & Conciliation Courts Review, 33*, 415–425.

Johnston, J. R., Kline, M., & Tshann, J. M. (1991). Ongoing post-divorce conflict in families contesting custody: Do joint custody and frequent access help? In J. Folberg (Ed.), *Joint custody and shared parenting* (2nd ed.). New York: Guilford Press.

Kalter, N., Pickar, J., & Lesowitz, M. (1984). School-based developmental facilitation groups for children of divorce: A preventive intervention. *American Journal of Orthopsychiatry, 54*, 613–623.

Kalter, N., Schaefer, M., Lesowitz, M., Alpern, D., & Pickar, J. (1988). School-based support groups for children of divorce: A model of brief intervention. In B. H. Gottlieb (Ed.), *Marshaling social support: Formats, processes, and effects* (pp. 165–185). Newbury Park, CA: Sage.

Kelly, J. B. (1994). The determination of child custody. *The Future of Children: Children and Divorce, 4*, 121–142.

Kelly, J. B. (2000). Children's adjustment in conflicted marriage and divorce: A decade review of research. *Journal of American Academy of Child and Adolescent Psychiatry, 39*, 963–973.

Kelly, J. B., & Wallerstein, J. S. (1977). Brief interventions with children in divorcing families. *American Journal of Orthopsychiatry, 47*, 23–26.

Kelly, J. B., & Wallerstein, J. S. (1979). Children of divorce. *The National Elementary Principal*, October, 52–58.

Kurdek, L. A., & Berg, B. (1983). Correlates of children's adjustment to their parents' divorce. *New Directions for Child Development, 19*, 47–60.

Lindemann, E. (1944). Symptomatology and management of acute grief. *American Journal of Psychiatry, 101*, 141–148.

Maccoby, E., Mnookin, R., Denner, C. F., & Peters, H. E. (1992). *Dividing the child.* Cambridge, MA: Harvard University Press.

Mahler, M., Pine, F., & Bergman, A. (1975). *The psychological birth of the human infant.* New York: Basic Books.

McLanahan, S. S. (1999). Father absence and the welfare of children. In E. M. Hetherington (Ed.), *Coping with divorce, single parenting, and remarriage: A risk and resiliency perspective* (pp. 117–145). Mahwah, NJ: Lawrence Erlbaum Associates.

McLanahan, S. S., & Sandefur, G. (1994). *Growing up with a single parent: What hurts, what helps.* Cambridge, MA: Harvard University Press.
McNeal, C., & Amato, P. R. (1998). Parents' marital violence: Long-term consequences for children. *Journal of Family Issues, 19*, 123–139.
Neal, J. H. (1983). Children's understanding of their parent's divorces. *New Directions for Child Development, 19*, 3–14.
Neighbors, B., Forehand, R., & McVicar, D. (1993). Resilient adolescents and interpersonal conflict. *American Journal of Orthopsychiatry, 63*, 462–471.
Nord, C. W., Brimhall, D., & West, J. (1997). *Fathers' involvement in their children's schools*. Washington, DC: National Center for Education Statistics.
Norton, A. J., & Miller, L. F. (1992). *Marriage, divorce, and remarriage in the 1990's*. Washington, DC: Bureau of the Census.
Pedro-Carroll, J. (1985). *Children of divorce intervention program procedures manual*. Unpublished manuscript, University of Rochester-Center for Community Study, Rochester, NY.
Pedro-Caroll, J. L., & Cowen, E. L. (1985). The children of divorce intervention project: An investigation of the efficacy of a school-based prevention program. *Journal of Consulting and Clinical Psychology, 53*, 603–614.
Pedro-Carroll, J. L., Sutton, S. E., & Wyman, P. A. (1999). A two-year follow-up evaluation of a preventive intervention for young children of divorce. *School Psychology Review, 28*, 467–476.
Peterson, G. W., Leigh, G. K., & Day, R. D. (1984). Family stress theory and the impact of divorce on children. *Journal of Divorce, 7*(3), 1–20.
Pleck, J. H. (1997). Parental involvement: Levels, sources, and consequences. In M. E. Lamb (Ed.), *The role of the father in child development* (pp. 66–103). New York: Wiley.
Ricci, I. (1979). Divorce, remarriage and the schools. *Phi Delta Kappan*, 509–511.
Roseby, V., & Johnston, J. (1997). *High-conflict, violent, and separating families*. New York: The Free Press.
Shaw, D. S., Emery, R. E., & Tuer, M. D. (1993). Parental functioning and children's adjustment in families of divorce. *Journal of Abnormal Child Psychology, 21*, 119–134.
Springer, C., & Wallerstein, J. S. (1983). Young adolescents' responses to their parents' divorces. *New Directions for Child Development, 19*, 15–27.
Stolberg, A. L., & Cullen, P. M. (1983). Preventive interventions for families of divorce: The divorce adjustment project. *New Directions for Child Development, 19*, 71–82.
Stolberg, A. L., & Garrison, K. M. (1985). Evaluating a primary prevention program for children of divorce: The divorce adjustment project. *American Journal of Community Psychology, 13*, 111–124.
Vandewater, E., & Lansford, J. (1998). Influences of family structure and parental conflict on children's well-being. *Family Relations, 47*, 323–330.
Wallerstein, J. S. (1983). Children of divorce: The psychological tasks of the child. *American Journal of Orthopsychiatry, 53*, 230–243.
Wallerstein, J. S. (1984). Children of divorce: Ten-year follow-up of young children. *American Journal of Orthopsychiatry, 54*, 449–458.
Wallerstein, J. S., & Kelly, J. B. (1980). *Surviving the breakup: How children and parents cope with divorce*. New York: Basic Books.
Winnicott, D. W. (1971). *Playing and reality*. London: Tavistock.
Zill, N., Morrison, D., & Coiro, M. (1993). Long term effects of parental divorce on parent–child relationships, adjustment, and achievement in young adulthood. *Journal of Family Psychology, 7*, 91–103.

CHAPTER

# 6

# Bullying

Dorothea M. Ross
Bainbridge Island, Washington

Bullying is a form of terrorism. It is an unprovoked attack intended to cause distress and discomfort in the victim. This form of antisocial aggression may involve a 1:1 interaction or several bullies against one or more victims. The problem of bullying has long been with us, in the workplace (Adams, 1992; Dean, 1995), the home (Bowers, Smith, & Binney, 1992; Dishion, 1990), in prisons (Ireland & Archer, 1996; Williams, 1995), and particularly in schools (Ahmad & Smith, 1990; Batsch & Knoff, 1994; Olweus, 1985). From historical (Ariès, 1962; Burk, 1897) and fictional (Hughes, 1857) accounts it seems probable that bullying has been a part of school life, especially boarding school life, for as long as schools have existed (Smith & Sharp, 1994).

Bullying affects everyone in the school–those who are bullied, the bullies themselves, bystanders who witness the bullying, and the children who hear about it. It creates a climate of fear and anxiety that acts as a deterrent to learning (Greenbaum, 1989). Bullying often begins in the preschool period (Moffitt, 1993; Schwartz, Dodge, & Coie, 1993) and may continue well into adulthood (Eron & Huessman, 1990). It is one of the most stable of human behaviors (Olweus, 1979), a characteristic that is reason for concern because many people, such as school teachers (Dean, 1995), must confront some form of bullying during their adult lives (Namie & Namie, 1999).

Although bullying has been a problem for centuries, it is only since the late 1970s that it has become a topic of research interest, first in Scandinavia (Olweus, 1978, 1979) and later in other parts of Europe and the world.

When a new topic appears on the behavioral research agenda there are invariably problems that must be resolved. A recurring problem is the failure of investigators to agree on definitions of behavioral problems, and bullying is no exception. Although it is regarded as a common problem there is not a widely accepted definition of it. Many investigators use minor variants of the definition proposed by Olweus (1993): "A student is being bullied or victimized when he is exposed *repeatedly and over time* to negative actions on the part of one or more other students" (p. 9).

Included under the rubric of negative actions is a broad spectrum of behaviors ranging from nonverbal harassment such as stares and glares, through cruel teasing, social ostracism, sex harassment, ethnic slurs, unreasonable territorial bans, destruction of property, extortion, and serious physical assault (Besag, 1989; Olweus, 1993; Ross, 1996). In emphasizing "repeatedly and over time" Olweus (1993) stated that his intention is to exclude "occasional nonserious negative actions" that are directed against one child at one time and against another on a different occasion. At the same time he concedes that a single instance of more serious harassment can be regarded as bullying under certain (unspecified) circumstances. The problem with the repeated occurrence requirement is that the waiting period heightens the negative effects on the victim, allows the bully to feel rewarded, increases fear in onlookers, and makes intervention a more lengthy process.

It would be helpful to see actual examples of the "certain circumstances" under which Olweus would regard single instances of more serious harassment as bullying. For example, a 9-year-old girl described the following incident that occurred on her first day in a new school (Carmichael, personal communication, June 4, 1991): "I was walking along the hall and some girls tripped me and then they grabbed hold of me and pushed me into a broom closet and they said I would be locked in there all weekend unless I gave them all my money for the Friday movie." Would this incident be regarded as bullying? Or must it happen repeatedly and over time in order to qualify? The problems inherent in Olweus' definition have resulted in other investigators not insisting on the repetitive aspect (see, e.g., Askew, 1989; Stephenson & Smith, 1989; Tattum, 1989).

A second problem is the diversity of characteristics attributed in the literature to bullies and victims. Hazler and his associates (Hazler, Carney, Green, Powell, & Jolly, 1997) have taken a first step toward clearing up some of the confusion by quantifying the extent of agreement among a worldwide group of 14 experts in this field. Their purpose was to determine which of a list of 70 potential characteristics experts saw as being most typical of bullies and victims. Those chosen as most typical are ones that occur frequently in descriptions of aggressive bullies and passive victims. The results demonstrated strong agreement among the participating experts on

19 characteristics for bullies and also 19 characteristics for victims. Hazler et al. (1997) made an important contribution with this research report; it should be mandatory reading for those interested in the problem of bullying and victimization.

## INCIDENCE AND PREVALENCE

Figures regarding the frequency of bullying during the school years vary greatly. Comparisons across studies may be largely invalidated by marked differences in definitions of bullying, whether teasing is included, types of questionnaire, wording of items, sampling, and other methodological differences. Keeping these caveats in mind, the literature clearly supports the following statements: 15% to 20% of all students will experience some form of bullying during their school years (Olweus, 1993; Ross, 1996: Smith & Sharp, 1994); between 10% and 20% of children are bullied often enough for them to consider it a serious problem (Boulton & Smith, 1994; Perry, Kusel, & Perry, 1988); and bullying in the 1990s is more lethal and occurs more frequently than it did in the previous two decades (Olweus & Alsaker, 1991). It follows that bullying may be the most prevalent form of violence in American schools and one that is likely to affect the greatest number of students.

Following Olweus' (1985) estimate that 15% of the students in Norwegian schools were actively involved in the bullying sequence, investigators in other countries became interested in the problem. Their findings show clearly that the problem of bullying exists in many countries representing a wide spectrum of cultures including England (Smith & Sharp, 1994), Ireland (O'Moore & Hillery, 1989), Canada (Bentley & Li, 1995), Australia (Rigby & Slee, 1991), Spain (Ruiz, 1992), Finland (Salmivalli, Lagerspetz, Bjorkqvist, Osterman, & Kaukiainen, 1996) and Japan (Hirano, 1992; Murakami, 1985).

Although bullying is clearly a major problem in American schools it is only since the 1990s that it has become a matter of concern on the educational agenda. Investigative interest in bullying has been slow to develop here because many Americans regard it as a *normal* occurrence, a part of the inevitably turbulent process of growing up. For these people, the bully is fondly (or fatuously) described as "all boy" and the victim is thought to benefit by having to endure it, by being "toughened up" and thus better prepared for the adverse events of life. The fallacies here are that if many children are bullied, then bullying becomes a normal behavior; even more destructive is the idea that in the end bullying benefits the victim. In fact, there is unequivocal evidence that the effects of being bullied are frequently severe throughout the school years although they may become significantly milder in adulthood (Olweus, 1993; Ross, 1996).

## BULLIES

One of Olweus' (1978) major contributions was his finding that boys who bully are not a homogeneous group. His distinction between aggressive and anxious bullies is important because different subgroups require different kinds of intervention.

### Aggressive Bullies

Most bullies belong to this group (Olweus, 1993). They are stronger than average, very active, impulsive, assertive, threatening, and are easily provoked; a positive attitude to violence underlies their behavior. As Dodge (Greenbaum, 1989) stated, they see their world with a paranoid eye. They have no empathy for their victims and feel no remorse about their actions, partly due to their perception of bullying incidents being significantly less severe than that of their victims (Besag, 1989; Olweus, 1993; Ross, 1996). They are noted for their skillful avoidance of any blame: Exasperated school personnel often describe them as "slippery." Olweus (1993) found that the most common form of bullying in this group begins with nonphysical actions such as words, gestures, and looks. That even a look can strike terror in the victim, is evident in the following quote of a 9-year-old-boy (Carmichael, personal communication, June 4, 1991):

> I try hard not to catch his eye in class but it's like he's pulling me, it's an awful feeling. I'm helpless and when I do look at him he gives me this look and I know what it'll be like at recess and what's going to happen to my lunch money.

In the study by Hazler et al. (1997) bullies were perceived as focusing on others rather than being self-focused: They had a need to be punished by others for their bullying rather than blaming themselves.

A common misconception about bullying is that it is a transient problem of childhood and early adolescence that disappears with increasing age. Nothing could be farther from the truth: Olweus (1979) reported a remarkable persistence into adulthood of the aggressive behavior that manifests itself in childhood as bullying. Although many children who bully do outgrow this behavior (Olweus, 1993), many others do not. Of interest here are the findings of Moffitt (1993) on another antisocial behavior, delinquency. She distinguished between two categories of delinquents: a small group in her study who engaged in *life-course-persistent delinquency* (delinquency of one kind or another at every life stage), and a larger group who did so only in late middle childhood and adolescence (*adolescent-limited delinquency*).

At first glance a similar pattern appears to be characteristic of children who bully. However, following an outstanding critique of misconceptions and controversies concerning the development of aggression (Loeber &

Stouthamer-Loeber, 1998), it is apparent that Moffit's (1993) life-course-persistent category should be expanded for children who bully to accommodate *two* age-of-onset groups: a preschool-onset and a childhood–adolescence-onset group with the behavior of some children from both groups worsening in severity from childhood to adulthood. Loeber and Stouthamer-Loeber (1998) have added a *limited duration type* that is consistent with Moffitt's (1993) *adolescent-limited delinquency* and also a *late-onset type* that accounts for the emergence of aggression in individuals during adulthood who do not have an earlier history of aggression. It would be interesting to know about the late-onset bullying group. For example, are some of the school principals, military personnel, and prison guards who are bullies individuals who secretly envied aggressive bullies in childhood and adolescence? It is possible that they were deterred from exhibiting bullying behavior until they found themselves in positions of power, coupled with low supervision and subordinates who were in no position to complain.

For children who do not outgrow their bullying behavior, the outlook is bleak. In 1960 Eron and Huessman began a longitudinal study of an entire group of third-grade children ($n = 870$) in the Midwest. In 1990 they reported that children who bullied others at age 8 had a 1:4 chance of ending up with a criminal record by age 30, as compared to the 1:20 chance that most children have. In addition, the childhood bullies were more likely to have been convicted of crimes, including a higher number of more serious crimes. They had not achieved well educationally and were more often high school dropouts. Professionally and socially they were below the nonbully group. They were more abusive to their wives and children and, perhaps most serious of all the problems, their children were often bullies so, in effect, they were raising a whole new generation of bullies. Contrary to common expectations, the results for the bullies in adulthood were independent of their IQ's and social class level at age 8.

Recently there have been encouraging signs of researcher attention directed to the accuracy of firmly established beliefs about bullies as well as to unexpected new characteristics of this group. The first of these was the finding by Forero, McLellan, Rissel, and Bauman (1999) in a study of 3,918 Australian school children in Grades 6, 8, and 10 that bullying was significantly associated with psychological and psychosomatic problems such as headache, stomach-ache, backache, and feeling irritable, nervous, or dizzy. Bully/victims had the most psychological and psychosomatic symptoms and liked school; aggressive bullies also had very high scores on psychosomatic problems and disliked school. Psychosomatic problems are rarely attributed to bullies by health practitioners. Perhaps they should consider being a bully and the school environment a possible cause of common psychological and psychosomatic symptoms (Williams, Chambers, Logan, & Robinson, 1996).

Another unexpected finding came from a study of 410 Finnish adolescents aged 14 to 16 (Kaltiala, Rimpelä, Mattunen, Rimpelä, & Rantanen, 1999). Both bullies and victims were found to be at increased risk for depression and suicide, which led Kaltiala et al. to conclude that bullies were more like victims than is commonly thought. When symptoms of depression were controlled for, suicidal ideation occurred most often among bullies. Yet in the literature and the mass media, it is almost always the victims who commit suicide.

Current interventions targeting school bullying have met with only a modicum of success: Not one has succeeded in reducing bullying by more than 50% (Olweus, 1993; Smith & Sharp, 1994). The consensus among school personnel is that there is a hard core of bullies who are highly resistant to the forms of intervention currently in use. Two recent studies provide some support for this statement. The first study, by Sutton, Smith, and Swettenham (1999) concerns the popular stereotype of the oafish bully as a not too bright, somewhat clumsy individual whose success is largely a function of physical strength, combined with the ability to identify victim potential in others, and the indifference of many school personnel to the problem of bullying. Sutton et al. started with the question, What empirical proof is there for this assessment of the bully? To investigate the validity of the belief that children who bully are lacking in social perspective-taking skills, Sutton et al. used a set of 11 stories designed to assess the theory of mind ability (Taylor, 1996) of 7- to 10-year-old children ($n$ = 193) involved in bullying. The question was How well do bullies understand the mental states, beliefs, and emotions of others?

The findings do not lend credence to the view of the bully as stupid and oafish. Instead, they provide support for a subgroup among aggressive bullies, a group who are cold, manipulative, highly skilled experts in social situations. They organize top level groups of loyal followers with real skill and foresight, and generally use subtle, indirect methods in their interactions with others. They scored higher on the stories than did anxious bullies, victims, and peers who stepped in to help victims of bullying.

The authors raise the question of where might these highly skilled children end up in adulthood, and speculate on the possibility of a *negative* effect on social cognitive skills in adult bullying (Sutton et al., 1999, p. 445).

Victims of bullying in the workplace often refer to managers who cunningly manipulate their workers, for example, creating "furtive alliances" and using "entrapment," and who also manage to hide their behavior from their superiors, passing it off as an "autocratic style." Subgroups of bullies with these social cognitive skills could be identified early in the school system and taught positive uses of this set of skills. With this training, these skills would become a definite asset, particularly on the work front.

Data from a second study (McBurnett, Lahey, Rathouz, & Loeber, 2000) provided further support for the existence of a hard core of bullies who are impervious to the current educational and counseling interventions. In this 4-year study McBurnett et al. found that extreme antisocial behaviors, including bullying, were strongly associated with lower than expected levels of salivary cortisol in 7- to 12-year-old boys ($n = 38$).

Cortisol typically is released in response to fear such as fear of punishment for misbehavior. Its low level in antisocial boys suggests that they do not fear negative consequences for misbehavior. Consequently, the usual deterrents to misbehavior are ineffective. Because their misbehavior may be biologically based, current treatment regimens may be of little use. McBurnett (personal communication, January 10, 2000) speculated that the drug programs used with hyperactive children might prove effective. He has also speculated that it might be necessary to discard traditional approaches to treatment of these children and instead focus on helping them to find a niche in society where their aggressiveness and lack of a sense of danger would be an asset.

What is unique about McBurnett et al.'s study is the concern that is voiced about helping the child to use his particular talents effectively rather than focusing on interventions designed to force him into a mold at odds with his own potentially strong assets. This positive approach also has implications for a number of other childhood behavior problems.

## How Children Become Aggressive Bullies

The major cause of bullying lies in the home. The parents of bullies are frequently aggressive and abusive to each other and model behaviors that could lead to their children becoming bullies (Bandura, 1977). On the mother's part, there is often a notable lack of warmth and caring for the child (Olweus, 1993). The parental style of discipline is noncontingent, that is, one day the child is punished for some misbehavior, the next day he does it again and nothing happens. Even when he behaves well there often is no reward. With this pattern of child-rearing, the child never knows what to expect. In any situation where there is uncertainty, he or she expects the worst and reacts immediately. It is reasonable that he or she would lash out at an accidental collision with another child. When the parents do punish the child they use power-assertive disciplinary methods such as severe corporal punishment. The child learns that might is right, so at school he makes sure that he is in the power spot. To this end he gathers a group of less effective children as "friends." Both parents have an unusually high tolerance for their child's inappropriate aggression towards other children. In the face of complaints from school or neighbors, they praise the child. Further, they often insist that the child handle conflict situations with physical aggression. In a study by Bandura and Walters (1959) of high aggressive vs. normally aggressive teenagers a comparison of parental attitudes toward

TABLE 6.1
Parental Pressure to Use Aggression

| | |
|---|---|
| 1. Threatening punishment for not fighting | |
| | Mother (p. 111): So I told him one night, the next time he came crying, he was going to get a spanking. |
| | Father (as reported by mother) (p. 107): You're going to whip these boys or else I'm going to whip you. |
| 2. Giving direct advice to fight | |
| | Mother (p. 116): I told him, "Go out and fight it out yourself." |
| | Father (p. 115): I told him many times that if someone wanted to fight with him and started the old idea of the chip on the shoulder, "Don't hit the chip, hit the jaw, and get it over with." |
| 3. Labeling not fighting as unmasculine or immature | |
| | Mother (p. 115): I've told him to look after himself and don't let anybody shove him around or anything like that, but not to look for trouble. I don't want him to be a sissy. |
| | Father (p.108): I don't want him to be a baby and have somebody push him around. |

From Bandura and Walters (1959). *Adolescent Aggression.* New York: Ronald Press.

aggression in their sons showed that compared to parents in the control group, one or both parents of the aggressive boys actively encouraged and sometimes even insisted that their sons use aggression outside the home. Table 6.1 shows that this parental pressure took several different forms.

## Other Potential Factors

***Temperament.*** Some infants are high active, impulsive, easily angered, and have a low tolerance for frustration. A child with this temperament *could* become a bully. However, he or she could also be helped to modify and channel these responses into acceptable behaviors (Thomas & Chess, 1977).

***Y Chromosome.*** Boys with an extra Y chromosome (XYY) are rare. They are also often more aggressive, impatient, and amoral than boys in general. Although this pattern of behavior is consistent with antisocial aggression, there is no convincing evidence directly linking the extra Y chromosome to bullying (Brock & Goode, 1996).

***Testosterone.*** Until recently bullying was believed to be the result of a high level of testosterone. This belief was based on data from animal studies of dominance behavior in which the testosterone level was positively correlated with level of aggression. Researchers studying human aggressive behavior extrapolated this finding to high-aggressive boys. It was reasonable then to attribute bullying, especially in the case of young children, to a substance in the body. However, Tremblay (Marano, 1995), who has been conducting long-term studies of more than 1,000 bullies and other aggressive children, decided to check the hormone–behavior links in 178 adolescent boys. To his surprise the boys who had been rated most aggressive at ages 6 to 12 had lower testosterone levels at age 13 than their normally aggressive peers, and the real bullies had the lowest levels of all. Tremblay found that a group he described as "tough leaders" had the highest testosterone levels of all. Although, these boys were aggressive, they also had prosocial skills, that is, they did not stay in control by using physical or verbal aggression. Instead, in new situations they quickly took control with verbal fluency. In Tremblay's studies, they were the most socially successful and the most popular.

Of relevance here is an investigation linking the etiology of antisocial behavior to the gestation period and first two years of life. In *Ghosts from the Nursery: Tracing the Roots of Violence*, Karr-Morse and Wiley (1997) began with the question, Why are children violent? Using evidence from case histories, crime statistics, and recent research in neurobiology, they present a convincing argument for the role of pregnancy, infancy, and parental behavior in the genesis of violence; they show why this 33-month period is so crucial in brain development. Whether alcohol, drugs, or violence against the mother traumatizes the fetal brain, or whether the infant suffers from outright physical abuse, other trauma, or prolonged neglect, the effects of all these negative experiences are cumulative at each subsequent stage of development.

There is unequivocal evidence that the developing brain must have a steady stream of certain positive experiences to establish the circuits for thinking, feeling, and relating, and some infants are seriously deprived of these experiences. Long before the beginning of language and memory, the brain and body store traces of positive and negative experiences and these become the basis for subsequent behavior. Karr-Morse and Wiley (1997) noted that the disruptive behavior that is first *reported* in the primary grades was often noticeable before the child was 3 years old.

## Anxious Bullies

These bullies are mainly male, with an anxious personality pattern and a notable lack of confidence. Altogether, they are a sad group. They have few likable qualities, low self-esteem, and home problems. They often have disruptive temper outbursts contributing to peer problems, and at school they have great difficulty concentrating. They appear to bully in an attempt to compensate for their feelings of inadequacy (Olweus, 1978, 1993).

Anxious bullies rarely take the initiative in a bullying incident, but once the bullying is underway, usually at the instigation of an aggressive bully, they actively participate. The actions of the aggressive bully have a disinhibitory effect by appearing to legitimize the bullying and this effect is strengthened in the anxious bullies on seeing the aggressive bully frequently rewarded (Bandura, 1977). The fact that the anxious bullies are so eager to align themselves with the more powerful and more popular aggressive bullies has earned them the description "camp followers." They buy the approval of the aggressive bullies with intense loyalty. If, for example, adults intervene in bullying that is initiated by the aggressive bully and impose sanctions, the anxious bullies are often blamed and then accept the punishment without any attempt to implicate the aggressive bully (Olweus, 1993; Ross, 1996).

### Gender Differences in Bullying Behavior

Although boys are more often identified as bullies, girls also bully. They are more likely to engage in verbal (malicious gossip) and psychological (social ostracism) forms of bullying, but are not exempt from physical harassment (Besag, 1989; Crick & Grotpeter, 1995). Roland (cited in Besag, 1989) concluded that the prime goal of girls is to be affiliated with other girls, so that by using alienation tactics they are "in" and their victims are "out." Crick and her associates (Crick, Casas, & Mosher, 1997; Crick & Grotpeter, 1995) described this behavior as "relational aggression." They assume that to hurt a girl, it is important to target something that she values. One logical choice is to target the relationship that a girl has with other girls, thus destroying the intimacy that girls value. A group of girls, for example, may give another girl the silent treatment, making sure that she knows that she is being excluded. A particularly vicious form that girls' bullying may take is the slam book. Each page has a heading in the form of a question, for example, Who is the stupidest girl in this class? Who is the ugliest, Who sleeps around the most, Who is the most disliked . . . and so on. When all nominations are complete, the book is passed around in the class and also to other classes.

Although boys are generally believed to bully more than girls, this is not the case. Bullying in girls has been greatly underestimated because it is a more covert, subtle, and complex form of bullying (Besag, 1989; Forero et al., 1999; Olweus, 1993) than the overt physical aggression typical of boys. When the frequency of relational aggression in girls is compared with overt aggression in boys, the difference is insignificant. Contrary to what Olweus (1978) first thought, girls are just as capable of bullying as boys are.

## METHODS FOR THE IDENTIFICATION OF BULLIES AND VICTIMS

There is increasing concern in the literature about the accuracy of methods for the identification of bullies and victims. A variety of methods have been used including peer nominations, teacher nominations, questionnaires, anonymous self-nominations, direct observation, and individual interviews. Although individual interviews would appear to be promising, there is some evidence that they are problematic. For example, Ahmad and Smith (1990) compared a number of different methods on middle school and junior high school students and found that only half of the respondents who admitted to bullying on a questionnaire also admitted to it in an interview. They concluded that self-reports were more valid than individual interviews or teacher and peer nominations.

Peer nominations offer several advantages, the most important one being that peers are more aware of which students bully others, because a substantial amount of bullying occurs when no school personnel are present (Crick & Grotpeter, 1995; Perry et al., 1988). However, Perry et al. have cautioned that a limitation of peer nominations is that there is no corroborative information of peer reports. They also believe that for extreme forms of bullying and victimization teachers may be the most reliable informants because they differ markedly from peers in threshold for perceiving victimization.

Of relevance here is a recent study on the identification of peer bullies and victims. Leff, Kupersmidt, Patterson, and Power (1999) examined multiple elementary and middle-school student and teacher characteristics to determine whether they influenced teachers' ability to identify peer-reported bullies and victims. Sixty-one teachers and 1,139 third- to sixth-grade students participated.

The accuracy of teachers' identification of peer-reported bullies was increased by several student and teacher characteristics. That the teachers were better able to identify bullies and victims in the elementary school than in the middle school is not surprising because bullying at the later level is likely to be more subtle and covert. When the nominations of general education teachers and related arts teachers were combined, identification was more accurate than those obtained from general education teachers alone. Other factors that were investigated, such as student gender, teacher–student ethnicity, and socioeconomic status, were of minimal importance.

## VICTIMS

No theory adequately explains why one child and not another becomes the target of bullies. For a long time it was assumed that the *difference theory*, being different in some way, was the criterion. Then, in 1984, Olweus introduced the *victim theory*, that is, that children are bullied because their whole demeanor labels them as easy targets who are unlikely to retaliate. Olweus (1993) has never suggested that this theory explains all bullying, however, popular acceptance of it has tended to obscure its limitations. The fact is that both theories make a contribution to understanding bullying (Ross, 1996).

One of the best statements on becoming a victim comes from Thompson and Smith (1991).

> ... some children and adolescents find themselves pushed into playing the role of victim in the emerging social pattern. Like the children who ... learn to behave in a bullying manner in social groups, so many victims enter social life as children with a lesser tendency to behave aggressively or even assertively and what seems to be a slightly greater difficulty in making effective social relationships with peers ... and find that the patterns of social interaction leave them on the margins of groups, waiting to be "picked on" by children interested in demonstrating dominance at very little cost to themselves. (p. 141)

Olweus (1984) identified two types of victims: the passive victim and the provocative one. He reported that the passive victims outnumbered the provocative ones 4:1. Perry et al. (1988), however, believe that the two groups are approximately equal.

## Passive Victims

Passive victims typically are lacking in self-confidence, are cautious, sensitive, and physically weaker and smaller than their same-age peers. They often have poor self-concepts, fears of inadequacy, ineffective social skills, poor interpersonal skills, no sense of humor, and a serious demeanor. They feel inadequate and usually blame themselves for their problems (Olweus, 1993; Perry et al., 1988; Ross, 1996). In the study by Hazler et al. (1997) the ratings by experts suggested that the passive victim focuses inwardly on his own deficiencies. They felt that each time the passive victim failed in a difficult situation he made less effort in the next one, thus steadily diminishing his chances of success.

***How Children Become Passive Victims.*** Children may become passive victims partly as a result of temperament. Some present a pervasively submissive demeanor (Olweus, 1978; Schwartz et al., 1993) that is often apparent at an early age. They are hesitant about entering group activities; sometimes their reluctance is the result of a general lack of interpersonal skills, social skills, and physical abilities through no fault of their own. In some cases there has been too much family involvement in the victim's life, with a consequent inability to handle situations on his own (Hazler et al., 1997). Some victims, for example, have been grossly overprotected, usually by their mothers. That maternal overprotection has the potential to seriously disrupt the young child's social development is evident in the following letter (Landers, 1995) about maternal infantilization and the discouragement of autonomy in a young boy:

> We have a grandson who is probably two or three years behind his peers. This child is not retarded or brain-damaged. The problem is that "Terry's" mother refuses to allow him to interact with other children. She would not allow him to start school until the age of 6 because she believed he would not be able to handle it. He used a pacifier until he was 5 years old.
>
> Terry is afraid of his own shadow . . . Terry's mother is crippling him in a way that could impact the rest of his life. Terry's mother is setting up her son for victimization, bullying, and high dependency. (p. 35)

***Short-Term Effects on Passive Victims.*** The effects on the victim of being bullied are immediate and severe throughout the school years (Besag, 1989; Ross, 1996). This is assuming that the victim is a "good" victim: He rewards the bully's need for power by becoming visibly upset when bullied, pays for protection promptly and outwardly willingly, and does not report being bullied to his parents or teachers. When these conditions exist, the bullying could go on for several years (Olweus, 1993). The victim's whole life becomes a rapid downward spiral: He is in deep trouble with being bullied at school and the social support that would normally be provided by family and friends is not forthcoming. One 8-year-old victim whose efforts to obtain such support were ignored told a counselor, "I've never felt so alone."

Strategies used by passive victims include avoidance of the bullies by using fugitive-like behavior (taking the long way to school, hiding at recess, professing illness to avoid going to school, and truancy). Their grades fall along with their self-esteem (Hazler, Hoover, & Oliver, 1993). They feel worthless and their friends drift away leaving them with no peer support when they most need it. Victims often come to see themselves as to blame for the bullying and reach an all-time low of total misery and hopelessness (Ross, 1996). In this framework, the idea that "If I kill myself, the bullying will go away" has a certain rational basis. Leach (1986) reported the following case:

> This 15-year-old boy lived with his mother, his father having left the family. . . . During the school year which ended in his death he had been continually bullied by other boys and had confided this to his principal, his mother, and the truant officer following inquiries into his frequent absences. His note said: "Day after day it's the same with no way out. I can't stop them; I ought to be able to stand up for myself but I can't. Nobody will stand up for me because nobody really cares about me and I can see why." (p. 654)

Only adults who are trapped by circumstances from which there is no escape, such as prisoners and sometimes those in the armed forces, experience the bullying and consequent misery that many victims encounter daily in school. Smith (1991) has accurately described it as "the silent nightmare."

***Long-Term Effects on Passive Victims.*** As adults, many former victims manage competently because they can choose their own work, friends, and social environment. Although they sometimes have problems with social relationships, having missed the social activity of the teen years, and may lack confidence, overall they are much happier than they were in school. However, some victims suffer long-term damage. The erosion of self-esteem in childhood is so severe that even in adulthood the social interactions of these victims are adversely affected (Besag, 1989). Gilmartin (1987) reported that the majority of heterosexual men who were bullied in school had great difficulty in interactions with women.

## Provocative Victims

A small percentage of victims are provocative, volatile, and quite aggressive. They tease and taunt, are hot-tempered, and often create considerable management problems in school. They are far more assertive, confident, and active than other victims and are noted for prolonging a fight even when they are losing. The following is a typical example of this category of victim (Ward, personal communication, January 15, 1986):

> Stevie is an impatient, quick-tempered, impetuous nine-year-old. School tasks frustrate him ... he's a constant disrupter in the classroom. His classmates try to "get Old Stevie going," because he provides good theater value. Whenever he starts a fight, a crowd gathers. Stevie often goads Adam, the indisputable "king of the playground." Adam first ignores Stevie, then he threatens to beat him up. Stevie is not deterred, he dances around Adam, taunting him, "Just try, Adam, just try." A fight starts. Within seconds Adam has Stevie on the ground with his nose bleeding badly, but Stevie keeps on fighting.

In a prospective study of the early family experiences of provocative victims (Schwartz, Dodge, Pettit, & Bates, 1997) there was evidence that these victims had experienced more punitive, hostile, and abusive family treatment than boys in the normative, passive victim, and nonvictimized aggressive groups. Of the four groups, only the provocative victims had a history of violent victimization by adults. This difference in socialization was consistent with the Schwartz et al. hypothesis that early experiences of victimization and harsh treatment by adults serve to dysregulate children emotionally, leading to later hyperreactive anger and victimization by peers.

### Bully/Victims

One small group of children exhibit a pattern of behavior akin to the Freudian mechanism of displacement. They are bullies in one situation and victims in another. Olweus (1985) reported that 6% of children who were seriously bullied in turn bullied others, a finding that was confirmed by Stephenson and Smith (1989). In the self-report study by Forero et al. (1999), a substantial number of subjects reported that they were bully/victims. These children typically are weaker than their bullies and stronger than their victims. They resemble provocative victims in that they often provoke others and are easily aroused themselves (Ross, 1996). They generally are unpopular with their peers. In the Forero et al. study, the bully/victims had the most psychological and psychosomatic symptoms of the four groups.

### Why Victims in General Do Not Complain

Although fear of retaliation and embarrassment are factors here, the single most important contributor to ongoing bullying is the *code of silence* that is operative in most peer groups. Being identified as an informer is the ultimate disgrace. Some victims do not tell anyone because they know on the basis of experience or observation that neither parents nor school personnel will handle the problem effectively; telling may lead to far more severe physical and psychological suffering if the adults fail to ensure the victim's anonymity.

## BYSTANDERS

The negative effects of school bullying are not limited to the main protagonists but, instead, spread out to include bystanders who witness the bullying and others in the school who hear about it. The anxiety engendered focuses on the question of who will be next. A climate of fear can permeate the school when there are no visible, clear-cut, and effective consequences for bullying. Such an atmosphere is highly detrimental to the learning process. Physical safety and psychological security are the essential elements of this process. Competent teachers, small classes, and a well-equipped school are of little value to the child who fears the daily bus ride to and from school, feels vulnerable and unsafe in the school building, is afraid to go alone into the bathrooms, and knows that school personnel are unlikely to help him. A bully-friendly atmosphere of this sort encourages absenteeism, truancy and, more seriously, early school dropout. When high-school dropouts were asked for their number one reason for not completing school, 10% reported fear of being bullied (Greenbaum, 1989).

Several researchers have advocated enlisting the help of bystanders to counteract bullying. Herbert (1989) strongly supports the idea: "Perhaps the most important factor in combating bullying is the social pressure that can be brought to bear by the peer group rather than the condemnation of individual bullies by people in authority" (p. 80). Olweus (1993) noted that 60% to 70% of the students in a given semester were not involved in bullying at all. He recommended using this group to counteract bullying problems.

Meanwhile, an increasing number of concerned experts have suggested that one deterrent to the kind of teenage violence that erupted at Littleton, Colorado in April, 1999, may be curbing bullying, as there is reason to believe that bullying is an antecedent of violence. On the basis of this premise one school near Littleton is trying a bully-intervention program: At Highline Community School in Aurora, Colorado, it is against the rules for a student to watch another student being bullied without intervening or seeking help. Apparently as a result of this program, misconduct reports primarily of bullying have dropped in this school by almost 50%. This program is now serving as a model for 300 schools in the nation (Mulrine, 1999).

## WHAT THE SCHOOL COULD DO ABOUT BULLYING

### Whole School Campaign

The school can initiate a *whole school campaign* against bullying. The basic premise of such an undertaking is that bullying is intentional, a purposeful act, and consequently, one that can be controlled provided that there is a strong commitment and willingness to work together on the part of all those involved: school personnel, other professionals, parents, and children (Olweus, 1993). To stop bullying, intervention is needed that can accomplish two changes. First, the bullying must be stopped and firm comprehensive action taken to ensure the safety of the victims. Second, the social behavior of the bullies and victims must be changed. The bullies must stop attacking other children and redirect their energy in more positive directions. The victims must learn to be more assertive and to acquire the verbal and social skills appropriate to their age and grade level. Some of the social behavior problems can be modified in the classroom but others, such as the victim learning to be more assertive, would require support group intervention, (Katz, 1993), ideally in the school setting but not in the classroom.

Before a whole school campaign is initiated, it is essential to have a *code of conduct* operating smoothly in the school. A code of conduct is a whole school disciplinary policy with a clearly stated set of rules for behavior in

TABLE 6.2
Advice to Pupils About Being Bullied

| |
|---|
| *When you are being bullied:* |
| Be firm and clear – look them in the eye and tell them to stop |
| Get away from the situation as quickly as possible |
| Tell an adult what has happened straight away |
| *After you have been bullied:* |
| Tell a teacher or another adult in your school |
| Tell your family |
| If you are scared to tell a teacher or an adult on your own, ask a friend to go with you |
| Keep on speaking up until someone listens |
| Don't blame yourself for what has happened |
| *When you are talking about bullying with an adult, be clear about:* |
| What has happened to you |
| How often it has happened |
| Who was involved |
| Who saw what was happening |
| Where it happened |
| What you have done about it already |

From Burstall (1995, September 8). The English Department for Education's Anti-Bullying Pack: Advice to pupils about being bullied. *Times Educational Supplement*, Primary Update Section, p. 3.

and around the school, effectively communicated to all students, and enforced without exception. For violations of the code, nonphysical sanctions such as deprivation of privilege should be used (Olweus, 1993).

There is a cluster of antisocial behaviors that thrive on a bed of secrecy, and bullying in schools is one such behavior (Besag, 1989). It follows that an important part of the code of conduct is to make the school a *telling school*. Any child who is bullied by another child or adult, or who sees another child being bullied, is urged to report the incident to designated school personnel (Harrison, 1993). Burstall (1995) provided specific advice to pupils concerning what to do when bullied and how to describe it to adults (see Table 6.2).

Children who report such incidents must be guaranteed anonymity. It is the responsibility of *everyone* in a telling school to help stop bullying. There are no passive bystanders. There is a designated teacher to report to along with a comprehensive reporting routine. It is essential to distinguish between *legitimate telling* (for behaviors that injure others or damage property) and *tattling* (for rule-breaking such as reading a book in math class) that causes no injuries to others and no damage to property. Traditionally, "telling on" someone is viewed as bad behavior. To overcome this ingrained belief, the following rational could be used in presenting the idea to students.

Children have the right to feel safe in school in an atmosphere conducive to learning. Bullying is a violation of children's rights: Children who are bullied or who witness bullying incidents generally do not feel safe. Consequently, they neither benefit from school as they should, nor do they enjoy it. When bullying occurs in the workplace adults have some recourse: They can file a complaint and action should then follow against the wrongdoer. In a telling school, children have the same rights and they must report a child or teacher who bullies them. The telling school intervention is particularly important because children who are ardent but misguided supporters of the code of silence may also passively conform to sex molesters' demand for secrecy.

Specific interventions are available that could be incorporated into the whole school campaign against bullying. However, the foregoing aspects of the campaign must be functioning well before any specific interventions are introduced. To avoid overload, use discretion in adding specific interventions.

## Big Brother Programs

One source of stress for children entering kindergarten is fear of what might happen to them in their new school (Besag, 1989; Maccoby, 1980). This fear is a rational one: The children are making the transition from being the oldest in a small preschool group to the youngest in a large school. Their classmates will be more critical, demands will be greater, and restraints will increase. To ease the transition, some schools, particularly Roman Catholic schools for boys, pair all those entering kindergarten as well as first-grade boys who are new to the school, with a Big Brother, a student from an upper grade. The Big Brother meets the boy assigned to him on registration day and makes him feel welcome. At least once a day he checks to see how the new boy is getting along (but without ever suggesting that school is a problem-laden experience). The Big Brother is a good source of information for the kindergarten teacher because he is in a position to spot potential problems. His presence is a deterrent to bullying and teasing. He may also be a help to the child's mother: Usually he contacts her occasionally by phone.

## Use of Stories and Drama

One of the most popular activities that can be used in the classroom to combat bullying is the use of stories and drama. Teachers have access to many books that can be used to enhance awareness of the cruelty inherent in forms of bullying (such as social exclusion, extortion, and sexual harassment) and to encourage open discussion of these topics.

Drama is a powerful way to raise the level of awareness of students to the misery of being bullied. A good example occurred in the Seattle area when a drama troupe performed a play entitled, "Can't You Take a Joke?", that was designed to make fifth- and sixth-grade children aware of how much teasing hurts. Through vignettes that often hit close to home, the play demonstrated the painful side of teasing. One student said afterwards, "The play showed other people what you really feel inside." Some students appeared near tears during some scenes (Iwasaki, 1993).

## Telephone Hotline

The Hotline is an open line on which any student who is concerned about bullying may talk with designated school personnel. This telephone procedure allows students to voice anonymously their concerns and describe bullying encounters they have experienced without identifying either themselves or the bullies. Anonymity has great appeal for children who are troubled about being bullied but for some reason are unable to complain to their parents or teachers about it. The Hotline allows the student to talk to an adult and hopefully develop some plan for handling the bullying (La Fontaine, 1991). From a researcher's point of view it generates bullying information that is direct, spontaneous, and unsolicited, characteristics that are in sharp contrast to questionnaire surveys and other standard procedures for eliciting information (La Fontaine, 1991). Olweus (1993) recommended a contact telephone for use in Norwegian schools.

## Classroom Courts

Any child can lodge a complaint about another child in the class who has done something bad to the complainant. Complaints must be in writing and deposited in a special box. The class meets once a week to hear the complaints. First, both parties promise to tell the truth. Then the complainant describes the problem and the accused child rebuts. Both children can produce witnesses, and members of the class may ask questions. The protagonists are sent outside while the class discusses the case. A vote is taken to decide if the accused is guilty or innocent. If guilty, the class decides on the punishment, with the teacher acting as moderator to ensure that the meeting is orderly and the punishment an appropriate one that can be completed in the school setting. If the accused is judged to be innocent, the complainant must apologize (Yoshikawa-Cogley, 1995).

Other intervention procedures, including conflict resolution, peer mediation, student watch programs, peer counseling, quality circles, and no blame or punishment procedures, are discussed in detail in Ross (1996) and Smith and Sharp (1994).

## Counseling

The school should provide counseling services for any child who is concerned about the bullying. Bystanders are often quite upset at the sight of ongoing bullying and may feel guilty about their own reluctance to go to the victim's assistance. Counseling for bullies and victims has been found to be most effective when part of each session focuses on having each participant begin to understand the motivation and feelings of the other one (Hazler, 1996). Bullies need to consider why their victims behave as they do, as well as how they feel as victims; victims also need to have some insight into what has brought the bullies to their current unacceptable level of behavior in addition to considering ways (if any) in which they could try to handle the bullying problem themselves.

## METHODS OF WORKING WITH HIGH-RISK CLIENTS

### The Shy Child

Shy children who are beginning kindergarten and older children who are shy and entering a new school with a stable population are at high risk for bullying (Ross, 1996). Both groups need practice first in the body language of friendship. The idea here is to start with the grosser physical aspects before moving on to the more refined elements such as verbal approaches to others. Shy children (and also adults) are usually unaware of the message that is conveyed through body language. The shy child needs to be taught how to convey a welcoming and reasonably assertive impression through body language. The child should practice standing or sitting in a relaxed way and reasonably close to another child, as well as smiling at other children and making eye contact with them (Zimbardo, 1982). When these behaviors have become comfortable, the next step is to acquire skills and tactics for entering groups: he (or she) needs to feel comfortable introducing himself to other children and showing his interest with appropriate questions. At this point some time should be spent on understanding that sometimes it is reasonable for a group to refuse to let another child join in an activity. *Maintaining* friendships requires a new set of behaviors such as being supportive of one's peers, showing sensitivity and tact when appropriate, managing the inevitable conflicts, and being a loyal friend.

The ideal teaching situation for shy children is the small support group format (Katz, 1993) with meetings twice a week for about an hour at a time. The leader can do role playing with one child while the others watch and make approving or critical comments about the behavior demonstrated by the leader. Roles should be reversed sometimes so that the leader then plays the part of the not too competent new child and one of the others accepts or rebuffs the leader's overtures. Role playing is particularly useful for demonstrating positive and negative kinds of body language messages. Situations that the child is likely to meet in school, at lunchtime, on the playground, and on the school bus all provide excellent fodder for the role playing exercises. Children enjoy these role play demonstrations and typically pay very close attention to them (Ross, 1996).

For each session, children in the group should be given homework assignments. Encourage them to practice in front of a mirror such events as introducing themselves to another child, inviting another child to play a game at recess, showing another child something the shy one has brought to school, and so on. In the group meetings pairs of children should role play these incidents and then ask for comments on what went well and what needs to be changed. Spend some time in each session on reports by the children on how things went at school.

## The New Child Who Does Not "Fit In"

Phillips (1989) reported the case of Rachel, a 10-year-old girl whose problems started when she entered a new school. Although she was clearly intelligent and quite creative, all her fellow students saw was a short, underdeveloped, ordinary-looking girl who seemed to be a good target for teasing. She was teased wherever she went in school. A boy on her school bus told her, "You're ugly. You're the ugliest girl on the bus." A girl whose name she did not know said, "No boy will ever ask *you* out." Rachel's parents knew that she was terribly miserable about school and they sought professional help.

Phillips (1989) focused first on teaching Rachel to be more assertive, the goal being to help her feel stronger which, in turn, should make her more assured and confident, a demeanor that could be expected to discourage teasing. Through a combination of homework assignments, positive reinforcement, and empathic listening, Phillips was gradually able to get Rachel to express her feelings freely. Phillips proceeded cautiously on the teasing problem because she knew the child was very uncomfortable about it. She found that one of the great moments in Rachel's life had been getting a standing ovation for her performance in a school play. Phillips then taught Rachel how to use thought substitution about her success in the play whenever anything at school, such as being teased, bothered her. Phillips also found out who was teasing Rachel, what they said, and how she reacted. Using role play, including reversal of roles so that Rachel could see the folly of cringing and looking embarrassed when teased, Phillips taught her that when teased she was to stand up straight, not show any upset, make extended eye contact, never argue, and never respond verbally at all unless what the teaser said was true. If the tease was true, she was to agree in an unemotional way, for example, by saying, "You're right, I do have hundreds of freckles." Agreeing reduces the impact of the teasing on the target child and tends to confuse the teaser.

Keeping silent when teased is difficult for children (Ross, 1996). Phillips taught Rachel to use an *emotional shrug*, that is, to assume a demeanor that conveys "So what?" or "Who cares, I don't." Although this was hard for her to master, Rachel persevered and soon found that she was being teased less and less. At last report, Rachel was no longer being teased (Phillips, 1989).

## CRISIS COUNSELING

### Promoting Issues in Common

In *Breaking the cycle of violence*, Hazler (1996) described a three-step therapeutic technique called Promoting Issues in Common (PIC) specifically for counseling bullies and victims. This technique has limited application in that it is appropriate largely for bullies and victims in conflict who previously have had a neutral or positive relationship which they would like to re-establish. In any case, without help neither the bully nor victim is able to take the first step toward any level of reconciliation. Parts of the PIC are appropriate for victims with no previous relationship with their tormentors (Hazler, 1996). Hazler (1996) cautions that the probability of this counseling technique being effective is greatest when the PIC is one part of an established approach to dealing with the problem of bullying. The more appropriate and coordinated the ongoing discipline, the more effective the PIC should be.

***Gaining Control of the Conflict Situation.*** With the PIC the first step in gaining control of an ongoing conflict situation focuses on creating the conditions that will facilitate effective counseling at a later point in time. Counseling cannot begin until the therapist has gained control of the conflict situation. It cannot begin, for example, when one person is still actively bullying another. Top priority must be given to lowering the tension to a moderate level. The therapist must provide the requisite level of physical force or verbal intervention to halt ongoing conflict. To accomplish this the therapist must assess the conflict situation accurately while showing an appropriate amount of concern. It is important to withhold judgments of who is in the wrong in order to convey to the combatants and any onlookers that more information must be obtained before a final judgment is made. The emphasis here is on hearing all sides. By delaying a final judgment the therapist has more opportunity to develop positive working relationships with everyone involved.

***Evaluation of the Problem Situation.*** The second step in the PIC model focuses on an individual interview, first with the bully, then with the victim. Seeing the bully first should facilitate the building of a positive relationship between the bully and the therapist. It also protects the victim. The goal of these interviews is to assess each one's needs as well as the needs common to their relationship. The protagonists are likely to need individual counseling sessions to provide help with their own problems; help with the relationship problem is best handled with joint counseling. A major shift in the interviewing process occurs in the period when the therapist tries to help the student who is being interviewed to see the other person's point of view. The task of considering the other's feelings and situation is a difficult one for most clients. At this point any other individuals familiar with the situation should also be interviewed. Evaluating everyone's views of the problem is essential if the next step, the direct intervention process, is to begin with the greatest probability of success.

***Direct Intervention Stage.*** The third step in the PIC technique focuses on providing direct interventions rather than specific therapeutic tactics. Decisions on direct interventions are made on the basis of how much each individual is in need of personal, social, and psychological therapy. It is important to delay working in pairs or larger groups until the therapist is confident that the individual is independently prepared to do so.

Prior to joint meetings the protagonists must have their personal concerns clearly identified, understand how the joint meeting will help them, and know which issues they have in common. The primary therapy goal of each joint meeting is establishing a working, but not necessarily friendly, relationship between both parties. The PIC technique emphasizes an ongoing model for improvement that relies less and less on the therapist for improving the relationship and more and more on the clients to do so. The last two joint meetings signify the timing of the termination process. The next-to-last meeting sets the stage for the final one. The rationale for termination and a preview of the final session should be discussed. In the final meeting a review of the full extent of the clients' development is made and assurance is given that extra help is available if it proves to be necessary.

## Brief Therapy: Solution-Focused Counseling

Solution-focused counseling (Murphy, 1997) is a brief therapy technique that uses problem solving to promote change in school problems in a relatively short time. It focuses on small changes, such as a noticeable improvement in the problem, without necessarily aiming for the complete elimination of it. The therapist asks the student what he (or she) wants from counseling, instead of making assumptions about the student's goal. The therapist always seeks the student's input before offering any suggestions of his own and he *never argues* with the student. He does not lecture, probe, or persuade as some counselors do, and he never focuses on what the student is doing wrong. Instead of trying to challenge the student's position, the counselor cooperates with the student's beliefs. Solution-focused counseling maintains that students already have the resources and strengths necessary for improving a situation and effective counseling helps them discover and apply these resources to the problem at hand.

***Interviewing.*** This is the first step in intervention. A single interview sometimes results in a solution to the problem by shifting the way the student views the problem that is the reason for counseling. Tomm (1987) coined the term *interventive interviewing* to convey the idea that the interview itself can be a powerful mechanism of change. For example, a shift from a past-oriented focus on what is wrong, to a future-directed focus on possibilities of change is conveyed with the following questions:

> What would you like to change about what is happening in your life now?
> If this bullying problem suddenly disappeared what would you be doing tomorrow at school that would be different from what you usually do?

Note here that the counselor should take into account that bullies often have a positive attitude to bullying. Consider their answers in interviews with reporters as to why they bully:

> To have fun, to really have fun. (Priest, 1987)

> If you don't feel like you can do anything else and you can beat up everyone in the school, at least you can do something well. (Priest, 1987)

> They're just paying for protection, man, it makes them feel safe. (Stewart, personal communication, January 30, 1982)

***Ambassador Approach.*** This is a procedure that Murphy (1997) recommended for exploring the bully problem. It involves the use of curious, tentative, and non-threatening questions from a person who professes to know very little about the problem that is the reason for counseling, but is genuinely interested in hearing about it. The therapist explains that he has never been bullied and, in fact, has never known a bully, but would like to know more about this problem. The following kinds of questions could be used:

> When do you think children begin to bully others?

Is the only problem really the attitude of school personnel about bullying as a problem?

Describe a recent example of when bullying someone caused you trouble.

What would your life be like if you weren't a bully?

What is going right for you at school at this moment?

What is one thing that you'd like to be able to do that you cannot do now?

Another set of questions is aimed at clarifying the student's resources, the assumption being that some of his resources could provide useful information about him:

What do you like to do outside of school?

What does the person who helps you the most do or say that really helps you?

How would other students treat you if you weren't a bully?

What do you think it would take so that you don't have to come to counseling?

The therapist must accept the student's view of the problem as expressed in his answers. The most effective way to avoid a power struggle in this situation is to work *with* rather than *against* the student's position.

***Formulation of Specific Goals.*** During the first counseling session the formulation of specific goals is crucial for a successful outcome. During this session the counselor must decide if the student appears to be genuinely interested in stopping bullying. It is important to be aware of the forces that are against his stopping. Bullies are often respected and sometimes even admired by a sizable number of students, and they often have a group of loyal followers (Olweus, 1993). The bully may be apprehensive about losing face if he stops bullying. In any case, it would be unrealistic to expect him to come to a complete stop on bullying. Instead, it would be much better to set a more reasonably attainable goal such as stopping bullying completely on two specified days a week as a beginning, then gradually increasing the nonbullying days. In line with the principles underlying solution-focused counseling, this idea should be suggested in a tentative way possibly when you are discussing goals, for example, "What would you think of this idea for a start . . . ?" It would be helpful to discuss responses the bully could make to his cohorts on being asked why he is not engaging in his usual bullying pursuits. It is essential to have the student report any bullying he engages in on the nonbullying days and, if possible, have school personnel note any bullying activity on the student's part because bullies habitually tend to deny charges of bullying (Olweus, 1993; Ross, 1996).

In subsequent sessions the counselor must determine the social and temporal circumstances surrounding periods when the bullying does *not* occur, consider ways that the student's resources (skills, social support, etc.) might be useful in interrupting the bullying pattern, persuade the student to change the frequency of bullying (in this case he set a goal of two nonbullying days a week), and help the student to see the bullying in a less favorable light. For example, one high-school junior who was exceptionally strong and well coordinated was "picked" to become an assistant in an after-school self-defense class for men, and the combination of the resultant status and time commitments resulted in a decrease in frequency of bullying as well as a loss of interest in it.

The decision to terminate counseling should be made when the student is clearly on track toward resolving the problem. It must be a collaborative decision between the counselor and the student and it should be very clear that the student could return for further counseling if it seemed necessary.

Solution-focused counseling is especially suited to the time constraints and heavy caseloads of school counselors. It is conceptually simple and does not require extensive formal training. It is the author's opinion that parents of adolescents could benefit significantly from the approaches described by Murphy (1997).

## GROUP INTERVENTION METHODS

### Support Groups

Children with specific problems whose needs are not being met by existing organizations would benefit from participating in support groups (Katz, 1993). These groups satisfy a wide range of needs, such as the need for gaining peer acceptance, dealing with divorce, a recent death in the family, or physical disablement. Before joining a support group, many children feel that they are alone in their misery. Interacting with other children with similar problems markedly lessens their feeling of isolation. One 9-year-old girl with terminal leukemia lovingly described her support group as "my very own little family." The group consists of a leader, preferably with counseling training, who also has expertise in small-group work. The maximum number of participants is 12 for adolescents, 10 at the middle-school level, and 6 in the primary grades. In most cases, each group should be a same gender one.

***Children Who Are Bullied.*** A support group would be ideal for the victims of bullying and teasing (Arora, 1991; Besag, 1989). In addition to providing emotional support for the victims, one goal of the support group set-up is to introduce behavior changes that would provide them with protection against bullying and teasing. The group format is ideal for practice in role playing, along with reversal of roles as a way of showing the victim how it feels to be a bully or teaser. It is also excellent for assertive training as a means of changing the cringing demeanor typical of many victims. For approaches to the teasing problem see Ross (1996, pp. 179–207) and also Phillips (1989), who offers excellent advice on assertive training for individuals, which could also be applied to groups.

Arora (1991) reported impressive success with a small support group of severely bullied high-school students. She developed a 12-hour training program which focused on teaching assertiveness behavior. Over a period of several months, the participants were taught appropriate responses to bullying situations and given ample opportunity to rehearse them in role play. The skills and techniques taught included refusing to do what the bully wanted, handling name-calling and critical comments, resisting unwanted pressure, and seeking help from bystanders.

***Overprotective Mothers of Preschoolers.*** These mothers could also benefit from a support group. A major obstacle to changing their behavior is their entrenched belief that they are excellent mothers. So direct challenges to this belief would almost certainly result in failure. One place to start would be to introduce the concept of developmental tasks, with an emphasis on those that apply to the preschool period. The next topic would be a description of what children entering kindergarten should be able to do, along with the probable consequences if a child cannot handle these tasks with comparative ease. For example, he or she would likely be tagged as a failure, a "baby," and in the absence of any strong redeeming talents would become an isolate in the kindergarten setting. A next step would be to provide the mothers with a hierarchy of tasks that their children should master. Treat this as a homework assignment, with the group being required to introduce one or two tasks each week, with a follow-up on their success or failure at the next meeting.

## A PLAN FOR ACTION

In 1993 the National Education Goals Panel (Johnston, O'Malley, & Bachman, 1993) stated that their goal was to have every school in the United States free of violence and conducive to learning by the end of the century.

We have fallen far short of this goal and, if anything, deterioration in the situation has accelerated. It is our opinion that a program consisting of the following three components would have a realistic chance of meeting the Panel's goal by the year 2010.

First, a 2-year primary prevention program for 3- and 4-year-old children would be used to forestall the onset of bullying and victimization. Its goal would be to equip the children with the cognitive, social, and emotional skills that are considered the prerequisites for school entry. It would require some parent participation. An outstanding program that would fit this approach is the *Early Violence Prevention Program* developed by Ronald Slaby and his associates (Slaby, Roedell, Arezzo, & Hendrix, 1995). It combats bullying, victimization, and racism.

Next, all public schools would set into motion as soon as possible whole school campaigns against bullying similar to those of Olweus (1993) and Smith and Sharp (1994). Parental involvement would be of prime importance and should be encouraged with an enrichment program for elementary school children such as the *Fast Track Program* (Conduct Problems Prevention Research Group, 1992). It offers parents many incentives, two of which are quite unusual. The parents are treated as expert members of the program team and are paid for their participation in the program.

Finally, a neighborhood watch program would be set up in each school district to mobilize the residents to take action against bullying and other kinds of violence by stopping it or reporting it. This neighborhood force could be a potent weapon against bullying in areas beyond the school's immediate jurisdiction. Community-wide interventions have proven to be effective with a variety of problems. One such intervention that focused specifically on bullying was set up in Hull, England by Randall and Donohue (1993) and has proven to be highly successful (Randall, 1995).

Note that for all three components of this proposed attack on the problem of bullying and violence in the schools, outstanding programs have already been developed, tested, and published. Their availability thus eliminates the need for costly program development with resultant delays in direct action to halt the spiral of increasing violence. Over the long haul, the financial costs of implementing this proposed course of action would be far outweighed by the costs of continuing to let the situation deteriorate. Prevention almost always costs less than treatment.

## REFERENCES

Adams, A. (1992). Holding out against work place harassment and bullying. *Personnel Management, 24*, 48–50.

Ahmad, Y., & Smith, P. K. (1990). Behavioral measures: Bullying in schools. *Newsletter of Association for Child Psychology and Psychiatry, 12*, 26–27.

Ariès, P. (1962). *Centuries of childhood: A social history of family life.* New York: Knopf.

Arora, T. (1991). The use of victim support groups. In P. K. Smith & D. Thompson (Eds.), *Practical approaches to bullying* (pp. 36–47). London: David Fulton.

Askew, S. (1989). Aggressive behaviour in boys: To what extent is it institutionalized? In D. P. Tattum & D. A. Lane (Eds.), *Bullying in schools* (pp. 59–71). Stoke-on-Trent: Trentham Books.

Bandura, A. (1977). *Social learning theory.* Englewood Cliffs, NJ: Prentice-Hall.

Bandura, A., & Walters, R. H. (1959). *Adolescent aggression.* New York: Ronald Press.

Batsch, G. M., & Knoff, H. M. (1994). Bullies and their victims: Understanding a pervasive problem in the schools. *School Psychology Review, 23,* 165–174.

Bentley, K. M., & Li, A. K. F. (1995). Bully and victim problems in elementary schools and students' beliefs about aggression. *Canadian Journal of School Psychology, 11,* 153–165.

Besag, V. C. (1989). *Bullies and victims in schools.* Bristol, PA: Open University Press.

Boulton, M. J., & Smith, P. K. (1994). Bully/victim problems in middle-school children: Stability, self-perceived competence, peer perceptions and peer acceptance. *British Journal of Developmental Psychology, 12,* 315–329.

Bowers, L., Smith, P. K., & Binney, V. (1992). Cohesion and power in the families of children involved in bully/victim problems at school. *Journal of Family Therapy, 14,* 371–387.

Brock, G. R., & Goode, J. A. (1996). *Genetics of criminal and antisocial behavior.* Chichester, UK: Wiley.

Burk, F. L. (1897). Teasing and bullying. *Pedagogical Seminary, 4,* 336–371.

Burstall, E. (1995, September 8). The English Department for Education's Anti-Bullying Pack: Advice to pupils about being bullied. *Times Educational Supplement,* Primary Update Section, p. 3.

Conduct Problems Prevention Research Group (1992). A developmental and clinical model for the prevention of conduct disorder: The FAST Track Program. *Development and Psychopathology, 4,* 509–527.

Crick, N. R., Casas, J. F., & Mosher, M. (1997). Relational and overt aggression in preschool. *Developmental Psychology, 33,* 579–588.

Crick, N. R., & Grotpeter, J. K. (1995). Relational aggression, gender, and social-psychological adjustment. *Child Development, 66,* 710–722.

Dean, C. (1995, March 17). 4,000 staff say they are bullied. *London Times Educational Supplement,* News, p. 6.

Dishion, T. J. (1990). The family ecology of boys' peer relations in middle childhood. *Child Development, 61,* 874–892.

Eron, L. K., & Huesmann, R. L. (1990). The stability of aggressive behavior—Even unto the third generation. In M. Lewis & S. M. Miller (Eds.), *Handbook of developmental psychopathology* (pp. 147–156). New York: Plenum Press.

Forero, R., McLellan, L., Rissel, C., & Bauman, A. (1999). Bullying behavior and psychosocial health among school students: cross sectional study. *British Medical Journal, 319,* 344–348.

Gilmartin, B. G. (1987). Peer group antecedents of severe love-shyness in males. *Journal of Personality, 55,* 467–489.

Greenbaum, S. (1989). *Set straight on bullies.* Malibu, CA: National School Safety Center.

Harrison, P. (1993, December 3). Adopting a more telling approach. *Times Educational Supplement,* p. 26.

Hazler, R. J. (1996). *Breaking the cycle of violence: Intervention for bullies and victims.* Bristol, PA: Accelerated Development.

Hazler, R. J., Carney, J. V., Green, S., Powell, R., & Jolly, L. S. (1997). Areas of expert agreement on identification of school bullies and victims. *School Psychology International, 18,* 3–12.

Hazler, R. J., Hoover, J. H., & Oliver, R. (1993). What do kids say about bullying? *Education Digest, 58*(7), 16–20.

Herbert, G. (1989). A whole-curriculum approach to bullying. In D. P. Tattum & D. A. Lane (Eds.), *Bullying in schools* (pp. 73–80). Stoke-on-Trent: Trentham Books.

Hirano, K. (1992). *Bullying and victimization in Japanese classrooms*. Paper presented at the European Conference on Developmental Psychology, Seville, Spain.

Hughes, T. (1857). *Tom Brown's schooldays*. London: MacMillan.

Ireland, J., & Archer, J. (1996). Descriptive analysis of bullying in male and female adult prisoners. *Journal of Community and Applied Social Psychology, 6*, 35–47.

Iwasaki, J. (1993, January 12). Play shows how teasing hurts. *The Seattle Post-Intelligencer*, pp. B1, B4.

Johnston, L. D., O'Malley, P. M., & Bachman, J. G. (1993). *Monitoring the future study for Goal 6 of the national education goals: A special report for the National Education Goals Panel*. Ann Arbor, MI: University of Michigan's Institute for Social Research.

Kaltiala-Heino, R., Rimpelä, M., Marttunen, A. R., Rimpelä, A., & Rantanen, P. (1999). Bullying, depression, and suicidal ideation in Finnish adolescents: School survey. *British Medical Journal, 319*, 348–351.

Karr-Morse, R., & Wiley, M. S. (1997). *Ghosts from the nursery: Tracing the roots of violence*. New York: Atlantic Monthly Press.

Katz, A. H. (1993). *Self-help in America: A social movement perspective*. New York: Twayne.

La Fontaine, J. (1991). *Bullying, the child's view: An analysis of telephone calls to Childline about bullying*. London: Calouste Gulbenkian Foundation.

Landers, A. (1995, February 17). Advice. *The Seattle Post-Intelligencer*, p. 35.

Leach, P. (1986). *Your growing child: From babyhood through adolescence*. New York: Knopf.

Leff, S. S., Kupersmidt, J. B., Patterson, C. J., & Power, T. J. (1999). Factors influencing teacher identification of peer bullies and victims. *School Psychology Review, 28*, 505–517.

Loeber, R., & Stouthamer-Loeber, M. (1998). Development of juvenile aggression and violence: Some common misconceptions and controversies. *American Psychologist, 53*, 242–259.

Maccoby, E. E. (1980). *Social development: Psychological growth and the parent–child relationship*. New York: Harcourt Brace Jovanovich.

Marano, H. E. (1995). Big. Bad. Bully. *Psychology Today*, 51–57, 65–70, 74, 76, 79, 82.

McBurnett, K., Lahey, B. B., Rathouz, P. J., & Loeber, R. (2000). Low salivary cortisol and persistent aggression in boys referred for disruptive behavior. *Archives of General Psychiatry, 57*, 38–43.

Moffitt, T. E. (1993). Adolescent-limited and life-course-persistent antisocial behavior: A developmental taxonomy. *Psychological Review, 100*, 674–701.

Mulrine, A. (1999, May 3). Once bullied, now bullies—with guns. *U.S. News & World Report*, p. 24.

Murakami, Y. (1985). Bullies in the classroom. *Japan Quarterly, 32*, 407–409.

Murphy, J. J. (1997). *Solution-focused counseling in middle and high schools*. Alexandria, VA: American Counseling Association.

Namie, G., & Namie, R. (1999). *Bullyproof yourself at work*. Benicia, CA: Doubledoc Press.

Olweus, D. (1978). *Aggression in the schools: Bullies and whipping boys*. Washington, DC: Hemisphere.

Olweus, D. (1979). Stability of aggressive reaction patterns in males: A review. *Psychological Bulletin, 86*, 852–875.

Olweus, D. (1984). Aggressors and their victims: Bullying at school. In N. Frude & H. Gault (Eds.), *Disruptive behaviors in schools* (pp. 57–76). New York: Wiley.

Olweus, D. (1985). 80,000 pupils involved in bullying. *Norsk Skoleblad*, p. 2, Norway.

Olweus, D. (1993). *Bullying at school: What we know and what we can do*. Cambridge, MA: Blackwells.

Olweus, D., & Alsaker, F. D. (1991). Assessing change in a cohort cohort—Longitudinal study with hierarchical data. In D. Magnusson, L. R. Bergman, G. Rudinger, & B. Rorestad (Eds.), *Problems and methods in longitudinal research: Stability and change*. Cambridge, England: Cambridge University Press.

O'Moore, A. M., & Hillery, B. (1989). Bullying in Dublin schools. *Irish Journal of Psychology, 10*, 426–441.

Perry, D. G., Kusel, S. J., & Perry, L. C. (1988). Victims of peer aggression. *Developmental Psychology, 24*, 807–814.

Phillips, D. (1989). *How to give your child a great self-image*. New York: Random House.

Priest, D. (1987, May 20). Why bullies do it: "To really have fun:" School violence being studied. *The Washington Post*, p. 16.

Randall, P. E. (1995, May). Beyond the school gates (bullying). *Special Children*, No. 84, 19–21.

Randall, P. E., & Donohue, M. I. (1993, October). Tackling bullying together. *Child Education*, 70, 79.

Rigby, K., & Slee, P. T. (1991). Bullying among Australian school children: Reported behavior and attitudes to victims. *Journal of Social Psychology, 62*, 415–448.

Ross, D. M. (1996). *Childhood bullying and teasing: What school personnel, other professionals, and parents can do*. Alexandria, VA: American Counseling Association.

Ruiz, R. O. (1992). *Violence in schools: Problems of bullying and victimization in Spain*. Paper presented at the Fifth European Conference on Developmental Psychology, Seville, Spain.

Salmivalli, C., Lagerspetz, K., Bjorkqvist, K., Osterman, K., & Kaukiainen, A. (1996). Bullying as a group process: Participant roles and their relations to social status within the group. *Aggressive Behavior, 22*, 1–15.

Schwartz, D., Dodge, K. A., & Coie, J. D. (1993). The emergence of chronic peer victimization in boys' play groups. *Child Development, 64*, 1755–1793.

Schwartz, D., Dodge, K. A., Pettit, G. S., & Bates, J. E. (1997). The early socialization of aggressive victims of bullying. *Child Development, 68*, 665–675.

Slaby, R. G., Roedell, W. C., Arezzo, D., & Hendrix, K. (1995). *Early violence prevention: Tools for teachers of young children*. Washington, DC: National Association for the Education of Young Children.

Smith, P. K. (1991). The silent nightmare: Bullying and victimization in school peer groups. *The Psychologist: Bulletin of the British Psychological Society, 4*, 243–248.

Smith, P. K., & Sharp, S. (Eds.). (1994). *School bullying: Insights and Perspectives*. London: Routledge.

Stephenson, P., & Smith, D. (1989). Bullying in the junior school. In D. P. Tattum & D. A. Lane (Eds.), *Bullying in schools* (pp. 45–57). Stoke-on-Trent: Trentham Books.

Sutton, J., Smith, P. K., & Swettenham, J. (1999). Social cognition and bullying: Social inadequacy or skilled manipulation? *British Journal of Developmental Psychology, 17*, 435–450.

Tattum, D. P. (1989). Violence and aggression in schools. In D. P. Tattum & D. A. Lane (Eds.), *Bullying in schools* (pp. 7–19). Stoke-on-Trent: Trentham Books.

Taylor, M. (1996). A theory of mind perspective on social cognitive development. In R. Gelman & T. Kit-Fong Au (Eds.), *Perceptual and cognitive development* (pp. 283–329). London: Academic Press.

Thomas, A., & Chess, S. (1977). *Temperament and development*. New York: Brunner/Mazel.

Thompson, D. A., & Smith, P. K. (1991). Effective action against bullying—The key problems. In P. K. Smith & D. A. Thompson (Eds.), *Practical approaches to bullying* (pp. 140–152). London: Fulton.

Tomm, K. (1987). Interventive interviewing. *Family Process, 26*, 167–183.

Williams, E. (1995, March 3). Drama out of a prison. *Times Educational Supplement*, p. 4.

Williams, K., Chambers, M., Logan, S., & Robinson, D. (1996). Association of common health problems with bullying in primary schoolchildren. *British Medical Journal, 313*, 17–19.

Yoshikawa-Cogley, L. (1995). Children talk out problems. *The Seattle Post-Intelligencer*, pp. B1, B3.

Zimbardo, P. G. (1982). *The shy child*. Garden City, NY: Doubleday.

CHAPTER

# 7

# Child Maltreatment

**Robert Germain**
Private Practice, Hilliard, Ohio

**Jonathan Sandoval**
University of California, Davis

Allen was standing there sobbing and shaking, eyes bulging, nose running, and tears streaming down his face. His father was holding him tightly, holding a knife to his cheek. "This is what I'll do if you can't learn to act right," his father said. Allen could hardly listen; he'd been spanked pretty hard before, but the knife was terrifying. His mind was racing and he knew that he'd better start acting right. But he was confused; he thought he had been behaving.

Is this a scene from a soap opera or a cheap novel? It sounds like it, but such dramas may be fairly regular among the children attending any given school. How do we respond?

## PERSPECTIVES ON CHILD MALTREATMENT

### Distinctions

Although it is most common to think of maltreatment as physical and sexual abuse, another kind of maltreatment that can lead to crisis for children is *psychological* maltreatment. Allen's situation typifies only one type of psychological maltreatment—terrorizing. Psychological maltreatment includes other acts of commission such as humiliating, exploiting, rejecting, and corrupting, as well as acts of omission such as psychological neglect and unavailability of caregiving.

The term *maltreatment* is used most often in this chapter because it includes both acts of commission (abuse) and omission (neglect). Thus, maltreatment refers to physical and psychological abuse and neglect, and to sexual abuse. A commonly used definition of neglect is "A condition in which a caretaker responsible for the child, either deliberately or by extraordinary inattentiveness, permits the child to experience avoidable present suffering and/or fails to provide one or more of the ingredients generally deemed essential for developing a person's physical, intellectual, and emotional capacities" (Polansky, 1981, p. 15).

### Incidence of Maltreatment

The incidence and prevalence of maltreatment varies not only with the type of maltreatment under consideration, but also with the specific definitions and methodology used in any particular study. In 1998 the U.S. Department of Health and Human Services estimated that more than 900,000 children were maltreated, more than half of them victims of neglect and nearly one fourth the target of physical abuse. In this same year, 12% were sexually abused and 6% victims of psychological abuse or medical neglect. One fourth of the victims were subjected to more than one kind of abuse. This is an incidence of 12.9 cases out of 1,000 children (U.S. Department of Health and Human Services, 2000).

***Physical Maltreatment.*** Physical abuse is the infliction of physical injury by beating, burning, biting, kicking, or other means. Physical neglect is the failure to supply the normal physical necessities of life, such as food, clothing, sleep, bathing, or health care. It includes abandonment and exposure of children to avoidable hazard and danger (e.g., driving while intoxicated). In one study, 43% of the identified neglect was physical neglect, including inadequate housing, nutrition, or clothing. The next largest category of neglect was inadequate supervision of children (36.6%) and failure or delay in providing health care (20.8%). The estimated incidence of physical maltreatment varies between 200,000 and 2 million, with 1.4 to 1.9 million children at high risk for physical abuse (Gelles & Straus, 1979). There are approximately 60,000 cases reported nationwide per year. The 1981 National Study reported an incidence of 3.4 per 1,000 and physical neglect at 1.7 per 1,000.

***Psychological Maltreatment.*** Psychological or emotional abuse is behavior that results in emotional or cognitive disabilities or retardation. Psychological or emotional neglect is the withdrawal of contact and support that brings on similar developmental difficulties. The outcome of psychological abuse may often be more debilitating that physical abuse. In the 1981 National Study, emotional abuse was reported at a rate of 2.2 per 1,000 children and emotional neglect at 1.0 per 1,000 children. Psychological maltreatment constituted the primary problem identified in about 39% of the abuse cases and 18% of the neglect cases. Psychological maltreatment is difficult for outsiders to identify, and many cases may go unreported.

***Sexual Abuse.*** Sexual abuse simply viewed is criminal sexual activity of any kind with a child. It may range from inappropriate fondling to rape and sodomy, but it also includes indirect acts such as sexually exploiting children through prostitution and involvement in pornography. The Federal Child Abuse Prevention and Treatment Act (CAPTA) defines sexual abuse as "(a) The employment, use, persuasion, inducement, enticement, or coercion of any child to engage in, or assist any other person to engage in, any sexually explicit conduct or simulation of such conduct for the purpose of producing a visual depiction of such conduct; or (b) The rape, and in cases of caretaker or inter-familial relationships, statutory rape, molestation, prostitution, or other form of sexual exploitation of children, or incest with children." The traumatic impact of a sexual act depends on how it is interpreted by the child, although inappropriate acts leave a child with distorted understandings and beliefs. Abuse is usually related to a power differential, a knowledge differential or a gratification differential in favor of the abuser. The prevalence of sexual abuse is quite common. Perhaps 1 female in 4 will experience it at some point in childhood as well as 1 male in 10 (Finklehor et al., 1986). Incidence rates of sexual abuse in 1986 were estimated to be 21 cases per 10,000 children (U.S. Department of Health and Human Services, 1988). The subject of sexual assault by other than family members will be covered in chapter 17.

***Educational Neglect.*** Although only recently cataloged, it is possible also to define educational neglect. This form of neglect includes permitted chronic truancy, failure to enroll a child in school, and inattention to a special educational need, such as for special education. It may be subsumed under the other forms of neglect, however.

## Maltreatment as a Psychological Crisis

Although there may be both physical and psychological damage from abuse, in most cases it is the psychological damage that is generally considered to be the most devastating aspect of the experience (Garbarino & Vondra, 1983). That is, in most, although certainly not all cases, bruises and broken bones heal, and whipping may have little physical impact. But it is the psychological impact from these types of maltreatment that makes them particularly harmful to the child.

Relative to the categories of crises discussed by Sandoval (chapter 1), maltreatment can be viewed as an example of traumatic stress and shares much psychologically with terrorism. Maltreatment is often unexpected, uncontrolled, and emotionally overwhelming. What can make psychological maltreatment even more traumatic is an ongoing, rational fear of reoccurrence. The anticipation of maltreatment may be worse than the act itself. The child is often in a primary, dependent, long-term relationship with the perpetrator, and may believe there is no recourse or escape. The child believes, and others reinforce, that caregivers (which often includes the perpetrator) must be acting in the legitimate best interests of the child.

Maltreatment does not produce results that are linked to any one diagnostic category; the outcomes are varied. Research, however, suggests that maltreatment leads to psychological maladjustment, and may predict serious emotional and behavioral disorders (Faller, 1981; Kadushin & Martin, 1981). Reactions are emotional, physical, and social in nature and have an impact on school learning.

## Emotional Reactions

Common emotional reactions are *anxiety and fear* (Adams-Tucker, 1981; Anderson, Bach, & Griffith, 1981; Browning & Boatman, 1977; James, 1994); *guilt and shame* (Burgess & Holstrom, 1978; Weiss, Rogers, Darwin, & Dutton, 1955); *depression and grief* (Anderson et al., 1981; Burgess & Holstrom, 1978, Toth, Manly, & Cicchetti, 1992); *flashbacks* (Terr, 1991) and *decreased self-worth*. In addition, children's fears may revolve around *recurrence* (of maltreatment itself), *disclosure* (not being believed or being punished for disclosure), or *resolution* (possible loss of parent).

Anger may be directed not only at the perpetrator, but also at other family members and significant others who failed to provide protection. In later life, as parents, maltreated children are more likely than others to abuse their own children (Egeland, Jacobvitz, & Papatola, 1987; Kaufman & Zeigler, 1987).

## Physical Reactions

Physical maltreatment is not the only type that results in physical reactions. Most maltreatment may bring about *somatic complaints* (Adams-Tucker, 1981; Anderson et al., 1981; Browning & Boatman, 1977) although physical and sexual abuse will usually have *direct physical consequences* (e.g., internal bleeding). Physical reactions might also include regressive physical behaviors such as thumb sucking and bed-wetting.

### Social Behavior

Maltreatment typically acts to disturb attachment relations with others (Webster & Browning, in press). Attachment problems, in turn, create *dysfunctional sexual attitudes and behavior* (Rosenfeld, Nadelson, Krieger, & Backman, 1979), *avoidance of intimacy* (James, 1994), and *deviant behavior* (Justice & Justice, 1979). For example, a child might be disruptive, attempt suicide, or be overly compliant. Maltreated children also are often retarded in social development (Crittenden, 1989), at times manifesting social interaction problems and affective expressive and recognition skills (Azar, Breton, & Miller, 1998).

Many studies have sought to determine the long-term effects of abuse. The findings, in many ways, parallel those of short-term impact. The long-term outcomes include impaired functioning in the emotional, physical, and social domains. After reviewing clinical literature, Vevier and Tharinger (1986) identified four consistent sequelae of child sexual abuse. These consist of a lack of trust, low self-esteem, feelings of helplessness and depression, and self-destructive behavior. Finklehor et al. (1986) pointed out that long-term effects have been found even among survivors who were not seeking help, although many other studies found no differences between nonabused individuals and those abused individuals who had not sought therapy. They conclude that the long-term effects may be more subtle than the immediate impact.

## THEORIES REGARDING THE CAUSES OF MALTREATMENT

There are three approaches to understanding why people maltreat children. These consist of a focus on the abuser, the family, and the larger context of the community and culture (cf. Milner & Dopke, 1997).

### Factors Within the Child Abuser

Research focusing on abusers document that they tend to be a heterogeneous group. Investigators have paid particular attention to physical abusers. Although some studies have found no differences in personality functioning of abusers and nonabusers (Gaines, Sandgrund, Green, & Power, 1978; Milner & Wimberly, 1980; Spinetta, 1978; Starr, 1982; Wright, 1976), others have found explicit personality characteristics. Some of these include a history of low-frustration tolerance, nonempathetic relationships, unmet dependency needs, power–authoritarianism problems, low self-esteem, depressed emotions, learned helplessness, and an adverse and traumatic experience (Smith, 1984). Main and Goldwyn (1984) described the characteristics of abusers as controlling aggression differently and less effectively than others, tending to isolate themselves, and being unsympathetic to distress in others (see also Frodi & Lamb, 1980).

Other researchers have focused on cognitive characteristics rather than personality traits. They identify abusers as having unusually high expectations for children, distorted perceptions of a child's behavior (i.e., views behavior as a problem when others see behavior as acceptable, or makes internal and stable attributions of misbehavior), and a lack of awareness of children's needs (Larrance & Twentyman, 1983; Mash, Johnson, & Kovitz, 1983; Spinetta & Rigler, 1972; Steele & Pollock, 1968). Similarly, maltreating parents may fail to recognize improvements in a child's behavior and thus fail to modify their own punitive behavior (Bell & Harper, 1977; Egeland & Sroufe, 1981). This body of research on abusers has emanated from the perspective that there is some personality or characterological flaw in abusers (Melnick & Hurley, 1969; Steele & Pollock, 1968) that leads to maltreatment. On-going ecological factors are secondary to the individual's cognitive, affective, motivational, and behavioral factors.

Research from this perspective has been criticized on two grounds. First, although significant differences may appear in studies, findings reveal that only about 5% of abusers show signs of significant observable disorders (Friedman, Sandler, Hernandez, & Wolfe, 1981; Kempe, 1973; Spinetta & Rigler, 1972; Starr, 1979). Second, this research approach, which emphasizes the individual, undermines efforts directed at the family and community (Garbarino, 1982; Ross & Zigler, 1980).

### Factors Within the Family

As an alternative, many experts view maltreatment as a result of family dysfunction, for example, from the interaction between the level of parental competence and the demands of a situation. Belsky (1984) focused on the interaction among the personal psychological resources of the parents, characteristics of the child, and the contextual sources of stress and support. Parents not skilled in dealing with developmental characteristics associated with a young child or adolescent may experience greater stress than skilled parents.

Other research has focused on the influence of the child's behavior on the behavior of adults. Although two studies found no difference in the behavior of abused and nonabused children, several other studies found that abused children were more disruptive than those children in families without such problems (Bonsha & Twentyman, 1984; Lahey, Conger, Atkeson, & Treiber, 1984; Lorber, Felton, & Reid, 1984; Wolfe & Mosk, 1983).

It should be noted that some investigators have differentiated abusing from neglecting parents. It may be that specific child behaviors are important contributors to parental behavior in abusing families, but not in neglecting families. Rather, neglecting parents tend to be coping inadequately, failing to assume basic responsibilities and to meet their own emotional needs (Aragona & Eyberg, 1981; Gaines et al., 1978; Herenkohl, Herenkohl, & Egolf, 1983). Although neglecting parents interacted less frequently with their family than did abusers (Bonsha & Twentyman, 1984), the two groups did not differ with respect to either their child-rearing knowledge (Larrance & Twentyman, 1983; Spinetta, 1978) or the aversiveness of their interactions—aversiveness was highly prevalent in both groups (Burgess & Conger, 1978).

In addition to personal psychological resources of parents and characteristics of children, sources of stress within the family system has been identified as related to the incidence of abuse. Some of the endogenous factors include: (a) the presence of multiple problems without accompanying coping skills; (b) characteristics of enmeshed families, or where there is a great dependence on family relationships yet little support within the family; (c) individuals who are disengaged from family responsibilities; (d) power that is centered in one adult only, typically the male; and (e) marital stress (Emery, 1982; Straus, 1980). There sometimes appears to be a pattern of escalating power and coercion (Burgess & Richardson, 1984; Patterson, 1982; Reid, Taplin, & Lorber, 1981) or inappropriate disciplinary techniques (ineffective contingencies and consistencies) that eventuate in harm to the child (Kelly, 1983; Wolfe & Sandler, 1981). Wolfe (1985) concluded that abusive mothers and abused children seem to interact in a fashion that actively maintains aversive behavior.

In addition to factors within the family, exogenous factors that increase family stress might also contribute to the incidence of maltreatment. These factors include poverty, blue-collar (vs. white-collar) employment, unemployment (Gelles & Straus, 1979; Straus, 1980), and change in residence, income, or work schedules (Justice & Duncan, 1976). However, some researchers suggest that abusers may not be subjected to significantly more economic disadvantage than nonabusers (Gaines et al., 1978; Starr, 1982), but that any such disadvantage is perceived as more unpleasant and debilitating (Conger, Burgess, & Barrett, 1979; Mash et al., 1983; Rosenberg & Reppucci, 1983). Similarly, abusers may not have fewer social supports available, but may more typically fail to use these supports (Garbarino, 1976, 1982). Thus, maltreatment may not spring from a psychological disorder or an unusually stressful environment, but an interaction of psychological functioning and coping skills with stressful life events.

### Factors Within the Context of the Community and Culture

Whereas Garbarino (Garbarino & Vondra, 1983), for example, views economic stress and social isolation within the community as being associated with maltreatment, others have focused on more pervasive aspects of the culture, attempting to identify factors that lead to a greater number of individuals at risk to be perpetrators of maltreatment. Some of these community–cultural factors include:

1. The cultural endorsement of domestic violence and corporal punishment, for example, spanking and demeaning children are viewed as an acceptable way to enhance character and promote learning (Hyman, 1983);
2. Socialization of men to view sex as gratification only, to objectify sexual partners, to see partners inferior in size and age, and to be dominant in sex (Finkelor, 1984);
3. Institutional (e.g., schools) disrespect for culture, lifestyle, language, and cognitive style (Hyman & Snook, 1999; Jones & Jones, 1983).

Gil (1971, 1983), for example, identified a number of realities of the current socioeconomic–political system as leading to maltreatment. He believes maltreatment results from a failure to meet an adult's developmental needs. When certain individuals are necessarily excluded from a basic standard of living, or from making meaningful economic contributions through their work, maltreatment is inevitable. Any economic–political system based on inequality, such as patriarchy, slavery, feudalism, capitalism, imperialism, or totalitarianism, will lead to a significant portion of the population with unmet developmental needs. Therefore, such societies would be likely to have a high prevalence of maltreatment. Similarly, any society where children are viewed as parental property, and do not possess fundamental human rights, is guaranteed to have significant levels of maltreatment. Any culture where force and coercion are viewed as a legitimate means to an end is guaranteed to have significant maltreatment. These conditions create a large number of families with high levels of stress, and individuals who have learned to use violence as a coping strategy.

## INDIVIDUALS AT RISK FOR ENCOUNTERING MALTREATMENT

As in many other areas of study, determination of risk levels rests with statistically significant correlations between demographic or other descriptive variables and the behavior one is trying to predict. Given the data presently available, the following characteristics are associated with a higher incidence of maltreatment: poverty, blue-collar (vs. white-collar) employment, unemployment, single parent families (U.S. Department of Health and Human Services, 2000), large families (U.S. Department of Health and Human Services, 2000), families where parents experienced violence as a child

(Gelles & Straus, 1979), families going through acute periods of change (e.g., residence, income, composition, work schedules, health, marital relations; Justice & Duncan, 1976), and families who are more punishing and less supportive (Garbarino, Sebes, & Schellenbach, 1984) and low-income families (U.S. Department of Health and Human Services, 2000).

The purpose of determining risk levels is typically to provide differential treatment to those at risk. This might involve anything from closer monitoring of behavior to specially designed programs. The question, then, is not whether there is a statistically significant correlation, but whether the data just cited lend themselves to dichotomizing populations (i.e., classifying children as at risk, or not at risk) and providing differential treatment. Often, they do not. For example, for unemployed individuals the incidence of physical abuse is 22% as compared to 14% for employed individuals (Gelles & Straus, 1979). If one were to monitor children of unemployed parents, there would be little improvement over a random selection procedure, and much to be lost with the maltreated children of employed individuals. Even an equation adding together multiple factors in order to predict level of risk may not be useful with the present data. In a test for predicting abusive behavior using several different estimators, the majority of subjects earning scores above the cutoff (predicting abuse) did not abuse (Milner, Gold, Ayoub, & Jacewitz, 1984). Also, when considering psychological, and not just physical and sexual maltreatment, virtually all children are at risk of being abused.

## Special Populations

However, there are three groups of children that can be considered at risk and helped by differential service. The first are children whose families are experiencing significant stress, under conditions of isolation from social support networks and a deficit in coping skills.

The second are children who have been maltreated previously. It is fairly clear that when the perpetrator has not received significant help, and is still in contact with the child, or where other family members are likely to respond to the still-high level of stress, maltreatment is likely to recur. Of reported maltreatment cases, only 6% involve a single incident; 94% involve multiple incidents of maltreatment before detection (Gelles & Straus, 1979). Although there are some children that may be monitored more closely than others, it is still more appropriate to consider all children at risk when it comes to designing school based prevention activities.

Disabled children are a third group at risk. They are particularly vulnerable because of their disability, lack of ability to communicate, child behavior, the stress on their caregivers, other caregiver behaviors, such as substance abuse, parental attachment difficulties, and parental isolation

(Botash & Church, 1999). Teachers working with this population should be particularly targeted for training in identification and reporting of suspected abuse.

### Mitigating Factors

Webster and Browning (in press) pointed out six factors that can lessen the impact of maltreatment. First is the age of the child and the relationship to caregivers. Second is the severity and type of abuse, with long-term damage being more harmful. The third factor is the closeness of the relationship with the perpetrator and the forth is the duration of the maltreatment. Also important are the emotional climate and reactions of family members, and the child's mental health and resiliency. Depending on these factors, maltreatment may result in long-term and severe mental disorders, or may be coped with successfully.

## PRIMARY PREVENTION ACTIVITIES

### Individuals

***Adults.*** Adults need to be given training in parenting skills, dealing with emotions (particularly anger), differentiating appropriate from inappropriate methods of disciplining, developing social skills, and developing supports to deal with life stress (Forehand & McMahon 1981; Wolfe & Sandler, 1981). Jaffe, Thompson, and Wolfe (1984) suggested focusing on the dysfunctional family, reducing their distress.

***Children.*** School-based programs have been created to educate children about abuse, teaching them to avoid situations where they may be subject to abuse, and how to take action in an abusive situation. Children need information on what is acceptable caregiver behavior. For example, they need to know what differentiates appropriate from inappropriate touch (Brassard, Tyler, & Kehle, 1983), and appropriate from inappropriate physical and psychological treatment. At the completion of a successful program a child will be able to identify behavior as maltreatment, and will therefore be less likely to see it as legitimate and deserved, and be more likely to take action to put an end to it (Tower, 1999).

Some primary prevention activities aimed at children run the risk of seeming to "blame the victim." Although some theories presented earlier identify child characteristics that may positively correlate with incidence of maltreatment, it is nevertheless reasonable to conclude that children are not responsible for maltreatment. Programs also must take care not to frighten children unnecessarily about the potential to get hurt in the world. However, all children can be helped to identify some behaviors of maltreatment and to learn how to seek assistance.

***Teens.*** High-school parent education courses or child development courses may also be effective preventive programs. Young mothers are particularly vulnerable to becoming abusers and they can be helped with knowledge of effective child-rearing practices and with anger and stress management.

### Institutions

Garbarino (1982) argued that efforts at levels less broad than the society and culture can be effective. Efforts aimed at legal, educational, and community in situations will have important payoffs.

***Educational.*** Because the school is the one system, other than family, to which all children belong, schools can take a leadership role in the identification, prevention, and treatment of maltreatment. In the most recent national survey (NIS-3), school staff were responsible for nearly 60% of the children identified as maltreated (U.S. Department of Health and Human Services, 1996) and there is encouraging evidence more children are being reported. School psychologists can provide education about maltreatment and reporting laws to school staff, as well as provide consultation when staff or parents want to talk about their observations or experiences with certain children.

As mentioned earlier it seems plausible that courses in family planning, family life education, child development, and lifelong coping skills would prevent some stressors and provide some skills for parents and thus reduce the incidence of maltreatment. To date, no direct evidence exists as to the long-term outcomes of such educational programs.

***Legal.*** In balancing the rights of parents and schools with the rights of children, the basic constitutional rights of children have been curtailed. A number of existing statutes related to punishment of children, medical treatment of children, and legal rights of children, both reflect and create attitudes toward children that encourage maltreatment. For example, many rights, such as "privileged communication" relate only to adults unless specifically designated as applicable to children. Many states do not have such a designation. The creation of laws that respect the rights of children could be an important part of primary prevention.

***Communities.*** A neighborhood-based national health service would reduce one aspect of family stress. Within communities, there needs to be publicized means of obtaining help for a wide variety of problems. Collaborative efforts among social agencies, church groups, industry, and schools could more effectively safeguard the well being of individuals (Garbarino & Vondra, 1983).

### Society and Culture

Gil (1971, 1983) and Giovannoni (1971) believe that without a substantial change in our socioeconomic–political system, there will always be maltreatment. Therefore, any primary prevention activity aimed at individuals or families will fail to prevent maltreatment totally unless and until substantial sociocultural changes are made. Specifically, Gil maintains that we must put and end to poverty, change to an egalitarian and cooperative society, make work a meaningful experience, and change our culture to one where children are highly valued and violence and coercion are seen as illegitimate. School personnel must continue to work for changes in societal conditions that create a world that is safe for children.

Other cultures may have other child disciplinary practices and attitudes toward sexuality than do members of the dominant culture in the United States. Care must be taken in evaluating what appears to be maltreatment and consider how the child perceives the act in his or her cultural context. Nevertheless, we must expect those living in the West to abide by the law and become acculturated in their treatment of children. Cultural informants may help in the identification of abuse, but school-based professionals are bound by reporting laws.

## WORKING WITH CLIENTS AT RISK

For the purpose of this section, *adults at risk* are defined as those individuals who are going through significant stress in their lives or who have committed acts of maltreatment previously. Because any child might come into contact with potentially maltreating caregivers in family, educational, or recreational settings, *children at risk* are defined as all children.

### Parents and Other Caregivers

The main purpose of intervention with parents and other caregivers is to decrease the likelihood of them maltreating children. As part of this goal, the purpose would be to increase their self-esteem or ego strength, and thus decrease the likelihood of impulsive acting-out behavior when frustrated. A social worker, or some other mental health professional, can provide a variety of services in this regard. Such services include an evaluation of the safety of the home, intervention with and support of parents, and provision of on-going family treatment. To relieve family stress, community services such as daycare, homemaker services, home helpers, and respite care could be effective.

School professionals can play an important role in decreasing the likelihood of psychological maltreatment and corporal punishment occurring in schools. For example, they can provide emotional support for teachers and help them with classroom management and advocate for policies and procedures that reduce teacher stress. For example, an uncomfortable physical environment, inappropriate class size, and limited discipline options, might be factors that could be changed to reduce stress.

For both parents and teachers, the development of empathy, behavior management skills, and skills for coping with life stress are likely to be crucial in reducing the incidence of maltreatment. School psychologists or other school personnel can play important roles in direct and indirect service to teachers and parents. School psychologists and counselors educate these groups concerning what constitutes maltreatment, when to suspect it, and how to report it (which may include contacting professionals such as the school psychologist).

## Children

Although our view is that all children are at risk, children who have been abused previously, children in highly stressed and dysfunctional families, and children with disabilities require some extra attention. Research on resiliency suggests that a child needs to have one positive, stable, intimate relationship with an adult in or outside of the family. With open lines of communication, it makes it more likely that the child will be willing to confront the feelings, beliefs, and behavior resulting from maltreatment, rather than accepting any intimidation or engaging in long-term repression, denial, guilt, and so forth. This relationship also would provide an all important positive model of a relationship in contrast to the one in which the maltreatment occurred. There is no reason to think that this positive, stable, intimate relationship could not be with an adult in the school or other agency. As part of providing for the psychological well-being of all children, a school or agency professional might have as a goal to insure that each vulnerable child has at least one such relationship. In summary, if a child has a positive self-concept, one positive relationship with a significant adult, and adequate information about appropriate and inappropriate treatment, should maltreatment occur, the child will be more likely to seek help, to seek the help more quickly, and to use the help more effectively.

## INTERVENING WITH ABUSED CHILDREN AND THEIR PARENTS

Although the purpose of this chapter is not to present an exhaustive review of services and programs, several programmatic interventions, dealing with treatment are available.

### Intervening With and on Behalf of Children

***Legal Interventions.*** Two of the principles of crisis counseling, mentioned by Sandoval (chapter 1) are to take action quickly and to be directive rather than having the client assume most or all of the responsibility. One of the most important ways to do this in dealing with a child who has been maltreated is to provide legal interventions.

There is a child protection unit in every county. If maltreatment is suspected, the school personnel should contact this agency, and then maintain a liaison with them if it is appropriate for the case. A child protective services worker can inspect the state child abuse registry to note any previously reported incidents. Every state has a mandatory reporting law for helping professionals when they suspect sexual or physical abuse. No state requires proof of maltreatment, just a statement about the condition of the child. Helping professionals have immunity from civil liability and criminal penalty as long as the report was made in good faith, even if maltreatment did not occur. On the other hand, there can be civil action brought against school personnel who knew of, but did not report abuse. For an extensive treatment of suspected child abuse reporting, see Kalichman (1999).

Although legal actions are important, they are often avoided or not fully implemented. Often state statutes do not define maltreatment effectively, and few have provisions for psychological maltreatment (Corson, 1983). Additionally, Berliner and Barbieri (1984) cited four reasons why it is difficult to prosecute cases of sexual assault against children, many of which apply to all forms of maltreatment: (a) adults are skeptical that the incident took place; (b) adults believe that perpetrators are mentally disturbed and are better handled by the mental health rather than the legal system; (c) adults believe children will be traumatized by the legal proceedings, adding to the damage done by the maltreatment itself; and (d) prosecutors fear that the child will not perform adequately as a witness.

***Identification and Diagnosis.*** School personnel can help, and must legally help, by identifying children who have been abused. Through observation of the behavior of all children, certain children will come to the attention of school staff. For many children, direct questioning may elicit a direct and honest answer. Often, children are relieved to share their "secret" with someone they trust. With adolescents, one may ask, "Have you or anyone in your family ever been sexually molested? (or been physically hurt by another person)." Simpler questions may be asked of younger children, such as "How do people in your family give hugs to show love?" or "If someone in your family is angry at someone else, what do they do?" Sometimes a child gives verbal cues such as, "I don't want to be alone with ______."

For a young child, play techniques, such as general dollhouse play, may serve as both a diagnostic and therapeutic technique. Often, there are clues in other projective techniques, such as drawings of family or self (Sgroi, Porter, & Black, 1982). In order to identify victims, one possibility is to have self-identification through drop-in center. However, although drop-in centers work well for children who feel comfortable with the setting and personnel, not every maltreated child will "drop-in." Therefore, an outreach program should be developed as well.

***Individual Counseling.*** In the absence of psychological support, the child's most likely adjustment, that of accommodation to the maltreatment, may be to develop chronically low self-esteem. Therefore, some form of counseling is imperative. When a maltreated child is identified, an interview with the child should take place in a private setting. The reasons for this should be explained to child. Counseling should be an on-going process from the point at which the child is identified as having been maltreated. Germain, Brassard, and Hart (1985) and Webster and Browning (in press) have identified a number of strategies in counseling:

1. *Ventilation and clarification of feelings.* Survivors typically need consistent and substantial compassion and nurturance, in addition to help in labeling the various reactions to their experience.

2. *Repeated replaying of experience through verbal means, role plays, or puppets.* Often there is a need for a repetitive recounting of events in order to make sense of what occurred.

3. *Anticipatory guidance.* Victims need to have developmentally appropriate information about what will happen next. They need to know about the reporting process, the legal process, and medical interventions.

4. *Strategies for dealing with the potential of continued maltreatment.* Because of problems with the legal and social systems and the protection of the rights of parents, often a child who has been maltreated will be given no protection in the home; that is, the perpetrator will still be in the home with the child. When maltreatment is possibly going to reoccur, the goal is for the child to keep a vigilant awareness of the possibility of threats rather than

dealing with this possibility by avoidance, denial, or anxious preoccupation of pending disaster. Vigilant awareness would involve the child determining the warning cues (e.g., verbal and nonverbal behavior prior to more escalated maltreatment, alcohol consumption), and selecting among alternative strategies when warning cues are present (e.g., leaving the situation, calling a specific person for help).

5. *Cognitive and emotional re-appraisal of the experience.* Often, even when they know about the maltreatment, peers and significant others in the child's life err in one of two ways. They urge the child to forget it all and "return to normal" or they never facilitate the child's acceptance that the experience occurred and the need to move on.

Cognitive restructuring, involving the ideas presented here, and emotional re-working, through techniques such as systematic desensitization, are seen as crucial in facilitating the child's acceptance of the experience. There are five issues in the cognitive restructuring of individuals who have been maltreated, issues that are assumed to be crucial in minimizing the impact of maltreatment:

1. You are not responsible for the family break-up; the perpetrator is. Not all cases of maltreatment lead to break-up of the family, but many do. Very often, the victims see themselves as the betrayer of the family, because it is their actions that may have immediately precipitated the break-up of the family.

2. You did nothing wrong; you are not to blame. Children often believe that they are responsible for the maltreatment, that they behaved badly and deserve the maltreatment. They need to be told that the perpetrator's behavior was inappropriate and be told why it was inappropriate.

3. You are not the only one to whom this has happened. Children may feel alone, different, and isolated, and as a result be unsure about whether their peers would ever accept them. Realizing that they are one of many children to whom this happens can help them feel less "different."

4. You have another person to care about you. In view of the loss of trust in a significant other, the child especially needs to feel protected from maltreatment in other settings, such as school. It therefore can be important for some professional in the school to take responsibility for being this child's "significant other."

5. The perpetrator's behavior was inappropriate, but the person may still love you. This is probably the most complex aspect of the counseling; these are two feelings that are very difficult to reconcile. But it is important to recognize that even parents who maltreat are vitally important to their children.

***Group Counseling.*** Groups can be particularly important for the maltreated child of elementary school age or beyond. A group can help a child realize:

1. "I am not alone";
2. "Someone really understands what it feels like, because they've been through it, too";
3. "Maybe it's not my fault, because other good kids have been abused";
4. "I can work out my problem individually, with the support of others"; and
5. "If others can survive the experience effectively, so can I."

Several different kinds of group approaches have been used with abuse victims: Stress management training, interventions dealing with posttraumatic stress symptoms, social skills, and anger control training (Azar et al., 1998).

There are community-based support groups for abused adolescents that have been established in many communities. For example, "Sons and Daughters United," for incest victims, uses group techniques to decrease social isolation, and to reestablish self-control and self-respect (Giaretto, 1981). School psychologists with appropriate training can start or help facilitate the starting of such groups.

### Intervening With Abusers

For the purpose of this section, it is assumed that it is the parents who are suspected of having maltreated the child. Perhaps during a parent conference a school psychologist crystallizes a suspicion that a child has been maltreated. Under these circumstances, it might be helpful, in a private setting, to inform parents about the report and your legal responsibility, and not try to "prove abuse" (Broadhurst, 1979).

At times, the issue of whether the client is the child or the parent arises. For school-based professionals, the primary consideration is what is in the best interest of the child. A secondary consideration would be to provide therapeutic processes rather than punishment for the perpetrators. In this regard, Kempe and Kempe (1978) estimated that only 10% to 20% of the families who abuse are beyond the conventional rehabilitation and treatment models. These are parents who cannot or will not provide adequate care for children. In these instances, in the best interest of the child, immediate action to terminate parental rights should be started. However, for the other 80% to 90%, alternative programs may be warranted.

When maltreatment is discovered, generally a bad family situation is exacerbated. As a result of the identification and investigation of maltreatment, often, there are severe negative consequences for the victim as well as the offender and rest of the family. There may be job loss with accompanying economic pressures, marital or family separation, and there may be a loss of whatever social support had been available from friends of the family. Diversion of court-ordered therapy programs, rather than imprisonment, would allow for a possibly lower recidivism rate, avoidance of welfare, less reliance on foster care, and would possibly keep the family intact (Tyler & Brassard, 1984).

Taking an ecological perspective, Guterman (1997) suggested the following practice principles: (a) Targeting the context in which maltreatment occurs. Focus on what in the environment maintains maltreatment. (b) Develop neighborhood and community structures that proactively support parents in child rearing. (c) Provide interventions to help parents cope with burdensome stressors, and (d) Develop economic, political, and cultural structures that nurture the abilities of local communities to sustain families.

### *Parenting Skills*

Parents who have maltreated may need help in acquiring appropriate developmental expectations, skills in empathy, skills in dealing with anger, frustration, and dependency, and strategies for alternative disciplinary techniques. Community resources can be mobilized for parents in order to decrease their stress. Parents can be helped through agencies that provide group treatment by and for child abusers, for example "Parents United" or "Parents Anonymous." This not only provides a parent with models of other individuals who have overcome acting abusively, but also with a much-needed social support network.

***Family Preservation.*** Because there are not sufficient placements for children removed from the home, there has been a move to create more in-home and family-focused models of service. Nelson, Landsman, and Deutelbaum (1990) reviewed three programs providing service to the entire family, using a short-term intervention of 6 months or less, using well-trained caseworkers with small caseloads. Often the caseworker is available around the clock for the first month and has daily contact with families assisting them with behaviorally based parenting skills. Overall, these programs are more successful with abusive families than with neglectful ones (Guterman, 1997).

## CONCLUSION

Helping professionals have a vital role to play in the identification of maltreated students, and in working with them, their parents, the community, and the society as a whole. The school often is cited as an institution that has the potential for great impact in the area of maltreatment. Garbarino (1976, 1982) believes that the school must serve not only as an academic specialist, but also as a community support system. Schools can help in the identification of maltreated children, provide support, refer to appropriate agencies, and assist children and the foster or adoptive parents. School personnel can help in the provision of a stable, nurturing, interpersonal relationship. There needs to be an active policy and program to assess the quality of life for the school's families, in cooperation with other agencies. Schools need to join with other agencies in helping parents deal with the stresses of everyday life, and school professionals can stimulate the community to assume this responsibility as well.

## NOTE

A particularly useful resource on up-to-date information on this topic is The National Clearinghouse on Child Abuse and Neglect Information website: *http://www.calib.com/nccanch/index.htm.*

## REFERENCES


Adams-Tucker, C. (1981). A sociological overview of 28 abused children. *Child Abuse and Neglect, 5*, 361–367.

Anderson, S. C., Bach, C. M., & Griffith, S. (1981, August). *Psychosocial sequelae in intrafamilial victims of sexual assault and abuse.* Paper presented at the Third International Conference on Child Abuse and Neglect, Amsterdam, The Netherlands.

Aragona, J. A., & Eyberg, S. M. (1981). Neglected children: Mothers' report of child behavior problems and observed verbal behavior. *Child Development, 52*, 596–602.

Azar, S. T., Breton, S. J., & Miller, L. R. (1998). Cognitive-behavioral group work and physical child abuse: Intervention and prevention. In K. C. Stoiber & T. R. Kratochwill (Eds.), *Handbook of group intervention for children and families* (pp. 376–400). Boston: Allyn & Bacon.

Bell, R. Q., & Harper, L. (1977). *Child effects on adults.* Hillsdale, NJ: Lawrence Erlbaum Associates.

Belsky, J. (1984). The determinants of parenting: A process model. *Child Development, 55*, 83–96.

Berliner, L., & Barbieri, M. K. (1984). The testimony of the child victim of sexual assault. *Journal of Social Issues, 40*, 125–137.

Bonsha, D. M., & Twentyman, C. T. (1984). Mother–child interactional style in abuse, neglect, and control groups: Naturalistic observations in the home. *Journal of Abnormal Psychology, 93*, 106–114.

Botash, A. S., & Church, C. C. (1999). Child abuse and disabilities: A medical perspective. *American Professional Society on the Abuse of Children Advisor, 12*(1), 10–13, 18.

Brassard, M. R., Tyler, A. H., & Kehle, T. J. (1983). School programs to prevent intrafamilial child sexual abuse. *Child Abuse and Neglect, 7*, 241–245.

Broadhurst, D. (1979). *The educator's role in the prevention and treatment of child abuse and neglect* (DHEW Publication No OHDS 79-30172) Washington, DC: DHEW.

Browning, D. H., & Boatman, B. (1977). Incest: Children at risk. *American Journal of Psychiatry, 134*, 69–72.

Burgess, A. W., & Holstrom, L. L. (1978). Accessory to sex: Pressure, sex, and secrecy. In A. W. Burgess, A. N. Groth, L. L. Holstrom, & S. M. Sgroi (Eds.), *Sexual assault of children and adolescents* (pp. 85–98). Lexington, MA: Lexington Books.

Burgess, R. L., & Conger, R. (1978). Family interactions in abusive, neglectful, and normal families. *Child Development, 49,* 1163–1173.

Burgess, R. L., & Richardson, R. A. (1984). Coercive interpersonal contingencies as determinants of child abuse: Implications for treatment and prevention. In R. F. Dangel & R. A. Polster (Eds.), *Behavioral parent training: Issues in research and practice* (pp. 239–259). New York: Guilford Press.

*Child Abuse Prevention and Treatment Act* (P.L. 93-247), 42 USC 5101 et seq; 42 USC 5116 et seq.

Conger, R., Burgess, R., & Barrett, C. (1979). Child abuse related to life change and perceptions of illness: Some preliminary findings. *Family Coordinator, 28,* 73–78.

Corson, J. (1983, August). *A survey of the states' statutes: Do they include "emotional abuse" in their definitions of child abuse and/or neglect?* Paper presented at the International Conference on Psychological Abuse of Children and Youth. University of Indiana, Indianapolis, Indiana.

Crittenden, P. M. (1989). Teaching maltreated children in the preschool. *Topics in Early Childhood Special Education, 9,* 16–32.

Egeland, B., Jacobvitz, D., & Papatola, K. (1987). Intergenerational continuity of parental abuse. In J. Lancaster & J. R. Gelles (Eds.), *Biosocial aspects of child abuse* (pp. 255–278). San Francisco: Jossey-Bass.

Egeland, B., & Sroufe, L. A. (1981). Attachment and early maltreatment. *Child Development, 52,* 44–52.

Emery, R. E. (1982). Interparental conflict and the children of discord and divorce. *Psychological Bulletin, 92,* 310–330.

Faller, K. (Ed.). (1981). *Social work with abused and neglected children.* New York: The Free Press.

Finklehor, D. (1984). *Child sexual abuse: New theory and research.* New York: The Free Press.

Finklehor, D., Araji, S, Baron, S. Browne, L. Peters, A., Doyle, S., & Wyatt, G. E. (Eds). (1986). *Sourcebook on child sexual abuse.* Newbury Park, CA: Sage.

Forehand, R. L., & McMahon, R. J. (1981). *Helping the noncompliant child: A clinician's guide to parent training.* New York: Guilford Press.

Friedman, R., Sandler, J., Hernandez, M., & Wolfe, D. (1981). Child abuse. In E. Mash & L. Terdal (Eds.), *Behavior assessment of childhood disorders* (pp. 221–255). New York: Guilford Press.

Frodi, A. M., & Lamb, M. E. (1980). Child abusers' responses to infant smiles and cries. *Child Development, 51,* 238–241.

Gaines, R., Sandgrund, A., Green, A. H., & Power, E. (1978). Etiological factors in child maltreatment: A multivariate study of abusing, neglecting, and normal mothers. *Journal of Abnormal Psychology, 87,* 531–540.

Garbarino, J. (1976). The family: A school for living. *National Elementary Principal, 55,* 66–70.

Garbarino, J. (1982). *Children and families in the social environment.* Hawthorne, NY: Aldine.

Garbarino, J., Sebes, J., & Schellenbach, C. (1984). Families at risk for destructive parent–child relations in adolescence. *Child Development, 55,* 174–183.

Garbarino J., & Vondra, J. (1983, August). *Psychological maltreatment of children and youth.* Paper presented at the International Conference on Psychological Abuse of Children and Youth, University of Indiana, Indianapolis, Indiana.

Gelles, R. J., & Straus, M. A. (1979). Violence in the American family. *Journal of Social Issues, 35,* 15–39.

Germain, R. B., Brassard, M. R., & Hart, S. N. (1985). Crisis intervention for maltreated children. *School Psychology Review,* 14, 291–299.

Giaretto, H. (1981). A comprehensive child sexual abuse treatment program. In P. B. Mrazek & C. H. Kempe (Eds.), *Sexually abused children and their families* (pp. 179–189). New York: Pergamon Press.

Gil, D. G. (1971), A sociocultural perspective on physical child abuse. *Child Welfare, 50,* 380–395.

Gil D. G. (1983, August). *Institutional abuse: Dynamics and prevention.* Paper presented at the International Conference on Psychological Abuse of Children and Youth. University of Indiana, Indianapolis, Indiana.

Giovannoni, J. M. (1971). Parental mistreatment: Perpetrators and victims. *Journal of Marriage and the Family, 33*, 649–657.

Guterman, N. B. (1997). Parental violence towards children. In N. K. Phillips & S. L. A. Straussner (Eds.), *Children in the urban environment* (pp. 113–134). Springfield, IL: Thomas.

Herenkohl, R. C., Herenkohl, E. C., & Egolf, B. P. (1983). Circumstances surrounding the occurrence of child maltreatment. *Journal of Consulting and Clinical Psychology, 51*, 424–431.

Hyman, I. (1983, August). *Psychological correlates of corporal punishment and physical abuse.* Paper presented at the International Conference on the Psychological Abuse of Children and Youth, University of Indiana, Indianapolis, Indiana.

Hyman, I., & Snook, P. (1999). *Dangerous schools: What we can do about the physical and emotional abuse of our children.* San Francisco: Jossey-Bass.

Jaffe, P., Thompson, J., & Wolfe, D. A. (1984). Evaluating the impact of a specialized civilian family crisis unit within a police force on the resolution of family conflict. *Journal of Preventive Psychiatry, 2*, 63–69.

James, B. (1994). *Handbook for treatment of attachment-trauma problems in childhood.* New York: Lexington.

Jones, R., & Jones, J. (1983, August). *Institutional abuse.* Paper presented at the International Conference on the Psychological Abuse of Children and Youth, University of Indiana, Indianapolis, Indiana.

Justice, B., & Duncan, D. F. (1976). Life crisis as a precursor to child abuse. *Public Health Reports, 91*, 110–115.

Justice, B., & Justice, R. (1979). *The broken taboo.* New York: Human Sciences Press.

Kadushin, A., & Martin, J. (1981). *Child abuse: An interactional event.* New York: Columbia University Press.

Kalichman, S. C. (1999). Mandated reporting of suspected child abuse: Ethics, law, and policy (2nd ed.). Washington, DC: American Psychological Association.

Kaufman, J., & Ziegler, E. (1987). Do abused children become abusive parents? *American Journal of Orthopsychiatry, 57*, 186–192.

Kelly, J. A. (1983). *Training child abusive families: Intervention based on skills training principles.* New York: Plenum.

Kempe, C. H. (1973). A practical approach to the protection of the abused child and the rehabilitation of the abusing parent. *Pediatrics, 51*, 804–812.

Kempe, R. S., & Kempe, C. H. (1978). *Child abuse.* Cambridge, MA: Harvard University Press.

Lahey, B. B., Conger, R. D., Atkeson, B. M., & Treiber, F. A. (1984). Parenting behavior and emotional status of physically abusive mothers. *Journal of Consulting and Clinical Psychology, 52*, 1062–1071.

Larrance, D. T., & Twentyman, C. T. (1983). Maternal attributions and child abuse. *Journal of Abnormal Psychology, 92*, 449–457.

Lorber, R., Felton, D. K., & Reid, J. B. (1984). A social learning approach to the reduction of coercive processes in child abusive families: A molecular analysis. *Advances in Behavior Research and Therapy, 6*, 29–45.

Main, M., & Goldwyn, R. (1984). Predicting rejection of her infant from mother's representation of her own experience: Implications for the abused-abusing intergenerational cycle. *Child Abuse and Neglect, 8*, 203–217.

Mash, E. J., Johnston, C., & Kovitz, K. (1983). A comparison of the mother–child interactions of physically abused and non-abused children during play and task situations. *Journal of Clinical Child Psychology, 12*, 337–346.

Melnick, B., & Hurley, J. R. (1969). Distinctive personality attributes of child-abusing mothers. *Journal of Consulting and Clinical Psychology, 33*, 746–749.

Milner, J. S., & Dopke, C. (1997). Child physical abuse: Review of offender characteristics. In D. A. Wolfe & R. J. McMahon (Eds.), *Child abuse: New directions in prevention and treatment across the lifespan* (pp. 27–54). Thousand Oaks, CA: Sage.

Milner, J. S., Gold, R. G., Ayoub, C., & Jacewitz, M. M. (1984). Predictive validity of the Child Abuse Potential Inventory Journal of *Journal of Consulting and Clinical Psychology, 52,* 879–884.

Milner, J. S., & Wimberly, R. C. (1980). Prediction and explanation of child abuse. *Journal of Clinical Psychology, 35,* 875–884.

Nelson, K. E., Landsman, J. J., & Deutelbaum, W. (1990). Three models of family-centered placement preventive services. *Child Welfare, 69,* 3–21.

Patterson, G. R. (1982). *Coercive family processes.* Eugene, OR: Castilia.

Polansky, N. A. (1981). *Damaged parents: An anatomy of child neglect.* Chicago: University of Chicago Press.

Reid, J. B., Taplin, P. S., & Lorber, R. (1981). A social interactional approach to the treatment of abusive families. In R. B. Stuart (Ed.), *Violent behavior: Social learning approaches to prediction, management, and treatment* (pp. 83–101). New York: Bruner/Mazel.

Rosenberg, M. S., & Reppucci, N. D. (1983). Abusive mothers: Perceptions of their own children's behavior. *Journal of Consulting and Clinical Psychology, 51,* 674–682.

Rosenfeld, A., Nadelson, C., Krieger, M., & Backman, J. (1979). Incest and sexual abuse of children. *Journal of the American Academy of Child Psychiatry, 16,* 327–339.

Ross, C. J., & Zigler, E. (1980). An agenda for action. In G. Gerbner, C. J. Ross, & E. Zigler (Eds.), *Child abuse: An agenda for action* (pp. 293–304). New York: Oxford University Press.

Sgroi, S. M., Porter, F. S., & Black, L. C. (1982). Validation of child abuse. In S. M. Sgroi (Ed.), *Handbook of clinical intervention in child sexual abuse* (pp. 39–79). Lexington, MA: Heath.

Smith, S. L. (1984). Significant research findings in the etiology of child abuse. *Social casework. The Journal of Contemporary Social Work,* June, 337–346.

Spinetta, J. J. (1978). Parental personality factors in child abuse. *Journal of Consulting and Clinical Psychology, 46,* 1409–1414.

Spinetta, J. J., & Rigler, D. (1972). The child-abusing parent: A psychological review. *Psychological Bulletin, 77,* 296–304.

Starr, R. H., Jr. (1979). Child abuse. *American Psychologist, 34,* 872–878.

Starr, R. H., Jr. (1982). A research-based approach to the prediction of child abuse. In R. H. Starr, Jr. (Ed.), *Child abuse prediction: Policy implications* (pp. 105–134). Cambridge, MA: Ballinger.

Steele, B. F., & Pollock, C. (1968). A psychiatric study of parents who abuse infants and small children. In R. E. Helfer & C. Kempe (Eds.), *The battered child* (pp. 89–133). Chicago: University of Chicago Press.

Straus, M. A. (1980). Stress and child abuse. In C. H. Kempe & R. E. Helfer (Eds.), *The battered child* (3rd ed., pp. 86–102). Chicago: University of Chicago Press.

Terr, L. C. (1991). *Childhood traumas: An outline and overview. American Journal of Psychiatry, 148,* 10–20.

Toth, S. L., Manly, J. T., & Cicchetti, D. (1992). Child maltreatment and vulnerability to depression. *Development and Psychopathology, 4,* 97–112.

Tower, C. C. (1999). *Understanding child abuse and neglect.* Needham Heights, MA: Allyn & Bacon.

Tyler, A. H., & Brassard, M. R. (1984). Abuse in the investigation and treatment of intrafamilial child abuse. *Child Abuse and Neglect, 8,* 47–53.

U.S. Department of Health and Human Services. (1981). *National study of the incidence and severity of child abuse and neglect: Study findings.* Washington, DC: U.S. Government Printing Office.

U.S. Department of Health and Human Services. (1988). *Study findings: Study of national incidence and prevalence of child abuse and neglect: 1988.* Washington, DC: U.S. Government Printing Office.

U.S. Department of Health and Human Services. (2000). *Child maltreatment 1998: Reports from the states to the national child abuse and neglect data system.* Washington, DC: U.S. Government Printing Office.

Vevier, E., & Tharinger, D. J. (1986). Child sexual abuse: A review and intervention framework for the school psychologist. *Journal of School Psychology, 24*, 293–311.
Webster, L., & Browning, J. (in press). Child maltreatment. In S. E. Brock & P. J. Lazarus (Eds.), *Best practices in school crisis prevention and intervention*. Bethesda, MD: National Association of School Psychologists.
Weiss, M. D., Rogers, M. D., Darwin, M. R., & Dutton, C. E. (1955). A study of girl sex victims. *Psychiatric Quarterly, 29*, 1–27.
Wolfe, D. A. (1985). Abusive parents: An empirical review. *Psychological Bulletin, 97*, 462–482.
Wolfe, D. A., & Mosk, M. D. (1983). Behavioral comparisons of children from abusive and distressed families. *Journal of Consulting and Clinical Psychology, 51*, 702–708.
Wolfe, D. A., & Sandler, J. (1981). Training abusive parents in effective child management. *Behavior Modification, 5*, 320–335.
Wright, L. (1976). The "sick but slick" syndrome as a personality component of parents of battered children. *Journal of Clinical Psychology, 32*, 41–45.

CHAPTER

# 8

# Helping Children Cope With Death

Pamela Green Hawkins
Private practice, San Francisco and Corte Madera, CA

This chapter addresses the role of the school mental health professional when a child's life has been touched by death. Because of an increased interest in issues related to death and dying since the 1960s, there is now a greater understanding of the bereavement process in general. Much consideration has been given to the special needs and problems faced by children in mourning. Special attention to their conceptions of death and how they relate to the resolution of grief has provided both prevention and intervention strategies for a variety of circumstances. In addition, attention to the role of available support systems has suggested the potential significance of the social context of the school. An informed professional can effectively use the school environment to offer understanding, stability, and support to a child in mourning and can monitor and respond to the progress of the grieving process.

Although people have been going through the grieving process for thousands of years, special circumstances of our present culture place an extra burden on the resolution of the process. We are acutely aware of the high price in mental distress and illness paid by those individuals with unresolved grief. Numerous retrospective studies and many anecdotal records relate bereavement to various physical and psychological stresses and impairments. The empirical evidence suggests that increasingly people seek help with grieving and turn to mental health professionals. Whether because of the secularization of the age or the increased mobility of the population, people less often look to religious leaders or institutions for healing or to extended family for support and guidance. The sense of community—spiritual, secular, and familial—has diminished for the individual and family, for the adult and the child. Therefore, people turn more and more to health-care and social systems for assistance. As a primary caretaking institution, the school can offer significant predictability, stability, and guidance for many children and families, solely or in conjunction with other support systems.

Sadly, every child is vulnerable to the loss through death of someone close. It is not possible to predict which child will be faced with such a loss. Statistics are not available for the numbers of children who experience the loss of a mother, father, both parents, or a sibling. Nor are such figures available for the loss of extended family members, friends, teachers, or other significant people in a child's life. Nevertheless, because the worries and fears engendered by death are also stirred in the friends, classmates, families, and community members close to a mourning child, it is clear that a very large, undetermined group of individuals can be variously affected by a single death.

Bereavement is a very complex issue, and people experience and respond to death in predictable as well as idiosyncratic ways. Grieving children are especially at risk of being misunderstood or overlooked. In order to employ meaningful prevention strategies and to respond effectively with direct and institutional interventions, it is necessary to understand the tasks of the mourning process and how children respond to their understanding of death.

## Tasks of Mourning

An integral component of the study of death and dying is the nature of human attachments, both what they are and how they develop. Bowlby (1960), a British psychiatrist, has been a central figure in the development of attachment theory. His conceptualization of the human tendency to make strong emotional bonds credits a need for security and safety that develops early in life. These attachments are usually directed toward a small number of specific people and tend to last throughout most of the life cycle. The early availability of these attachment figures provides a foundation of basic trust (in the Eriksonian sense) and a source of strength from which to venture and explore the world outside the relationship (Erikson, 1950). The patterns established with these attachment figures provide a basis for relationships later in life. When the early attachment is disrupted or threatened or severed, the child's response is one of intense anxiety. The greater the attachment and the vulnerability without it, the greater the distress when it is threatened or lost. Others (notably Engel, 1961) have suggested that injury to affectional bonds is traumatic in a way similar to physical injuries and that comparable healing processes must follow both wounds. Healing requires attention, corrective action, and time. It follows that the mourning process—the adaptation to loss—is necessary to the restoration of the bonding process (Worden, 1991). When considered developmentally, it is essential that the entire process of mourning be completed before an individual can be free to re-attach and to continue growing. When the process is incomplete, future bonds will be anxiety-laden, tenuous, or nonexistent. At the same time, the grieving process is "work," and difficult work. Often, it cannot be accomplished alone and is left partially undone. It can be especially difficult for children.

A number of models have been proposed to describe the mourning process. Kubler-Ross (1969), Matz (1979), Bugen (1977), and Parkes (1972) have each used a succession of stages or emotions to define the process. Although conceptually helpful, these approaches do not translate clearly to individual bereavement. A more clinically useful conceptualization is that offered by Worden (1991).

Worden has postulated four tasks of mourning. The first task is to accept the reality of the loss, to face directly the reality that the person is dead, is gone and will not return. The initial response to death, even when it is expected, is centered on the sense that it has not happened. Denial can take many forms. It can be manifested in a belief that reunion is possible, if not in this life, then in an afterlife. Thus, the meaning of the loss can be dismissed through focusing on its reversibility or on reunification. The meaning can also be denied by dismissing the significance of the dead person. For example, "Oh, well, he wasn't such a good father anyway." Others minimize the loss by removing any tangible reminders of the person or will not tolerate mention of the person in their presence; the person no longer exists physically or psychologically. An opposite phenomenon, labeled *mummification* by psychiatrist Gorer (1965), denies the death by keeping the person alive through having the deceased's possessions ready and waiting for his or her return and more generally acting as if the deceased would reappear. Certainly, it is normal to wish for a reunion or that one had been misinformed about the death; however, if such spiritual, magical, or distorted responses are maintained, the bereaved will be unable to progress to the second stage of grieving.

The second task is to experience the pain of grief. If the emotional and behavioral pain is not acknowledged or experienced, it will be manifested through some physical symptom, aberrant thinking or behavior. Often, there is considerable tension between social norms and the nature of this task. There can be subtle and overt pressure not to feel and not to express the sadness, anguish, and pain following death. Often, people try to distract themselves or use thought censoring devices. Friends often act out this role for a mourner, either in the best interest of their friend or because they cannot tolerate such strong feelings. Some people focus only on positive feelings or memories and thereby both idealize the deceased and deny their negative or painful feelings. Although a temporary flight from the pain is normal, prolonged denial will be accompanied by psychological or behavioral maladaptations. The sooner the pain can be faced and felt, the sooner and more easily its effects can be worked through and movement can proceed to the next task.

Once the pain of the death has been experienced, it is possible to adjust to a new environment that does not include the deceased. This third task may mean learning to function more independently, or learning new skills, or otherwise coming to terms with living differently. Not adapting to the lost means remaining immobilized, helpless, withdrawing from the world and its requirements.

The final task of mourning is to withdraw emotional energy from the deceased and to reinvest it in another relationship. People are often troubled by the prospect of reinvolvement because they fear another loss and consider that the risk is too great. Others feel that attachment to a new person would be disloyal to the deceased, a betrayal, or somehow dishonor his or her memory. Thus, by not loving and by instead holding onto the past attachment rather than forming new ones, one does not complete the tasks of mourning.

There is no definitive measure of the end of mourning. Worden (1991) contends that it is reached when the tasks of mourning are accomplished and when the person is able to think of the deceased without pain. Although one can always expect a sense of sadness when thinking about the loss of a loved one, it is also expected that such thoughts will not have a wrenching quality and will not cause physical manifestations of anguish such as intense crying or stomach pains. At the same time, one will be able to reinvest emotions in present and future relationships without guilt or remorse and with an acknowledged awareness of the loss.

There has been considerable controversy throughout the years stemming from the psychoanalytic schools, as to whether children are capable of mourning. Working from the adult model of grieving are those (Wolfenstein, 1966) who contend that it is not possible to mourn without the complete identity formation that comes at the end of adolescence. On the other hand, others (Furman, 1974) believe that children can mourn at the age when object constancy is achieved: as early as 3 years of age. Bowlby (1960) cited mourning behaviors as early as 6 months of age. A third view (Worden, 1991) builds a model of mourning to conform to the cognitive development and understanding of the child. A child's ability to proceed through the grieving process is dependent on a number of factors. His or her response will vary according to developmental level because that will largely determine the conceptualization of death. It also will be affected by the relationship to the deceased and by the nature of the death. The structure and the stability of the family before and after the death will be significant determinants in the grieving process and its outcome.

Knowing how children conceive of death can help adults to understand their behavior and to respond in a supportive manner following the loss of a significant person. Most research on bereaved children accepts the theory that there are three stages to their understanding of death. These parallel Piaget's stages of cognitive development and focus on children's ability to grasp the concept that some things cannot be reversed. Their understanding of causality is also significant to their reaction to a death (Piaget & Inhelder, 1969). Empirical studies have examined the behavioral responses of infants following the death of a significant caretaker, usually the mother, and have demonstrated visible distress, considered by some to be mourning. However, in the current understanding of child development, children who are less than 18 to 24 months form intense subjective images of objects, not concepts. They do not fully understand that an object has no existence apart from their sensory perception (Flavell, 1977). Thus, although infants do respond to the absence of a caretaker, it does not follow that they comprehend death. Three to 5-year-olds tend to think that dead people live on "under changed circumstances" (Lonetto, 1980). Their reasoning includes four types of causality that are particularly relevant to understanding their concept of death. Their animistic thinking assumes that the whole world and everything in it is alive. Because inanimate objects can move, think, feel, and be at rest, it follows that people too are always alive. Death is likened to a deep sleep, a hibernation, loss of mobility, or departure. Children are concerned about the comfort and physical care of dead persons; they might be hungry, need a doctor, or some fresh air. Their magical thinking imparts a power to everyone and everything to command at will. This kind of causal thinking allows anything to happen—mountains open upon command, pears tell secrets, princes turn into frogs. Within this system, people can die because of another's wish and can return to life just as readily; just as the bite of an apple can induce sleep for 100 years, a kiss can revive one. Artificialistic thinking is the belief that things exist for people's convenience. Because toys can be fixed upon request, so, too can dead people. Finally, children of this age ascribe personal motives to certain events. Bad dreams are brought on by misbehavior; bad falls are brought on by eating too much candy; death can also be caused by wrong thoughts or deeds.

As a result of understanding death to be temporary, reversible, and caused magically, children at this stage tend to respond in varied, often contradictory and unpredictable ways. The dead person is missing, and when he or she does not return, not only are children hurt and angry at being abandoned, they are also anxious that others might abandon them. They are frequently convinced that some thought or action of their own caused the death and so experience tremendous guilt. This can also lead to fears that "bad" wishes or actions will be punished by the child's own death. Children at this stage of development, while they are frequently able to play happily, tend to experience brief, intense outbreaks of anxiety or distress.

From about age 6 to 8, children frequently conceive of death as a person (Lonetto, 1980). As a result, Death can be fought and mastered if one's magic is strong enough. Young and healthy people do not die; only the old and sick are too weak to hold off Death. Many fears are associated with the fate of the corpse, for the dead are still invested with the ability to see, hear, and receive messages, as well as to eat and breathe. Thus, many children worry about being trapped in coffins. They are fascinated by what happens to bodies after death and tend to be preoccupied with decomposition and decay.

During the years from 9 to 12 the earlier modes of causal thinking are being replaced by logical and naturalistic thinking. The child's objective observation of objects and events, their concrete physical and mechanistic operations and the laws governing them become the basis of their logic. By their observations they now know that plants, animals, and people are alive and that what lives also dies. Death is understood as final and irreversible. Nevertheless, it still has a capricious quality and is something they do not expect to happen to them until they are very old. If one is lucky, it is possible to escape death. Although children at this stage still mention external forces such as physical violence, disasters, or accidents as causes of death, they more frequently understand internal bodily causes. They list illness and old age, or give careful descriptions of the physiological details they have heard (Lonetto, 1980).

Anxieties related to separation and loss are still experienced in children at this stage. However, fears are not so much related to abandonment and retribution as they are to the physical consequences of death. Because thinking processes at the developmental level are concerned with physical causality and the laws of nature, many fears are focused on bodily mutilation, being buried alive, and on the physiological process of death. Limericks and rhymes about these processes ("the worms crawl in, the worms crawl out . . .") are perennial favorites of children at this age and may be understood as attempts to release anxieties. Another source of anxiety at this stage is the belief that life and death is a matter of luck. Death is capricious and can happen if you are unlucky. This is an age filled with superstitions to prevent such bad luck: holding one's breath passing a cemetery, not stepping on cracks in the sidewalk, knocking on wood. Because children can understand the irreversibility of death, they are able to consider possibilities after death. Beliefs about immortality and life after death and reincarnation become meaningful and can offer comfort. However, some children have difficulty reconciling the physiological aspects of death with religious teachings; if a body is in the grave forever, how can it go to Heaven (Grollman, 1976; Lonetto, 1980)?

During adolescence, children come to understand that death is not only final and irreversible, it is also both universal and personal. They are now capable of grasping, adopting, and formulating abstract conceptualizations. Concerns about life after death are no longer about the physical state of the body and whether it can be in the ground and in Heaven simultaneously, but rather focus on abstract theological beliefs or explanations. Rather than concrete and physical, death is remote and spiritual. It is inevitable, but not immediate. They are concerned with their present life and plans and deny the possibility that death could interfere with their fulfillment. Thus, with the comprehension of personal death comes an emotional and cognitive distancing that protects against the personal threat and anxiety. Their concerns are frequently about how others might respond. For example, they might attend to the appearance or the physical dignity of the dead person; they might glorify or idolize the event or the person when a peer dies (Grollman, 1976).

Thus, children's conceptions of death move from an initial understanding that is magical, reversible, and personified, which evokes fears of abandonment, personal responsibility, and guilt. The next state accepts the finality of death but attributes it to chance despite an increased awareness and understanding of the physical causes and effects of death. Finally, the adolescent is capable of comprehending personal death but distances the possibility, focusing instead on immediate life and aspirations. A child's particular concept of death is one of the major factors involved in his or her response to death. Another significant element is his or her relationship to the deceased.

## THE CHILD'S RELATIONSHIP WITH THE DECEASED

Among the most significant determinants of grief are the relationship between the mourner and the deceased, who the person was and the nature of their attachment. Certain relationships are especially significant to children. A child's dependent, vulnerable state necessarily means that the loss of caretaking people—whether parents, grandparents, or teachers—will have special weight and meanings. The loss of a sibling or a peer will have comparable noticeable effects. Moreover, the nature of the attachment has several relevant components.

The strength of the attachment is directly related to the intensity of the grief. The security of the attachment is a factor in the child's sense of continued well being and self-esteem. In addition, the degree of ambivalent feelings, the manner in which they were expressed or manifested, and the way they were handled will affect the grieving process.

## Death of a Parent

The death of a parent is one of the greatest catastrophes that can befall a child. It is a unique and shocking experience, especially to a young child who has no background for coping with such a situation or the range of strong emotions it evokes. The child's dependence on a parent leaves him or her with an overpowering sense of despair, helplessness, abandonment, and threat that is not always recognized. Children are not equipped with the cognitive or psychological understanding of death to cope alone with a crisis of such magnitude. When a parent dies, there are manifold increases in the child's needs. Among those most essential are continued love, comfort, and support from family members and others, as well as reassurance of continued care. Tragically, the remaining parent is often unable to care adequately for the grieving child as a result of his or her own grief, especially in the early period of bereavement. This is a time when other available caretaking adults can "adopt" the child until the surviving parent is able to cope and respond. In addition, the child needs the stability and security of a familiar environment. All too often, the death of a parent means relocating, possibly for financial reasons, to be closer to other family members or to avoid painful memories. Whatever the reason, relocating the home necessitates even more losses as well as the stress of making new friends, meeting new teachers and neighbors (see chap. 9).

The death of either parent is a shattering event for a child of any age, evoking a host of emotions. The child feels shocked, stunned, bewildered, overwhelmed, frightened, abandoned, desolate, helpless, hurt, angry, and guilty. Not all children experience all these feelings or with the same degree of intensity. To a great extent, the response is a function of the child's developmental level. Infants perceive a parent's death as a separation and loss; they respond with anxiety, anger, and apathy. First described by Spitz (1945) as *hospitalism*, this syndrome originally applied to orphaned infants who reacted to separation from their mother first with anger and then with a kind of quiet, resigned despair. Some refused nourishment and eventually died. Further studies have demonstrated that infants and young children can recover from this primary loss if another caretaker will provide a quality of nurturing comparable to that of the mother.

Preschool children consciously experience feelings of abandonment and frequently verbalize them. They are hurt and angry at being left. They are afraid they might also lose the other parent and be completely abandoned.

Their magical thinking may lead to irrational guilt for the death and to fears of punishment. If these fears are not addressed and the child is not reassured and helped with the guilt and anger, the child's development may well be seriously impeded.

Young elementary aged children may still feel a deep sense of abandonment, but more commonly they are overwhelmed by sadness and loneliness. Some children withdraw both physically and emotionally from their families and peers. Their isolation is sometimes interpreted as a plea for privacy, but more often is a flight from anger or guilt. Their thoughts and fears need attention and understanding and reassurance (Furman, 1974).

Older children and adolescents often feel extremely angry with the parent for dying and for leaving them bereft. Sometimes they are angry with the surviving parent for "allowing" or "not preventing" the death, or for being alive instead of the parent who has died. They are sometimes angry with other children because they have not lost a parent, or with God for letting it happen. Often, they feel unworthy or diminished, less valued by their peers and have lower self-esteem. Quite frequently they feel embarrassed and ashamed. The sense of being different and not understood can lead to a variety of behaviors that likely will exacerbate their isolation and frustration. Opportunities to exchange common grief reactions with others, whether adults or peers, who have experienced a recent death can be especially healing (Christ, 2000; Worden, 1996; Zeligs, 1974).

Death of a parent carries special significance to children in other ways. The extent to which the parent is seen as responsible for the financial support of the family will affect the child's sense of immediate and future security. If the parent is of the same sex as the child, there is a greater likelihood of identification with the fate of a similar early death. The death of any family member will alter the roles and alliances of other members, but they are most powerfully affected by the death of a parent. Frequently, the process of realignment is itself painful and confusing for children. And finally, completion of the grieving tasks can be impeded by the fact that the child may have no control over, or limited access to, a replacement for a dead parent. The remaining parent may or may not remarry; that parent's choice may or may not be accepted by the child; the child may reinvest in a relationship outside the family (Bowen, 1978).

### Death of a Sibling

The task of childhood mourning over a sibling is also related to the child's age and his or her perception and awareness of the meaning of death. In addition, it is very much affected by the ways in which the parents cope with the loss and the nature of the sibling relationship before the death (Brenner, 1984). A child's bereavement over a dead sibling is often overshadowed by the parent's intense reaction. The loss of a child is such a trauma to the parents that they can be so overwhelmed and depleted that there is little strength left to attend to the living child. Frequently, the attention and resources of other family and friends are directed to the parents as well, so the surviving child is overlooked or an afterthought while the parents are intensely fragile. Thus, to protect the parents, childhood mourning often goes underground. It can remain suppressed forever, or until a time when it can be dealt with without fear that it will further hurt the parents.

Parents often attempt to protect surviving siblings from the realities of death. Family members might use religious or philosophical speeches or posturing to obscure or deny the death. Children might be denied the opportunity to view the body in the belief that it would be too painful or would cause nightmares. They might be told an incomplete or distorted story of the death. Such attempts to shield the surviving child usually fail to protect and instead cause other problems for the children. The vacuum of information is easily filled with fantasies about how the death occurred, and usually intensifies whatever sense of guilt or responsibility they may have about their role in the death.

A number of studies of children's disturbed reactions to a sibling loss (Cain, Fast, & Erickson, 1963; Rosen & Cohen, 1981) indicate that avoidance is exactly the wrong thing to do. Krell and Rabkin (1979) hypothesized that three profiles of children emerged from families who participated in conspiracies of silence.

*Haunted* children are those who live in fear of what may happen to them or what feelings they may arouse in their parents. These children are the caretakers of their parents' feelings and are constantly vigilant lest they remind their parents of the dead child. Although they are constrained and on guard at home, they often misbehave at school or develop phobias or somatic symptoms.

*Bound* children are overprotected because their parents live in fear that they may lose another child. As a result of the parents' real and imagined fears, they develop a new family system that is closed, guarded, overprotective, and restrictive. In this system, children are prevented from being inquisitive and risk-taking and often withdraw into a constrained household occupied by their fearful parents, the ghost of their dead sibling, and themselves. A common outcome is initial angry behavior outside the family and, ultimately, rejection of the parents.

*Resurrected* children are seen as substitutes for their dead sibling. They are treated as though they were the dead child with a limited chance of establishing their own identity. The more the parents undermine their attempts to develop a unique personality, the greater the risk of psychological disturbance.

Preschool children often experience the death of a sibling as the loss of a best friend and companion, an abandonment that is puzzling and hurtful. They often are guilty for wishes they had to eliminate their competitor or rival or because they did not share their toys. Young elementary aged children are often overwhelmed with sadness and loneliness and tend to withdraw from social interactions at home and at school. Frequently, to compensate for their sense of responsibility in the sibling's death, or because of a historically conflict-ridden relationship, the surviving child will misbehave and, thus, be punished. Older children and adolescents often feel extreme discomfort with their friends. They feel different, misunderstood, rejected, isolated, and often freakish. They may avoid their peers and, thus, school can become a painful experience to be avoided as well (Schumacher, 1984).

The circumstances of the death are relevant to the surviving child's response. In the case of prolonged illness, the death is somewhat easier for the parents to cope with than a sudden death because of the period of "anticipatory grief." For the surviving child, however, this period may well be one of prolonged anguish, of feeling neglected, rejected, and increasingly resentful of the dying sibling. They may feel relieved and glad at the actual death, emotions that often are misunderstood, considered unacceptable and punished. In the case of a sudden death, the surviving child is often left with an incredible sense of guilt because he or she has not had the opportunity to resolve old issues. The guilt, fear, and self-blame that may result from any of these dynamics can be expressed through misbehavior, depression, overly solicitous behavior, overeating, and other forms of self-destructive behavior (Bank & Kahn, 1982).

## Death of a Grandparent

There is often a special affinity between grandchildren and grandparents. In many cases, both live outside the mainstream of productive society. Grandparents do not carry the responsibility of raising the child and so are not sources of frustration or targets of rebellion. Both parties have everything to gain and nothing to lose; this can allow for a relatively carefree and mutually satisfying relationship that can be a profound loss to a child when the grandparent dies. Additionally, a grandparent represents a sense of continuity and tradition that are central to a child's construction of an ordered world, especially in today's transient culture. The older the child at the time of the loss, the more meaning the death will potentially have. It can be a personal loss and a symbolic loss as mentioned. Additionally, it can be an opportunity to observe the relationship between parent and grandparent, to learn from the parent's grieving how to acknowledge and resolve losses.

## Death of a Friend

The effects of the death of a close peer on a child have not been systematically studied and are not often reported in the literature. One can assume that children will react much as they might to the death of a sibling, with a great sadness and loneliness, with a sense of abandonment and hurt. They are not so likely to experience intense guilt because it is unlikely that they would have the same or a comparable conflict-ridden history or the sense of responsibility that a sibling's death would evoke. However, should these factors be central to the predeath relationship, then the bereaved child could experience profound guilt and could exhibit disturbed thinking or behavior.

## The Dying Child

Terminally ill children of all ages need love, care, comfort, and the assurance that they will not be left to die alone. This reassurance, as well as the consistent nurturing and attention that will confirm it, are essential to the alleviation of the major fears of dying children. Natterson and Knudsen (1960) studied the fear of death in hospitalized fatally ill children and their mothers and found that the predominant causes of fear and distress were related to the child's developmental age.

Children younger than 5 were most afraid of separation from their mother, of being alone, abandoned, or lost. Frequently, these young children respond by becoming extremely clinging, with demands for the constant physical presence of an adult, and often with an intense fear of going to sleep, yet another form of separation.

Terminally ill preschool children often experience the abandonment of hospital placement, the pain and physical changes in their bodies, and the medical procedures as punishment for being bad. Their frantic attempts to "be good" to avoid further punishment are difficult to sustain, only making them more vulnerable to feelings of guilt and more punishment. Children from age 5 to 10 had the strongest reaction to the medical procedures. At this stage of development, children can understand the relationships between the disease and its effects on the body, as well as the specific purposes of various medical procedures. They usually become quite knowledgeable about the disease and become experts on its effects and treatments. Consistent with their developmental level, they have concerns about bodily functions and malfunctions and so are filled with anxieties about disfigurement in life and the processes of death and decay after death.

Children usually use their age-appropriate interest in concrete information to help master their fears of death. Denial is a common defense of children under the age of 10. These children need extra reassurance and support that they will not be alone without taking away their defensive stand. In such instances, health professionals are needed most by the parents so that they can meet their child's desperate need.

Terminally ill adolescents share the same fears of abandonment and physical disfigurement as do younger age groups. Unlike younger children, however, they have a greater awareness of the enormity of their impending loss. They have a sense of their own future and plans to fulfill it. As a result, their anger and bitterness are much stronger and tend to overshadow their sadness and sense of loss. They, also, consider their death to be a punishment, but they see it as cruel and undeserved. At a time when independence is central to emotional and cognitive development, a terminally ill adolescent is increasingly dependent on the old world, parents, and home, and increasingly isolated from what should be the new world of friends and school. It is not surprising that the dying adolescent is so often bitter and enraged, loses self-esteem and self-assurance, and alienates him or herself from those closest as a desperate attempt to prove independence. Parents need considerable support to deal with the massive despair, rejection, and rage of these adolescents.

## PUBLIC DEATHS

In our age of information, many deaths of public figures and public deaths of private citizens are present in children's lives. In addition, violence is a factor in many of these well-publicized deaths, including deaths that happen at schools. These losses pose special problems for children, parents, and school personnel. In general, schools have responded according to the immediacy and the impact of these public deaths on children. Thus, discussions of current events can include and address responses to more emotionally distant public deaths, whereby teachers and counselors can provide opportunities for students to express concerns and needs. The greater the emotional closeness, by virtue of the personality or stature of the person who died or because of the nature of the loss, the greater the attention that must be paid. Children who have already been touched by loss or by other trauma are most likely to be affected by such news and events. Families and school administrators need to be mindful of the potential retraumatization and intervene quickly for those children.

## MANIFESTATIONS OF GRIEF

Since the first systematic study of normal grief reactions done by Lindemann (1944), an extensive and varied list of behaviors have become associated with the grieving process. Worden (1991) grouped them in the four general categories of feelings, physical sensations, cognitions, and behaviors. Although his work was not limited to children, most of the phenomena included apply to the responses of grieving children.

Among those feelings most common to the grief process, sadness is the most pervasive. It is often expressed through crying, but the absence of tears does not mean that these feelings are being denied. Young children especially have difficulty sustaining intense sad feelings and often experience brief intermittent times of sadness. Anger is very commonly felt and generally comes from one of two sources: either from a sense of frustration that one was powerless to prevent the death or from the anxiety associated with the loss. In either case, it is essential that the anger be appropriately identified and directed toward appropriate external objects, including, at times, the deceased so that it is not turned against the self. Anger turned inward can lead to depression and to suicidal behavior.

Guilt and self-reproach are also commonly experienced. Guilt can be related to past misbehaviors or omitted expressions of care, or it can be related to a specific event related to the death. Most often, the guilt is irrational and will be mitigated through continued reality testing. Anxiety usually stems either from the fear that the child will not be able to take care of him or herself or from heightened awareness of one's own mortality. The first source of anxiety is common to children of all ages; the second is more common among adolescents. Feelings of loneliness, helplessness, and numbness are often experienced by children of all ages. Yearning is particularly associated with younger children's searching behavior, but is also connected to the more passive pining of older children. A sense of emancipation or relief may be felt by some older children or adolescents, especially after a long or painful illness or a death that can allow for a dramatic, healthy shift in family structure or dynamics.

Children quite often report physical sensations and somatic complaints during the grieving process. These sensations may be stomachaches, lethargy, shortness of breath, oversensitivity to noise, or weakness in general. They may also take the form of constipation or bedwetting, vomiting, or loss of appetite. Children will often report symptoms related to the cause of death, both from anxiety and from identification with the deceased.

Certain thought patterns are commonly experienced during the grieving process, especially in the early stages. Disbelief is often the first response to news of a death. For children, the disbelief is easily re-experienced upon awakening or when first exposed to a new situation. Children are often very confused, cannot seem to keep track of things or maintain the order of the day and have trouble concentrating. They are frequently preoccupied with thoughts about the deceased, including fantasies of recovering the lost person. Sometimes, children report feeling the presence of the deceased watching over them or helping them with a difficult task or experience. Occasionally, children report auditory or visual hallucinations, particularly a short time after the death.

The following behaviors are commonly reported among grieving children and usually correct themselves over time. Children frequently experience sleep disorders, especially during the early stages of grief. They may have difficulty falling asleep, may wake frequently or may wake very early in the morning. Changes in eating patterns are also common. Although appetite disturbances can be manifested in either overeating or undereating, undereating is more often reported. Confused and preoccupied thinking can lead to absent-minded behavior. Among children, this is more often a source of irritation or an inconvenience than problematic, as it can be among adults. Children can respond by withdrawing from involvements with others or by sustained, restless activity. Both are efforts to avoid painful feelings, as are efforts to avoid any reminders or mention of the deceased. On the other hand, some children try to maintain the deceased by focusing on mementos or treasured memories or through searching behavior. Crying and sighing are very common responses for children of all ages, as are dreams of the dead person. Both normal dreams and nightmares frequently serve a number of purposes psychologically for the child in mastering the tasks of grieving and can be instructive to adults by providing clues to the course of the bereavement process.

The aforementioned manifestations of grief are considered to be within the normal responses of children immediately following a death and during the grieving process. The line of separation between normal and dysfunctional mourning reactions is not in symptom, but intensity and duration. It is the continued denial of reality even many months after the funeral that indicates a disturbed reaction. Similarly, prolonged bodily distress or persistent frenzy, unceasing apathy, consistent self-condemnation or hostility are all indications of a distorted grief reaction. Although the intensity and duration of any of these reactions is idiosyncratic, professional consultation is advisable when there is any question. Other signals that indicate the need for professional advice include delinquency, unwillingness to attend school, difficulties in learning, sexual perversion, unreasonable withdrawal, friendlessness, excessive anger, or intense suspicion (Grollman, 1976).

Those children who would be expected to be most vulnerable during bereavement share one or more of the following experiences or characteristics. Children who have experienced previous losses, whether through death or divorce, are especially likely to be devastated and overwhelmed by another loss. Children without reliable, available support from their immediate or extended family will have greater difficulty moving through the bereavement process. Socially isolated children and those with dysfunctional peer relations will also most likely have a more difficult time. A child experiencing any of the other stresses of childhood—such as a recent move, academic difficulties, birth of a sibling–will be especially vulnerable at the death of someone close. These children may all be considered at risk and potential recipients of secondary prevention efforts.

## INTERVENTION STRATEGIES

Based on understanding of children's conceptions of death and on the tasks of grieving, there is considerable agreement on strategies to help children cope with death (Brenner, 1984; Christ, 2000; Worden, 1996). For the most part, these have been developed by clinicians to be used by the adults in the child's home or school environment. There is general consensus that children should receive clear, honest information about the death. Responses to questions should be direct, brief, and repeated only when the child seems ready for more. It is important for adults to take the time to understand how the child understands what has happened in order to confirm, clarify, or correct his or her views. Children gain from preparation for a participation in those rituals or ceremonies associated with the death. These events, although difficult, offer opportunities for shared grief, public confirmation, and acknowledgment of the deceased's life and death, and closure to the physical presence of that person. Adults can be helpful by encouraging children to express and share the whole range of feelings stirred by the death as well as by being available to console and comfort. Support and assistance to the other bereaving family members can provide indirect help to a child. When parents are themselves so overwhelmed that they are unable to be available to their child, other adults can often provide more direct "surrogate parenting."

The following is a review of typical ways in which children attempt to deal with their grief and a synthesis of recommendations for therapeutic responses (Bank & Kahn, 1982; Bowlby, 1960; Cain et al., 1964; Christ, 2000; Grollman, 1976; Jewett, 1982; Lonetto, 1980; Worden, 1996). Although not all of these behaviors will be evidenced directly at school, the child may talk about them. They may also be of concern to other students or to school personnel.

In working on the first task of bereavement, accepting the reality of the loss, it is not uncommon for children to act dazed upon learning of a death or to appear as if they have not heard or understood. In such cases, it is helpful for the adult to repeat the news of the death later in the day, to answer questions clearly and honestly when they arise, and to wait for the news to "sink in." Some children flatly deny that the death has occurred and sustain an unusually high activity level to avoid thinking about it. It is generally agreed to accept this denial initially, but, if it persists, consultation with a therapist is recommended (Christ, 2000; Jewett, 1982). Sometimes, children will insist on being the one to tell everyone else the news;

usually their need to be the center of attention in this way will not last long and can be allowed without causing a problem for the child.

Dreams and nightmares are frequent after hearing of a death and are instrumental in accepting the loss. Nevertheless, many children panic at the dreams, are afraid of being alone and of going to sleep. In such cases, it is helpful to maintain usual routines as far as possible and to review any changes with the child frequently. Their fears of abandonment add to the terrors of the dreams, so children need reassurance that they will be cared for as well as comforted for the dreams or nightmares. It is often comforting to hear music or the sounds of life and activity during the night.

The consistency and predictability of the school routine is usually a source of comfort to children. Here, too, changes should be anticipated and reviewed to reinforce the predictable component of school life. School personnel can be very helpful to families by continued communication around the child's behavior and interactions at school related to accepting the reality of the death (Charkow, 1998; Lenhardt, 1997).

A variety of behaviors can be associated with the task of experiencing the pain of grief. Children are helped with their sadness and tears, their longing and loneliness, by sharing their feelings with adults and hearing of the adults' sadness. It is also helpful to review memories, both pleasant and unpleasant, of the dead person. Joint projects such as scrapbooks or collections of writings help to concretize shared and personal memories and experiences. When a death is close to an entire class of children (e.g., one of the students or a highly involved parent), such projects serve to support the grieving needs of all the children and often the teacher, too. It is not uncommon for children to regress to earlier behavior after a death. At such times, children need acceptance of such behavior as a means to achieve comfort or recreate past times, yet they also need support for their attempts to regain their more mature level of functioning. Searching behavior also needs to be supported and allowed to continue until children feel they have made a thorough search and have had ample opportunities to discuss the repeated disappointments encountered.

Anger and guilt often interfere with the experience of pain and deflect attention from the grieving process. Children often direct their anger toward their parents and other caretakers, or toward siblings and peers. It is important to empathize with these feelings, to respect their source, and to reassure the child that such hurting is part of grieving and will eventually subside. It is helpful to emphasize the value of conversation about guilty and angry feelings and encourage their expression through drawing, writing, and playing them out as well. Expressions of anger and guilt often surface at school. They can be manifested in a social context in both acting out and withdrawn behaviors, in peer conflicts, and in relation to school tasks, by an inability to concentrate or obsessive work habits. Again, this aspect of the grieving process can be facilitated by consistent monitoring on the part of school personnel in order to respond effectively to the child and to inform the family of difficulties and progress. In addition to individual counseling, school-based group work focused on bereavement is often a highly effective forum for expressing, sharing, and "normalizing" emotions.

The third task, adjusting to a new environment that no longer includes the deceased, can be facilitated by discussions that explore the feelings around such an adjustment. The negative feelings, the guilt and anger, that might impede the process need expression; the success of adjustment can also be anxiety provoking. Many children feel uncomfortable and guilty at being able to feel happy again; they may feel disloyal and a sense of betrayal that may constrain them and prevent their moving through this task. Rather than adapt to the new situation, they may withdraw, become immobilized, or feel helpless. Such manifestations of grief are frequently seen in the school setting. They can operate in both the social and academic world of the child and need to be addressed so that the grieving child does not suffer further losses by falling behind academically or socially with peers.

The school setting can help foster a child's ability to reinvest in new relationships. It is a natural environment for children to learn about relationships, to experience the process of losing and making friends, to acknowledge and share group feelings and memories, and to recognize and foster transitions and growth.

The school also offers a structured and formalized curriculum that validates experiences and processes related to life and death, growth and change. Such support comes from the life science studies, from social studies, and from literature. By its very nature as both a socializing and educational institution, the school system supports the grieving process. The mental health professionals within the system, whether teachers, administrators, counselors, or psychologists, can further support grieving children by monitoring their progress and communicating with family about it, by continuous support and responsiveness in their needs individually and as part of a class, by offering group counseling and by referring the child and family for therapy when it is indicated. Participation in bereavement groups for children has been associated with a significant decrease in symptomatology. Noted effects have included a range of protective processes. These have included a reduction in the impact of the loss, a reduction of a chain of negative reactions, the establishment of self-esteem and self-efficacy, and the opening of a sense of new possibilities. They may provide a useful surrogate support system for children and may contribute new social meanings for the loss (Leenaars & Wenckstern, 1996; Zambelli & De Rosa, 1992). In addition to private therapists or public agencies, local communities offer a number of specialized referral agencies (see Wass & Corr, 1984, and Wass, 1980, for extensive listings of resources).

## PREVENTION

Just as the school's social environment and curricula can be healing to a grieving child, so can these factors serve preventative functions for all children. Both elements of the school setting can provide lessons in bereavement. Certainly, children will learn from directly observing the grieving process of a friend or classmate. They also learn from discussions in science classes, from the elementary curriculum's lessons on living things and their requirements to the more complex biology and physics classes of adolescents. Social studies classes provide information on living in society and functioning as an individual, on the family, and personal development. Growth and change are fundamental to both these physical and social aspects of life. They are also frequent topics in children's reading and literature classes. There is a wide range of books available to children of all ages that address concerns of dying and grieving. (Wass, 1980, and Thomas, 1984, provide extensive bibliographies.)

All these elements serve the prevention of mental health problems by providing a base of information and of predictability of thoughts, feelings, and behaviors associated with grieving. The greater the child's cognitive awareness of death and its effects on the survivors, the better prepared he or she will be for losses throughout life. Specialized curricula in "Death Education" have been organized and are available for a wide range of elementary school aged children (Deaton & Berkan, 1995; Thomas, 1984). Their major purpose is to counterbalance a perceived avoidance of the subject of death in the classroom through a focused program. Whether such a formalized program is more effective than ongoing acknowledgment and discussion of issues related to death and bereavement is not clear. Nevertheless, the support that can be provided to children, families, and staff by knowledgeable, responsive mental health professionals in the school setting has been demonstrated.

## CONCLUSION

A child's experience with death can have profound effects on future intrapsychic development and interpersonal relationships. The school setting provides unique opportunities to mental health professionals to serve bereaved children, their families, peers, and teachers. An ever-increasing understanding of children's intellectual and psychological conceptions of death allows for effective prevention programs for all children and for significant observations and interventions for grieving children. The curriculum offers ongoing opportunities for prevention by addressing death issues in a variety of content areas and with methods appropriate to the full range of age and developmental levels. The structure of the academic and social school routines are both a support for grieving children and a gauge by which to measure their course through the grieving process. Awareness of bereaved children's needs and perceptions, understanding of their reactions, and communication with families and teachers about their progress are a sure form of prevention of mental health problems in the future.

## REFERENCES


Bank, S. P., & Kahn, M. D. (1982). *The sibling bond.* New York: Basic Books.

Bowen, M. (1978). *Family therapy in clinical practice.* New York: Aaronson.

Bowlby, J. (1960). Grief and mourning in infancy and early childhood. *Psychoanalytic Study of the Child, 15,* 9–52.

Brenner, A. (1984). *Helping children cope with stress.* Lexington, MA: Heath.

Bugen, L. A. (1977). Human grief: A model for prediction and intervention. *American Journal of Orthopsychiatry, 47,* 196–206.

Cain, A. C., Fast, I., & Erickson, M. E. (1964). Children's disturbed reactions to the death of a sibling. *American Journal of Orthopsychiatry, 34,* 741–752.

Charkow, W. B. (1998). Inviting children to grieve. *Professional School Counseling, 2,* 117–122.

Christ, G. H. (2000). *Healing children's grief.* New York: Oxford University Press.

Deaton, R. L., & Berkan, W. A. (1995). *Planning and managing death issues in the schools.* Westport, CT: Greenwood Press.

Engel, G. L. (1961). Is grief a disease? A challenge for medical research. *Psychosomatic Medicine, 23,* 18–22.

Erikson, E. H. (1950). *Childhood and society.* New York: Norton.

Flavell, J. H. (1977). *Cognitive development.* Englewood Cliffs, NJ: Prentice-Hall.

Furman, R. (1974). Death and the young child: Some preliminary considerations. *Psychoanalytic Study of the Child, 19,* 321–333.

Gorer, G. (1965). *Death, grief and mourning in contemporary Britain.* London: Cresset.

Grollman, E. A. (1976). *Talking about death.* Boston: Beacon.

Jewett, C. L. (1982). *Helping children cope with separation and loss.* Harvard, MA: Harvard Common Press.

Krell, R., & Rabkin, L. (1979). The effects of sibling death on the surviving child: A family perspective. *Family Process, 18,* 471–477.

Kubler-Ross, E. (1969). *On death and dying.* New York: Macmillan.

Leenaars, A. A., & Wenckstern, S. (1996). Postvention with elementary school children. In C. A. Corr & D. M. Corr (Eds.), *Handbook of childhood death and bereavement.* New York: Springer.

Lenhardt, A. M. C. (1997). Disenfranchised grief/sorrow: Implications for the School Counselor. *School Counselor, 44,* 264–270.

Lindemann, E. (1944). Symptomatology and management of acute grief. *American Journal of Psychiatry, 101,* 141–149.

Lonetto, R. (1980). *Children's conceptions of death.* New York: Springer.

Matz, M. (1979). Helping families cope with grief. In S. Eisenberg & L. E. Patterson (Eds.), *Helping clients with special concerns* (pp. 218–238). Chicago: Rand McNally.

Natterson, J. M., & Knudson, A. G. (1960). Observations concerning fear of death in fatally ill children and their mothers. *Psychosomatic Medicine, 22,* 456–465.

Parkes, C. M. (1972). *Bereavement: Studies of grief in adult life.* New York: International Universities Press.

Piaget, J., & Inhelder, B. (1969). *The psychology of the child.* New York: Basic Books.

Rosen, H., & Cohen, H. (1981). Children's reactions to sibling loss. *Clinical Social Work Journal, 9,* 211–219.

Schumacher, J. D. (1984). Helping children cope with a sibling's death. In J. C. Hansen & T. T. Frantz (Eds.), *Death and grief in the family* (pp. 82–94). Rockville, MD: Aspen Systems Corp.

Spitz, R. (1945). Hospitalism: An inquiry into the genesis of psychiatric conditions in early childhood. *Psychoanalytic Study of the Child, 1,* 53–72.

Thomas, J. L. (Ed.). (1984). *Death and dying in the classroom: Reading for life.* Phoenix, AZ: Ornyx Press.

Wass, H. (1980). *Death education: An annotated resource guide.* Washington, DC: Hemisphere.

Wass, H., & Corr, C. A. (1984). *Helping children cope with death.* Washington, DC: Hemisphere.

Wolfenstein, M. (1966). How is mourning possible? *Psychoanalytic Study of the Child, 21,* 93–123.

Worden, J. W. (1991). *Grief counseling and grief therapy* (2nd ed.). New York: Springer.

Worden, J. W. (1996). *Children and grief.* New York: Guilford Press.

Zambelli, G. C., & De Rosa, A. P. (1992). Bereavement support groups for school-age children: Theory, intervention and case example. *American Journal of Orthopsychiatry, 62,* 484–493.

Zeligs, R. (1974). *Children's experiences with death.* Springfield, IL: Thomas.

CHAPTER

# 9

# Illness: A Crisis for Children

Margaret S. Steward
University of California, Davis

A second-grade teacher called to ask me about the wisdom of putting Billy into a small reading group. I started to inquire about his reading skills, but the teacher interrupted me saying, "No, you don't understand, Dr. Steward, Billy has diabetes, and I don't want the rest of the children to catch it!" That phone call was an indirect result of three factors. First, changes in public law including the enactment of Public Law 94142 and the 1997 reauthorization of the Individuals with Disabilities Education Act that guarantees children a place in the public classroom. Second, there have been important advances in modern medical practice so that when Billy adheres to his treatment regimen he will have sufficient health and energy to cope with school. Third, there was inadequate communication between home, school, and health care. The clue to this was the fear in the teacher's voice. There had not been adequate lines of communication set up among the adults in Billy's life—his parents, his pediatrician, and his teacher. In these changing times school personnel need to make a concerted effort to understand the physical capacities and limitations, and medical needs of each of the children in their midst who must deal everyday with chronic illness, injury, or physical disabilities. At the same time medical personnel need to know more about the educational demands and opportunities of the specific classroom into which their young patients are going. We all need to be brought up to running speed with respect to what it means for a child to cope with illness.

Unfortunately the teacher who called me was not quite ready for Billy in her class. Once I understood her concerns, there were a number of avenues to explore. One obvious issue was the teacher's need for accurate information to quell her concern that Billy's metabolic disease might be contagious and therefore that the other students (and possibly she herself) might be vulnerable. Of course, there were other issues. For example, did she have a feel for how Billy's diabetes might influence his behavior during the school day to interrupt or compromise his learning? Had she learned to scan for behavioral clues such as uncharacteristic irritability and uncooperativeness that might suggest that his blood sugar was too low, or understand that increased requests for drinks of water and trips to the bathroom suggest that his blood sugar was too high? Had his parents told her that he might need special supervision at lunch or snacktime? Could Billy's pediatrician be invited to conduct an inservice session so that the whole school staff would know how to identify a medical emergency, which for Billy might mean seizures or a coma, and what to do about it?

We know that it is also important to understand what Billy thinks is wrong with him. Does he believe, as some young children with diabetes have told us, that he got the disease by eating too much candy, or that he will die because he has "die-a-beasties"? If he is being treated with the latest medical technology, he will be involved in testing his own blood sugar level several times a day, and making judgments about what to do with the fluctuations he finds. Does he see his role in his own medical care as a burden or a privilege? Does he feel physically vulnerable and therefore avoid engaging in activities with other boys his age? What does he tell classmates who ask? His disease—chronic, at times life-threatening, but for all practical purposes "invisible"—can be a source of much confusion, misapprehension, and anxiety for Billy and his classmates.

## INCIDENCE AND PREVALENCE OF DISEASE IN CHILDHOOD AND ADOLESCENCE

Although advances in medical research and technology have changed the face of children's health, it is a fair assumption that every child has a direct experience with brief, acute disease. The frequency of colds, the flu, and respiratory diseases, recurrent events in children's lives, is dependent in part on family size and the inevitable sequential spreading of infection through a family or a classroom (Parmelee, 1986). In the United States, the typical child is absent due to health about 5 school days a year. Although the incidence of "common childhood diseases" is dropping, the accident rate is climbing and children under 15 years are the most likely victims of accidental injury, disability, and death. Approximately one in four children experiences a medically attended injury each year with boys and poor children sustaining the majority of the injuries (Scheidt, Harel, Trumble, Jones, Overpeck, & Bijur, 1995). It is striking to note that for adolescents, accidents are the leading causes of mortality and morbidity, followed by homicide, suicide, drug abuse, venereal disease, and teen-age pregnancy—all behaviorally determined. As a result of disease or injury, one person in two will require hospitalization during childhood or adolescence.

Of the children and adolescents in America 10% to 20% have a chronic health condition; 1% to 2% have a condition severe enough to interfere with their daily activities (Wallander & Thompson, 1995). It is estimated that an elementary school teacher will have six children with chronic disease in her classes over a 10-year period, whereas the typical high school teacher will have approximately 30 youngsters with chronic disease over the same 10-year period. Given the current prevalence of chronic diseases, half of these children will have asthma; the other half will have one of a dozen other chronic diseases such as congenital heart disease, diabetes, sickle cell anemia, hemophilia, or cancer. There are demographic differences in the incidence of chronic conditions of childhood: juvenile rheumatoid arthritis is more common in girls, whereas asthma and leukemia are more common in boys and hemophilia affects boys exclusively. Cystic fibrosis, diabetes, and leukemia are more common in Caucasians than other ethnic groups, whereas sickle cell disease is more common in African American children (Kliewer, 1997).

Children with severe chronic diseases share a number of characteristics and experiences that are highly stressful, regardless of the specific diagnosis (Wallander & Thompson, 1995). Most chronic diseases of childhood are costly to treat, require care over an extended period of time, and require medical services intermittently. The daily burden of care falls on the family and the child. Most chronic diseases leave children intermittently fatigued and in pain and some require episodic treatments that are also painful and require hospitalization. Many chronic diseases entail slow degeneration and although children's lives are being extended through vigorous treatment protocols, most children with chronic disease—even if they live into young adulthood—face premature death.

Today for children, their classmates, and their teachers, chronic disease means something different than it did in the past. For example, since the 1970s, survival rates of children with acute lymphocytic leukemia (ALL), the most prevalent of the childhood cancers, are reported to have jumped from less than 1% to nearly 70% (Bearison & Mulhern, 1994)—and to 85% at our medical center. In the past a diagnosis of cancer often meant swift withdrawal from school, hospitalization, and inevitable death. Schooling was seen as relatively unimportant because children usually did not survive to graduate. By contrast, today a child with that same diagnosis may be back in his or her own second-grade classroom, postchemotherapy, struggling with an arithmetic assignment, and wearing a T-shirt proclaiming that "Bald is Beautiful."

Most children diagnosed with a chronic disease can be and are mainstreamed, as their diseases do not impair intelligence. But that does not mean that they will always be in the classroom. As an example, a recent study by Rynard and his colleagues (Rynard, Chambers, Klinck, & Gray, 1998) reported that children with cancer missed one third of the total school days while they were on treatment (a protocol that can last 2 to 3 years). In addition, many experience interference in their school work while they are in the classroom as a direct result of limited stamina and attention, indirectly as a result of medication, or as a result of lowered self-esteem and self-assurance. When there is lack of clarity, or disagreement, between parents and teacher about the academic expectations for a child with chronic disease, there is increased stress for the child and the teacher (Strong & Sandoval, 1999). Unfortunately, sometimes children's performance is lowered by protective stances of their physicians, their parents, or even their teachers who inadvertently ask for less than a child could deliver academically, and therefore get less. School staff are in a unique position to offer children and their families medical crisis counseling. How, when, and why to do so is discussed next.

## THEORIES

In this section, we first discuss the issue of disease versus illness in order to offer a framework for providing medical crisis counseling. We then look at illness as a learning experience, illness as a stressor, and finally diagnostic and treatment experiences that have the potential to contribute to childhood trauma.

### Disease Versus Illness

The literature in behavioral medicine differentiates *disease* from *illness* (Eisenberg, 1977; Kleinman, 1988). The former designates biological pathophysiology that results in symptoms and signs that are commonly recognizable in everyone who is diagnosed with the disease. The latter refers to the experience of the individual. Put more simply, *disease* is a term that belongs to the medical system, whereas *illness* belongs to the personal, family, and social systems. Parmelee (1986) pointed out that one can have a disease without feeling ill, as well as feeling ill without having a disease. In the case of the child in the classroom, both disease and illness must be dealt with. Anna Freud (1952) described the dramatic psychological withdrawal of some children who had only harmless sore throats, upset stomachs, raised temperatures, or common infectious diseases of childhood. She correctly observed that, as with adults, there is not a direct correlation for children between the severity of the physical disease and the intensity of the child's emotional response, the illness experience. Those of us trained to work with children know that the same experiences will be viewed differently at different physical, cognitive, and emotional age/stages. In addition, the growing child, well or ill, faces developmental challenges and will be expected to continue to meet and master developmental milestones.

## Illness as a Learning Experience

Parmelee (1986, 1996) asserted that there are real cognitive, social, and emotional benefits in the natural ebb and flow of a child's experience with his or her own brief illness and in the participation of caretaking when siblings or parents are ill. He suggests that recurring illnesses of short duration provide children with expanded experiences of their physical selves and with associated mood changes, feelings of distress, and loss of vigor. It is within the family that the child learns the "sick role" (Parsons, 1958), and begins to model the family's use of medical resources (Lewis & Lewis, 1989; Lewis, Lewis, & Palmer, 1977). Our own longitudinal research on children's drawings of the body (Steward, 1987) revealed that during illness children's usual sense of self is altered and then restored. Physical recovery preceded psychological recovery for some children by as much as a month. It is probable that a successful voyage through a time-limited illness in childhood acts as a psychological inoculation against "learned helplessness" when the wear and tear of adulthood increases our vulnerability to the illness role (Reich, Steward, Rosenblatt, & Tupin, 1985; Seligman, 1975).

Coping with acute disease, in addition to the eliciting of an affective response, usually demands the exercise of cognitively based skills as well. The intellectual accommodation that a child must make to mild illness meets the Piagetian criteria of "moderate novelty" that facilitates cognitive growth and development (Snyder & Feldman, 1977). Vernon, Foley, Sipowicz, and Schulman (1965) found that although some mothers reported that their children demonstrated troublesome behaviors during and following illness, others reported that the behavior of their children actually improved.

In the school setting, as in the family, children not only experience their own illness, but also see teachers, staff, and other children move through illness and back into health. Children can test their own and their family's explanatory models (Campbell, 1975; Kleinman, 1988) on classmates, teachers, and school staff. This gives them the opportunity to develop an appreciation for the multiple potential causes for feeling ill, and enables some to differentiate the "math headache" or the "history test stomach ache" from virus induced symptoms with great accuracy.

### Illness as a Stressor

More than 30 years ago Wolff (1970) identified illness as the universal stress of childhood. A compelling argument can be made that school personnel in order to tailor a child's educational experience, must understand the child's medical diagnosis, treatment protocol, and the ramifications of the specific disease process that the child is undergoing. It is also critical to understand the relative stressfulness of the child's experience of illness. In order to do that it is helpful to assess a child's appraisal of the potential stressors of the specific disease and to review the child's selection and use of coping processes. There has been less research on children's appraisal than their coping strategies (Sandler, Wolchik, MacKinnon, Ayers, & Roosa, 1997), but we believe that before designing intervention strategies, it is worth pausing to assess the child's appraisal of the events. There are three phases of the appraisal process identified in the current research and clinical literature. Lazarus (1991) identified primary appraisal, in which the person makes a judgment about whether a particular event or experience is stressful, benign, or potentially irrelevant. Stressful events can be seen as potentially harmful, or a challenge that offers the potential for mastery or gain. Events that might be stressful to one child, may be seen as benign or essentially irrelevant to another.

For Lazarus, secondary appraisal involves the assessment of coping resources (a child's own resources and others that can be tapped). Coping should be seen as a strategy or set of strategies that may either facilitate problem solving—or may actually get a child deeper into trouble (Lazarus & Folkman, 1984). Children can often use some help in identifying alternative coping strategies, and sometimes help in practicing them (Fassler, 1978; Genevro, Andreasson, & Bornstein 1996). The selection and use of coping strategies change across the life cycle, with younger children employing more action-oriented, external strategies, while adolescents and adults are increasingly able to employ internal cognitive and affective strategies (Altschuler & Ruble, 1989; Band & Weisz, 1988; Steward & Steward, 1981). There is also evidence that as children, girls employ a broader range of coping strategies than do boys (Spirito, Stark, & Vyk, 1989). Unfortunately, the opportunities for young patients to use developmentally appropriate action strategies in the face of stress (e.g., escaping, running away, and so on) are sharply limited when there is a need to provide medical care. Action strategies are further limited by the drain on children's physical energy and well-being that results from the disease process and the direct and indirect effects of treatment, treatment-related pain, or medication.

Janoff-Bulman (1992) proposed a third kind of appraisal that occurs over time, involving interpretation and redefinition of an event that occurs over the course of coping and adjustment. This third type of appraisal uses cognitive strategies that ultimately contribute to the re-establishment of personal integrity and emotional equilibrium following a crisis. Children can often use help with this third process; for some it will come quickly whereas for others it will involve a life-long struggle for meaning. Kliewer (1997) suggested that parents influence their children's threat appraisals and coping strategies by coaching them to react emotionally and to use particular coping strategies; parents model their own emotional responses and coping efforts in the face of stress; and they create an environment at home which either invites open communication or stifles it.

Following is a generic matrix that may help us focus on some of the facets contributing to a child's appraisal of the experience of illness. In this matrix there are two intersecting dimensions: (a) duration of illness (ranging from chronic to acute) and (b) relative visibility of the disease–treatment process (ranging from invisible to clearly visible). As seen in Fig. 9.1, each of the quadrants created by the dimensions of duration and visibility can have diseases of quite different etiologies. However, we believe that children within the same quadrant will share many common illness experiences, struggle with some of the same demons, and may benefit from similar interventions.

Our clinical experience with children suggests that the quadrants can be rank ordered with respect to the stressfulness of the illness experience (all

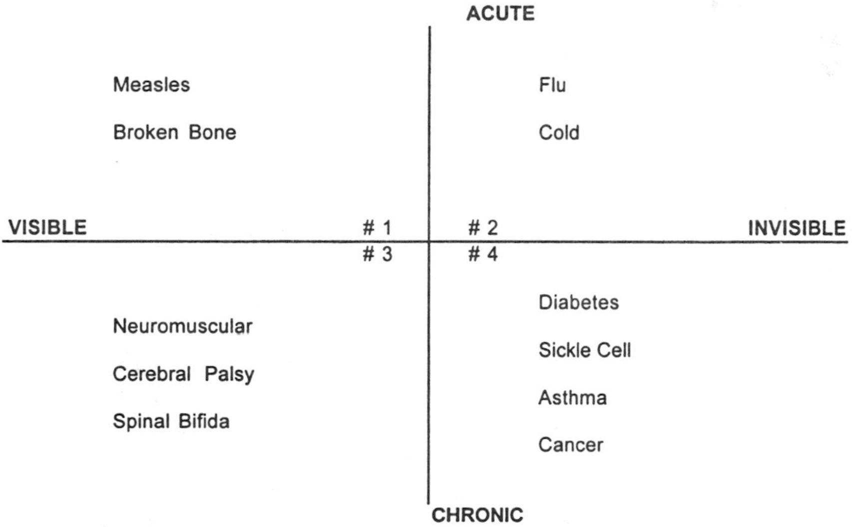


FIG. 9.1. Child's appraisal of illness utilizing variables of duration and relative visibility of the disease or injury.

other things being equal—which they never really are). Children with diseases in quadrant #1 who experience a brief illness or injury that gives visible clues that change or normalize as recovery occurs will have the least difficulty explaining the experience to themselves and others. They will be given the most validation in the patient role by peers, teachers, and parents (because all can see for themselves that the child is sick) and they will have the easiest time monitoring their own healing process. Measles with spots that recede, and the skin rash of poison oak fit this descriptive experience. So too does a broken bone, complete with cast, traction, and so on. Therapeutic intervention with children in this quadrant could include opportunities for replaying the experience, and assurance of the body's power to heal.

Children with diseases in quadrant #4 who must live with chronic, invisible disease find the experiences that result from this kind of disease very confusing. Many, diagnosed in infancy have lived with the disease "from forever," and have never experienced life disease free. However, outside the medical setting it is hard for these children to retain the patient role because "You don't look sick to me!" Children often have difficulty complying with medical regimens because it is sometimes impossible to tell when they are getting better, or even getting control of the invisible symptoms. Children often create or select clues that are irrelevant to the actual disease process and act in response to them. Compliance with medication or other treatment regimes is especially low for children in this quadrant (LaGreca & Schuman, 1995). It should be noted that children are not alone here. Leventhal (1986) demonstrated that when physicians and nurses became patients, they were unsuccessful in medicating their own high blood pressure because it is a disease process with few if any sensory cues. Therapeutic intervention activities using such expressive techniques as story, drawing, and free play can usefully focus on a child's theories of causality, and beliefs about the efficacy of treatments. It is also useful to consult with medical personnel to check out the accuracy of the child's understanding, and to identify sensory clues that accurately monitor fluctuating disease process.

Of the remaining two quadrants, children with diseases in quadrant #2 who have invisible but brief illness tend to experience more initial cognitive and affective disruption than children with diseases in quadrant #3 who can see what is going on. Many children with diseases in quadrant #2 feel like they have been "tricked" by their bodies and initially are quite angry. Yet the time-limited nature of their experience rarely strains the coping capacity of most children. Some develop strange little rituals for a brief time after they have returned to physical health in order to protect themselves from reoccurrence. However, especially younger children who have found the experience, for example, of vomiting with the flu particularly distasteful, make strong resolve "never to do that again!" Should the child's reaction reach crisis proportions, focus on the self-healing power of the body can be helpful.

The difficult assignment for children with disease or injury in quadrant #3 with visible, but chronic conditions is not only that they must live everyday with the debilitating condition, but that they must also transform their understanding of their disease as their minds and bodies grow. However, we are beginning to find that many physically handicapped children cope exceptionally well, developing an accurate body image, and satisfactory compensatory strategies and move through childhood and adolescence with their self-esteem intact (Harter, 1985; Wallander & Thompson, 1995). But Massie (1985) reminds us that when a disability is visible to a child and to others, the child "must endure the frightened looks that mark every initial encounter" (p. 17). Strategies for coping with other people's reaction to the child with visible, chronically disabling conditions becomes increasingly important in the elementary school years. Reverse role play—with the child playing the critical, embarrassing, gawking stranger—often generates some marvelous responses that a child can store in his or her growing repertoire of responses.

## TRAUMA INDUCED BY ACUTE INJURY OR NECESSARY BUT PAINFUL MEDICAL OR DENTAL PROCEDURES

Terr (1991) defined childhood trauma as "the result of one sudden, external blow or series of blows rendering the young person temporarily helpless and breaking past ordinary coping and defensive operations" (p. 10). Terr differentiated among three categories of trauma: (a) a one-time occurrence, that is, an unanticipated "single blow" (Type I); (b) repeated exposure to extreme external events (Type II); and (c) cross-over stressors, which are one-time events that have long-term catastrophic consequences (Type III). In the context of childhood illness, we believe that Terr's definition of Type I childhood trauma matches some children's experience of physical injury, dental extractions or surgery. Examples of Type II trauma include children's experience of repeated, painful medical procedures administered to treat childhood cancer including spinal taps and bone marrow aspirations, debridement of burned tissue, or surgical procedures. It may also apply to recurrent pain associated with chronic diseases such as arthritis, hemophilia, sickle cell disease and cancer or the experience of asthma attacks. An example of Type III trauma might be an experience of loss of a limb, or accidental facial disfigurement.

Terr (1991) reported that the characteristic sequelae of childhood trauma—strongly visualized or otherwise repeatedly perceived memories, repetitive behaviors, trauma-specific fears and a sense of severely limited future—are found regardless of the source of the traumatic event or the age of the child. Each of these behavioral sequelae could interrupt the child's ability to function in the classroom cognitively and socially and can be seen in children's written work, disruptive or negative behavior, and the inability to play with pleasure by oneself or with others. The most dramatic sequelae of childhood trauma, from a psychosocial perspective, is the development of multiple personality disorders. The absence of comfort or reparative experiences after traumatic experience plays a critical role in the development of this form of psychopathology. Koocher and his colleagues (Bronfman, Biron, Campis, & Koocher, 1998; Koocher & Pollin, 1994; Shapiro & Koocher, 1996) made a strong argument for medical crisis intervention with a child who has been traumatized by extreme physical injury, repeated pain of aggressive treatment, or recurrent pain of chronic disease.

One of the reasons that necessary medical care is potentially so traumatic is that the child is in a classic "double-bind" (Bateson, Jackson, Haley, & Weakland, 1956). The doctor and the young patient are involved in an intense relationship in which a contradictory message is given ("This won't hurt," or "I'm doing this to make you better"). The child can't effectively challenge the message, nor can the child escape. As Terr (1991) suggested, "ordinary coping" will not work for the child in this situation—the experience is overwhelming, in fact, traumatic. Children who are hurt call out for their parents, yet Varni (Varni, Blount, Waldron, & Smith, 1995) pointed out that, unfortunately, strategies parents use to help a child cope with a scraped knee on the playground may not be beneficial in the medical setting. Although it is true that some parents can facilitate children's coping, others actually increase their children's distress, for example, by looking on passively or even assisting in restraining their children during the administration of a painful procedure (Blount, Corbin, Sturgis, Prater, & James, 1989; Bush, Melamed, & Cockrell, 1989; Morgan & Steward, 1996; Peterson, Oliver, & Saldana, 1997). Furthermore, adults—parents and medical staff—frequently underestimate the amount of pain a child experiences, or wrongly believe that with experience a child will adapt to the pain of a repeated medical procedure.

There are options available to make many medical procedures less traumatic (such as Zofran for control of nausea and vomiting, behavioral strategies taught to parents and children to increase the sense of control or distract attention, and EMLA cream to take the sting out of venipunctures). We have found that interventions to lessen the pain of the physical trauma of necessary procedures are not always offered, and even if offered, are not always accepted by children or their families (Steward, O'Connor, Acredolo, & Steward, 1996). Thus the diagnosis and treatment of injury and of many chronic diseases still present children with painful experiences falling well outside the normal range of tolerance and well beyond the parameters of most children's coping strategies.

The matrix in Fig. 9.2 portrays children's experiences with necessary medical care. It has three intersecting dimensions that we have identified from the clinical literature and from our observation and interviews of children in medical settings: (a) the relative painfulness of the experience (ranging from no pain through excruciating pain); (b) the proximity of instruments or equipment to the body (ranging from treatments that do not touch the body to those that penetrate body boundaries, e.g., breaking the skin or penetrating an orifice), and (c) the cognitive congruence of the experience of the medical care with a child's understanding of the need for that care (ranging from consonant with the child's understanding to totally incongruent and incomprehensible to the child).

Using this matrix we would predict that any procedure that could be described as painful, breaking body boundaries, and incongruent, unnecessary or harmful from the child's perspective would be maximally disruptive both cognitively and emotionally. "The needle" fits that description, and indeed clinical experience and survey research confirm that children fear and dislike needles more than any other experience during clinic visits or hospitalization. It is a common theme in hospital playrooms as children give their dolls hundreds of shots, reversing roles and replaying what has happened with a vengeance. Any time research protocols include a blood draw (e.g., to check the level of medication to determine compliance), there are very few volunteers! Some children do adapt to the necessity of needles,

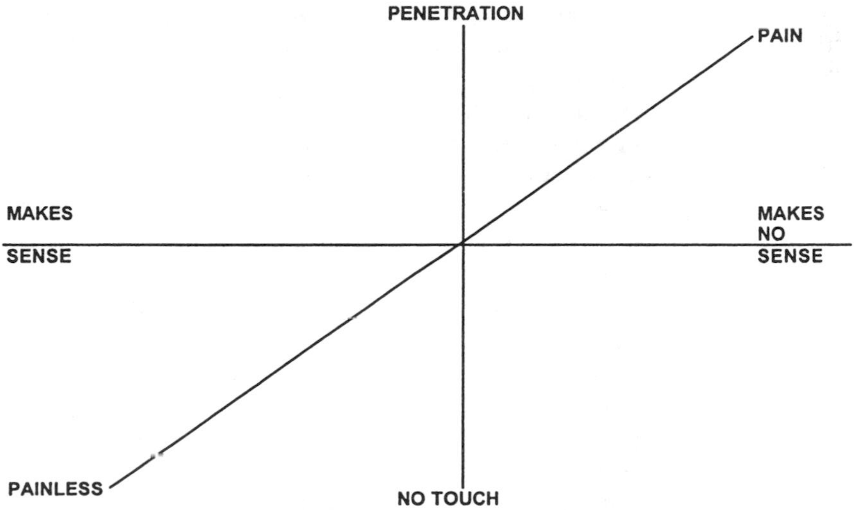


FIG. 9.2. Child's appraisal of medical care utilizing variables of pain, touch, and child's comprehension of intent of diagnostic or treatment procedure.

like the 10-year-old boy who said, "I remember when I thought finger sticks hurt, Man, I must have been crazy! They are nothing more than a tired mosquito bite!" (Ross, 1989). Others report the opposite experience with repeated painful procedures, like this 6-year-old boy who told Dr. Ross, "I was more braver when I was little than when I was big."

Any procedure that falls at the extreme of any of the three variables will probably cause a child emotional or behavioral disruption. Thus an X-ray or CT scan, which does not hurt, and does not touch the body can still be traumatic to a child who believes that the purpose of the procedure is so that "the doctors can read the bad thought in my mind." We found that the stethoscope was not feared because its touch is cold, but because the doctor might find out "that I be dead" (Steward & Regalbuto, 1975). As we noted earlier, children do not adapt to pain—some procedures hurt every time they are administered (Steward, Steward, Joye, & Reinhart, 1991).

A fourth dimension, not shown on the matrix, but of growing importance with advances in medical technology, is the child's role in administration of a medical procedure. Jaime, a 14-year-old with diabetes reflected on the control issue this way, "When I give myself my shot, you're doing it from both ends. You feel it from the doctor's side pushing it in, and you feel it from the patient's side going in. This way I feel the pain that you feel. It's best this way." We believe that while the actual pain of the medical procedure may be the same, by increasing the child's participation and control in administration the potential trauma of the experience will be lessened.

School psychologists and other nonmedical school personnel can use this matrix to help prepare children for medical procedures, such as vision and hearing screening and vaccinations completed on school sites. To use this model effectively, one must understand exactly what will be happening to the child, so that you can address the questions: Will it hurt? What equipment will be used and will it touch or go inside me? And why are they doing it to me? Given this information, a variety of coping strategies can be introduced (Genevro et al., 1996; Ross, 1984; Varni et al., 1995). Although medical staff are likely to be involved in preparing a child for rare, dramatic, usually painful procedures that often accompany the treatment of chronic disease, the matrix may be useful in the emotional debriefing of a child returning to school following medical procedures, the work of Janoff-Bulmann's Appraisal III (Bronfman et al., 1998).

## WHO IS AT RISK?

There are several groups of individuals in the classroom who are at risk as a result of a medical crisis and could benefit from counseling: children who have been diagnosed with chronic and life-threatening diseases, children who are prone to acute injury, and children who live with chronic, life-threatening disease in their families. In conceptualizing the risk status of an individual child, the stressors and resources of both the child and of the family need to be considered. Many children not only experience a medical crisis, but also live with families who have limited social, economic, and personal resources to cope or have developed maladaptive coping strategies that may actually increase the negative health and psychosocial outcomes for the child. The co-occurrence of multiple stressors on these families is not rare. Finally, the school staff themselves are also at risk as they work through a medical crisis with a student and the student's family.

### Children With Chronic and Life-Threatening Disease

We have already described that many of the diagnostic and treatment procedures that children experience, while medically necessary, are very painful and highly distressing. School re-entry is potentially distressing as well, regardless of whether the cause of the absence is following the initial diagnosis of a chronic disease, a prolonged treatment series, or a serious injury. Ross (1989) proposed an assignment for the teacher of the "re-entry child." She believes it is critical for the child re-entering school after a medically related absence to experience specific and visible academic success. This strikes me as a fine recommendation, for it offers the child the opportunity to re-exert control and demonstrate skills in the cognitive domain in the familiar world of the classroom, after receiving unwelcome body touch and handling by staff in a foreign and often dis-empowering hospital setting. One 10-year-old boy who had lost his hair and was extremely pale told Ross, "I'm way behind now, and when I go back [to school], all the kids will think I'm dumb as well as a weirdo" (p. 84). Ross has an assignment for the school counselor as well: She believes that each child needs to be equipped to confront and handle teasing (Ross & Ross, 1984; Ross, chap. 6, this volume). For example, Ross notes that children with leukemia often report that their "worst pain ever" is being teased when they return to school. Each child should be prepared to deal with classmates' questions and comments—regardless of whether they are motivated by cruelty or simply curiosity. In addition, at the elementary school level it is very useful, in consultation with the child and his or her parents, to offer special preparation for the whole class prior to a child's return. Sometimes parents want to participate, sometimes they prefer that a teacher talk with the class after being briefed by medical staff or a hospital child life worker. Sometimes the child wants to talk with classmates, especially if there is special medical apparatus or equipment to show. Peer contacts are often difficult for children with chronic disease to maintain so that fragile peer relationships need to be supported and nurtured by teachers. Jonathan, an 8-year-old whose best friend has asthma told him, "It kind of worries me a lot when you're in the hospital, you're there for a long time. I sometimes think you're dead" (Rich & Chalfen, 1999). One adolescent reported to Bearison (1991) that on his return to class after a 6-week absence for cancer treatment, his teacher arranged a little conference in a private room during the lunch period "between me and my friends ... she asked me who I wanted to talk to ..." His friends asked dozens of questions, including asking if they could catch his cancer by drinking from the same cup! Most importantly, they welcomed him back to school.

For many children with chronic illness, the transition to adolescence is very difficult and constitutes a more subtle version of a medical crisis. Billy, the child with diabetes that we introduced at the beginning of the chapter, will experience some changes in relationship to his chronic disease as he moves from middle childhood into adolescence. Often this developmental shift means the youngster will be expected to assume increased responsibility for his or her treatment regimen (La Greca & Skyler, 1995). To the astonishment and dismay of his parents and his pediatrician, the cooperative elementary-aged child may become less rather than more reliable in "managing" his illness as the child makes the transition to adolescence (Gudas, Koocher, & Wypij, 1991). Adolescents stop taking their medications and don't tell their physicians; or they do tell their physicians, "... you can write the prescriptions all you want, I won't do it!" (Rich & Chalfen, 1999). The increased cognitive flexibility of adolescence will make the uncertainty of his disease more starkly clear and therefore more stressful. One teenager with severe asthma confessed, "... it's really scarey to think, what if I didn't get to the hospital in time? Or, what if I wasn't in the right place? And then you start playing the 'what if' game, and that becomes even more of a torment" (Rich & Chalfen, 1999). The temptations of "teenage" food, activities, and the strong pull for identification with his healthy classmates will make him even more painfully aware of his differentness and dangerously vulnerable to peer pressure. In addition to the psychological and developmental stressors, Wysocki et al. (1992) found in survey research that professionals tend to overestimate adolescents' competence about necessary treatment regimens. Some children with chronic conditions may experience new complications as they move into adolescence—a result of physical development and/or deteriorating health. It is important to keep in touch with youngsters during this developmental transition, for their appraisal of their health condition and their coping strategies may be up for renegotiation.

Finally, we believe that children who are long-term survivors of childhood cancer are an especially vulnerable group of youngsters. Most are diagnosed as small children when they have neither the cognitive capacity to understand their predicament, nor the language to express their thoughts or feelings. Their experiences of medical procedures are painfully traumatic, with most treatment protocols lasting 2 to 3 years. Nir (1985), reflecting on 5 years of providing psychiatric liaison services to families and children in treatment for cancer, observed that "post-traumatic stress disorders accompanied, almost without exception, the diagnosis of cancer" (p. 131). Our (Steward et al., 1996) recent pilot study of survivors, diagnosed as 2- to 4-year-olds and interviewed as 7- to 11-year-olds, revealed that the children who had survived cancer were remarkable in their secrecy and social isolation. Few had told their friends or teachers of their earlier bout with cancer, although their memories of the events and places and people on our medical staff were fully intact and often intrusive. There was little or no communication with their families about their traumatic experiences possibly because families believed (or wanted to believe) that the children had forgotten. One mother reported, "M doesn't have any disturbing memories, she was too young." Her daughter, contradicting, said, "I wish I could forget the whole thing." Another child, whose mother told us her daughter didn't remember, reported her memories of her treatment-related pains and said, "I still wake up screaming!" Many children reported anxious rumination about their parents or siblings being diagnosed with cancer or other life-threatening diseases, or even re-occurrence of cancer in themselves. Some reported the sense of a foreshortened future that has been identified by Terr (1991) as a sequela of posttraumatic stress. To our question about growing up one child said, "If I ever think about growing up I always think that I will die before I ever grow up." These children are often invisible to the school staff, but no less in need of thoughtful and compassionate psychosocial intervention.

## Injury-Prone Children

Every teacher and every parent knows that some children are more prone to injury than others. Boyce (1996) confirmed that this observation is supported by incidence studies with animals and humans. Research by Boyce and his colleagues, focusing on the contribution of unique biological and temperamental characteristics of the child to the likelihood of injury, makes the picture more interesting. He asserts that there is a subset of children who are not only *more vulnerable* than other children to injury and acute illness in some situations; in other situations they are actually *more resilient.* These children can be characterized by their sensitive cardiovascular response at the biological level, their risk-taking at the behavioral level, and their exquisite sensitivity to psychosocial and environmental stress. These children are more likely than other children to be injured or catch the current flu bug when they experience high stress, yet are actually less likely than other children to experience injury or illness when their stress level is low. His work has focused on multiple "mundane, low-intensity" sources of stress that school children must deal with on a regular basis (what Lazarus would call "hassles"). For example, there are personal experiences like losing your lunch or jacket or a toy, having to ride in a different carpool, getting to bed too late or getting up too early; and there are ecological stressors in the school environment like having to deal with a substitute teacher, "vacation days," the student–teacher ratio, relative ease of access to supportive staff. Many children will roll with the punches and take both the personal and environmental stressors in stride—but this subset of children will not, and that is exactly what puts them at risk for acute illness and injury. There are data to support the link for this subset of children between stress and injury across the school years from preschoolers (Barr, Boyce, & Zeltzer, 1994; Liang & Boyce, 1993) to high-school athletes (Smith, Smoll, & Ptacek, 1990). A school environment in which teachers and counselors provide an ambiance that is positive and supportive, offer quick response to personal stress, and model effective problem solving can be a win–win situation. It will make an enormous difference to these children and they will thrive, and teachers will feel more effective and enjoy their role as well.

### Children With Chronic, Life-Threatening Illness in Their Families

I saw a big billboard from the train recently, picturing a three generational family—mom, dad, the kids, grandma, uncle Joe. The caption was "One of us has MS, it affects all of us!" True, and one of the children pictured could be in your classroom, since it is estimated that 5% to 15% of children and adolescents have parents who suffer from significant medical conditions (Worsham, Compas, & Ey, 1997). Children who live with illness in the family often carry invisible burdens of anxiety and worry, as well as extra care-taking responsibilities that take time away from homework, play, and even rest. This is a relatively new area for clinical research and just a handful of studies have been completed. The initial findings suggest that age of the child, and gender of both the sick parent and child make a difference in the patterns of stress and coping in these families. Adolescents experience more stress than younger children—possibly because the younger children do not understand the nature or meaning of their parent's illness, nor do they understand the possible hereditary features for themselves of their parent's disease. Adolescent girls whose mothers are seriously ill experience specially high stress, often picking up the burden of household management, being emotionally available to the mother, and having to play the role of informational conduit about their mother's condition to other family members and friends (Worsham et al., 1997). Work with individual adolescents may be especially helpful, because parents do not see or at least do not report the distress that their children reveal through self-report (Compas et al., 1994; Wellisch et al., 1992).

### School Staff

Our recent review of research conducted with children across a broad range of troubled and traumatic family and community settings revealed that many adults (parents and professionals) have difficulty relating to traumatized children, and often employ denial or inattention to shield themselves from what such children are thinking and feeling (Steward & O'Connor, 1994). No getting around it–it is very hard work to teach in a classroom with one or more of the children identified earlier. The challenge is that each child so identified is unique and requires an individual educational and psychosocial plan, demands the establishment and nurturance of a complex communication network with adults outside the classroom walls, and necessitates constant monitoring in relation to the other students in class. It is also hard work because frequently the child touches the teacher's heart. At our medical center a study on adult stress was completed with the medical staff (Dr. Mark Servis, personal communication, December, 1999). The focus of the study was on those working in the Emergency Room who cared for children who were seriously injured, victims of violent physical or sexual abuse, or who died while in their care. It was found that 80% of the staff reported physical symptoms of their own in the first 24 hours after their shift, and 50% of the staff reported that they had physical symptoms that continued for at least 3 weeks. Based on my 30 years of experience as a supervisor for psychotherapists working with young abused children, I believe that if you have children of your own either the same age or younger, then having a child in medical crisis in your classroom will also increase your worry about your own children and stress your relationship with them.

## PRIMARY PREVENTION

### Seat Belts and Helmets

I have already noted that accidents were the primary cause of injury and death in children under the age of 15 years. Head injuries were the most common type of injury among children treated in the emergency room of our medical center in 1996. Most of those head injuries could have been prevented! Of those children injured in car crashes fewer than one third were wearing seat belts, and only 10% of the children hit while riding a bike were wearing a helmet. Safety curriculum is mandated for elementary school children in most but not all states, but changing human behavior obviously requires a highly focused campaign. Schools can and should mount campaigns not only in the classroom, but work in cooperation with other community agencies and hospitals at local health fairs. Primary prevention time, energy, and dollars spent on this issue with school children could prevent irreversible brain damage and spinal cord injuries. But, words alone are not sufficient. Campaigns for behavioral change, like remembering to snap seat belts closed and to wear helmets, requires monitoring, feedback, and reinforcement in order to be effective. Adults and children need to buy in, and Peterson and Oliver (1995) noted that evaluations of prevention programs across the country reveal that there must be real consequences for safer behavior.

## Three Way Communication

Teachers and parents who participated in the focus groups designed by Strong and Sandoval (1999) called for more communication about the needs and school progress of chronically ill youngsters with neuromuscular disease. The call was for teacher–parent sessions that were more consistent, with more frequent exchange of views, information, and problem solving. This same request could be made by the parent of every child with a chronic disease or who is recuperating from a major injury. The daily course of these children can change episodically and unpredictably. Sometimes it feels like just when you "get it right," then a medical crisis occurs or a child's treatment protocol changes and you need to make new accommodations or lesson plans or even shift your academic expectations for a child. The initiation and maintenance of this kind of communication network takes time. If you feel stressed and unrewarded for the efforts, that will be communicated to the other participants and you could undo some of your good work in the process. You need to make sure that your school administration is aware both of the necessity of it, and your allocation of time for it.

## In-Service Training

If you anticipate or currently have a child with special medical needs in your classroom, there are a number of different people who can help you tailor your educational plans for that child. Sometimes the district special education consultant can be helpful. Given the parent's permission, the child's physician is definitely one person to contact. You might offer to meet the physician at his or her office for an initial consultation; then let the physician see the specific classroom where their patient will be. Another idea, if you live near a major medical center or children's hospital, would be to make contact with the director of the pediatric child life program, the art therapist and the hospital teacher might come. These folk often have a wealth of information—from a psychosocial and developmental perspective—that can be very helpful. They also often have some marvelous very practical suggestions for eliciting cooperation from children who, due to illness or injury, initially seem withdrawn or reticent to re-engage in the rough and tumble of the classroom. You might invite these people to meet with you, or with you and the parents; but you might also create a school-wide or district wide in-service for you and your colleagues. Asking for help is a sign of strength and professionalism, not a sign of weakness.

You can also do some reading. Bearison (1991) published an extraordinary book in which 8 children with cancer speak directly to you, the reader. His conversations with some children cover more than a 3-year period. In addition, he has organized common narrative themes that arise in conversations with children who have been diagnosed with cancer, again presented in the children's own voices, including "why me?", God and prayer, losing your hair, advice for others who have cancer. The children's perspective, fears, and wisdom are instructive for those of us who have personally escaped life-threatening disease, and are generalizable well beyond any specific diagnostic category. Another view of children's experience of illness is powerfully presented in the book, *I Will Sing Life: Voices from the Hole in the Wall Gang Camp*, by Berger, Lithwick and Seven Campers (1992), which features seven children who attended a summer camp and follows them home. I've used this book with medical students and they have found it medically accurate and the children's stories compelling. Although discussion of individual infectious and chronic diseases is beyond the scope of this chapter, you may wish more information. Gold (1996) published information on infectious diseases aimed at the teacher. Information about specific chronic diseases is well presented in a recent book, edited by Phelps (1998), *Health-Related Disorders in Children and Adolescents*. Each chapter includes a description of the etiology, the disease process, behavioral manifestations, discussion of the educational consequences and identification of resources that would be helpful for teachers, families, and the child.

## METHODS THAT WORK WITH HIGH-RISK CHILDREN

### Listen Actively

Every child who is living with disease or injury has a story to tell of his or her illness experiences and that child needs someone who will listen. Werner and Smith (1988) documented the critically important role of a caring adult in the lives of vulnerable children. In their research those children who survived and thrived into a productive adulthood, although born at risk and into a risky environment, had a teacher or a grandparent or a priest who listened to them during their childhood. Half a century ago Carl Rogers (1951) proposed that the effective counselor should listen actively and be warm and respectful. He called the therapeutic stance "unconditional positive regard." The purpose of the listening is to understand and empathize. Rogers advocated the use of silence, to give the individual space to explore their thoughts and feelings. Unlike the conversational expectation to "take turns," the counselor's job is to validate, or clarify, or summarize what he or she has heard. From my clinical experience, his advice is still right on! Medical staff have busy schedules that often mean that they seek information about the physical symptoms or the disease process, but they often fail to listen to their young patients' personal experience of illness. Parents own emotional turmoil may also distract them from hearing their child's narrative. Children sometimes decide not to discuss either disease or illness issues with their parents, because of the distress it obviously causes their parents. In the picture that one child drew for me of her family, she was lying on her hospital bed while her parents and both brothers were looking down at her with sad faces and tears streaming from their eyes. Teachers and counselors at school are in a unique position to fill a void.

What should you listen for? Koocher and Pollin (1994) suggested that there is a set of core fears or concerns that emerge, often in sequence, in the midst of a medical crisis. They have identified the following: fear of loss of control, loss of self-image, fear of dependency, fear of stigma, fear of abandonment, fear of expressing anger, fear of isolation, and fear of death. They believe that failure to address these issues can result in a patient being immobilized, depressed, withdrawn, or anxious. Addressing these issues offer patients opportunities for exploration and review of their experiences and incorporation of them into their own life story. Loss of control, stigma, death—these are difficult areas even for adult patients to discuss, and may seem so for child patients as well. Fortunately, children can communicate in many modalities. Their illness narratives can be expressed in words, phrases, and songs (I have given some children a tape recorder and let them record while their back is to me—to preserve their sense of privacy, and their control of the timing of the disclosures). Children can also work graphically by drawing and painting or sculpting with clay to tell you their story. I had the privilege of supervising a gifted artist and photographer, Johanna Russell, as she honed her skills as an art therapist in our medical center. I was astonished at the stark reality of collages that the children from the burn unit made from their own bloody bandages, and the poignant emotions drawn on the plaster gauze masks of the children's faces that she made with the children in the pediatric unit. The common key is the focus on a sensory mode of cognitive processing, thus increasing access to sensory modalities for communication. That should be easy for those of us who have been trained to work therapeutically with children. A school art teacher or an art therapist, especially one who is based in a medical facility, may be a very useful consultant.

Visual narrative techniques, employed in two innovative research projects to study the life experiences of children with chronic disease, offer a very promising avenue for school counselors to facilitate discussion of core concerns identified by Koocher and Pollin (1994) with children. Clark (1999) gave 36 children and their families cameras so that the children, who were 5 to 8 years old, could "show what it is like to have diabetes (or asthma)." Clark then conducted "autodriven interviews" in which the photos served as the basis of the interview. One child with diabetes chose to have himself photographed at a Halloween party standing in line with his empty plate—in stark contrast to the overflowing plates of his classmates, while a child with asthma asked his mother to photograph all of the flowers in the garden to which he was allergic. Some children refused to have themselves photographed in vulnerable positions (such as when they were getting a shot), while others were delighted to demonstrate their prowess in "doing my own shot," and still others showed coping and comforting strategies such as sleeping with a stuffed animal or wearing a charm on their medical identification bracelet. Rich and Chalfen (1999) gave camcorders to 19 subjects, aged 8 to 19 years, for a month to document for their physicians what it was like to live with asthma. In each of these studies children pictured pain, terror, and distress and were able to remember and discuss their thoughts and feelings about the "bad times." Rich and Chalfen found that fear of sudden death from asthma was a consistent theme touched on by almost all of the participants in their study. I believe that visual narrative techniques are highly promising ways to focus the discourse between the child and the counselor about tough issues especially if the photos and videotape are in the child's control. Then, as with other narrative material, the child's own sense of pacing and ability to cope with the emotion surrounding the events is respected.

In addition to listening for the reality with which chronically ill or injured children must cope, all of us who have lived and worked with children know that they can use imagination and fantasy for coping with anxiety and stress. And there are many reports in the clinical literature about the use of imagination specifically with children in hospital settings (Beuf, 1979; O'Connor, 1991; Zeltzer & LeBaron, 1986). You don't have to generate the imagery, follow a recipe from a treatment manual, or superimpose some clever fantasy of your own—children do that spontaneously. What you must do, if you are working with high-risk children is give them an opportunity to tap into their fantasies and share them with you. They will tell you that their teddy bear has sickle-cell anemia, or that their baby doll's "count is too low." Most young children identify and then outgrow transition objects, the blankets and soft toys that uniquely comfort them (Winnicott, 1971). Ill children hold on to them longer and the importance of the transition object, especially in times of high medically induced distress, is often missed by medical staff and families. Clark (1998) reported the importance of a toy car to a child with diabetes. It was so important that his mother bought several of them, keeping one in her own car, she sent one to school each day in his backpack, and the child took the car with him to medical appointments.

## Body Work

When the integrity of the body has been insulted through injury or disease, words will only go so far in the process of reintegration. I believe these children need to reclaim control of their physical body, and to find areas of physical competence, whatever their level of fitness. Too often, elementary and middle-school physical education programs are only for the physically fit, and have little flexibility for children with special physical needs. I urge you to explore programs in your community. One promising option in our own community has been the development of self-defense training specifically for children who have physical limitations. I also believe that for children who have been injured or sick, but have returned to health, martial arts training is very valuable. Akido, the only martial art that is purely defensive, has training programs for children as young as 5 years. When a child has been hurt and handled by others, it is very easy to learn the victim role. There are children, such as those with cystic fibrosis, asthma, arthritis, or hemophilia, whose symptoms may be exacerbated by physical activity that is wrongly paced, or where performance criteria are set for healthy children. Most children whose chronic disease process is well-controlled with medication can participate more fully than they believe in physical activity. Exercise, self-defense, and the martial arts give a child the opportunity to learn physical skills to gain control, increase personal and physical autonomy, and improve self-image. Consultation with the child, parents, and the child's physician is useful to determine how to tailor a program to fit a child's specific need and physical skill level.

## The Internet

The Internet may offer a special resource to children who must live with sickness or injury, and their parents, teachers, and counselors. A national organization has been formed that is dedicated to almost every major childhood disease and most now have their own web sites and links to relevant additional sites. Beyond the obvious access to information and education about diagnosis and treatment of specific diseases are a range of possibilities that are being developed. It is only fair to warn you that currently many of the web sites identified by topical searches are actually appeals for program and research funding or product advertisements. But exploring the resources on the web is worth the effort—and might well be a project that you could do with a child, or that a child and a classmate could do together. Chat rooms may have a special appeal for the child who looks funny or smells peculiarly or moves slowly—the anonymity and uncritical acceptance will be welcomed. We used to link children undergoing similar treatment protocols by phone with one another—and this is just a more sophisticated, and less expensive strategy.

### Encourage and Nurture Friendships

This suggestion is much more difficult than it seems at first blush—and the word should really be "friendship," not plural. Children with chronic diseases or serious injury often have honed skills with adults, but not other children. Sometimes their social–relational skills with peers are immature, pseudomature or just a bit clumsy for their age/stage. Peer acceptance may be dependent on two factors: (a) how obvious a child's symptoms are, and (b) how much the disease interferes with a child's participation in regular school activities (Healey, McArvey, Saaz von Hippel, & Jones, 1978). The more visibly symptomatic and impaired the child, the more difficult it will be to gain peer acceptance or to initiate friendships. The classroom teacher is in a good position to identify a child who has the social skills and emotional capacity to reach out in friendship to the sick child. Call the parents of both children and let them know that you are concerned, see if they might help you in the task of linking the two children together. The two children can be teamed up within the classroom on a number of assignments. The establishment and maintenance of a friendship will have added power if there is occasional after school or weekend contact as well.

## GROUP INTERVENTION

### Summer Camp

Summer camps for children with chronic and life-threatening disease give children a wonderful opportunity to spend time with kids "just like me!" Some camps are created for children and adolescents with a specific disease—cancer, diabetes, etc., whereas other camps take children with a variety of medical diagnoses. Although there are often educational sessions about their disease from the biomedical model, Clark (1998) noted that the scientific information is far less important to the children than the opportunity to get acquainted with other children who live with similar restrictions, physical limitations, medical regimes. They learn they are not unique. At camp the familiar medical equipment used in dreaded and daily treatment can be transformed into playful tools and objects that bring laughter. Hypodermic needles can be used to shoot out paint for art projects and nebulizers can be used to blow up balloons. Asthmatic children teach each other such valuable skills as how to cheat on a breathing test, by holding their thumb on the back of the device! For some children, it is the highlight of their year. Even very ill children can be accommodated, and some will hold off death for the opportunity to return just one more time to their beloved camp counselors and friends. School staff can and should be strongly supportive of the chance for chronically ill children to attend a special summer camp. In fact, you may be the person to persuade a cautious parent that it is a great idea to let their child attend.

## Social Skills Training

Varni and his colleagues (Varni, Katz, Colegrove, & Dolgin, 1993) working on the problem of re-integrating children newly diagnosed with cancer back into the classroom, added a social skills training component to the standard re-entry program (education and support for children returning to school, school conferences, and classroom presentations for peers and teachers). The social skills training focused on social–cognitive problem solving, assertiveness training and ways of handling teasing and name calling. The rationale for the addition of this component was the observation that young children with cancer typically have not developed the social competence necessary to cope with the stressors associated with their disease. A 9-month follow-up confirmed that social skills training was helpful in lowering parent report of behavior problems, decreasing externalizing problems and increasing self-esteem.

The program designed by Varni and his colleagues is typical of many hosted and run out of the medical–clinical setting where there are sufficient children with common medical conditions to benefit from the group process. However, Rynard and his colleagues (Rynard et al., 1998) reported the success of a school-based support program created for children with cancer. One group was for children currently on treatment, the second for children who had completed the treatment protocol. Parents and teachers both reported high satisfaction with the program. Parents rated their children as displaying a greater number of negative behaviors than did teachers. It may be that children display more symptomatic behavior at home (there is a strain on siblings of ill children—sibling rivalry for scarce family resources may have been one stimulus), and parents may also have been functioning under more daily stress and seen the same behaviors as more negative than teachers did.

## Focus Groups

Strong and Sandoval (1999) reported the results of a series of focus group conversations with teachers, parents, and individuals with neuromuscular disease, a rare but debilitating disease, to gather information about coping issues and teacher attitudes. Analysis of these conversations resulted in a "map of concerns"—essentially a Ven diagram displaying those issues identified uniquely by each of the three groups, and those overlapping, shared concerns. The results are fascinating, and the technique worth replicating, for example, within a local school or school district. The authors included both teachers who had children with neuromuscular disease in their classroom and those who did not. This is a feature of the model that definitely should be replicated.

In summary, as laws are implemented and medical technology increases there will be more children with chronic disease and serious injury mainstreamed in our classrooms. Informed compassionate school staff in consultation with families and medical personnel can be pivotal. The devil, of course, is in the detail—for each child's need is unique. The teacher who anticipates the embarrassing physical changes a child with cancer will experience as a result of chemotherapy can turn a stimulus for teasing into a sensitive greeting for a returning classmate (Ross, chap. 6, this volume). Yet, a principal, with the best intentions in the world, may warn other students not to touch a hemophilic child, leaving that child not only "untouchable" but also feeling powerless and humiliated (Massie, 1985). A school nurse can mistakenly support an asthmatic child's immature dependency on adults for health care, or can encourage independent observations and judgments about necessary medical intervention (Lewis & Lewis, 1989; Lewis et al., 1977). A school psychologist can passively listen as a child retells his or her story about necessary, repeatedly painful medical procedures or can actively work with the child on coping strategies (Bronfman et al., 1998). School staff have the power to create an atmosphere that could contribute to a child's low self-esteem and stimulate troubling or avoidant coping strategies resulting in school phobia or school failure, or they can insure that school is one of the child's best experiences. In fact, the classroom may be "the only place where I'm normal!"

## REFERENCES

Altschuler, J. L., & Ruble, D. N. (1989). Developmental changes in children's awareness of strategies for coping with uncontrollable stress. *Child Development, 60*, 1337–1349.

Band, E. B., & Weisz, J. R. (1988). How to feel better when it feels bad: Children's perspectives on coping with everyday stress. *Child Development, 24*, 247–253.

Barr, R. G., Boyce, W. T., & Zeltzer, L. (1994). The stress-illness association in children: A perspective from the biobehavioral interface. In R. J. Haggerty, L. R. Sherrod, N. Garmezy, & M. Rutter

(Eds.), *Stress, risk and resilience in children and adolescents: Processes, mechanisms, and interventions* (pp. 182–224). New York: Cambridge University Press.
Bateson, G., Jackson, D. D., Haley, J., & Weakland, J. H. (1956). Toward a theory of schizophrenia. *Behavioral Science, 1*, 251–264.
Bearison, D. J. (1991). *"They never want to tell you."* Cambridge, MA: Harvard University Press.
Bearison, D. J., & Mulhern, R. K. (Eds.). (1994). *Pediatric psycho-oncology: Psychological perspectives on children with cancer.* New York: Oxford University Press.
Berger, L., Lithwick, D., & Seven Campers (1992). I will sing life: Voices from the hole in the wall gang camp. Boston: Little, Brown.
Beuf, A. H. (1979). *Biting off the bracelet: A study of children in hospitals.* Philadelphia, PA: University of Pennsylvania Press.
Blount, R. L., Corbin, S. M., Sturges, J. W., Wolfe, V. V., Prater, J. M., & James, L., D. (1989). The relationship between adults' behavior and child coping and distress during BMA/LP procedures: A sequential analysis. *Behavior Therapy, 20*, 585–601.
Boyce, W. T. (1996). Biobehavioral reactivity and injuries in children and adolescents. In M. H. Bornstein & J. L. Genevro (Eds.), *Child development and behavioral pediatrics* (pp. 35–58). Mahwah, NJ: Lawrence Erlbaum Associates.
Bronfman, E. T., Biron Campis, L., & Koocher, G. P. (1998). Helping children cope: Clinical issues for acutely injured and medically traumatized children. *Professional Psychology: Research & Practice, 29*(6), 574–581.
Bush, J. P., Melamed, B. G., & Cockrell, C. S. (1989). Parenting children in a stressful medical situation. In T. W. Miller (Ed.), *Stressful life events.* Madison, CT: International Universities Press.
Campbell, J. D. (1975). Illness is a point of view: The development of children's concepts of illness. *Child Development, 46*, 92–100.
Clark, C. D. (1998). Childhood imagination in the face of chronic illness. In J. de Rivera & T. R. Sarbin (Eds.), *Believed-in imaginings: The narrative construction of reality.* Washington, DC: American Psychological Association.
Clark, C. D. (1999). The autodriven interview: A photographic viewfinder into children's experience. *Visual Sociology, 14*, 39–50.
Compas, B. E., Worsham, N., Epping-Jordan, J. E., Howell, D. C., Grant, K. E., Mireault, G., & Malcarne, V. (1994). When mom or dad has cancer: Markers of psychological distress in cancer patients, spouses, and children. *Health Psychology, 13*, 507–515.
Eisenberg, L. (1977). Disease and illness. *Culture, Medicine and Psychiatry, 1*, 9–23.
Fassler, J. (1978). *Helping children cope.* New York: The Free Press.
Freud, A. (1952). The role of bodily illness in the mental life of children. *Psychoanalytic Study of the Child, 7*, 69–80.
Genevro, J. L., Andreassen, C. J., & Bornstein, M. H. (1996). Young children's understanding of routine medical care and strategies for coping with stressful medical experiences. In M. H. Bornstein & J. L. Genevro (Eds.), *Child development and behavioral pediatrics* (pp. 85–104). Mahwah, NJ: Lawrence Erlbaum Associates.
Gold, R. (1996). What every teacher should know about infectious diseases. In R. H. A. Haslam & P. J. Valletutti (Eds.), *Medical problems in the classroom* (pp. 53–69, 3rd ed.). Austin, TX: pro-ed.
Gudas, L. J., Koocher, G. P., & Wypij, D. (1991). Perception of medical compliance in children and adolescents with cystic fibrosis. *Journal of Developmental and Behavioral Pediatrics, 12*, 236–242.
Harter, S. (1985). Processes underlying the construction, maintenance and enhancement of the self concept in children. In J. Suls & A. Greenwald (Eds.), *Psychological perspectives on the self* (Vol. 3, pp. 137–181). Hillsdale, NJ: Lawrence Erlbaum Associates.
Healey, A., McAreavey, P., Saaz von Hippel, C., & Jones, F. H. (1978). *Mainstreaming preschoolers: Children with health impairments.* Washington, DC: U.S. Department of Health, Education and Welfare.

*Individuals with Disabilities Education Act Amendments of 1997.* (P.L. 105–17). (1997). 20 U.S.C. Chapter 33 Secs. 1400–1485.

Janoff-Bulman, R. (1992). *Shattered assumptions: Towards a new psychology of trauma.* New York: The Free Press.

Kleinman, A. (1988). *The illness narrative: Suffering, healing and the human condition.* New York: Basic Books.

Kliewer, W. (1997). Children's coping with chronic illness. In S. A. Wolchik & I. N. Sandler (Eds.), *Handbook of children's coping: Linking theory and intervention* (pp. 275–300). New York: Plenum Press.

Koocher, G. P., & Pollin, I. (1994). Medical crisis counseling: A new service delivery model. *Journal of Clinical Psychology in Medicine, 1*, 291–299.

La Greca, A. M., & Schuman, W. B. (1995). Adherence to prescribed medical regimens. In M. C. Roberts (Ed.), *Handbook of pediatric psychology* (pp. 55–83). New York: Guilford Press.

La Greca, A. M., & Skyler, J. S. (1995). Psychological management of diabetes. In C. J. Kelnar (Ed.), *Childhood diabetes* (pp. 295–310). London: Chapman & Hall.

Lazarus, R. S. (1991). *Emotion and adaptation.* New York: Oxford University Press.

Lazarus, R. S., & Folkman, S. (1984). *Stress, appraisal and coping.* New York: Springer.

Leventhal, H. (1986). Symptom reporting: A focus on process. In S. McHugh & T. M. Vallis (Eds.), *Illness behavior: A multidisciplinary model* (pp. 219–237). New York: Plenum Press.

Lewis, C. E., & Lewis, M. A. (1989). Educational outcomes and illness behaviors of participants in a child-initiated care system: A 12-year follow-up study. *Pediatrics, 84*, 845–850.

Lewis, C. E., Lewis, M. A., & Palmer, B. (1977). Child-initiated care: The use of school nursing services by children in an "adult free" system. *Pediatrics, 60*, 499–507.

Liang, S. W., & Boyce, W. T. (1993). The psychobiology of childhood stress. *Current Opinion in Pediatrics, 5*, 545–551.

Massie, R. K. (1985). The constant shadow: Reflections on the life of a chronically ill child. In N. Hobbs & J. M. Perrin (Eds.), *Issues in the care of children with chronic illness* (pp. 13–23). San Fransicso: Jossey-Bass.

Morgan, J., & Steward, M. S. (1996). Nondisclosure of pain by young children following invasive medical procedures. In M. S. Steward & D. S. Steward, Interviewing young children about body touch and handling. *Monographs of the Society for Research in Child Development, 61*(4–5), 144–152.

Nir, Y. (1985). Post-traumatic stress disorder in children with cancer. In S. Eth & R. S. Pynoos (Eds.), *Post-traumatic stress disorder in children* (pp. 123–132). Washington, DC: American Psychiatric Press.

O'Connor, K. J. (1991). *The play therapy primer.* New York: Wiley.

Parmelee, A. H. (1986). Children's illnesses: Their beneficial effects on behavioral development. *Child Development*, 57, 1–10.

Parmelee, A. H. (1996). Commentary: Children's health and the development of social knowledge. In M. H. Bornstein & J. L. Genevro (Eds.), *Child development and behavioral pediatrics* (pp. 155–165). Mahwah, NJ: Lawrence Erlbaum Associates.

Parsons, T. (1958). Definitions of health and illness in light of American values and social structure. In E. G. Jaco (Ed.), *Patients, physicians and illness: Sourcebook in behavioral science and medicine* (pp. 165–187). New York: The Free Press.

Peterson, L., & Oliver, K. K. (1995). Prevention of injuries and disease. In M. C. Roberts (Ed.), *Handbook of pediatric psychology* (pp. 185–199). New York: Guilford Press.

Peterson, L., Oliver, K. K., & Saldana, L. (1997). Children's coping with stressful medical procedures. In S. A. Wolchik & I. N. Sandler (Eds.), *Handbook of children's coping: Linking theory and intervention* (pp. 333–360). New York: Plenum Press.

Phelps, L. (Ed.). (1998). *Health-related disorders in children and adolescents.* Washington, DC: American Psychological Association.

Reich, J. H., Steward, M. S., Rosenblatt, R., & Tupin, J. P. (1985). Prediction of response to treatment in chronic pain patients. *Journal of Clinical Psychiatry, 46*, 425–427.

Rich, M., & Chalfen, R. (1999). Showing and telling asthma: Children teaching physicians with visual narratives. *Visual Sociology, 14*, 51–72.

Rogers, C. R. (1951). *Client-centered therapy: Its' current practice, implications and theory.* Boston: Houghton Mifflin.

Ross, D. M. (1984). Thought-stopping: A coping strategy for impending feared events. *Issues in Comprehensive Pediatric nursing, 7*, 83–89.

Ross, D. M., & Ross, S. A. (1984). Teaching children with leukemia to cope with teasing. *Issues in Comprehensive Pediatric Nursing, 7*, 59–66.

Ross, S. A. (1989). Childhood leukemia: The child's view. *Journal of Psychosocial Oncology, 7*(4), 75–90.

Rynard, D. W., Chambers, A., Klinck, A. M., & Gray, J. D. (1998). School support programs for chronically ill children: Evaluating the adjustment of children with cancer at school. *Children's Health Care, 27*, 31–46.

Sandler, I. N., Wolchik, S. A., MacKinnon, D., Ayers, T. S., & Roosa, M. W. (1997). Developing linkages between theory and intervention in stress and coping processes. In S. A. Wolchik & I. N. Sandler (Eds.), *Handbook of children's coping: Linking theory and intervention* (pp. 3–40). New York: Plenum Press.

Scheidt, P. C., Harel, Y., Trumble, A. C., Jones, D. H., Overpeck, M. D., & Bijur, P. E. (1995). The epidemiology of nonfatal injuries among US children and youth. *American Journal of Public Health, 85*(7), 932–938.

Seligman, M. E. P. (1975). *Learned helplessness: On depression, development and death.* San Fransicso: Freeman.

Shapiro, D. E., & Koocher, G. P. (1996). Goals and practical considerations in outpatient medical crisis intervention. *Professional Psychology: Research and Practice, 27*, 109–120.

Smith, R. E., Smoll, F. L., & Ptacek, J. T. (1990). Conjunctive moderator variables in vulnerability and resiliency research: Life stress, social support and coping skills, and adolescent sport injuries. *Journal of Personality and Social Psychology, 58*(3), 360–370.

Snyder, S. S., & Feldman, D. H. (1977). Internal and external influences on cognitive-developmental change. *Child Development, 49*, 937–943.

Steward, M. S. (1987). Affective and cognitive impact of illness on children's body image. *International Journal of Psychiatric Medicine, 5*, 107–113.

Steward, M. S., & O'Connor, J. (1994). Pediatric pain, trauma and memory. *Current Opinion in Pediatrics, 6*, 411–417.

Steward, M. S., O'Connor, J., Acredolo, C., & Steward, D. S. (1996). The trauma and memory of cancer treatment in children. In M. H. Bornstein & J. L. Genevro (Eds.), *Child development and behavioral pediatrics* (pp. 105–128). Mahwah, NJ: Lawrence Erlbaum Associates.

Steward, M. S., & Regalbuto, G. (1975). Do doctors know what children know? *American Journal of Orthopsychiatry, 45*, 146–149.

Steward, M. S., & Steward, D. S. (1981). Children's conceptions of medical procedures. In R. Bibace & M. E. Walsh (Eds.), *Children's conceptions of health, illness and bodily functions* (pp. 67–84). San Fransicso, CA: Jossey-Bass.

Steward, M. S., Steward, D. S., Joye, N., & Reinhart, M. (1991). Pain judgments by young children and medical staff. *Journal of Pain and Symptom Management, 6*(3), 202.

Strong, K., & Sandoval, J. (1999). Mainstreaming children with neuromuscular disease: A map of concerns. *Exceptional Children, 65*, 353–366.

Terr, L. (1991). Childhood traumas: An outline and overview. *American Journal of Psychiatry, 148*, 10–20.

Varni, J. W., Blount, R. L., Waldron, S. A., & Smith, A. J. (1995). Management of pain and distress. In M. C. Roberts (Ed.), *Handbook of pediatric psychology* (pp. 105–123). New York: Guilford Press.

Varni, J. W., Katz, E. R., Colegrove, R., Jr., & Dolgin, M. (1993). The impact of social skills training on the adjustment of children with newly diagnosed cancer. *Journal of Pediatric Psychology, 18*, 751–768.

Vernon, D. T., Foley, J. M., Sipowicz, R. R., & Schulman, J. L. (1965). *The psychological responses of children to hospitalization and illness*. Springfield, IL: Thomas.

Wallander, J. L., & Thompson, R. J. (1995). Psychosocial adjustment of children with chronic physical conditions. In M. C. Roberts (Ed.), *Handbook of pediatric psychology* (pp. 124–141). New York: Guilford Press.

Wellisch, D. K., Gritz, E. R., Schain, W., Wang, H.-J., & Siau, J. (1992). Psychological functioning of daughters of breast cancer patients. Part II: Characterizing the distressed daughter of the breast cancer patient. *Psychosomatics, 33*, 171–179.

Werner, E. E., & Smith, R. S. (1988). *Vulnerable but invincible: A longitudinal study of resilient children and youth*. New York: McGraw-Hill.

Winnicott, D. W. (1971). *Playing and reality*. London: Tavistock.

Wolff, S. (1970). *Children under stress*. London: Penguin Press.

Worsham, N. L., Compas, B. E., & Ey, S. (1997). Children's coping with parental illness. In S. A. Wolchik & I. N. Sandler (Eds.), *Handbook of children's coping: Linking theory and intervention* (pp. 195–214). New York: Plenum Press.

Wysocki, T., Meinhold, P. A., Abrams, K. C., Barnar, M. U., Clarke, W. L., Bellando, B. J., & Bourgeois, M. J. (1992). Parental and professional estimates of self-care independence of children and adolescents with IDDM. *Diabetes Care*, 15, 43–52.

Zeltzer, L. K., & LeBaron, S. (1986). Fantasy in children and adolescents with chronic illness. *Developmental and Behavioral Pediatrics, 7*, 195–198.

CHAPTER

# 10

# Children of Parents With Disabilities

Mari Griffiths Irvin (emeritus)
University of the Pacific

The passage of Public Law 94-42, The Education for All Handicapped Children Act, in the mid 1970s brought increased attention not only to the needs of children with disabilities but to the needs of their parents and siblings as well. Since the 1970s discussions of the various needs of members of the "family with disability" have increasingly been found at professional conferences and in the literature. School personnel now often take the lead in providing interventions designed to attend to the specific needs of children adversely affected by a particular disability in the family.

The needs of many such children remain more hidden, however, as the disability within the family is less visible to school personnel. These children, the children of parents with disabilities, are not a homogeneous group as the disabilities incurred by their parents and their family situations are varied. But in each instance the child lives a life in relationship to a parent or parents who have incurred significant impairment or disability. Who among these children needs supportive intervention?

The purpose of this chapter is to (a) help the school pupil personnel services practitioner develop an awareness of this particular population of children; (b) provide preliminary information about the critical variables that must be considered in the determination of the needs of these children; and (c) suggest ways in which the school pupil personnel services staff might better serve these children and their parents.

## WHO ARE PARENTS WITH DISABILITIES?

### Handicap or Disability?

Many professionals do not uniformly distinguish between the use of the terms *disability* and *handicap*. The United Nations "Declaration on the Rights of Disabled Persons" (1975) defined a person with a disability as "any person unable to ensure by himself or herself wholly or partly the necessities of a normal individual and/or social life, as a result of a deficiency, either congenital or not, in his or her physical or mental capabilities." Hamilton (1950) stated that the actual limitations of the individual, the disability, does not necessarily handicap the individual. English (1971a), using Goffman's (1963) definition of "stigma," an attribute that is highly disturbing to others and suggestive of less than human or normal, summarized a body of literature that indicated that most physically disabled persons are stigmatized to some extent. English (1971b) also noted that stigma implied human devaluation and depreciation and included "the negative perceptions and behaviors of so-called normal people to all individuals who are different from themselves" (p. 1).

Battle (1974) went beyond the disability–handicap distinction and cited Susser and Watson as distinguishing among three components of handicap: organic, functional, and social.

> "Impairment" is the organic component, a static condition of the process of disease. "Disability" is the functional component, or the limitation of function imposed by the impairment and the individual's psychologic reaction to it. "Handicap" is the social component, the manner and degree in which the primary impairment and functional disability limit the performance of social roles and relations with others. (Battle, 1974, p. 131)

As a reflection of the aspirational societal value which does not diminish a person by virtue of attributes beyond one's control, contemporary literature favors the use of term *disability* to that of the term *handicap* in describing individuals. Nonetheless, most persons with disabilities have experienced the reality of the stigma effect resulting in attributions directed toward the disabled person by a society that highly values the "normal." It is unfortunate but highly probable that Geis' (1977) observation made more than two decades ago holds true: Most persons with disabilities must struggle with the question of their self-worth at some point in their lives. Thus, although the term *disability* is used in this chapter to underscore the value of persons regardless of their life situations, Battle's (1974) distinctions regarding the interactive effects of the actual impairing condition, societal attributions about that condition, and the subsequent psychological effects on all involved persons should not be ignored.

### Types of Disabling Conditions

Perhaps the individual with a physical anomaly or sensory deficit is most readily associated with the term disability as it is within the life experience of most adults to have had personal interaction with an individual with significant physical, visual, or hearing deficit. Mental retardation and mental illness are also commonly perceived as disabling conditions, especially when the degree of impairment is sufficient to be readily observable behaviorally. Less immediately observable may be those individuals who experience disability as a result of substance abuse. Individuals whose lives are seriously affected by the use of alcohol or drugs may often appear normal to the casual observer, although members of their immediate families or close work associates are likely to experience the negative effects of their addiction. Perhaps most invisible to the life experience of the majority of persons are those individuals whose physical health is seriously impaired through chronic illness. The invisibility of the illness may be related to one of two conditions. Either the individual with a chronic illness may be in the early state of a debilitative disease process in which the individual appears relatively normal, or the chronically ill person may be so impaired as to be only in social contact with members of the immediate family.

It is probable that every public school serves children who have parents with a variety of disabling conditions. It is also likely that school instructional, administrative, and support personnel are not aware of the total number of children attending any given school who have parents with disabilities. It may be argued that it is not necessary, nor perhaps even desirable, to identify those children who have parents with disabilities unless the behavior of the children commands the attention of school personnel. However, it is reasonable to hypothesize that some unidentified children who have parents with disabilities are at-risk children who will have difficulty learning to their potential in school. Preventive interventions for such children cannot be made unless these children can be identified prior to "problem referral" for school special services.

## WHO ARE AT-RISK CHILDREN OF PARENTS WITH DISABILITIES?

The professional literature is sparse regarding children of parents with disabilities. The effects of physical disability and chronic illness upon the individual have had a longer history of study (Garrett & Levine, 1973; Marinelli & Dell Orto, 1977; Schonz, 1975; Wright, 1960) and have provided some insight into the variables that must be considered if the needs of children of parents with disabilities are to be well recognized. In addition, the study of the ability of the family to cope with the experience of major illness has been recognized (Eisenberg, Sutkin, & Jansen, 1984; Gallagher & Vietze, 1986; Hill & Hansen, 1964). Four categories of specific factors related to the family's ability to cope were identified by Hill and Hansen (1964): (a) characteristics of the disabling event; (b) the perceived threat of the disability to family relationships, status, and goals; (c) resources available to the family; and (d) the past experience of the family in dealing with the same or similar situation.

The publication of Thurman's (1985) *Children of Handicapped Parents: Research and Clinical Perspectives*, represented a significant contribution to both the practitioner and the researcher in that it explicitly set forth the complexity of the potential impact of parental disability in the lives of children. In the Thurman book, Coates, Vietze, and Gray (1985) discussed the methodological issues specifically involved in the study of children of disabled parents. The authors presented a systematic discussion of the variables that must be considered in determining the impact of parental condition upon a given child. This chapter has heuristic value for the school practitioner who is concerned about children of parents with disabilities both at the problem prevention and problem resolution levels.

Coates et al. (1985) identified the onset of the disabling condition of the parent (i.e., is the condition congenital or "adventitious") as the first question that must be answered. If the parental disability is not congenital, the time relationship of the disability and the arrival of the child must then be considered a critical question. Other variables of importance—type of disability, family status, child status, and family process—assume differing relationships to each other, dependent on the time of onset of the disabling condition in the life of the child under consideration.

## Significance of Time of Onset of Parental Disability

It may seem obvious that the time of onset of a disability in the life of an individual would play a large role in the determination of the personal self-awareness and manner in which the person with a disability is able to relate to others and to fulfill social roles. Individuals who have congenital disabilities develop self-awareness with the impairment or disability as a "given" in their lives. That is not to say that there may not be grieving for what might have been. But such individuals have experienced themselves in no other way and the process of self-development in some way includes the reality of the disability. Similarly, the significant others in the lives of persons with congenital disabilities have known the individual in no other way.

Although the developmental process of persons with congenital disabilties proceeds with the disability woven into the fabric of the lives of both the person with the disability and the persons of significance in his or her life, the stigma referred to earlier by Goffman (1963) and English (1971b) may serve to transform the impairment or disability into handicap to a greater or lesser degree. The point here, however, is that the ability of the person with the disability to take on the social roles of spouse and parent is "negotiated" with the perceived handicapping condition already present as a part of the "life space" of the involved parties. For persons with congenital disabilities who become parents, the disability and how it is perceived by all parties involved operates more as an independent variable that directly affects both family process and child outcomes as dependent variables.

In contrast, in the case of noncongenital disabilities, regardless of the time of onset, the disability is experienced by the self and significant others as an assault, an intrusion to which there must be coping and adaptation. The loss, or continuing loss in the case of individuals with degenerative disease process, of function brought about by the disabling condition represents a type of "death" that needs to be acknowledged and truly grieved if subsequent optimal living is to occur (Keleman, 1974; Kubler-Ross, 1969; Matson & Brooks, 1974).

The person who has incurred the impairment or disability is not the only individual who is experiencing loss and needs to grieve. Family members who have strong emotional ties to the person with the disability, especially when dependency or interdependency of some type is involved, are likely also to experience traumatic loss (Cole, 1978; Feldman, 1974). Family members go through a period of emotional turbulence subsequent to the disabling event as each seeks to accommodate the reality of the personal loss experienced (Shellhase & Shellhase, 1972). The five-stage developmental sequence (denial, bargaining, anger, depression, and acceptance) introduced by Kubler-Ross (1969) to characterize personal reactions of the individual to dying is also applicable to the process each parent must undergo in dealing with the reality that she or he is the parent of a child with a disability. This model may also have utility in understanding the behavior and needs of the child who has a parent with a disability. Behavior of family members can easily be misinterpreted during this indefinite period of "coping" (Duncan as cited in Seligman, 1979). Unfortunately, the needs of family members are often overlooked or ignored as energy is directed toward the person who is impaired or disabled. This exclusive focus on the person with the disability is sometimes true even when members of the family unit are involved in the rehabilitative process (Lindenberg, 1977).

Regretfully, there can be no hard and fast rules to guide school personnel in the determination of whether a specific parental disability necessarily results in a negative outcome for a given child. Physical impairment and disability may result from a variety of causes and always are interactive with the personality dynamics of the individual with the disability and each member of the affected family. Thus, great care should be taken to avoid stereotyped descriptions or prognostic statements about either persons with disabilities or the significant others in their lives. Nonetheless, the precipitous onset of parental disability is more likely to have a negative impact upon the child, at least temporarily, until the family has the opportunity to reorganize itself with the parental disability as a component of the family's reality. This is surely a time when school personnel need to demonstrate sensitivity to the varied and multiple needs of the child and the family.

## Significance of Parental Disability Variables

Do specific parental disabilities result in specific outcomes for children or are children likely to be affected simply by the fact that they have a disabled parent? This issue was raised by Campion (1995) in her book entitled *Who's Fit to Be a Parent?* Written primarily for a British audience, Campion suggested that inadequate parenting may result from parental illness or disability. The passage of the Children Act 1989 into British law focused attention on the rights of children as individuals and stressed the responsibilities that parents have in raising children. Ironically, at about the same time, the American Disability Act was passed in the United States, which underscored the rights of all individuals regardless of impairment or disability. Earlier, the 1977 White House Conference on the Handicapped had affirmed the rights of persons with disabilities to assume the responsibilities of marriage and childrearing (Proceedings, 1977).

In her analysis of the fitness of parents, Campion differentiated between ideal and actual conditions regarding parenting fitness and approached the questions she raised with a social policy focus. Social policy questions about the fitness of parents have also been addressed through several court decisions in recent years despite the assertion of Coates et al. (1985) that the research has not adequately dealt with the critical questions regarding child outcomes and parental disability. Glass concluded her 1985 review of the literature relating to the impact of parental disability on the child and the family by citing Buck and Hohmann's (1981) conclusions that little objective research is available. Glass referenced Romano's (1984) observation that "much of what appears in the literature indicates that ablebodied health professionals project their own negative fantasies upon families where there is a disabled parent, as if it were fact" (p. 151).

> Much of the available literature depends on highly selected and biased samples, anecdotal case descriptions, or opinion based on personal experience. . . . There is a great need for well-developed and well-grounded research using sound, scientific methods with application of standardized measurement and adequate controls. Of great interest and value would be cooperative longitudinal studies of families with a disabled parent, using a systematic and uniform method of obtaining data; controlled empirical studies of effects of pa-

> rental disability on children of different ages and stages; comparison of the responses and adjustment of children to an already disabled parent with the responses of children to a parent who later acquired a disability; study of children of families with one disabled parent compared with children in families where both parents are disabled, and comparison of the characteristics of coping and noncoping families. (Glass, 1985, p. 153)

The professional literature now contains an increasing number of studies that point to certain outcomes for children based on a specific parental disability variable. Bornstein's (1995) four volume "handbook" represents a major contribution to the diversity of issues affecting parenting. His fourth volume includes extensive chapters on three conditions of parental disability: sensory and physical disability (Meadow-Orlans, 1995), depression (Field, 1995) and substance abuse (Mayes, 1995).

Earlier research literature, which often utilized case study methodology based on a few subjects, has described outcomes for children of parents with a variety of disabilities (e.g., Evans, 1978; Gluckman, 1991; Greene, Norman, Searle, Daniels, & Lubeck, 1995; Hawley & Disney, 1992; Pomerantz, Pomerantz, & Colca, 1990; Power, 1977). In addition, there is a growing body of literature on children of parents who abuse alcohol and other drugs. Much of the earlier literature on the topic was primarily descriptive and self-report with strong and predictable, primarily negative, child outcome effects. However, more empirical studies have been published in recent years which have both reported outcomes but also have acknowledged the complexity of the interaction of the number of variables involved in predicting outcome effects on children whose parents are substance abusers (Mayes, 1995). This literature is particularly important because of the large number of children affected by substance abuse of various kinds and the social policy directed toward substance abuse offenders including parents.

Although the empirical research base is growing on the relationship of parental disability to child outcome effects (Buck & Hohmann, 1983; Coates et al., 1985; Downey & Coyne, 1990; Greer, 1985) there continues to be a need for research that methodologically addresses specific critical parental disability factors.

***Severity.*** The severity of the parental disability, the degree to which the parent has independent living skills, is likely to affect the child. How the parent with the disability is cared for, the amount of family energy, both financial and emotional, which must go toward providing direct care for that family member, may have decided implications for the needs of other family members, particularly children. The severity of the parental disability is also likely to be related directly to the amount and kind of nurturance that the child is able to receive from the that parent.

***Stability.*** Certain disabling conditions, regardless of the severity of the condition, are relatively stable throughout the lifetime of the person. That is not to say that the disability may not have different significance for the person at various times throughout the individual's lifetime; rather, the condition does not itself result in deterioration of function over time. For example, the individual who loses a leg as the result of an automobile accident can be contrasted with an individual who has multiple sclerosis (MS). Although both disabilities are for the lifetime of the persons involved, the person with the amputated leg has incurred a one-time "assault" whereas the person with MS is likely to experience an unpredictable disease pattern with episodic loss of various types of physical function and the possibility of gradual physical deterioration resulting in total or near-total physical dependency. The person who has lost a leg has incurred a sudden loss for which there has not been an opportunity to prepare. However, the rehabilitative task is usually one with good prognosis as the disability is not degenerative. In contrast, the person with MS is likely to experience continual adjustment and readjustment to the physical losses resulting from a characteristically erratic disease process. It seems likely that children growing up in families with a parent whose disability results in the experience of periodic, major negative changes or gradual deterioration of function might be living in a more stressful home environment than children who grow up in families wherein the parental disability is the result of a one-time event.

Such children will need support in school, particularly during times of disruption, but school personnel need also to be aware that the child who is experiencing the slow death of a parent may be undergoing a continuous grieving process over a period of months or even years. In such a situation, the child is likely to experience many "little deaths" as the disease process continues and the limitations of the parent with their attendant implications for child–parent interaction become more global. The actual death of such a parent may at last provide closure for the child, so that the grieving can be completed.

Similarly, the spouse of a person with a debilitating disease will be experiencing a series of losses as well as increases in family responsibilities which may also involve negative economic changes. It is possible that some of the priorities of school personnel may become less urgent in such a family situation given this increase in parental responsibility and the very real limitations of parental time and energy. What may appear to be lack of parental concern in response to a given perceived need of the child by school personnel may be, in reality, a reflection of the cumulative effects of parental stress. Sensitivity to the less apparent, more subtle variables operating upon the family experiencing a parental debilitative disease process may be a major contribution to the ability of such a family to cope with its various problems and stresses.

***Chronicity.*** Related to the stability variable in conditions involving parental disability is chronicity; that is, how long has the parent been disabled and for how long is it anticipated that the parent will be disabled? Some conditions involving disability are "forever," but some "forevers" are longer than others. For example, the life expectancy for individuals with major diseases may vary from a few weeks to several decades. Support may be more available for individuals in "acute" rather than "chronic" situations because of the ability and willingness of many individuals to respond to "emergencies" that require an immediate and focused response.

Less energy may be available for the sustained support both of the family member with the disability and other members of the family if there is no immediate resolution of the problem. Thus, it is probable that the effects of parental disability in the lives of children may vary based on the length of time the parent is afflicted with the disability. School personnel should not, however, make any assumptions about the specific effects of this time variable upon a given child or family; rather, each instance needs to be reviewed carefully with attention given both to the child's various needs and to sources of ongoing support available to the child and the family.

***Involved Processes.*** What functions of the individual are affected by the disability? Is the person primarily restricted in physical movement but mental processing remains unimpaired? Is cognitive processing affected? Is the primary condition a mental illness or are emotional responses such as depression secondary to a physical disease or disability? Does the disability result in mood changes or volatile behavior on the part of the affected individual? Answers to these questions may have definite implications for the risk status of children whose parents experience disabling conditions.

***Visibility.*** How visible, literally, is the disability? The degree of impairment resulting from some disabilities is signaled by a commonly understood aid (e.g., white cane or wheelchair). In contrast, some individuals with disabilities use supports that alert the observer to a problem but provide much less information about the extent of the person's condition (e.g., a hearing aid). It is difficult to state globally whether the visibility of a person's disability serves to help or hinder interpersonal relationships. The visibility of the ability, on one hand, may serve as a stigma in that it alerts observers to the differences between such individuals and the so-called normal persons. As such, the individual with the disability may experience stereotypic behavior as relational responses from persons. On the other hand, the visibility of the disability may prevent misinterpretation of certain behaviors. As an example, a person with MS who is experiencing problems with balance while walking might be perceived as intoxicated or on drugs by unaware observers.

***Societal Acceptance.*** Because of the stigma that may be assigned to disability and impairment (Goffman, 1963), it is probable that the person with a disability will experience questioning of self-worth subsequent to the awareness of the disabling condition. "Depression, self-blame and self-hatred, blocked motivation, slowed behavior or pathological compensatory activity, and difficulties progressing on the rehabilitation program and in community adjustment—these are all concomitants of feelings of low worth" (Geis, 1977, p. 131). Thus, it is possible that the primary variable for children whose parents have disabilities, at least for those with adventitious disabilities, relates to the living in a family situation that is struggling with the emotional sequella of the experiencing of the disability.

In addition, some disabling conditions are more readily acceptable societally. For example, an individual impaired by heart disease is usually afforded more understanding and acceptance than an individual who is battling AIDS or recovering from an accidental overdose of an illegal addictive substance. It is possible that the type of disability experienced by the parent will have implications for the sensitivity of the school community to the child's needs, but it is difficult to predict whether more or less support will be afforded the child dependent on the values placed on the parental disability. The existing perception of the child by the teacher may be a critical variable in determining the degree of support given the child. Particularly vulnerable, then, may be the child whose behavior is already disturbing to the teacher. Conversely, knowledge of the parental condition may be useful to the teacher in understanding the problematic behavior of a child. Clearly, in each instance of a child whose parent experiences disability, school personnel should accept the child's needs for in-school support independent of their evaluation of the condition of the parent with the disability.

## Family Status Variables

Family status variables, background information about the family, are assumed to contribute to child outcome behavior. The answers to specific contextual family questions can be helpful in ascertaining the diverse needs of family members, especially children. Does the child have two parents or is the parent with the disability a "single parent"? If the child lives within an extended family unit, does this family pattern represent internal family support or is it an additional source of stress? Does the family have external support through close friends or religious affiliation? Does the community in which the family lives provide support to the family through the provision of needed medical or social services? Is the economic status of the family stable? Have roles within the family changed as the result of parental disability; are roles presently stable or does the nature of the disability result in ongoing change in role function that must continuously be assimilated by family members?

### Child Status Variables

The assumption should not be made that all children in a family with a parent who has a disability will experience similar effects. In such families, the age and birth order of children may be critical variables in assessing the impact of the effect of the disabling condition upon a given child. The gender of the parent with the disability, particularly in combination with the gender and age of the child, may also have a differential effect. Child status variables may be particularly important when the onset of the disabling condition is adventitious, when the disability serves as an unwelcome intrusion in the family's developmental pattern.

### Family Process Variables

Coates et al. (1985) summarized family process or interaction variables as falling into three general categories: (a) power-decision-making style, (b) communication, and (c) problem-solving effectiveness. Again, the time of disability onset, congenital or adventitious, tends to determine whether independent or dependent variable status is assigned to the parental disabling condition in relation to these processes and the effects of the disabling condition on the child.

## ROLE OF SCHOOL PUPIL PERSONNEL SERVICES STAFF

Specifically, what can and should be done in schools for at-risk children of parents with disabilities? Who should provide those services?

### Use of a Team Model

Perhaps the best vehicle for potential use in identifying at-risk children of parents with disabilities is the Multidisciplinary Team (MDT). Since the passage of Public Law 94-142 and its mandate of the team approach to the identification of children with disabilities, MDTs have assumed a primary coordinational responsibility in schools for the identification of children with special needs. Although the literature points to limitations in team effectiveness (Abelson & Woodman, 1983; Yosida, 1983), it can be argued that some of the difficulties experienced in using the team model are a function of the relative skill of team members in using a collaborative process for problem identification and resolution. The model offers considerable potential for usage beyond that of decision making for children with disabilities.

Pfeiffer and Tittler (1983) presented a model of team functioning based on a family systems orientation. This model appears to have particular utility in serving children of parents with disabilities in that it assumes that school and family are "intimately interrelated and reciprocally influential" (p. 168). The determination of risk status of any given child whose parents have disabling conditions cannot be done by relying on existing research outcomes, but there is ample evidence of critical variables that need to be considered. This exploration can only be done if school personnel and family members are able to share information systematically. A school–family systems orientation is needed to provide for the generation of the kind of data needed to make appropriate child-specific recommendations for children of parents with disabilities.

## Identification of At-Risk Children

A twofold approach is recommended for the determination of at-risk children of parents with disabilities—specific child referral and school screening.

***Specific Child Referral.*** Follow-up to each child problem referral to the MDT should include sufficient family and health information to determine whether either of the child's parents or immediate caregivers does, in fact, experience impairment or disability. This task may not be as easy as it may appear, given the variety of conditions, some more invisible than others, that may constitute a parental disability. School personnel who have had contact with the family over time should be interviewed, and the contact with the family subsequent to the referral of the child should be made by personnel who are sensitive to the presence of disabling conditions in families. Pfeiffer and Tittler (1983) recommended that the focus of any formal assessment should extend beyond the child and include data regarding the family. Ideally the involvement with the family should begin before the time of a "problem referral" on a child.

***School Screening.*** When screening occurs in a school, for whatever purpose, the intention is to identify those students for whom preventive intervention may be appropriate. Thus, it is hoped that the number of problem referrals can be reduced or, more ideally, eliminated. The objective is to prevent times of school crisis by anticipating need rather than reacting to it. In such a model, data are gathered on all children so that a determination might be made as to which children are in need of more extensive follow-up and services. A "family interview" would be one means by which such screening could occur to identify children of parents with disabilities. The child's first teacher within a given school system could be a primary person in arranging for such a home or school contact. The logistics of an every-child family interview are significant, given contemporary working patterns both of parents and school professionals. It is unrealistic to expect that such an opportunity for interaction between family and school representatives will occur without the use of released time specifically designated for such a purpose. Only those administrators who regard the use of time for this purpose as a long-term investment in successful child outcomes are likely to implement such an approach.

A second, less-ideal approach to screening for the purposes of identifying children of parents with disabilities would be to include some critical questions about the family in the data-gathering done by the school for other purposes, such as vision and hearing screening. The disadvantage to this approach is that it relies heavily on "hearsay" information and does not necessarily include the interviewer as an observer. However, even limited data gathered in such a way, if reliable, would afford the opportunity to determine whether additional involvement with the family is warranted for the purposes of identifying at-risk children of parents with disabilities.

***What Next?*** Gathering data on families about the possible presence of a parent with a disability in the family unit should not be seen as an end unto itself. The mere fact that a child has a parent with a disabling condition does not necessarily warrant atypical services by the school district to that family or to the child. Rather, it is one "bit" of data that must be integrated with other known information about the child and then used for decision making in determining whatever "appropriate" educational services are for that child.

## INTERVENTION STRATEGIES

### Prevention of Crisis Situations

Sandoval (chap. 1, this volume) identified several strategies that can be used in schools to prevent crises. One of them, anticipatory guidance, has much possibility for use with children of parents with disabilities. Such guidance provides the opportunity for children to prepare for events that are likely to occur in their future. School personnel, especially if working together with family members, can on a child-specific basis, help a given child prepare for events and situations that have the potential for disruption for the child. Similarly, teachers who work regularly with the child can be provided information so that they might also prepare for specific changes in the child's life. If, for example, school personnel can be alerted to the absence of a parent from the home for an extended period of rehabilitation, school personnel can help the child deal with this event both factually and emotionally. The focus in such guidance is to provide the child with the emotional resources needed to cope well with the necessary life changes that are occurring for the large part outside of the child's control. Such guidance can be more easily provided when there is a collaborative school–home relationship. However, some parental disabling conditions do not as easily lend themselves to such collaboration. If both parents are addicted to alcohol, for example, the child cannot depend on the parents to work collaboratively with school personnel, as denial may be a component of their disease process. In such instances, school personnel may need to work directly and only with the child, to the degree that the parents will support such involvement. Similarly, when the parental disabling condition involves the possibility of child abuse and child protective services need to be involved, school personnel will be limited in their choices. However, in most situations throughout the period of the child's public school enrollment, parents have the right to be advised, even if they need not consent, before supportive services can be provided to the child.

## The Developmental Variable

Generally speaking, the younger the child the more probable that significant others will be needed to provide support. The provider of support services to the child needs to attend carefully to the child's level of understanding of the parental disability. What feelings are elicited by this experience? How are they different, if they are, from the feelings expressed by other children of comparable chronological age in regard to their parents? Is the child developmentally ready to relate to other children in a group situation designed to strengthen coping skills? How much "information" can the child handle about the parental disability? Persons who work with the children of persons with disabilities need to be sensitive to the ways in which the child receives information about the disability. It is quite possible that the individual child is experiencing difficulty in decoding parental behavior. One cannot assume that the child has specific information about the parent's impairment. Often children in the family are "protected" from knowledge about the parental disability. Even when the condition is signaled in some visible manner, the child may not have the life experiences to enable appropriate interpretation. When the behavior of a child of a parent with a disability suggests that the child is receiving mixed messages about the parental disability or when the child gives evidence of confusion or concern about the parental condition, school personnel may find it helpful to discuss this matter explicitly with one or both of the parents. It is possible that the parents may not be aware of the child's particular understanding of the situation.

It is also possible that the parents may need help in deciding what the child should be told or how to discuss with the child what may be a particularly painful topic for them. Again, no assumptions that are not checked out carefully should be made about the feelings or the needs of the parents in this matter. Rather, school personnel should attempt to work as supportive partners with the parents in the process of helping the child acquire the information, emotionally loaded that it is, about the parental disability appropriate for the child's developmental level. In addition, school personnel may be able to serve as resources to the child as the child makes decisions about what or how to share information about the parental condition with friends.

### Support for the Supporters

A parental disabling condition is usually a long-term experience in the lives of children. The passage of time does result in changes within the family unit, many of which may reflect the adaptation and adjustment that alleviate certain types of stress. But it is possible that family helpers may need their own support resources to enable them to continue to work well with persons undergoing a chronic type of stressful condition. When energy is put into helping people deal with crisis, there may be an expectation, recognized or not, that change will occur in a relatively short period of time. The problems affecting many families with parents who experience disabling conditions tend to be slow to resolve in a satisfactory manner.

Teachers who work for a limited period of time, usually one academic year, with a given child may be able to receive adequate support from the school pupil personnel services staff, support that will enable them to work productively with a child and parents who are experiencing significant difficulty related to parental disability But school pupil personnel services staff may find themselves working for several years with a given family that is experiencing chronic stress related to parental disability. It may indeed be a frustrating and painful experience to "watch" a family struggle with the ongoing effects of disability over time. Such school staff need to be particularly aware of the possibility of "blaming the victim" for lack of satisfactory resolution of difficult problems. Staff support groups may be one vehicle for the "working through" of issues related to serving as providers of services to families experiencing chronic and difficult problems related to parental ability.

## CONCLUSION

As the number of children affected by similar adverse conditions are recognized societally, interventions have been designed to attend to the needs of these children. The needs of other children, however, remain more hidden because the source of their stress is not as apparent. One such group of children are those who have parents with disabilities. Although not a homogeneous group, many of these children experience significant loss or distortion of parenting care as the result of the disability incurred by one or both of their parents. School pupil personnel services staff are encouraged to work with teachers and administrators in the identification of families incurring stress as the result of parental disability. Interventions should be designed for such children and families that will provide for ongoing support. School personnel need to be sensitive to their own needs in working with families whose problem situations continue over time.

## REFERENCES

Abelson, M. A., & Woodman, R. W. (1983). Review of research on team effectiveness: implications for teams in schools. *School Psychology Review, 12*, 125–136.

Battle, C. U. (1974). Disruptions in the socialization of a young, severely handicapped child. *Rehabilitation Literature, 35*, 130–140.

Bornstein, M. H. (Ed.). (1995). *Handbook of parenting: Vol. 4. Applied and practical parenting.* Mahwah, NJ: Lawrence Erlbaum Associates.

Buck, F. M., & Hohmann, G. W. (1981). Personality and behavior of children of disabled and nondisabled fathers. *Archives of Physical Medicine and Rehabilitation, 62*, 432–438.

Buck, F. M., & Hohmann, G. W. (1983). Parental disability and children's adjustment. In E. L. Pan, T. E. Backer, & C. L. Vash (Eds.), *Annual Review of Rehabilitation: Vol. 2*, (pp. 203–241). New York: Springer.

Campion, M. J. (1995). *Who's fit to be a parent?* New York: Routledge.

Coates, D. L., Vietze, P. M., & Gray, D. B. (1985). Methodological issues in studying children of disabled parents. In S. K. Thurman (Ed.), *Children of handicapped parents: Research and clinical perspectives* (pp. 155–180). Orlando, FL: Academic Press.

Cole, C. M. (1978). The role of brief family therapy in medical rehabilitation. *Journal of Rehabilitation, 44*, 29–42.

Downey, G., & Coyne, J. C. (1990). Children of depressed parents: An integrative review. *Psychological Bulletin*, 108, 1–27.

Eisenberg, M. G., Sutkin, L. C., & Jansen, M. A. (Eds.). (1984). *Chronic illness and disability through the life span, effects on self and family.* New York: Springer.

English, R. W. (1971a). Combating stigma toward physically disabled persons. *Rehabilitation Research and Practice Review, 2*, 19–27.

English, R. W. (1971b). Correlates of stigma toward physically disabled persons. *Rehabilitation Research and Practice Review, 2*, 1–17

Evans, R. (1978). Children of dialysis patients and selection of dialysis setting. *American Journal of Psychiatry, 125*, 343–345.

Feldman, D. J. (1974). Chronic disabling illness: A holistic view. *Journal of Chronic Diseases, 27*, 287–291.

Field, T. (1995). Psychologically depressed parents. In M. H. Bornstein (Ed.), *Handbook of parenting: Vol. 4. Applied and practical parenting* (pp. 85–100). Mahwah, NJ: Lawrence Erlbaum Associates.

Gallagher, J. J., & Vietze, P. (Eds.). (1986). *Families of handicapped persons: Current research, treatment, and policy issues*. Baltimore, MD: Paul Brookes.

Garrett, J., & Levine, E. (Eds.). (1973). *Rehabilitation practices with the physically disabled.* New York: Columbia University Press.

Geis, H. J. (1977). The problem of personal worth in the physically disabled patient. In R. P. Marinelli & A. E. Dell Orto (Eds.), *The psychological and social impact of physical disability* (pp. 130–140). New York: Springer.

Glass, D. D. (1985). Onset of disability in a parent: Impact on child and family. In S. K. Thurman (Ed.), *Children of handicapped parents: Research and clinical perspectives* (pp. 145–154). Orlando, Fl: Academic Press.

Gluckman, C. (1991). The normal child with disabled parents: Mary. *Journal of Child Psychotherapy, 17,* 95–106.

Goffman, E. (1963). *Stigrna.* Englewood Cliffs, NJ: Prentice-Hall.

Greene, B. F., Norman, K. R., Searle, M. S., Daniels, M., & Lubeck, R. G. (1995). Child abuse and neglect by parents with disabilities: A tale of two families. *Journal of Applied Behavior Analysis, 28,* 417–434.

Greer, B. G. (1985). Children of physically disabled parents: Some thoughts, facts, and hypotheses. In S. K. Thurman (Ed.), *Children of handicapped parents: Research and clinical perspectives* (pp. 131–143). Orlando, Fl: Academic Press.

Hamilton, K. W. (1950). *Counseling the handicapped in the rehabilitation process.* New York: Ronald Press.

Hawley, T. L., & Disney, E. R. (1992). Crack's children: The consequences of maternal cocaine abuse. *Social Policy Report of the Society for Research in Child Development, 6*(4), 1–22.

Hill, R., & Hansen, D. A. (1964). Families under stress. In H. T. Christensen (Ed.), *Handbook of marriage and the family* (pp. 782–819). Chicago: Rand McNally.

Keleman, S. (1974). *Living your dying.* New York: The Free Press.

Kubler-Ross, E. (1969). *On death and dying.* New York: Macmillan.

Lindenberg, R. (1977). Work with families in rehabilitation. *Rehabilitation Counseling Bulletin, 21,* 67–76.

Marinelli, R. P., & Dell Orto, A. E. (1977). *The psychological and social impact of physical disability.* New York: Springer.

Matson, R. R., & Brooks, N. A. (1974). Adjusting to multiple sclerosis: An exploratory study. *Social Science and Medicine, 11,* 245–250.

Mayes, L. C. (1995). Substance abuse and parenting. In M. H. Bornstein (Ed.), *Handbook of parenting: Vol. 4. Applied and practical parenting* (pp. 101–126). Mahwah, NJ: Lawrence Erlbaum Associates.

Meadow-Orlans, K. P. (1995). Parenting with a sensory or physical disability. In M. H. Bornstein (Ed.), *Handbook of parenting: Vol. 4. Applied and practical parenting* (pp. 57–84). Mahwah, NJ: Lawrence Erlbaum Associates.

Pfeiffer, S. I., & Tittler, B. I. (1983). Utilizing the multidisciplinary team to facilitate a school-family systems orientation. *School Psychology Review, 12,* 168–173.

Pomerantz, P., Pomeantz, D. J., & Colca, L. A. (1990). A case study: Service delivery and parents with disabilities. *Child Welfare, 69,* 65–73.

Power, P. (1977). The adolescent's reaction to chronic illness of a parent: Sosme implications for family counseling. *International Journal of Family Counseling, 5,* 70–78.

*Proceedings from the White House Conference on the Handicapped.* (1977, May). Washington, DC.

Romano, M. (1984). Impact of disability on family and society. In J. V. Basmajian & R. L. Kirby (Eds.), *Medical rehabilitation* (pp. 273–276). Baltimore, MD: Williams & Wilkins.

Schonz, F. C. (1975). *The psychological aspects of physical illness and disability.* New York: Macmillan.

Seligman, M. (1979). *Strategies for helping parents of exceptional children: A guide for teachers.* New York: The Free Press.

Shellhase, L., & Shellhase, F. (1972). Role of the family in rehabilitation. *Social Casework, 53,* 544–550.

Thurman, S. K. (Ed.). (1985). *Children of handicapped parents: Research and clinical perspectives*. Orlando, FL: Academic Press.

United Nations. (1975, December 9). *Declaration on the Rights of Disabled Persons, General Assembly Resolution 3447* [XXX]. New York.

Wright, B. A. (1960). *Physical disability—A psychological approach*. New York: Harper & Row.

Yosida, R. K. (1983). Are multidisciplinary teams worth the investment? *School Psychology Review, 12*, 139–143.

CHAPTER

# 11

# Moving

Jonathan Sandoval
University of California, Davis

Who among us enjoys moving? The process of giving up an established home and friends and relocating to another neighborhood, city, or geographical region is often accompanied by fatigue, feelings of loss and alienation, and fear of the unknown. Moving for adults may be made more pleasant by the anticipation of a more challenging or rewarding occupation, or by the intellectual stimulation of relocating to a new environment. Unfortunately, most moves are not made to improve one's life. Many moves are dictated by other life events such as deaths and divorces, and come as an added burden to those experiencing life's catastrophes. Nevertheless, for many individuals, moving is a normal part of adult life, as with the civilian and military employees of the Department of Defense who routinely relocate every 2 to 5 years. Although there is a connection between adult attitudes and children's reactions, we cannot assume children will experience a move the same way parents do.

"I don't want to move, Dad, all my friends are here!" "What will it be like in my new neighborhood?" "I'm going to get my own room in our new house when we move, aren't I, Mom?" "Boy, I'll be glad to get out of this school!" These are some of the reactions of children to the announcement of a family move. On balance, children do not like to move any more than do adults. Under the right circumstances, however, moving can lead to growth in intellectual, social, and emotional development.

For children, moving means separation. In many cases children will be giving up friends, a neighborhood, and a school environment with which they have become familiar. According to Bowlby (1960, 1961), separation and the emotions attached to it are the most difficult events with which children must deal. Relations with significant others form the core of emotional development, and disruptions in the separation and individuation process can lead to life long personality problems. Children who have already experienced separation difficulties will find moving much more traumatic than others. Moving may also be a problem for the *friends* of a child who is relocating. Rubin (1980) found that friends of moving children suffered increases in loneliness, irritability, and anger following their companion's departure.

There are studies of stress in humans that attempt to quantify various life events as to their stress value. On Holmes and Rahe's (1967) scale, for example, changes in residence and a change in school each receive a value of 20 on a scale of 100. (The death of a spouse received a full 100 points.) On this scale, life-event scores may be added together to yield a total life crisis value. Almost always a move will add to a person's stress when it accompanies events such as family disintegration, loss of job, or death. All things being equal, a move in the absence of other negative situations would appear to have less of a negative impact on individuals than moves accompanied by events such as illness or divorce. All too often, however, a move does come about as a result of another life crisis.

## EXTENT OF THE PROBLEM

Moving has become a fact of life for modern Americans. Between March 1998 and March 1999, 16% of the U.S. population, moved to a new residence, the majority (59%) within the same county (U.S. Department of Commerce, Census Bureau, 2000). Eighteen percent of those moving were between 1 and 17 years of age. A reasonable estimate would be that almost 50% of the population in an elementary school had moved at least once during their lifetime. Of those children who do move, they are more likely to be poor, come from single-parent homes, have parents who are unemployed or are migrant workers, and are limited English proficient (U.S. General Accounting Office, 1994).

We do not know for what percentage of these children moving turns into a crisis. Certainly it does not negatively impact all children and youth as indicated by the next section. Nevertheless, depending on the reason for the move and the individual child's makeup, moves may be quite traumatic and require intervention from school mental health personnel such as a school psychologist. Children who move will be at some risk for developing severe learning and behavior problems in the schools.

**Is Moving Always Detrimental to Children?**

There is some evidence that children are not uniformly opposed to moving (Bekins, 1976; Bush, 1977; Lehr & Hendrickson, 1968). More than half of the children in a survey sponsored by Bekins, for example, did wish to move. This upper middle-class sample perceived making new friends, going to a new school, traveling and learning about new localities to be exciting prospects. The minority, however, did not look forward to moving, citing the loss of friends as the major problem.

A number of studies have been done attempting to discover whether moving has a negative affect on children's academic, social, or emotional development. Before examining these outcomes, we must consider that the effects of moving are very different for different populations.

A sizable amount of this research has focused on children of military dependents. Research has particularly focused on whether or not the stereotype of the "Military Brat" has any validity. Very little research has contradicted the early findings of Sackett (1935), who discovered that the children of military officers in Panama were performing better or equal to their stateside civilian counterparts. When the proper control base rates are considered, military children seem to have fewer intellectual and social emotional problems than other children (Gerner, Perry, Moselle & Archbold, 1992; Gordon & Gordon, 1958; Greene & Daughtry, 1961; Kenny, 1967; Marchant & Medway, 1987; Pederson & Sullivan, 1964; Seagoe, 1932). On the other hand, military dependent children and others living abroad have to cope with geographic mobility, transcultural experiences, father's episodic absence, and stressful other factors placing some of them at risk for adjustment problems (Shaw, 1987). In a study of Air Force adolescents, Pittman and Bowen (1994) examined the role of various predictors in three kinds of adjustment following a move: personal adjustment, adjustment to the new environment, and parental relations. Important features contributing to adjustment were the adolescents' perceptions (attitudes toward the move), and level of social support.

One problem in the research of military children, besides the lack of suitable control groups, is in distinguishing between the children of officers and enlisted men. Pittman and Bowen (1994) found that father's rank was correlated with positive outcomes for adolescents. For officers, a move may be perceived as a positive part of a career and leading to advancement, whereas for enlisted personnel a move may simply be an annoyance.

In a study of primarily officer's children, Pederson and Sullivan (1964) found that normal children had mothers who were more accepting of frequent relocation and parents who were strongly identified with the military than did children who were diagnosed emotionally disturbed (see also Marchant & Medway, 1987).

It may be unfair to generalize from military to civilian children because military moves are scheduled and supported economically and with various planned interventions for those who have moved. Personnel who move are given time and careful orientations to their new assignments. In addition, it is sometimes the case that military children move with a cohort and do not necessarily lose all of their friends in a move. They simply find themselves in a different part of the world with some of the same classmates, and relationships are maintained.

Research on nonmilitary children has more often shown that children suffer ill effects from moving, although the findings are not unanimous in detailing negative outcomes. Much of the research has examined academic outcomes. Although frequent moves are clearly correlated with low achievement (Benson, Haycraft, Steyaert & Weigel, 1979), when previous achievement and socioeconomic status is controlled, the effect of moving on achievement is often reduced or eliminated (Heinlein & Shinn, 2000; Temple & Reynolds, 1999), particularly in children from low-socioeconomic status homes. In addition, Wright (1999) found that low achievement outcomes from a move were associated with children moving within the school district rather than with children moving outside of the district. Many poor children move within a school district as a result of evictions and other changes in life circumstance.

Other studies have focused on self-concept, depression, and emotional well-being as outcomes of moves (Brown & Orthner, 1990; Calabrese, 1989; Hendershott, 1989; Kroger, 1980). These studies have generally suggested moving is related to adjustment problems, at least in the short run. One study even demonstrated mobility and its incumbent stress to be related to subsequent burn injuries (Knudson-Cooper & Leuchtag, 1982)!

Again, researchers have not always distinguished between children's moves that are supported and planned (presumably leading to positive outcomes for the family) and those moves that are a result of negative economic or social conditions. The emotional effect of moving on children of a high-level executive is obviously going to be different (and likely more positive) than the effect of moving on the children of a seasonal worker or unskilled laborer who must travel from job to job. In this latter group, particularly, moving may be a result of life problems rather than a cause of them. In general, researchers have had difficulty in distinguishing cause and effect in the study of moving. Attention to interactions may facilitate the understanding of moving research findings. For example, Blane and Spicer (1978) found that mobility had little or no effect on children from high-socioeconomic status (SES) homes but was detrimental for children from most low-socioeconomic homes.

Examining another individual variable, Whalen and Fried (1973) found that mobility improved test scores of intelligent children but depressed scores of children with lower IQs. Perhaps the exposure to new environments, the pride that comes from mastering the challenges of moving to a new place, and the introduction to different values and ways of living that travel brings may have positive effects on children. This beneficial effect is no doubt magnified for bright children in families who perceive the move to be in their best interests and are optimistic and enthusiastic about the changes (Fassler, 1978, Stroh & Brett, 1990).

### Children at High Risk of Academic, Emotional, or Social Problems

One might hypothesize that those children with a sense of separation anxiety would have the most difficult time with a move and be more prone to exhibit the features of a crisis. Psychiatric researchers estimate that a large number of the childhood population has some vestiges of separation and related anxiety. Who else is at risk for developing a crisis? As already mentioned, children for whom a move is not a planned or economically favorable situation are probably at risk of having negative outcomes from moving.

Children for whom moving is a result of another life crisis are probably at greater risk for developing a crisis around the event. For example, South, Crowder, and Trent (1998) argued that parental divorce sharply increases the likelihood that children will move out of their neighborhoods to significantly poorer neighborhoods (see also Tucker, Marx, & Long, 1998). In their 1995 review of the literature, Humke and Schaefer (1995) identified additional factors contributing to postmove emotional adjustment, such as poor premove adjustment, number of moves, distance of move, and multiple stressors. They suggest that one of the most influential factors was parental attitude toward the move, because children are often sensitive to their parents' attitudes. In addition, however, moving may have different consequences depending on the age or developmental level of the child.

***Developmental Considerations.*** Generally speaking, most researchers have observed very little ill effects occurring from moves in the preschool population (Inbar, 1976; Tooley, 1970). Because the major effect of a move on preschoolers is a change of environment and usually not a loss of significant others, moves may be easy for infants and toddlers. Because preschoolers have formed attachments mainly to family members, and only secondarily to places and peers, they may be protected from stress. To the extent that important family members stay with the child during the move, there are perhaps superficial impacts of a move on young children. Placing the child out of the home with relatives and babysitter while settling in is probably not a good idea (Stubblefield, 1955). Nevertheless, one might speculate that because a major life crisis centers around separation at the preschool age, the extent to which the move causes parents to become preoccupied with the details of the move and to ignore the child's needs for comfort and emotional support, a move will create additional problems for the very young child. A move coupled with the loss of a parent through divorce or death will be especially difficult. There is no doubt that moves can cause great stress for one or another parent, although one might speculate that mothers bear the brunt of the problems of packing, finding new housing, and so on. Depending on the child's closeness to the mother and the stress-induced changes in her reactions to the child, problems might be anticipated for preschoolers, because this is the age when children are most attuned to their parents' mental state.

Others have argued that middle childhood represents a time of great vulnerability (Inbar, 1976; Matter & Matter 1988, Tooley, 1970). Inbar (1976) suggested that because children in elementary school are transferring their close relations from the family to friends, moving may be a severe handicap for the socialization process. In addition, according to Erikson (1962), young elementary school children are involved in establishing a sense of industry that occurs primarily in mastering the tasks in schools such as learning to read and write. Consequently, the disruption in school progress brought about by a move may cause considerable emotional difficulties as well as learning problems. It may be argued that the curriculum across the United States is more uniform than it is different, and that children can easily make the transition to related curriculum materials or even find the same reading series, for example, that they left behind them.

The problem may be much easier for higher achievers, in this regard, than for learning disabled or other children who have difficulty learning and who depend on the interpersonal relationship with the teacher to facilitate learning. Although individual educational plans (IEPs) may have been developed for exceptional children, these plans may not be as easy to transfer from one locale to another as IEP proponents hope. Also, the problem of re-qualifying for special education may crop up to the extent that different standards for special education exist in different regions of the country. As a result, a child with learning handicaps may not encounter a sympathetic environment when he or she moves.

Other researchers believe that adolescents experience the most trauma during moves (Hendershott, 1989; Pinder, 1989; Tooley, 1970). The task of adolescents, according to Erikson (1962), is to establish an identity through the use of interpersonal relations with peer groups. To have the continuity of such relations with peers disrupted by a move will obviously lead to difficulties. Adolescents most fear the loss of a social group as an ego support system. Because the group facilitates role playing and experimentation that leads to identity, the loss of close friends brought about by a move is particularly destructive. In addition, adolescents often are in conflict with parents as they seek to reject family values and parental authority in the process of creating their own values as individuals. The move may provide a focal point for conflict and rebellion leading the adolescent to attempt to use the move as a way of achieving independence (e.g., by asking to remain behind, or by simply refusing to cooperate in any way with the moving plans).

Cause and effect is not always clear in moves with adolescents. Some moves may be occasioned by school problems. Rumberger and Larson (1998) believe that school mobility may represent a less severe form of educational disengagement similar to dropping out. Adolescents in their study who made even one nonpromotional school change between 8th and 12th grades were twice as likely to not complete high school as were adolescents who did not change schools.

Other adolescents may welcome a move as an opportunity to start over again in a secondary school with a new group of peers. They see the move as facilitating role experimentation by providing a new audience and setting for them to try different ways of acting. Moves may be viewed positively by these adolescents who wish to start over. Kroger (1980), examining 11 intact middle-class homes found little or no negative impact on self-concept as a result of moving.

## PREVENTION ACTIVITIES

When one knows that a move is in the offing it is possible to prepare the child for the move in a way that will facilitate adjustment. There are a number of anticipatory guidance activities that can be planned for a child that will help him or her think through in advance changes that will occur and prepare for the accompanying strong feelings. To remove the fear of the unknown, children should preview the new house, actively participate in its selection, and tour the new neighborhood, school, and community. The American Movers Conference, a moving trade organization, sponsored a conference on moving and children and produced an excellent pamphlet (American Movers Conference, n.d.) designed for parents to help them prepare their child for moving. Many of their suggestions are very relevant.

First, they encourage parents to talk about the move with their children. Children should not learn about the move from another source (Switzer, Hirschberg, Myers, Gray, Evers, & Forman, 1961). They advise the parent to explain to each child at his or her own level of understanding the reason for the move and to anticipate what the new home and community will be like. They also suggest that parents inform their children about how they can make the move a successful one and assign them a role in the move. Additionally, they recommend that parents be accepting of children's feelings, even their particularly negative ones about the move. They believe that parents should be truthful and share their misgivings as well as hopes for the new move. Obviously, the further in advance of the move the conversations take place, up to a point, the more successful they will be (Stubblefield, 1955). A child who has moved before may have some residue of feelings about the previous move and past experiences that should also be explored openly.

The American Movers Conference pamphlet also offers some age-appropriate suggestions. For infants, they emphasize the importance of disrupting the infant and toddler's normal routine as little as possible. Preschoolers, they suggest, may be helped by directly addressing any fears that the child may be left behind, and reassuring the child that favorite toys and special objects such as teddy bears or beds and chairs will be taken along. Although they will be packed and out of sight, the special objects will be restored to an appropriate place in the new house. The movers warn against leaving preschoolers with babysitters for a long period of time during the moving period. To do so might cause them to experience more separation than usual. They also suggest the preschooler be allowed to pack and carry along some of their own special possessions during the move. They suggest that a move is not a good opportunity to discard a number of battered and broken toys that a child has become attached to. As inconvenient as this may seem, it is probably better to wait until the child is settled to throw things away.

Children of elementary school age can be reasoned with more effectively. The pamphlet urges parents to allow them to express their concerns and to talk about the challenges of fitting in with a new group of friends and schoolmates. The pamphlet suggests that frank discussions with teenagers may allow them to express their potential anger at the move but also to consider the advantages, such as the opportunity of meeting new people and new activities. It suggests that parents be active in finding organizations and groups in the new area that are involved in interesting activities and encourage the teenager to bring friends into the new home, even though the new house may not be as settled and presentable as the parents may like.

Additional specific ideas for making the transition as smooth as possible for children are found in Fig. 11.1. These ideas embody a number of good preventive principles such as anticipatory guidance and emotional inoculation.

## Prevention in the School Setting

One of the prevailing notions that parents have is that it will be easier on their child if they move their school-aged children during the summer rather than interrupting their school year. This notion is based on the idea

1. If you are moving to a distant place, help your children learn about the new area. Moving companies, the local Chamber of Commerce, tourist bureaus, and state agencies are possible sources of information.
2. By using dolls, boxes, and a wagon children can get a feeling for concept of moving through play acting.
3. Let children help decide how their rooms are to be arranged and decorated.
4. Take the time to make a last visit to places your family is particularly fond of.
5. Encourage the children to exchange addresses with their friends. If practical, give thought to allowing them to have their old friends visit at the new home. A telephone call to an old friend is a low cost way to relieve post move depression.
6. Prepare a package for each child containing favorite toys, clothing, and snacks. Label with the child's name.
7. Survey your new home for loose steps, low overhang, and other possible accident procedures. Keep your eye on the children until they become familiar with the new home's peculiarities.
8. Take your break with the family as soon as the major unpacking is done. Don't try to do everything as soon as you arrive.
9. Both parents should spend time with all their children after the move listening to what they've learned in new school, new friends.
10. The first week in a new school may be difficult your child. Follow his or her progress closely and if any problems increase or don't go away in time don't hesitate to visit with the teacher. Accompanying him or her to school the first few days may ease everyone's minds.
11. Younger children may react to the move by reverting to babyish actions. Be reassuring, not scolding. They will soon relax and return to normal behavior.
12. Any abnormalities that linger, particularly physical ones such as loss of appetite and constipation, menstrual disorder—should be referred to a doctor. Point out to the doctor that your family recently relocated.

FIG. 11.1. Suggestions for parents from the American Movers Conference Pamphlet. Reprinted with permission from American Movers Conference.

that children will find it difficult to maintain continuity in learning if they shift from one set of curriculum materials to another in midyear. Although there is a certain amount of truth that missing school and changing teacher's curriculum materials will interrupt learning, a move during the summer may bring about a number of more serious problems. Children moving during the summer will find themselves in a new neighborhood without friends and without activities to occupy their time. They are isolated and bored until school opens in September, allowing time for anger and frustration to build. In addition, when school does open, most teachers are faced with a new classroom and will not be able to identify children who have moved. As a result, the teacher will not be able to give the newly arrived children the special attention they may require.

If the child moves during the school year, he or she will move from one social setting to another. The teacher and the classmates will recognize that the child is new to the school and make some allowances for the fact.

Sensitive teachers will be able to engage the new child in a number of activities to assist in the establishment of a peer group and in an appropriate curriculum that is challenging but not overwhelming or repetitive.

***Helping the Child Who Is Leaving.*** When it is known that a child will be leaving the school there are a number of activities teachers or others can engage in that will assist in the transition. Ceremonies are very important in marking passages. Making sure that children have an opportunity to say goodbye is very important. Allowing the child time to say goodbye to former teachers and others in the school besides immediate classmates may allow the child to make the separation easier.

Encouraging the child to write to former classmates may be a useful activity, not only for the creative writing involved, but in helping the child realize that friendships can endure time and distance. Departing children can also be encouraged to take with them a folder of previous work and work in progress. Taking a record of past and present accomplishments helps the child maintain a sense of continuity with the old classroom but also has the advantage of providing the new teacher with an idea of the child's level of academic functioning. A note to the new teacher along with an evening telephone number and encouragement to call can also help the moving child find appropriate placement in the new school.

As always, giving a child an opportunity to express both positive and negative feelings about the move in the classroom can be a useful exercise for the entire class. Such classroom meeting discussions should be planned for a period when there is time for a complete discussion because other children in the group, and not just the departing child, may have feelings they wish to explore about moving. No doubt there will be a number of moves each year in a classroom and these occasions present excellent opportunities for social studies lessons ranging from geography to anthropology.

Bibliotherapy is another activity that may be very helpful for the child leaving a school (Smardo, 1981a). With the help of the librarian, teachers and school psychologists can identify reading materials that focus on the experience of moving and the adjustments to a new environment. A number of children's books have been written on this topic (Bernstein, 1977; Fassler, 1978; Smardo, 1981b). When doing bibliotherapy it is important to identify materials that are relevant, are at an interest level that will engage the child, and are at an appropriate level of reading difficulty so that the child may read the materials on his or her own. Once the child has had an opportunity to read the materials, some discussion should follow. The point of bibliotherapy is to provide the child with models for effective coping and problem solving. Besides books on moving per se, stories concerning making friends and adapting to new customs and circumstances may also be particularly relevant.

Splete and Rasmussen (1977) suggested that school guidance personnel routinely hold "exit interviews" of departing students to discuss their fears and apprehensions about a move. Part of this interview might be providing factual information about the new school and community if it is available.

Work with parents is also possible. Splete and Rasmussen recommend work with parents and other family members to resolve conflicts connected to the move, based on the notion that parent attitude toward moving is an important variable in child adjustment. Counselors can also give parents strategies and advice for how to be proactive in working with the new schools their children may enter. Parents can set up meetings at the new school and accompany their child on a tour of the school and meet school personnel prior to enrollment (Holland-Jacobsen, Holland, & Cook, 1984).

***Helping the New Child in the Classroom.*** The first necessity for helping a new child become integrated in the classroom both socially and academically is to find out as much information about him or her as possible. A phone call to a previous teacher coupled within a close inspection of academic records will offer an excellent opportunity to prepare for educational planning for a new child. Often, educational records take months to arrive, if they ever do. Therefore, a phone call may prove a particularly good investment. Previous teachers may be asked about interests and preferred activities, information that can be used to help the child establish friendships with similarly inclined peers in the classroom, as well as to motivate academic performance. Of course, academic strengths and weaknesses as well as successful pedagogic technique should be inquired about.

Research on friendships suggests that those of like ability are inclined to associate together and form lasting friendships (Rubin, 1980). If possible, the teacher might seat the new child with like-minded peers or include them in the same work or play groups. In secondary schools, various interest groups such as music, art, hobbies, and the like can form the basis for forming friendships. Because the curriculum in the secondary school often includes elective courses, it is in these subjects that adolescents are likely to meet potential friends.

Teachers receiving new pupils in the new classroom must be educated (by school psychologists) about possible signs of maladaption to the move. They should look for symptoms of depression, withdrawal, fatigue, even loss of appetite and bring students who are suffering some form of depression to the attention of school psychologists and counselors. Teachers seem to appreciate that moving is a crisis for children so they will be open to assistance in this regard. In the next section, I discuss crisis counseling interventions on the part of guidance personnel should teachers identify children in need of extra assistance.

Switzer and his colleagues (Switzer et al., 1961) noted that often school personnel harbor hostility for new children in general. New children are perceived to be threats to the accomplishment of important goals such as building cohesive classroom groups, keeping student–teacher ratios low, and maintaining high levels of classroom achievement. To the extent that this hostility affects the new student, consultation with the teacher directed at eliminating this theme will be necessary.

It is an open question as to whether new children should be singled out and introduced to classmates. Verbal and extroverted children probably can handle this situation well and will be comfortable in front of groups and able to tell new classmates about their previous location and the circumstances of their move. Other children will be far too shy to engage in open classroom discussions in spite of the positive outcomes that might occur in making themselves known to potential friends and integrating themselves in the classroom. Orientation programs in which new children may simply watch the classroom and familiarize themselves with procedures and practices may be best for some (Levine, 1966). Levine reported a program in which upper grade children are recruited and trained to serve as guides to children entering school. The guides show the new pupils the building, inform them of school rules, and discuss age-appropriate resources in the school and community.

Holland-Jacobsen, Holland, and Cook (1984) recommended five ways a counselor can be helpful:

1. Providing inservice sessions for teachers on how to facilitate adaptation of students to the new school
2. Arranging "get-to-know-the-school" night for new students and parents
3. Arranging special tutoring "catch-up" sessions at the beginning of the year and throughout the year as necessary
4. Setting up a buddy system by assigning a peer to each new student
5. Setting up periodic meetings with new students.

These suggestions seem easy to implement and likely to be of help.

## CRISIS COUNSELING CHILDREN WHO HAVE MOVED OR ARE ABOUT TO MOVE

At some point, the school psychologist will encounter a child who is in a state of crisis as a result of a move. A first step, of course, is to determine what has brought about the move and whether it represents a radical change in the child's home environment or parental relations. If the move was occasioned by another hazardous life event, perhaps the counseling should be directed primarily at this circumstance and secondarily at the issues associated with the move. On the other hand, the impact of the move should not be ignored in helping, for example, the child adjust to a parental divorce.

### Individual Interventions

Assuming the major issue is the move and the change from one school and neighborhood to another, the focus of counseling for younger children should be on the expression of feelings of loss and the experience of apprehension at establishing new routines and friendships. The child can be led to examine the old situation and encouraged to enumerate both positive and negative aspects of his or her relationships. If the child attempts to idealize the old, it will be important to question the child carefully to create a more balanced view.

Next, the child may explore the new situation. If the child is in crisis before the move, the counselor may ask about what ideas the child has of the new environment. By being on the lookout for mistaken ideas and by inquiring about new opportunities and advantages of the move, the helper may assist the child to establish a more favorable outlook.

Many times, the crisis will arise after the move when the child finds him or herself alone and isolated. Because the loss of friendship is so devastating at middle childhood, it may prove effective in counseling to help the child maintain or reestablish the old friendships through telephone calls, letter writing, and visits.

If the child is having trouble making new friends, it may be important to determine if the child has the social skills necessary for establishing friendships or if he or she is failing to use them. If the problem is lack of skill, a number of social skills programs have been developed that may prove useful (Gresham, 1981). If the child has the skills but fails to use them, a different tactic is called for. Pointing out to the counselee how he or she has not used opportunities when they have presented themselves may facilitate action. By being an interested adult and by reinforcing prosocial behaviors, the child may soon establish an important social network.

Counseling adolescents will call for many of the same approaches modified to fit their higher level of cognitive functioning and their unique type of egocentrism (Elkind, 1974). As mentioned previously, adolescents, with help, can come to see a move as a new chance to try out different styles of behaving and to play new roles. A counselor can point out this relevant notion, and help the student consider what the premove social status had been and what it might be in a new setting.

The adolescent's egocentrism creates a condition of extreme self-consciousness and sense that they are constantly being observed and judged by others (Elkind's, 1974, imaginary audience). Another aspect of counseling will be to help the adolescent test how realistic it is to be afraid and inhibited in the new social situations they are encountering at the new school. The client must learn to distinguish between his or her preoccupations and sensitive points and what is of interest and of concern to others. Role playing may be a useful technique to get the adolescent to be aware of another's frame of reference.

## Group Intervention

Mutual support groups have been used successfully to help individuals with common problems explore feelings and discuss ways of overcoming them and coping. They are a way to gain information from credible sources about unusual situations. Interaction with peers experiencing the same hazardous situation, can reduce a sense that reactions are unique and abnormal. Such feelings lead to alienation, isolation, and poor adaptation. Support group may be an ideal mechanism for helping adolescents with the stress of relocation.

Strother and Harvill (1986) described a six session (once a week) model support group they have used successfully. The recommend 90-minute groups for 8 to 20 voluntary participants. The first session is designed to help the students feel comfortable with the group and to become acquainted. Participants are asked to describe their move and their initial reactions. Most of the discussion is focused on answering questions about the new school and providing information. Following the first session, students meet for a group lunch to encourage cohesion of the group.

The second session focuses on providing members with skill to build a new support system. Students share thoughts and feelings about their recent loss, discuss fears about forming new social supports, and explore how they have made friends in the past. In dyads, they discuss feelings of sadness at loosing old friends as a result of the move. The session closes with brainstorming about how to make new friends and a request to maintain a journal of their experiences in meeting new people at school.

The next three sessions are devoted to sharing again feelings of loss, discussing common family concerns, and encouraging mutual support among group members. Increasingly the group shifts from providing information to providing emotional support. A number of exercises are used to achieve these ends, as well as shared homework assignments.

The final session summarizes the previous weeks, and promotes the exchange of strategies for coping with the move. The group evaluates itself, and is encouraged to continue supporting each other after the group concludes. Any group members who require further counseling are also identified for individual follow-up.

Group work offers the advantage of working with several individuals at once, but also has the advantage of restoring a sense of belonging that may be lost in a move. Students can become more easily assimilated into to the new school environment if they are given knowledge and emotional support along the way.

## CONCLUSION

In summary, moving is a hazardous time for children. Moving presents a number of opportunities to build new skill and competencies, however. With the right preparation on the part of parents, and with sensitive school personnel, a child may experience a move as a natural part of growing up. If the move is a part of another crisis, careful attention to helping the child resolve the issues of moving can leave the child with more resources to cope with other life events.

## REFERENCES

American Movers Conference. (n.d.). *Moving and children.* Arlington, VA: Author.

Bekins Co. (1976). *Youth consumer survey.* Glendale, CA: Author.

Bernstein, J. E. (1977). *Books to help children cope with separation and loss.* New York: Bowker.

Benson, G. P., Haycraft, J. L., Steyaet, J. P., & Weigel, D. J. (1979). Mobility in sixth graders as related to achievement, adjustment, and socioeconomic status. *Psychology in the Schools, 16,* 444–447.

Blane, D., & Spicer, B. (1978). Geographic mobility, educational attainment and adjustment—which children are at risk? *Education Australia, 3,* 51–64.

Bowlby, J. (1960). Separation anxiety. *The International Journal of Psychoanalysis, 41,* 89–113.

Bowlby, J. (1961). Separation anxiety: A critical review of the literature. *Journal of Child Psychology and Psychiatry, 1,* 251–269.

Brown, A. C., & Orthner, D. K. (1990). Relocation and personal well-being among early adolescents. *Journal of Early Adolescence, 10,* 366–381.

Bush, S. (1977). Newsline: Moving can be fun. *Psychology Today, 11,* 28.

Calabrese, R. L. (1989). The effects of mobility on adolescents' alienation. *High School Journal, 73,* 41–46.

Elkind, D. (1974). *Children and adolescents* (2nd ed.). New York: Oxford University Press.

Erikson, E. (1962). *Childhood and society* (2nd ed.). New York: W. W. Norton.

Fassler, J. (1978). *Helping children cope: Mastering stress through books and stories.* New York: Macmillan.

Gerner, M., Perry, F., Moselle, M. A., & Archbold, M. (1992). Characteristics of internationally mobile adolescents. *Journal of School Psychology, 30,* 197–214.

Gordon, R. E., & Gordon, K. K. (1958). Emotional disorders of children in a rapidly growing suburb. *International Journal of Social Psychiatry, 4,* 85–97.

Greene, J. E., & Daughtry, S. L. (1961). Factors associated with school mobility. *The Journal of Educational Sociology, 35,* 36–40.

Gresham, F. M. (1981). Social skills training with handicapped children: A review. *Review of Educational Research, 51*, 139–176.
Heinlein, L. M., & Shinn, M. (2000). School mobility and student achievement in an urban setting. *Psychology in the Schools, 37*, 349–357.
Hendershott, A. B. (1989). Residential mobility, social support and adolescent self-concept. *Adolescence, 24*, 217–232.
Holland-Jacobsen, S., Holland, R. P., & Cook, A. S. (1984). Mobility: Easing the transition for students. *The School Counselor, 32*, 49–53.
Holmes, T. H., & Rahe, R. H. (1967). The social readjustment rating scale. *Journal of Psychosomatic research, 11*, 213–218.
Humke, C., & Schaefer, C. (1995). A review of the effects of residential mobility on children and adolescents. *Psychology: A Journal of Human Behavior, 32*, 16–24.
Inbar, M. (1976). *Social science frontiers: The vulnerable age phenomenon*. New York: Russell Sage.
Kenny, I. A. (1967). The child in the military community. *Journal of the American Academy of Child Psychiatry, 6*, 51–63.
Knudson-Cooper, M. S., & Leuchtag, A. K. (1982). The stress of a family move as a precipitating factor in children's burn accidents. *Journal of Human Stress, 8*, 32–38.
Kroger, J. E. (1980). Residential mobility and self concept in adolescence. *Adolescence, 15*, 967–977.
Lehr, C. J., & Hendrickson, N. (1968). Children's attitudes toward a family move. *Mental Hygiene, 52*, 381–384.
Levine, M. (1966). Residential change and school adjustment. *Community Mental Health Journal, 2*, 61–69.
Marchant, K. H., & Medway, F. J. (1987). Adjustment and achievement associated with mobility in military families. *Psychology in the Schools, 24*, 289–294.
Matter, D. E., & Matter, R. M. (1988). Helping young children cope with the stress of relocation: Action steps for the counselor. *Elementary School Guidance & Counseling, 23*, 23–29.
Pedersen, F. A., & Sullivan, E. J. (1964). Relationships among geographical mobility, parental attitudes and emotional disturbances in children. *American Journal of Orthopsychiatry, 34*, 575–580.
Pinder, C. C. (1989). The dark side of executive relocation. *Organizational Dynamics, 17*, 48–58.
Pittman, J. F., & Bowen, G. L. (1994). Adolescents on the move: Adjustment to family relocation. *Youth & Society, 26*, 69–91.
Rubin, Z. (1980). *Children's friendships*. Cambridge, MA: Harvard University Press.
Rumberger, R. W., & Larson, K. A. (1998). Student mobility and the increased risk of high school dropout. *American Journal of Education, 107*, 1–35.
Sackett, E. B. (1935). The effect of moving on educational status of children. *The Elementary School Journal, 35*, 517–526.
Seagoe, M. V. (1932). The transient child. *Journal of Juvenile Research, 16*, 251–257.
Shaw, J. A. (1987). Children in the military. *Pediatric Annals, 17*, 539, 543–544.
Smardo, F. A. (1981a). Books about moving. *Childhood Education, 58*, 37–39.
Smardo, F. A. (1981b). Geographic mobility: How do we help children cope? *Childhood Education, 58*, 40–45.
Splete, H., & Rasmussen, J. (1977). Aiding the mobile child. *Elementary School Guidance and Counseling, 11*, 225–228.
South, S. J., Crowder, K. D., & Trent, K. (1998). Children's residential mobility and neighborhood environment following parental divorce and remarriage. *Social Forces, 77*, 667–693.
Stroh, L. K., & Brett, J. M. (1990). Corporate mobility: After the move, what do children think? *Children's Environments Quarterly, 7*, 7–14.
Strother, J., & Harvill, R. (1986). Support groups for relocated adolescent students: A model for school counselors. *Journal for Specialists in Group Work, 11*, 114–120.

Stubblefield, R. L. (1955). Children's emotional problems aggravated by family moves. *American Journal of Orthopsychiatry, 25*, 120–126.

Switzer, R. E., Hirschberg, J. C., Myers, L., Gray E., Evers, N. H., & Forman, R. (1961). The effect of family moves on children. *Mental Hygiene, 45*, 528–536.

Temple, J. A., & Reynolds, A. J. (1999). School mobility and achievement: Longitudinal findings from an urban cohort. *Journal of School Psychology, 37*, 355–377.

Tooley, K. (1970). The role of geographic mobility in some adjustment problems of children and families. *Journal of the American Academy of Child Psychiatry, 9*, 366–378.

Tucker, C. J., Marx, J., & Long, L. (1998). "Moving on": Residential mobility and children's school lives. *Sociology of Education, 71*, 111–129.

U.S. Department of Commerce, Census Bureau. (2000). PPL-132 Geographical Mobility: March 1998 to March 1999 (Update), (Series P-20, No. 531). Atlanta GA: Author.

U.S. General Accounting Office. (1994). Elementary school children: Many change schools frequently, harming their education (GAO/HEHS-94-95, pp. 1–55). Washington, DC: Health, Education, and Human Services Division.

Whalen, T. E., & Fried, M. A. (1973). Geographic mobility and its effect on student achievement. *Journal of Educational Research, 67*, 163–165.

Wright, D. (1999). Student mobility: A negligible and confounded influence on student achievement. *Journal of Educational Research, 92*, 347–353.

CHAPTER

# 12

# School Violence and Disasters

Jonathan Sandoval
University of California, Davis

Stephen E. Brock
Lodi Unified School District, Lodi, CA

This chapter discusses two categories of hazardous events that lead to crisis responses in adults and children, and which most often come to mind when we think of crises in the school. We examine reactions to natural and man-made disasters, such as hurricanes, floods, and fires, and we discuss reactions to terrorist attacks or other acts of violence that may occur at school. We view such incidents as drive-by shootings, sniper attacks, and bombings as acts of terrorism. All of these events are likely to cause traumatic stress.

One feature that these two categories share with others is that they are typically sudden and unanticipated. Some exceptions are impending war, floods, and tornadoes and hurricanes where storm warnings can be delivered in anticipation. Earthquakes, fires, dam breaks, come with no warning. However, even with warnings, those involved often do not anticipate the severity of the event, and often discount the warning as only indicating a chance of personal involvement. Another similarity between disasters and terrorist attacks is that adults in the school as well as the children are affected. The teachers, administrators, and guidance staff would be equally traumatized by a schoolyard shooting or an airplane crashing into the school, for example. The normal caretakers in the school can be as traumatized as the children, and they too will need assistance in coping with the aftermath of the crisis. It is much more likely that outside crisis response assistance will be needed to help an entire community deal with disaster and mayhem associated with violence than with many of the crises described in this book.

Fortunately, these two kinds of hazardous events, acts of school violence and disasters, are also similar in that they are very rare. Although there is an impression that acts of violence are increasing, in fact, the incidence of violent crime is dropping (Kaufman et al., 2000). What has increased is the amount of national press coverage that is given to these events when they do occur. This increased publicity results in more attention to the event, which can lead to societal reforms, such as gun control. But there is also a regrettable aspect to increased attention. With acts of violence there comes publicity, and the chance that other deranged and impressionable individuals will attempt a copycat reenactment of the crime to gain the same attention (Lazarus, Brock, & Feinberg, 1999).

The rarity of these events also leads to problems in prevention. Prevention usually is based on understanding the dynamics and causes of the precipitating event. Because these events are unusual, and many disasters are considered "Acts of God," it may not be very cost effective to address preventing the specific event. This does not mean there are not things to be done with respect to primary prevention (e.g., upgrading building codes to reduce the impact of earthquakes and hurricanes); rather the focus of prevention is secondary, and more directed toward generic preparation to respond to crises in general rather than on preventing unknown events from occurring.

In chapter 2 Brock reviewed the process of establishing crisis response teams in schools, and we will not review that material here. Drawing heavily from our earlier account of crisis response planning (Brock, Sandoval, & Lewis, 2001), in this chapter we discuss several related topics. First, we explore what can be done to prevent acts of violence (including identifying and responding to potentially violent youth). Next we discuss how to prepare for the crisis response following acts of violence or natural or man-made disaster. Finally, we examine the actual crisis intervention response to acts of violence and to disaster (including the processes of identifying and responding to psychological trauma victims).

## PREVENTING TERRORISM AND CREATING SAFER SCHOOLS

Individuals who are not part of the school community often commit acts of terrorism and violence. They come from the outside and commit their crimes on the school site. Aside from making it difficult to enter the school grounds, it is difficult to do more in terms of prevention for these types of events. More can be done, however, in reducing the violence that takes place in schools instigated by students. Chapter 6 on bullying discusses the causes and potential responses to aggressive children. But school violence does not only come from children who are bullies; alienated, isolated, and rejected children are also capable of explosive violence. To create safer schools, there must be a close examination of student discipline, the openness of the school to outsiders, the school climate, and the physical arrangement of the campus.

### Student Discipline

The *School Safety Check Book* (National School Safety Center, 1990) advocated the establishment of written discipline rules that clearly differentiate between an infraction (unacceptable behavior such as lying and inappropriate language) and a crime (behavior that violates the law such as assault and vandalism). Rules need to identify specific unacceptable behaviors and their consequences. Rules must be reasonable, and should allow for due process and appeal. In particular, school disciplinary codes must cover school fights. There is a fine line between a schoolyard altercation involving pushing and shoving and assault or battery. Increasingly schools are moving the line to declaring fights battery. Poland (1997) reported that the Houston schools experienced a dramatic decrease in the number of fights after implementing a policy requiring students involved in fights to make a court appearance and pay a $200 fine.

### Campus Visitors

Schools as public institutions are open to visitors, but the school can require that visitors identify themselves and can set guidelines for access. Signs should be posted at all school entry points directing visitors to check in at the school office. It is important to establish policies that ask all staff members to approach and identify unfamiliar campus visitors (Stephens, 1994; Trump, 1998) and ask them to sign in, if they have not already done so. After having signed in, all campus visitors should be issued identification badges. Staff should be trained in, and comfortable with, challenging visitors without badges.

### Employee and Student Identification

To further assist in the identification of campus visitors, it is also helpful if students and employees are issued their own personal identification cards. If funds are available, a system of photo-identification badges increases security.

### School Climate

Positive school climates are both the result of, and contribute to, secure and safe schools. Stephens (1994) advocated creating a positive school climate by building pride and ownership in the school, making the campus welcoming (by having staff greet students as they arrive and being present during class changes), and having high administrator visibility (including class visitations and attendance at special events).

On the other hand, Hyman and Snook (1999) argued that educator policies and practices, such as corporal punishment, and discipline that is administered inconsistently, can contribute to student misbehavior. These practices lead to student alienation, which in turn leads to acts of violence.

Resiliency research and school climate research provide important data regarding factors influencing the climate of the school. Resiliency and school climate improves as children are able to form positive relationship with a caring adult (Masten, 1994; Werner & Smith, 1982). Many vehicles are available for making this kind of adult–child interaction possible, including schools within schools, use of community mentors, and providing sufficient numbers of school counselors. Dwyer, Osher, and Warger (1998) and Strepling (1997) have reviewed the school climate literature. Their findings on the characteristics of effective schools, and safe and secure classrooms are summarized in Table 12.1. Students feel secure when there is a sense of community and there is sufficient routine for students to know what to expect.

TABLE 12.1
Characteristics of Effective Schools and Safe/Secure Classrooms

| | |
|---|---|
| 1. | Focus on academic achievement and foster enthusiasm for learning. |
| 2. | Involve families in meaningful ways. |
| 3. | Develop links to the community. |
| 4. | Emphasize positive relationships among students and staff. Teachers and students learn and use each other's names. |
| 5. | Treat students with equal respect. |
| 6. | Discuss safety issues openly. |
| 7. | Create ways for students to share their concerns and help students feel safe expressing t heir feelings. |
| 8. | Have in place a system for referring children who are suspected of being abused or neglected. |
| 9. | Offer extended day programs for children. |
| 10. | Promote good citizenship and character, and build a community of learners (using collaboration between students and teacher, school and home). |
| 11. | Identify problems and assess progress toward solutions. Classroom meetings are held to discuss issues and solve problems. |
| 12. | Support students in making the transition to adult life and the workplace. |
| 13. | Develop and consistently enforce school wide rules that are clear, broad-based, and fair. |
| 14. | Classroom management includes firm, fair, and consistent rules and procedures. |
| 15. | Use of learning centers and the opportunity for cooperative group work. |
| 16. | Leisure areas exist for discussions, downtime, and reading. |
| 17. | Books and magazines readily available. |
| 18. | Displays of students' in-progress and completed work. |
| 20. | Plants and objects that assist students in developing an identity of the classroom space as "ours." |

*Note.* From "Early Warning, Timely Response: A Guide to Safe Schools" by Dwyer, Osher, and Warger (1998) and Striepling (1997).

### School Environment

Often a relationship exists between student and staff behavior, and their surroundings. Crowe (1990) described the *Crime Prevention Through Environmental Design* theory, which asserts that the appropriate physical "design" and effective use of the "built environment" decreases the incidence of crime and prevalence of fear. Crowe identifies significant problem areas on school campuses, including parking lots and lockers, and suggests potential remedies.

Brooks (1993) suggested evaluating patterns of student congregation, paying particular attention to shifts in clusters of students, rival groups binding together, students attending events they normally do not attend, sudden appearance of underground publications, and parents withdrawing their children from school due to a fear that something might happen. These are warning signs from the physical environment that should be monitored.

### School Security

Many schools have their own security personnel or have become "beats" for local police. Models of campus security, described by Grant (1993), include "officer friendly" and "campus cop." In the former the police officer has a public relations role; educates children on safety, gangs, and substance abuse; and is viewed as a positive role model. In the later model, the officer's role is to enforce laws. Combining both models Grant described the development of the *School Liaison Officer Program* in Richmond, British Columbia. In this program police officers attend sporting events, dances, field trips; have casual conversations with students; investigate school crimes; follow-up on disclosures; and provide enforcement. Schools have also invoked technology for surveillance as part of their security approach. The ultimate, perhaps, is the use of metal detectors to screen for weapons. A balance must be struck between adequate monitoring for safety and the establishment of a friendly, caring school climate. There is a tradeoff between control and sensitivity to educational needs and traditions.

## IDENTIFYING AND RESPONDING TO POTENTIALLY VIOLENT STUDENTS

The school environment can be made as safe as possible, and still an act of violence can suddenly occur. An important additional step in the prevention of acts of violence is to recognize the warning signs of students who may be a danger to others and prone to terrorism. We now take up the topic of the warning signs of antisocial aggression.

## Warning Signs of Violence

School staff, students, and parents should be helped to recognize the early warning signs of potentially violent students. Several resources are now available to help. One of the most prominent is *Early Warning, Timely Response: A Guide To Safe Schools* (Dwyer et al., 1998). Developed at the request of President Clinton, and mailed to every school in the nation, it reflects the views of experts in the fields of education, psychology, mental health, criminal justice, and law enforcement. Other helpful resources include materials developed by the American Psychological Association (1999), and the National School Safety Center (1998). Both of these organizations provide documents that were developed from analysis of school-associated violent deaths. For a summary of warning signs provided by these and other sources, see Table 12.2. Most of these signs seem obvious indicators of problems with anger control, but unfortunately they are often dismissed as normal adolescent behaviors, especially in males. A history of displaying signs and the existence of several signs should probably be taken more seriously than a single behavior in isolation.

We strongly recommend that when publicizing these warning signs, professionals or training programs emphasize that they be attended to with great caution. Students who display these warning signs might, or might not, commit a violent act. Warning signs should *only* be used to identify students who may require further assessment to evaluate risk and to guide interventions. They should not be viewed as perfect predictors of violent behavior, nor should they be used to exclude students from school (Brock, 1999). Dwyer et al. (1998, pp. 6–7) provided several principles designed to help schools avoid the misuse or misinterpretation of warning signs. These principles include the following.

TABLE 12.2
Imminent Warning Signs of Violence

1. Serious physical fighting with peers or family members.
2. Severe destruction of property.
3. Severe rage for seemingly minor reasons.
4. Detailed threats of lethal violence.
5. Possession and/or use of firearms and other weapons.
6. Other self-injurious behaviors or threats of suicide.

*Note.* From "Early Warning, Timely Response: A Guide to Safe Schools," by K. Dwyer, D. Osher, and C. Warger, 1998, p. 11.

***Do No Harm.*** The intention of early warning sign screening should be to facilitate the identification of students who are troubled and in need of supportive interventions. They should not be used to label, exclude, punish, or isolate. In addition, information about early warning signs must be kept confidential.

***Avoid Stereotypes.*** It is essential not to use stereotypes (e.g., race, socioeconomic status, learning ability, or appearance) to identify students. Even if the purpose of the identification is to provide "helpful" interventions, labeling can do harm. Another area of potential misuse is invasion of privacy and discrimination by overidentifying certain groups of children (Nelson, Roberts, Smith, & Irwin, 2000). Biased school staff may consciously or unconsciously target individuals from a particular group. Nelson et al. also express concern over the possibility that students labeled as dangerous might be denied access to after school programs.

***View Warning Signs Within a Developmental Context.*** It is important to place the student's behavior within the appropriate developmental context. Developmentally typical behavior should not be interpreted as a warning sign. Always remember that troubled students typically display many warning signs, repeatedly, and with increasing intensity over time. Thus, it is important not to overreact to a single sign.

## Responding to Warning Signs

It is critical that referral procedures be in place if any screening for potential violence is done. Any procedures developed should be sensitive to the level and intensity of the warning signs being observed. Specifically, at least two levels of referrals need to be in place, one for "at-risk" and another for "high-risk" students.

***At-Risk Referral Procedures.*** The first level of referral procedures should be designed to facilitate the assessment of students who display relatively low intensity and short duration early warning signs. Vehicles for these referrals may include traditional school resources such as Student Study Teams or Student Assistance Programs. Through these resources, the appropriate school staff members (e.g., administration, school mental health staff, other support staff, or teachers) can be informed about the status and progress of the at-risk students, and appropriate interventions recommended.

***High-Risk Referral Procedures.*** The second level of referral procedures should be designed to facilitate the assessment of students who display several imminent warning signs of violence (see Table 12.2). Obviously, a school's response to these signs must be immediate. School procedures must specify that when any of these behaviors are noted, the observer should make an immediate referral to a school administrator, to a school mental health professional, or both. An initial assessment procedure should be to determine the nature of the suspected violence and to determine if the means for such behavior are available (e.g., does the student have a weapon). If the means are at hand, responsible and trusted adults should removed them as soon as possible. If the student refuses to relinquish the means of threatened violence, school staff will need to discretely call for assistance from local law enforcement. Next, once immediate safety is assured; a mental health professional should conduct a careful risk assessment. While waiting for this evaluation, a responsible and trained adult should keep the student under close supervision. Under no circumstances should a high-risk student be left alone.

### Intervening With Potentially Violent Students

There are a variety of strategies that may help the student at risk for violence. Among them are individual counseling, behavioral programming, and social skills and anger management training.

***Counseling.*** One of the most important interventions for troubled children is individual and group counseling. This support is typically provided by a mental health professional. Depending on specific student needs, a referral might also be made to an outside agency or a private practitioner. With potentially violent youth, counseling may focus on teaching skills such as anger management (e.g., Goldstein & Glick, in press) and social skills (e.g., Elliot, McKevitt, & DiPerna, in press) rather than traditional psychotherapy. As with all counseling interventions, a plan should be developed that is unique to the individual. With the student at risk for violence, however, this plan will necessarily need to include provision for immediate assistance when needed. For example, there may need to be provisions for responding to and calming the student who is on the verge of losing control.

***Positive Behavioral Programming.*** A second individual intervention are positive behavior plans which identify an undesirable behavior and then determining its function or purpose. Once the purpose of the behavior has been identified, the next step is to identify a replacement behavior. Ideally, this replacement behavior is not only more socially adaptive, but also provides an alternative way for the student to achieve his or her behavioral goal.

***Conflict Resolution and Management.*** Training of students and staff in conflict resolution and management can decrease violence and provide alternative methods of solving problems (Petersen & Straub, 1992). Conflict resolution programs, when implemented well, help students to develop empathy to control their own emotions. They also facilitate the development of communication and problem solving while showing students how to settle disputes among peers. Program graduates, called conflict managers, may be used by schools to help resolve student conflicts. Like peer tutoring, conflict management is helpful both for the mediators and the students in conflict. Not only do students in conflict receive assistance resolving their problem, but also the mediators will feel empowered to resolve differences without adult assistance.

***Social Skills and Anger Management Training.*** Larson (1994) reviewed several social skill and anger management programs. Examples include *Adolescent Anger Control: Cognitive-Behavioral Techniques* (Feindler & Ecton, 1986), *Aggression Replacement Training: A Comprehensive Intervention for Aggressive Youth* (Goldstein, Glick, Reiner, Zimmerman, & Coultry, 1985), and *Think First: Anger and Aggression Management for Secondary Level Students* (Larson, 1990, 1992). Larson's (1994) review article provides additional information on these training programs.

## PREPARING FOR ACTS OF VIOLENCE AND DISASTERS

Schools have a history of preparing for disasters, with the most obvious example being drills (e.g., fire, tornado, earthquake drills). Recently, schools have also begun to develop drills for responding to acts of violence. Elements of these drills and other preparedness considerations are discussed in this section.

### Danger Signals

Poland (1994) advocated that schools develop clear "danger" signals. These signals or code words can be used by individuals to notify the central administration of acts of violence or by the administration to alert individual teachers to danger. Ideally, these codes communicate the need for assistance without alerting individuals, who might be making threats of violence, to the staffs' intended actions.

Another danger signal procedure that needs to be established is one that can alert an entire school's staff of a hazardous situation (California Department of Education, 2000), either violence or impending disaster. This danger signal (which could make use of a code word or specific bell sequence) would communicate the kind of danger that is imminent, and that all students are to be moved to a secure location. Using codes is helpful in reducing panic among the student body, but adults in the school must understand these codes and know how to respond. Clearly, it is essential that all school staff members must know the meaning of danger signals. Finally, it is important to note that in addition to danger signals, an "all clear" signal be established (California Department of Education, 2000).

### Danger Procedures

Complementary to training in the danger signals described earlier, school staffs need to be trained regarding exactly what to do when a signal indicates that an act of violence or disaster is occurring. During a terrorist attack, for example, staff must know that students are to be directed to a secure room, doors locked, cover taken underneath tables or desks, windows closed, and curtains drawn (California Department of Education, 2000). Drills will be helpful in reinforcing these instructions.

### Emergency Evacuations

Some acts of school violence and many disasters (e.g., fire, plane crash, toxic waste or chemical spills, bomb threats, and so forth) may necessitate the evacuation of students from one location to another. The first step in developing an evacuation plan is to identify potential safe areas that students could be moved to in the event that their school or their classrooms are no longer safe. Ideally, the area chosen would be large enough to accommodate the entire student body. Examples of such locations include shopping centers, community recreation facilities, business offices, and churches. In most cases, existing fire drill evacuation routes can be adapted to other potential emergencies requiring evacuation. However, the evacuation procedure should contain alternative evacuation routes in the event that the primary evacuation routes or safe areas are affected by the crisis event. Also be aware that terrorists have been known to study these evacuation routes and cause an evacuation in order to concentrate potential victims in a particular location.

### Accounting for Students and Staff

It is also important to develop plans and procedures that will allow the school to quickly and efficiently account for students and staff members following acts of violence. Reporting methods may include the use of alphabetical listings of all students and staff or class lists.

### Reuniting Students With Parents

Facilitating the development of procedures for reuniting students with their families following crisis events is yet another task. We have seen literally hundreds of parents arriving simultaneously to locate their children following a school shooting, which resulted in incredible confusion and great emotional distress when reunification did not occur efficiently.

## Crowd Control

Crowd control procedures complement student and parent reunion procedures. In advance of a crisis areas need to be designated where parents can wait until they can be reunited with their children. Possible locations may include school cafeterias, multipurpose rooms, playground areas, and libraries. The school will need to be able to communicate with large groups of people at one time. This will mean making sure that bullhorns or public address systems are available.

## Traffic Management

Traffic management issues include plans for keeping driveways clear to allow emergency response vehicle access to school grounds. As a rule, traffic management procedures should encourage school visitors to park on side streets during times of crisis. The need to clear a location for an emergency medical helicopter landing site may also play a role in traffic management.

## Involving Community Resources

The California Department of Education (2000) recommended obtaining a prior written agreement regarding coordination of the law enforcement or medical personnel in response to school crisis events. This document should detail the point at which responsibility for a situation would be assumed by law enforcement or other civil agencies. When preparing for the involvement of law enforcement in school crisis events (such as school shootings), it is important to provide them with a detailed floor plan of the school showing entrances, windows, roof latches, ventilation systems, and so on, and current estimates of the number and identities of staff and students in each class area (Petersen & Straub, 1992; Trump, 1998). Often school yearbooks or class pictures become handy tools for helping law enforcement to identify students. Police should also have a master key to the school and know if there are parking permits used to identify student and staff cars (Neal, 1999).

## Referral Planning Procedures

Preparing for the crisis intervention response to psychological trauma victims is yet another critical crisis preparedness procedures. Clearly, it will be difficult to meet the needs of those who have been psychologically traumatized by acts of violence or disaster without carefully developed crisis intervention referral options.

Referral planning procedures will typically involve staff in-service and training. Given that an effective crisis intervention provides such support immediately, it is clearly desirable to have as many staff members as possible receive in-service instruction. At a minimum, every member of the school's guidance staff should have a clear understanding of the principles, goals, and limitations of psychological first aid. In addition, professional mental health counseling resources need to be identified. The identification of community resources will involve the survey of both community mental health agencies and private practitioners. Community agencies are typically well known to most school psychologists, social workers, and counselors. School district personnel should have little difficulty developing a comprehensive list of local community mental health agencies, but it will be important to verify expertise in crisis intervention. The identification of private mental health practitioner referrals is more difficult, especially in urban communities where there are large numbers of licensed professionals.

Referral planning must acknowledge that not all individuals exposed to acts of violence or disaster will require immediate individual assistance or eventually require a professional mental health referral. Depending on circumstances and resources, many students and staff members may be able to independently integrate the trauma into their lives. Although individuals not obviously in crisis or at high risk will not be made priorities when it comes to making treatment decisions, there are clearly ways in which schools can and should facilitate the process of crisis resolution. Large numbers of students can effectively be intervened with through group and classroom discussions of the crisis event. With preparation, and if comfortable in the role, the classroom teacher can be an effective provider of this type of crisis intervention.

## RESPONDING TO VIOLENCE AND DISASTER

The common goal of responding both to acts of violence and to victims of disaster is to prevent the formation of Post-Traumatic Stress Disorder (PTSD). This syndrome, first identified among combat veterans, does have a manifestation in children similar to that in adults, although children's reactions may be somewhat different and the symptoms will vary with age. Three clusters of symptoms are typically associated with PTSD, re-experiencing, numbing/avoidance, and hyperarousal. Anthony, Lonigan, and Hecht (1999), studying children and adolescent survivors of Hurricane Hugo found reactions characterized by (a) intrusive phenomena coupled with active avoidance of negative experiences (bad dreams, repetitive images, upset thoughts, fear reactions), (b) emotional numbing along with passive avoidance of emotionally unrewarding activities (anhedonia, isolation, avoidance), and (c) arousal (somatic complaints, easy startling, sleep disturbance, and attention problems). They note that anhedonia (the absence of pleasurable feelings in situations where they are normally present), learning/memory problems and attention problems, although common, are associated problems and do not predict later PTSD status. Children are more likely than adults to have symptomotolgy related to aggression, anxiety, depression, and regression (Mazza & Overstreet, 2000).

By no means all children, if untreated, will develop PTSD. Estimates vary by extent and type of trauma, but a conservative estimate is that 12%–15% of children may develop PTSD six or more months following a disaster (La Greca, Silverman, Vernberg, & Prinstein, 1996; McDermott & Palmer, 1999). Some may even develop long-term characterological patterns of behavior following a disaster (Honig, Grace, Lindy, Newman, & Titchener, 1999). These character traits, exhibited later in life, may originate as coping responses to the trauma.

In addition to exposure to the event itself, symptoms may be more severe if there is parental discord or distress (Swenson et al., 1996; Wasserstein & La Greca, 1998), and if there are subsequent stressors, such as lack of housing following a disaster (La Greca et al., 1996). The traumatic death of a family member, also increases the risk of stress reactions (Bradach & Jordan, 1995). Symptoms may also be heightened among Latino and Black children (La Greca et al., 1996). La Greca and her colleagues discussed five factors that are related to the development of severe symptomatology: (a) exposure to disaster-related experiences, including perceived life threats, (b) pre-existing child characteristics such as demographics, (c) the recovery environment including social support, (d) the child's coping skills, and (e) intervening stressful life event during recovery. With this model in mind, intervention must proceed to supply an appropriate recovery environment that is suited to a child's characteristics and facilitates coping. The first response, is the provision of psychological first aid to those most in need.

## Triage

Following acts of violence or a disaster, the medical workers who first arrive and find widespread injury will first perform medical triage. Triage, derived from the French for "sorting," is defined as:

> The screening and classification of sick, wounded, or injured persons during war or other disasters to determine priority needs for efficient use of medical and nursing manpower, equipment, and facilities.... Use of triage is essential if the maximum number of lives is to be saved during an emergency situation

> that produces many more sick and wounded than the available medical care facilities and personnel can possibly handle. (Thomas, 1993, p. 1767)

This concept is also applicable to the identification of psychological trauma victims.

## Initial Psychological Triage Following Acts of Violence or Disaster

The process of psychological triage involves deciding who is at risk for psychological trauma following the hazard of an act of violence. The following are guidelines for psychological triage decision making.

***Physical Proximity.*** All individuals directly experiencing or witnessing an act of violence or an injury or loss during a disaster should be considered to be at high risk to be significantly affected by the event. The physically closer the individual is, the greater the likelihood of the person becoming a psychological trauma victim. Conversely, the greater the physical distance between the individual and the place in which the crisis event occurred, the less the likelihood of psychological trauma. This fact has been documented in several studies (Bloch, Silber, & Perry, 1956; Green, Grace, & Lindy, 1983; Green et al., 1991; Nader, Pynoos, Fairbanks, & Frederick, 1990; Pynoos et al., 1987; Shore, Tatum, & Vollmer, 1986).

***Emotional Proximity.*** In addition to physical proximity, emotional proximity is also a consideration when attempting to identify the psychological victims of violence. Individuals who have an emotional attachment to someone who was injured or killed are at risk for psychological trauma. The stronger the attachment, the more likely it is that the individual will be traumatized. The importance of attachment has been demonstrated by Nader et al. (1990), who found that greater acquaintance with the victim of a schoolyard shooting was significantly related to higher scores on a measure of posttraumatic stress reactions.

Perception of danger or threat may also increase emotional proximity. Following a disaster or violence, children who have developed a concern for the wellbeing and safety of themselves, a family member, or other emotionally significant person may also be at risk for psychological trauma. The trauma is likely to heighten the fears for others, as there is concrete evidence now available that bad things can happen to people.

***Previous Trauma.*** Individuals known to be vulnerable because of previous trauma, loss, or preexisting psychopathology should be considered at high risk. Special attention needs to be given to students who have experienced other traumas within the past year or those who have experienced prior crises similar in nature to the current crisis event (American Psychiatric Association, 1987). How an individual perceives a crisis event will have a lot to do with his or her frame of reference at the time of the event. If the individual had experienced numerous recent significant traumas and losses, a relatively minor or remote crisis event might be sufficient to cause psychological trauma. For example, Nader et al. (1990) reported that children who have experienced previous traumas had renewed Post-Traumatic Stress Disorder symptoms related to the previous experience, following a sniper attack at their school.

***Acute Stress Reactions.*** Any individual whose response to the event is out of proportion to the degree of exposure to the crisis event should be evaluated next. These individuals may not have the intellectual or emotional problem-solving skills necessary to cope with the experience. Those conducting psychological triage must determine whether the psychological victims are either *over-* or *under*reacting to the event based on their degree of exposure. Denial, blocking, or emotional numbing of the unpleasant reality of an act of violence and is often part of the early reactions to a crisis event (Gillis, 1992; Horowitz, 1976). For example, individuals directly exposed to a shooting and are not reacting to it, should be monitored closely. We should also be aware, as Gillis reports, that delayed stress reactions are possible following a trauma.

***Psychopathology.*** Although the acute stress associated with psychological trauma is not a sign of mental illness (it is a normal reaction to abnormal circumstances), a history of emotional disturbance can lower one's capacity to cope with an unforeseen crisis (American Psychiatric Association, 1994). A preexisting psychopathology can also make it more difficult to process information during crisis intervention.

The family's mental health should also be considered (Lystad, 1985). For example, following a school bus kidnapping, Terr (1983) found ". . . relationships between the clinical severity of the children's posttraumatic conditions and their preexisting family pathology . . ." (p. 1550). If family members are not functioning well to support the child's coping, it will obviously more difficult for the child to surmount a traumatic event.

***Lack of Resources.*** A lack of resources can make it much more difficult for children and adults to cope with violence or traumatic events. For example, a lack of material resources such as money, food, housing, and transportation can turn a moderately stressful event into a crisis. According to the American Psychiatric Association (1994), "There is some evidence that social supports . . . may influence the development of Acute Stress Disorder" (p. 431). Internal resources include intelligence, skill in problem solving, personality, and temperament. Individuals with disabilities may use up these resources in coping with their disability and not have extra resources available to deal with violence disasters and terrorism. These internal personal resources must also be evaluated in the attempt to identify children and adults at risk for psychological trauma.

### Initial Interventions and Secondary Screening

All individuals classified as being at risk should be closely monitored to assess their need for mental health referrals. Crisis intervention will be provided by school and community mental health professionals, unless the disaster is so widespread that state or national assistance is forthcoming. It may or may not be provided at the school site. The goals of triage include identification of students and staff members most significantly affected by crisis and then providing these individuals with immediate psychological first aid assistance. Secondary triage goals include identification of individuals mildly to moderately affected by the crisis, and the collection of data used in making crisis therapy referral decisions.

### Screening

After psychological triage has identified all individuals judged to be at risk due to either involvement and exposure or other risk factors, the next step is to survey the entire school population for signs of posttraumatic stress. Mass screening is especially important following crises that affect large numbers of students. During these situations it is unlikely that the crisis intervenors will be able to independently identify all students significantly affected by the event. Thus, teachers and parents should be enlisted in the process. Parents and teachers are the most likely to see and be affected by a student's crisis reactions. In his discussion of mass screening, Klingman (1988) suggested using "... observation of signs of behavior maladaptation, child paper-and-pencil products (e.g., free writing, drawing), anxiety scales administered to children, and the identification of absentees" (pp. 210–211). An effective referral system needs to educate care providers about reactions to look for among youth following a crisis. It would tell them what signs suggest the need for a crisis intervention. Staff in-service, both during and before a crisis event, would be important for teachers. School newsletter articles both before and during a crisis event would serve a similar purpose for parents. Finally, it is important to note that the media can be very helpful. Newspapers and broadcast media can quickly and efficiently alert parents and the community in general to signs, symptoms, and reactions suggesting the need for crisis intervention and where assistance can be obtained.

***Self-Referral.*** All students need to be informed about the availability of assistance in coping with acts of violence or disasters. Especially following crises affecting large numbers of students, it is possible that crisis workers, teachers, and parents may overlook or fail to recognize signs suggesting the need for a crisis intervention. Other students may not display behavioral signs of distress Thus, students need to know where to go for assistance on their own. This information can be disseminated in a variety of way, such as public address announcements, school assemblies, and teacher-led discussions.

***Parent Involvement.*** Because of the sudden and unexpected nature of situational crises, it is not always possible to contact a student's family right away. Some students will need to be seen immediately and in a crisis situation this is an appropriate action. However, we recommend that as soon as crisis intervenors obtain parent permission for referral or continuing crisis intervention. Parents also need to know about distress their children are experiencing so that they may participate in lending their child emotional and physical support.

Natural disasters often strike parents as well as children. Because parent adjustment is related to a child's recovery, seeing that parents get assistance and counseling will be important.

## CRISIS COUNSELING AND INTERVENTION FOLLOWING DISASTERS AND TERRORISM

Crisis intervention and counseling for children and youth subject to the traumatic stress of acts of violence is not greatly different from the generic principles of counseling and intervention outlined in the first chapter of this book and discussed in subsequent chapters. One obvious difference is the need to first secure the safety of the survivors. The crisis intervenor must first see to it that children are protected from further harm and are removed from exposure to traumatic stimuli (Young, Ford, Ruzek, Friedman, & Gusman, 1999).

The impact of disasters and acts of violence is typically a loss for the affected individual. The loss may be of human life or of a sense of safety and security or of shelter. Grieving and mourning these losses will be among the objectives of the counseling intervention. It is important, however, to acknowledge that the combination of traumatic stress and grief generated by a sudden traumatic loss create unique problems for crisis intervenors.

Associated with traumatic stress are emotional numbing and avoidance of trauma reminders. These symptoms can greatly interfere with the process of grieving. Given this reality it is typically a good idea that trauma work take precedence over grief work.

## Disaster Response

Young and his colleagues (Young et al., 1999) emphasized three concepts in intervention: Protect, Direct, and Connect (Myers, 1994). It is important to *protect* children from further harm by moving them to a secure location, and attending to their basic needs for food, drink and sleep, and shelter. To relieve tension, it is also helpful to provide a place for play and relaxation. Children need to be protected from the gaze of onlookers and the curious, and they need to be spared watching scenes of the traumatic event replayed on television.

Helpers need to be *direct* with children and take an active role in managing their environment. Because parents may be disabled by the disaster, it is comforting to see some adult taking control and making decisions.

*Connecting* means to establish a relationship through verbal and nonverbal means with the child. This relationship will be important to help the child manage fear, anxiety, panic, and grief. Simply by being physically present with the child, anxiety can lessen. Connecting also refers to the need to reunite children with parents and loved ones, and connecting children to knowledge and resources through anticipatory guidance.

Bibliotherapy may also be useful following a disaster. A particularly useful resource for children is book entitled *"I'll Know What to Do": A Kid's Guide to Natural Disasters* by Mark, Layton, and Chesworth (1997). The authors focus on four concepts they view as fundamental to recovery: information, communication, reassurance, and the reestablishment of routine. The authors explore children's feelings that often emerge in the aftermath of a disaster, and offer useful techniques to help young people cope with them.

An important intervention goal following a disaster is to restore psychosocial resources (Smith & Freedy, 2000). Providing social supports is particularly difficult during times of crisis. With a disaster, whole communities are affected. There is a disruption of both schools and social services. There is often an absence of adults with whom children can process feelings of loss, dread, and vulnerablity. Support groups can provide one vehicle for feeling connected to others and working through these feelings. Ceballo (2000) described a short-term supportive intervention group based in the school for children exposed to urban violence. Her groups are designed to (a) validate and normalize children's emotional reactions to violence, (b) help children restore a sense of control over certain aspects of their environment, (c) develop safety skills for dealing with the environment in the future, (d) understand the process of grief and mourning, and (e) minimize the influence of PTSD symptoms on educational tasks and other daily life events. Such structured support groups can promote resiliency and promote constructive coping with problems.

Galante and Foa (1986) worked in groups with children in one school throughout the school year following a major Italian earthquake. The children were encouraged to explore fears, mistaken understandings, feelings connected to death and injury from the disaster using discussion, drawing, and role playing. Most participants except those who experienced a death in the family showed a reduction in symptoms of disturbance.

Another feature of disasters and terrorist acts is a lowered sense of control over one's destiny and heightened fear of the unknown. Thus, a focus on returning a sense of empowerment to children will be important. If children can be directed to participate in restorative activities and take some actions to mitigate the results of the disaster, no matter how small, they can begin to rebuild an important sense of efficacy.

Finally, there may be issues of survivor guilt, if there is widespread loss of life or property. Survivor guilt is a strong feeling of culpability often induced among individuals who survive a situation that results in the death of valued others Those spared, but witnessing the devastation of others, may have extreme feelings of guilt that will need to be dealt with. Children, particularly, ascribe fantastical causes to the effects they see. They will need to explore their magical thinking in counseling or play therapy about why they escaped injury or loss (St. Thomas, 1993).

## CONCLUSION

Although stressful traumatic events such as natural and man-made disasters or act of violence come often without much warning, schools can be prepared to respond to them. Schools can be made safe and secure against outsiders, and increasingly strategies are being implemented to identify and treat potentially violent terrorists among the student body. In addition, following a traumatic event, a psychological triage can facilitate the delivery of crisis intervention and counseling, and in doing so facilitate the adaptive coping of trauma victims. We will never be free of violence or disaster, but we can do much to ameliorate its psychological impact.

## REFERENCES

American Psychiatric Association. (1987). *Diagnostic and statistical manual of mental disorders* (3rd ed., rev.). Washington, DC: Author.

American Psychiatric Association. (1994). *Diagnostic and statistical manual of mental disorders* (4th ed.). Washington, DC: Author.

American Psychological Association. (1999). *Warning signs*. Washington, DC: Author.

Anthony, J. L., Lonigan, C. J., & Hecht, S. A. (1999). Dimensionality of posttraumatic stress disorder symptoms in children exposed to disaster: Results from confirmatory factor analyses. *Journal of Abnormal Psychology, 108*, 326–336.

Bloch, D. A., Silber, E., & Perry, S. E. (1956). Some factors in the emotional reactions of children to disaster. *The American Journal of Psychiatry, 113*, 416–422.

Bradach, K. M., & Jordan, J. R. (1995). Long-term effects of a family history of traumatic death on adolescent individuation. *Death Studies, 19*, 315–336.

Brock, S. E. (1999, Summer). The crisis of youth violence: Dangers and opportunities. *CASP Today: A quarterly Magazine of the California Association of School Psychologists, 48*, 18–20.

Brock, S. E., Sandoval, J., & Lewis, S. (2001). *Preparing for crises in the schools: A manual for building school crisis response teams*. New York: Wiley.

Brooks, R. D. (1993, Winter). Signs of the times. *School Safety*, pp. 4–7.

California State Department of Education. (2000). *Crisis management and response* [On-line]. Available: *http//www.cde.ca.gov/spbranch/safety/crisis.html*

Ceballo, R. (2000). The neighborhood club: A supportive intervention group for children exposed to urban violence. *American Journal of Orthopsychiatry, 70*, 401–407.

Crowe, T. D. (1990, fall). Designing safer schools. *School Safety*, pp. 9–13.

Dwyer, K., Osher, D., & Warger, C. (1998). *Early warning, timely response: A guide to safe schools*. Washington, DC: U.S. Department of Education.

Elliot, S. N., McKevitt, B. C., & DiPernna, J. C. (in press). Promoting social skills and the development of socially supportive learning environments. In S. E. Brock & P. J. Lazarus (Eds.), *Best practices in school crisis prevention and intervention*. Bethesda, MD: National Association of School Psychologists.

Feindler, E. L., & Ecton, R. B. (1986). *Adolescent anger control: Cognitive-behavioral techniques*. New York: Pergamon Press.

Galante, R., & Foa, D. (1986). An epidemiological study of psychic trauma and treatment effectiveness for children after a natural disaster. *Journal of the American Academy of Child Psychiatry, 25*, 357–363.

Gillis, H. (1992, April). *A report on data collected following the Stockton Schoolyard Shooting*. Paper presented at the San Joaquin County Office of Education, Stockton, CA.

Goldstein, A. P., & Glick, B. (in press). Agression replacement training. In S. E. Brock & P. J. Lazarus (Eds.), *Best practices in school crisis prevention and intervention*. Bethesda, MD: National Association of School Psychologists.

Goldstein, A. P., Glick, B., Reiner, S., Simmerman, D., & Coultry, T. M. (1985). *Agression replacement training: A comprehensive intervention for aggressive youth*. Champaign, IL: Research Press.

Grant, S. A. (1993, Winter). Students respond to "campus cops." *School Safety*, 15–17.

Green, B. L., Grace, M., & Lindy, J. D. (1983). Levels of functional impairment following a civilian disaster: The Beverly Hills Supper Club Fire. *Journal of Consulting Clinical Psychology, 51*, 573–586.

Green B. L., Korol, M., Grace, M. C., Vary, M. G., Leonard, A. C., Gleser, G. C., & Smitson-Cohen, S. (1991). Children and disaster: Age, gender, and parental effects on PTSD symptoms. *Journal of the American Academy of Child and Adolescent Psychiatry, 30*, 945–951.

Honig, R. G., Grace, M. C., Lindy, J. D., Newman, C. J., & Titchener, J. L. (1999). Assessing the long-term effects of disasters occurring during childhood and adolescence: Questions of perspective and methodology. In M. Sugar (Ed.), *Trauma and adolescence* (pp. 203–224). Madison, CT: International Universities Press.

Horowitz, M. J. (1976). Diagnosis and treatment of stress response syndromes: General principles. In H. J. Parad, H. L. P. Resnik, & L. G. Parad (Eds.), *Emergency and disaster managment: A mental health source book* (pp. 259–270). Bowie, MD: Charles Press.

Hyman, I., & Snook, P. (1999). *Dangerous schools: What we can do about the physical and emotional abuse of our children.* San Francisco: Jossey-Bass.

Kaufman, P., Chen, X., Choy, S. P., Ruddy, S. A., Miller, A. K., Fleury, J. K., Chandler, K. A., Rand, M. R., Klaus, P., & Planty, M. G. (2000). *Indicators of school crime and safety, 2000.* Washington, DC: U.S. Departments of Education and Justice [NCES 2001–017/NCJ-184176.]

Klingman, A. (1988). School community in disaster: Planning for intervention. *Journal of Community Psychology, 16,* 205–216.

La Greca, A. M., Silverman, W. K., Vernberg, E. M., & Prinstein, M. J. (1996). Symptoms of posttraumatic stress in children after Hurricane Andrew: A prospective study. *Journal of Consulting & Clinical Psychology, 64,* 712–723.

Larson, J. D. (1990). *Think first: Anger and aggression management for secondary level students* [Video Tape]. Milwaukee, WI: Milwaukee Board of school Directors.

Larson, J. D. (1992). *Think first: Anger and aggression management for secondary level students* [Treatment manual]. Whitewater, WI: Author.

Larson, J. D. (1994). Violence prevention in the schools: A review of selected programs and procedures. *School Psychology Review, 23,* 151–164.

Lazarus, P. J., Brock, S., & Feinberg, T. (1999, September). Dealing with the media in the aftermath of school shootings. *Communiqué: National Association of School Psychologists, 28*(1), 1, 7–6, 10.

Lystad, M. (1985). Special programs for children. In M. Lystad (Ed.), *Innovations in mental health services to disaster victims* (pp. 151–160). Rockville, MD: National Institute of Mental Health.

McDermott, B. M. C., & Palmer, L. J. (1999). Post-disaster service provision following proactive identification of children with emotional distress and depression. *Australian & New Zealand Journal of Psychiatry, 33,* 855–863.

Mark, B. S., Layton, A., & Chesworth, M. (1997). I"ll know what to do": A kid's guide to natural disaster: Washington DC: Magination Press/American Psychological Association.

Masten, A. S. (1994). Resilience in individual development: Successful adaptation despite risk and adversity. In M. C. Wang & E. W. Gordon (Eds.), *Educational resilience in inner city America: Challenges and prospects* (pp. 3–25). Hillsdale, NJ: Lawrence Erlbaum Associates.

Mazza, J. J., & Overstreet, S. (2000). Children and adolescents exposed to community violence: A mental health perspective for school psychologists. *School Psychology Review, 29,* 86–101.

Myers, D. (1994). *Disaster response and recovery: A handbook for mental health professionals.* Rockville, MD : U.S. Department of Health & Human Services, Public Health Service, Substance Abuse and Mental Health Services Administration, Center for Mental Health Services. DHHS publication (SMA) 94-3010.

Nader, K., Pynoos, R., Fairbanks, L., & Frederick, C. (1990). Children's Post-traumatic Stress Disorder reactions one year after a sniper attack at their school. *American Journal of Psychiatry, 147,* 1526–1530.

National School Safety Center. (1990). *School safety check book.* Westlake Village, CA: Author.

National School Safety Center. (1998). *Checklist of characteristics of youth who have caused school-associated violent deaths.* Malibu, CA: Author.

Neal, C. (1999, September). *Keynote speaker: First responding officer, Columbine High School.*

Nelson, R., Roberts, M., Smith, D., & Irwin, G. (2000, February). The trouble with profiling youth at-risk for violence. *Communiqué, 28, 10.*

Petersen, S., & Staub, R. L. (1992). *School crisis survival guide: Management techniques and materials for counselors and adminiwstrators.* West Nyack, NY: The Center for Applied Research in Eduation.

Poland, S. (1994). The role of school crisis intervention teams to prevent and reduce school violence and trauma. *School Psychology Review, 23,* 175–189.

Poland, S. (1997). School crisis teams. In A. P. Goldstein & J. C. Conoly (Eds.), *School violence intervention: A practical handbook* (pp. 127–159). New York: Guilford Press.

Pynoos, R. S., Frederick, C., Nader, K., Steinberg, A., Eth, S., Nune, F., & Fairbanks, L. (1987). Life threat and post traumatic stress in school-age children. *Archives of General Psychiatry, 44*, 1057–1063.

St. Thomas, B. (1993). Too afraid to talk. In L. B. Golden & M. L. Norwood (Eds.), *Case studies in child counseling* (pp. 173–185). New York: Merrill/Macmillan.

Shore, J. H., Tatum, E. L., & Vollmer, W. M. (1986). Psychiatric reactions to disaster: The Mount St. Helens experience. *American Journal of Psychiatry, 143*, 590–595.

Smith, B. W., & Freedy, J. R. (2000). Psychosocial resource loss as a mediator of the effects of flood exposure on psychological distress and physical symptoms. *Journal of Traumatic Stress, 13*, 349–357.

Stephens, R. D. (1994). Planning for safer and better schools: School violence prevention and intervention strategies. *School Psychology Review, 23*, 204–215.

Strepling, S. H. (1997). The low-aggression classroom: A teacher's view. In A. P. Goldstein & J. C. Conoly (Eds.), *School violence intervention: A practical handbook* (pp. 23–45). New York: Guilford Press.

Swenson, C. C., Saylor, C. F., Powell, M. P., Stokes, S. J., Foster, K. Y., & Belter, R. W. (1996). Impact of a natural disaster on preschool children: Adjustment 14 months after a hurricane. *American Journal of Orthopsychiatry, 66*, 122–130.

Terr, L. C. (1983). Chowchilla revisited: The effects of psychic trauma four years after a schoolbus kidnapping. *American Journal of Psychiatry, 140*(12), 1543–1555.

Thomas, C. L. (Ed.). (1993). *Taber's cyclopedic medical dictionary* (17th ed.). Philadelphia: F. A. Davis.

Trump, K. S. (1998). *Practical school security: Basic guidelines for safe and secure schools*. Thousand Oaks, CA: Corwin.

Wasserstein, S. B., & La Greca, A. M. (1998). Hurricane Andrew: Parent conflict as a moderator of children's adjustment. *Hispanic Journal of Behavioral Sciences, 20*, 212–224.

Werner, E. E., & Smith, R. S. (1982). *Vulnerable but invincible: A study of resilient children*. New York: McGraw-Hill.

Young, B. H., Ford, J. D., Ruzek, J. I., Friedman, M. L., & Gusman, F. D. (1999). Disaster mental health services: A guidebook for clinicians and administrators [Online]. Available: *http://www.wramc.amedd.army.mil/departments/socialwork/provider/DMHS.htm*

# PART III

# ADOLESCENT CRISES

CHAPTER

# 13

# Suicide

**John M. Davis**
California State University, Hayward

**Stephen E. Brock**
Lodi Unified School District, Lodi, CA

This chapter addresses four aspects of suicidal behaviors among youth under the age of 19: the incidence, the underlying theory, basic research, and school-based strategies for responding to the problem of youth suicide. The incidence section presents the magnitude of the problem of youth suicide. The theory section provides a definition, nomenclature, and typology for suicide and suicide-related behaviors. It also reviews the development of the concept of death by suicide in children. The research section explores some of the risk factors of youth suicide. Finally, the responses section addresses school-based strategies for preventing and responding to suicidal ideation and behaviors.

## INCIDENCE OF SUICIDE IN CHILDREN AND ADOLESCENTS

The discussion that follows presents current data for the incidence of suicidal ideation and behaviors among young people. This is done to illustrate the magnitude of the problem. Specific variables discussed are age, gender, and ethnicity. Also presented are data regarding methods of suicide and information regarding the interpretation of suicide statistics.

## Age

Although estimates vary, it is generally agreed that completed suicides among young people are relatively rare, whereas suicidal ideation and behaviors are not (Davis, 1988). In 1996 (the most recent year for which data is available), no children under the age of 5 and only four children between the ages of 5 to 9 committed suicide in the United States (Peters, Kochanek, & Murphy, 1998).

However, as youth enter adolescence the risk of suicide increases. After the age of 10 suicide becomes a leading cause of death. In the United States, during 1996, 298 (of 18,949,000) 10- to 14-year-olds and 1,817 (of 18,644,000) 15- to 19-year-olds committed suicide (Peters et al., 1998). Currently, suicide ranks as the fourth leading cause of death in the 10- to 14-year-old age group (exceeded by accidents, cancer, and homicide) and as the third leading cause of death among 15- to 24-year-olds (exceeded by accidents and homicide; National Center for Injury Prevention and Control, 1998). Table 13.1 displays the current rate of suicide in the 5 to 9, 10 to 14, and 15 to 19 age groups according to gender and race.

Although the rate of youth suicide suggests this act to be relatively rare (less than 10 out of every 100,000 15- to 19-year-olds committed suicide in 1996), much concern has been expressed over increases in this rate. Since

TABLE 13.1
1996 Suicide Rates (per 100, 000) by Gender, Age and Race

| *Gender* | *Age* | *All Races* | *White* | *Black* | *All Other Races* |
|---|---|---|---|---|---|
| Both Genders | | | | | |
| | 5-9 | 0.02 | 0.03 | 0.00 | 0.00 |
| | 10-14 | 1.57 | 1.62 | 1.24 | 1.80 |
| | 15-19 | 9.47 | 10.26 | 6.72 | 10.87 |
| Males | | | | | |
| | 5-9 | 0.03 | 0.04 | 0.00 | 0.00 |
| | 10-14 | 2.28 | 2.31 | 1.90 | 2.95 |
| | 15-19 | 15.55 | 16.27 | 11.46 | 16.70 |
| Females | | | | | |
| | 5-9 | 0.01 | 0.01 | 0.00 | 0.00 |
| | 10-14 | 0.82 | 0.89 | 0.56 | 0.61 |
| | 15-19 | 3.55 | 3.81 | 1.82 | 4.86 |

*Note.* From Peters et al. (1998).

1950 there has been a 350% increase in the 15- to 19-year-old rate (2.7 to 9.47 per 100,000). Similarly, since 1979 there has been a 190% increase in the 10- to 14-year-old rate (0.82 to 1.57 per 100,00; Peters et al., 1998; O'Carroll, Potter, & Mercy, 1994). These frightening changes have previously been used to argue for increased attention to the problem of youth suicide. At least among our teenage population, it is possible that the increased attention has paid off. Recent data suggest the possibility that teenage suicide has reached a plateau. These trends in the suicide rates for youth are summarized in Figs. 13.1 and 13.2.

Although completed suicide is rare, other forms of suicidal ideation and behaviors are much more common. It has been estimated that there are more than 100 youth suicides attempts for every youth suicide (Ramsay, Tanney, Tierney, & Lang, 1996). Data from the Youth Risk Behavior Survey

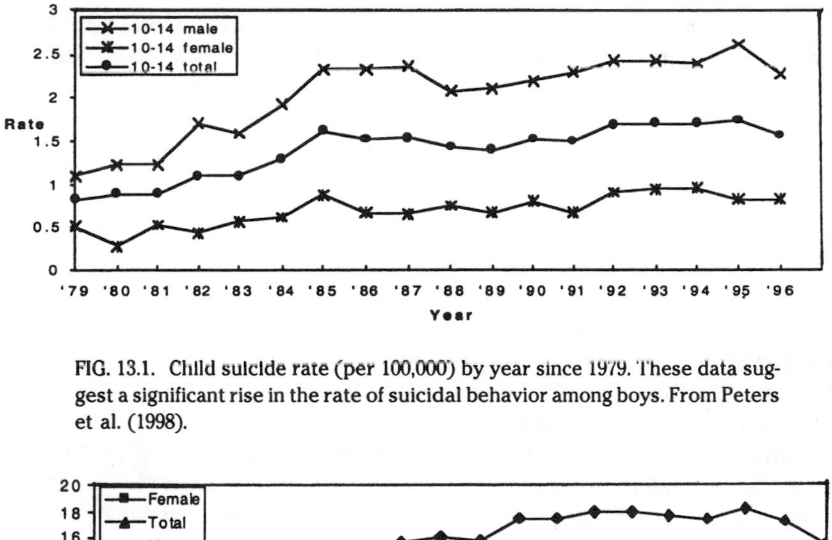


FIG. 13.1. Child suicide rate (per 100,000) by year since 1979. These data suggest a significant rise in the rate of suicidal behavior among boys. From Peters et al. (1998).

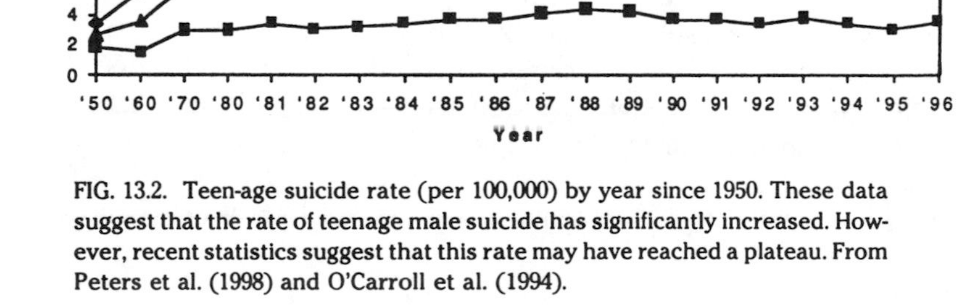

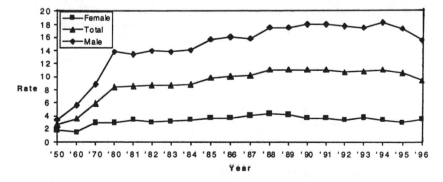

FIG. 13.2. Teen-age suicide rate (per 100,000) by year since 1950. These data suggest that the rate of teenage male suicide has significantly increased. However, recent statistics suggest that this rate may have reached a plateau. From Peters et al. (1998) and O'Carroll et al. (1994).

(Kann et al., 1998) found that 20.5% of high school students reported having seriously considered suicide, and 15.7% having made a suicide plan in the 12 months preceding the survey. Further, 4.5% reported having attempted suicide, with 2.6% indicating that the attempt required medical attention. Table 13.2 provides a further break down of these data by gender, race/ethnicity, and grade.

## Gender

As can be seen by analyzing Table 13.1 and Figs. 13.1 and 13.2, there are clear gender differences in suicidal behavior, suggesting that completed suicide is a largely male phenomenon. Among those in the 10- to 14-year-old group, there are 2.78 male suicides for every female completion. Similarly, in the 15- to 19-year-old group there are 4.3 male suicides for every female completion. However, as can be seen by analyzing Table 13.2, overall female high school students were significantly more likely to than male students to have considered, planned, and attempted suicide.[1]

## Ethnicity

The data regarding suicidal behavior among minority youth is very limited (Roberts, Chen, & Roberts, 1997). The data that is available suggest that in 1997 Hispanic students had the highest rates of suicidal ideation and behaviors (Kann et al., 1998; Table 13.2). Although Black youth tended to have the lowest rate of completed suicide (Peters et al., 1998; Table 13.1), between 1980 and 1992 suicide rates increased most dramatically among young Black males (Centers for Disease Control, 1995).

From a sample of more than 5,000 middle-school students in the Houston area Roberts et al. (1997) interpreted self-report questionnaire data as suggesting that minority status may increase the risk for suicidal behaviors. This finding is consistent with the data reported in Table 13.1 (Peters et al., 1998), which found the highest suicide rate to fall in the "all other races" category. Relative to Anglo American respondents several ethic groups reported elevated prevalences of suicidal thoughts (i.e., Mexican American, Pakistani American, and Mixed Ancestry groups), suicide plans (i.e., Mixed Ancestry group) and suicide attempts (i.e., Mexican American and Pakistani American groups). The ethnic groups that did not display elevated levels of suicidal ideation and behavior were African American, Central American, Indian American, Vietnamese American, and Chinese American.

[1]This gender difference did not hold true, however, for those suicide attempts that required medical attention.

TABLE 13.2

Percentage of High School Students Who Reported Having Seriously Considered Attempting Suicideand Who Reported Suicidal Behavior by Gender, Race/Ethnicity, and Grade

| | *Seriously Considered Attempting Suicide*[a] | | | *Made a Suicide Plan*[a] | | | *Attempted Suicide*[a, b] | | | *Suicide Attempt Required Medical Attention*[a] | | |
|---|---|---|---|---|---|---|---|---|---|---|---|---|
| *Category* | *Female* | *Male* | *Total* | *Female* | *Male* | *Total* | *Female* | *Male* | *Total* | *Female* | *Male* | *Total* |
| *Race/Ethnicity* | | | | | | | | | | | | |
| White[c] | 26.1 | 14.4 | *19.5* | 18.5 | 11.0 | *14.3* | 10.3 | 3.2 | *6.3* | 2.6 | 1.5 | *2.0* |
| Black[c] | 22.0 | 10.6 | *16.4* | 16.0 | 8.8 | *12.5* | 9.0 | 5.6 | *7.3* | 3.0 | 1.8 | *2.4* |
| Hispanic | 30.3 | 17.1 | *23.1* | 23.9 | 16.0 | *19.6* | 14.9 | 7.2 | *10.7* | 3.8 | 2.1 | *2.8* |
| *Grade* | | | | | | | | | | | | |
| 9 | 28.9 | 16.1 | *22.2* | 19.9 | 13.0 | *16.3* | 15.1 | 6.3 | *10.5* | 5.0 | 3.2 | *4.1* |
| 10 | 30.0 | 14.5 | *21.5* | 24.2 | 11.0 | *16.9* | 14.3 | 3.8 | *8.5* | 3.7 | 1.4 | *2.4* |
| 11 | 26.2 | 16.6 | *21.0* | 21.0 | 13.5 | *16.9* | 11.3 | 4.4 | *7.6* | 2.8 | 2.6 | *2.7* |
| 12 | 23.6 | 13.5 | *17.9* | 15.3 | 11.2 | *13.0* | 6.2 | 3.7 | *4.8* | 2.0 | 1.0 | *1.4* |
| *Total* | *27.1* | *15.1* | *20.5* | *20.0* | *12.2* | *15.7* | *11.6* | *4.5* | *7.7* | *3.3* | *2.0* | *2.6* |

*Data source.* Kann et al. (1998)

*Note.* United States, Youth Risk Behavior Survey, 1997

[a] During the 12 months preceding the survey.

[b] One or more times.

[c] Non-Hispanic.

### Methods

Not surprisingly, the methods employed in attempted suicide are usually less lethal than those of completed suicide. Although drug overdoses account for about 70% of all attempts (Moscicki, 1995), firearms account for about 63% of youth suicides (Peters et al., 1998). Within this age group during 1980 to 1992, the proportions of suicides by poisoning, cutting, and other methods declined and the proportions by firearms and hanging increased. Among teenagers, 81% of recent suicide rate increases can be attributed to firearms (Centers for Disease Control, 1995).

### Interpreting Suicide Statistics

But what about the accuracy of these statistics? Statistics can be inaccurate owing to over- or underreporting. It is safe to assume that suicides are not overreported because of the denial and social stigma associated with suicide, particularly with children (Toolan, 1975). It is unanimously agreed upon that underreporting is a problem (Potter, Powell, & Kachur, 1995). Ross (1985) stated that she felt suicides were underreported by about 4:1. Similarly, Jobes, Berman, and Josselsen (1986) estimated underreporting to range from 10% to 50%. Perhaps the most careful investigation of this phenomenon is Shaffer's (1974) research. In his study reviewing coroners' records for children, he found that under- or misreporting suicidal deaths as accidents probably occurred but the effect on the suicide statistics was relatively slight, the rate increasing from .98 to 1.44 in the 10- to 14-year-old group and from 8.87 to 10.7 in the 15- to 19-year-old group. Thus, a range of estimates exists.

In spite of a generally low rate of completions, given a high-school population of 2,000 students, a typical school could expect that in a given year more than 400 students would have had serious thoughts of suicide and as many as 50 would have made a serious suicide attempt. Most frighteningly, about once every 5 years a completed suicide might be expected.

## SUICIDE THEORY

What are "suicide" and "suicide-related" behaviors? Are all suicides the same or are there different "types"? What is the role of "development" in the youth's evolving understanding of suicide? These are the questions addressed within the discussion that follows. Having answers to these questions are critical for school-based mental health personnel. Knowing the definitions of suicide and suicide-related behaviors will facilitate communication and reduce confusion among school-based suicide prevention and intervention personnel. Knowledge of the different types of suicide provides a guide that can help to school professionals to conceptualize the level of mental illness, treatment types, and priority treatment issues. Finally, an understanding of the child's evolving understanding of suicide will help school professionals make their response to the suicidal crisis developmentally appropriate.

## Suicide Defined

Attempts to operationalize deaths as suicide are ongoing. Currently, the classification system used by coroners' offices to identify a death as suicide varies from one jurisdiction to another. The definition that is most appealing to the authors has been offered by Jobes, Berman, and Josselsen (1987). This definition has two components. First, it indicates that there must be evidence that the death was *self-inflicted.* Jobes et al. suggest that this may be determined by pathological, toxicological, investigatory, and psychological evidence. Statements from witnesses may also be used to determine if the death was self-inflicted. Second, this definition requires there be evidence of *intent* to die. In other words, at the time of the self-inflicted injury there was explicit or implicit evidence that the victim intended or wished to kill him or herself, and that the decedent understood the likely consequences of the behavior. Examples of implicit evidence, offered by Jobes et al. (1987) include preparations for death; expressions of farewell, hopelessness, and great pain; efforts to obtain or learn about means of death; rehearsals of the fatal behavior; precautions to avoid rescue; evidence that the victim recognized the lethality of the means of death; prior suicide attempts and threats; stressful events or significant losses; and serious depression or mental disorder (p. 322).

## A Nomenclature for Suicidal Behaviors

As has already been suggested, the topic of this chapter is broader than completed suicide. It also includes a variety of suicide-related behaviors. In this section, the authors review a nomenclature for suicidal behaviors recently proposed by O'Carroll, Berman, Maris, Moscicki, Tanney, and Silverman (1996). It attempts to define a set of basic terms for suicidology, and is designed "to facilitate communication and minimize confusion among those who work to understand and prevent suicide" (p. 239). In this nomenclature, a distinction is made between suicide-related thoughts and suicide-related behaviors. The former includes suicidal ideation. The latter includes instrumental suicide-related behaviors (e.g., suicide threats) and suicidal acts (i.e., suicide attempts and completed suicide). The O'Carroll et al. definitions for each of these behaviors are provided in Table 13.3.

TABLE 13.3
Nomenclature for Suicidology

I. *Suicidal Ideation:* Any self-reported thoughts of engaging in suicide related behavior.

II. *Suicide-Related Behavior:* Potentially self-injurious behavior for which there is explicit or implicit evidence *either* that (a) the person intended at some level to kill himself/herself, *or* (b) the person wished to use the *appearance* of intending to kill himself/herself in order to attain some other end. Suicide-related behavior comprises instrumental suicide-related behavior and suicidal acts.

A. *Instrumental Suicide-Related Behavior:* Potentially self-injurious behavior for which there is evidence (either implicit or explicit) that (a) the person did not intend to kill himself/herself (i.e., had zero intent to die), *and* (b) the person wished to use the *appearance* of intending to kill himself/herself in order to attain some other end (e.g., to seek help, to punish others, to receive attention).

1. *Suicide Threat:* Any interpersonal action, verbal or nonverbal, stopping short of a directly self-harmful act, that a reasonable person would interpret as communicating or suggesting that a suicidal act or other suicide-related behavior might occur in the near future.

B. *Suicidal Act:* A potentially self-injurious behavior for which there is evidence (either implicit or explicit that the person intended at some level to kill himself/herself. A suicidal act may result in death (completed suicide), injuries, or no injuries.

1. *Suicide Attempt:* A potentially self-injurious behavior with a nonfatal outcome, for which there is evidence (either explicit or implicit) that the person intended at some level to kill him/herself. A suicide attempt may or may not result in injured.

a. *Suicide Attempt with Injuries:* An action resulting in nonfatal injury, poisoning, or suffocation where there is evidence (either explicit or implicit) that the injury was self-inflicted *and* that the decedent intended at some level to kill himself/herself.

2. *Suicide:* Death from injury, poisoning, or suffocation where there is evidence (either explicit or implicit) that the injury was self-inflicted *and* that the decedent intended to kill himself/herself. (Note: The term *completed suicide* can be used interchangeably with the term *suicide*.

*Note.* Adapted from "Beyond the Tower of Babel: A Nomenclature for Suicidology" (pp. 246-247) by P. W. O'Carroll, A. L. Berman, R. W. Maris, E. K. Moscicki, B. L. Tanney, and M. M. Silvermar 1996, *Suicide and Life-Threatening Behavior, 26*(3), 237-252. Copyright 1996 by Guilford Press. Adapted with permission.

## Types of Suicide

Clearly not all suicides are the same. In fact, it has been argued that there are probably as many motivations for suicide as there are people who commit suicide (Ramsay et al., 1996). However, there have been attempts to classify the different types of suicide. For example, Beebe (1975), Everstine and Everstine (1983), Gould (1965), and Maris (1992) have all offered typologies of suicide. The following is the authors' consolidation of their works. The "types" are indicative of the underlying rationale or processes occurring within the youth at the time of the suicide attempt. The typology serves as an informational diagnostic guide that can help to conceptualize the level of psychopathology, the type of treatment, and the first issues that would need to be addressed in treatment. Seven types are discussed.

***Psychosis or Personality Disintegration.*** This type is best represented by the youth experiencing auditory hallucinations ordering him or her to kill him or herself or to die. It is important to acknowledge that the self-inflicted deaths of some youth who are functioning under an active delusional system may not be classified as suicide. For example, the child or adolescent under the delusion of being Superman might leap off a tall building, killing him- or herself. However, such behavior would not be classified as suicidal unless there was an intent to die and an awareness that the behavior would result in death.

***Self-Homicide.*** The primary causative factor in this type of suicide is intense rage at another. However, for some reason, the rage cannot be outwardly expressed, so is turned inwards. Self-murder, then, symbolically represents the murder of someone else.

***Retaliation for Real or Imagined Abandonment.*** In this type, the youth hopes that the suicide will accomplish two things when he or she is threatened by rejection or abandonment. First, the youth beats the adult to the punch (e.g., "you can't kick me out, I'm leaving"). Second, the youth uses suicide as a demonstration of power to compensate for feelings of helplessness and lack of control.

***Blackmail or Manipulation.*** Suicide is used as the ultimate threat in this type: "If you don't treat me better you'll be sorry." This and the previous type are most often seen in families where suicidal threats or gestures are used as power ploys.

***Rejoining a Powerful Lost Love Object.*** In this type, death is thought of as a way to become reunited with a dead significant other, most often a parent or grandparent, but any significant other whose loss is experienced as insurmountable. This type of suicide occurs when the youth is unable to move through the grieving process concerning the loss of a loved one.

***Atonement of Unpardonable Sins.*** This type finds death being viewed as the only way to be relieved of the guilt and "badness" a youth feels he or she has engendered. Although this type of suicide is believed to be very infrequent, injury prone youth may fit into a less extreme version of this dynamic.

***A Cry for Help.*** This type is probably the most familiar and most successfully treated. Although overwhelmed, regardless of the kind of underlying problem, youth in this type are at least aware they have a problem and that they would like to have some other means of coping with it. They either know no other way to cope or to call for help; or other channels have been blocked to them by their guardians, so they turn to suicidal behavior.

## A COGNITIVE-DEVELOPMENTAL PERSPECTIVE

Unfortunately, there appear to be few studies on the evolution of children's ideas about suicide. A literature review, making use of the PsycINFO database, found only three such studies. The first, by Normand and Mishara (1992), suggested that understanding of the concept of suicide is clearly related to a child's age (as well as their concept of, and experiences with, death). Among a sample of 60 children, they found that 10% of first graders, 50% of third graders and 95% of fifth graders had a basic understanding of suicide. The second study, by Clark (1992), analyzed the retrospective reports of 16 undergraduates. These reports revealed that among this sample the average earliest reported suicide memory was 10.5 years. The average earliest reported suicidal thought was 13.8 years. However, the most recent study, by Mishara (1999), suggested that all school-aged children generally know about suicide. Although first and second graders may not recognize the word "suicide," this research suggested that most understood the concept of "killing oneself." By Grade 3, it was found that "children generally understand suicide quite well" (p. 114). However, primary grade children generally did not understand the dynamics that lead to suicide. By Grade 5 almost all understood that it is a psychosocial dynamic that leads to suicidal behavior. From these data, Mishara (1999) concluded that children know enough about suicide for their self-injurious behavior to be viewed as truly suicidal. He stated: "This study indicates that children generally know enough to knowledgeably commit suicide with a realization that this will result in permanent death" (p. 117).

Although studies of the progression of children's understanding of suicide are rare, there is a more substantial body of literature on the development of ideas about death that may be useful in further understanding the nature of the concept of suicide. Although helpful, the warning of Orbach and Glaubman (1979) should be remembered when considering these studies:

> Many children show a split in the death concept; they may have a mature concept of impersonal death, but a rather childish concept of their own personal death. Only the exploration of the emotional and personal aspects of the death concept is of value diagnostically and therapeutically. (p. 677)

Nagy (1959) and Anthony (1971) were the first to address the issue of the child's conceptions of death. Although not specifically Piagetian, their findings fit Piaget's theoretical framework. Koocher (1973, 1974) and Wass (1982) used the Piagetian framework to conceptualize their data. All agree that children proceed through at least three distinct phases that are roughly equivalent to Piaget's preoperational, concrete, and formal operational stages.

Safier (1964) claimed that the youngest children (those he considered preoperational) saw life and death in terms of flux or interchange. At this age, death is "sleeping" or "resting," and is temporary and reversible; therefore, the child cannot conceptualize death as nonexistence so could not be motivated to take his or her own life to achieve it. This perspective offers insight into why suicide is so rare among children under age 10.

During concrete operations, which is based on logical and naturalistic thinking, death is now understood as an irreversible event. However, children in this phase see death as something that is unlikely to happen to them until they are very old. That is, they see death as concrete and externalized, something that will eventually happen to them. It could be that these children are so strongly involved in rule learning and following that the rules seem immutable. The strength of the prohibitions on taking one's life then, would have more force in middle childhood than at other stages. However, no data on this possibility have yet been published.

During the formal operational period of development (approximately 12-year-olds and older), death is seen as not only irreversible, but also as personal. It is viewed as part of an internal principle which encompasses the self and others. As such, suicide would now be understood as a means to an end. This perspective offers insight into why suicide becomes a leading cause of death after the age of 10, and increases dramatically after age 15. Elkind's (1978) idea of "adolescent egocentrism" and the "imaginary audience" might also help to explain the rise in suicide in adolescence. He stated:

> The imaginary audience has other negative consequences as well. Suicide, which is rare in childhood, becomes more frequent in adolescence. Although such self-destructive behavior has many determinants, one of these is the imaginary audience. A common fantasy among suicidal persons is the imagined reactions of an audience. Many suicidal persons see their action as a way of punishing those they feel have rejected them. Such persons take pleasure

> in imagining the grief and remorse of those they leave behind. These imagined reactions are a powerful motive for carrying out the suicidal idea. (p. 124)

Thus, as in all other areas, the more developed cognition becomes, the more options are available. This includes negative options such as suicide.

## SUICIDE RESEARCH

Research investigating the dynamics of suicide and suicidal behavior have suggested that there are several significant risk factors for these behaviors. They include psychopathological, familial, biological, and situational factors (Brock & Sandoval, 1996; Moscicki, 1995). Each of these risk factors are now discussed.

### Psychopathological Risk Factors

Psychiatric disorders are arguably the most important risk factor for suicide. Research estimates indicate that 90% of all suicides are associated with addictive or mental disorders (Garland & Zigler, 1993). Among adolescents the most frequent disorders are affective and conduct disorders, and substance abuse. Alcohol intoxication has been found in approximately half of all youth suicides. Also, it appears that psychiatric disorders are a characteristic of most, but not all, suicide attempters (Moscicki, 1995).

### Familial Risk Factors

Family characteristics that increase youth suicide risk include a family history of suicide, and medical and psychiatric illness. Economic stress, significant family strife, and family loss are also associated with increased risk. Suicidal children experience more parental separations, divorces, and remarriages. Suicide attempters often view their parents as indifferent, rejecting, and unsupportive (Davis & Sandoval, 1991; Moscicki, 1995; Pfeffer, 1989).

### Biological Risk Factors

Research has found that persons who commit suicide, and violent suicide attempters (e.g., those who use more destructive means), often have a deficit in the functioning of the neurotransmitter serotonin (Davis & Sandoval, 1991). Reduced central serotongenic activity is correlated more highly with suicidal behavior than with any particular psychiatric diagnosis (Brown & Goodwin, 1986). However, a causal connection between serotonin and suicidal behavior has yet to be established. It is possible that the changes in this neurotransmitter are associated with characteristics such as impulsivity or violence, and not a cause of suicidal behavior per se (Moscicki, 1995).

### Situational Risk Factors

Although situational factors are popularly viewed as causing suicide, they are, by themselves, insufficient. It is only when combined with other risk factors, such as those just mentioned, that they create the conditions that lead to suicide (Moscicki, 1995). As many as 40% of youth suicidal behaviors appear to have identifiable antecedents (e.g., rejection, unwanted pregnancy, poor school performance, fights with friends, dispute or breakup with a romantic partner, or problems with parents). Among youth, the most frequent stresses leading to suicidal behavior are interpersonal loss or conflict (particularly in romance), economic problems, and legal problems. The most common event of this type is a disciplinary crisis (Pfeffer, 1989; Shaffer, 1974; Spirito, Overholser, & Stark, 1989). Perhaps the strongest situational risk factors in the United States is the presence of a firearm in the home. Even after other risk factors are taken into account, the presence of a gun increases the risk of suicide. This is true regardless of the type of weapon, or whether the weapon and ammunition are stored separately (Brent et al., 1991).

Knowledge of the risk factors for suicide, offered by suicide research, is of great importance to school-based mental health professionals. The fact that some of these factors are internal and may be difficult to observe (biological and psychopathological) highlights the importance of having school-based personnel involved in suicide prevention and intervention. Next to parents, school personnel are most likely to have the intimate knowledge of students needed to identify these risk factors. Also, the fact that some of these factors are external (familial and situational) highlights the importance of ensuring that school-based personnel are observant. Again, next to parents, school personnel are the best positioned to identify these risk factors. Making use of this knowledge, however, will require some preparation on the part of the school. Thus, in the section that follows the authors review strategies to prevent and respond to suicidal behavior.

## SCHOOL-BASED RESPONSES

This section examines a range of responses that schools can take to address the problem of suicide. Caplan's (1964) schema for "preventive psychiatry" is used to organize the material. Caplan defined preventive psychiatry as:

> ... the body of professional knowledge, both theoretical and practical, which may be utilized to plan and carry out programs for reducing (1) the incidence of mental disorders of all types in a community ("primary prevention"), (2) the duration of a significant number of those disorders which do occur ("secondary prevention"), and (3) the impairment which may result from those disorders ("tertiary prevention"). (pp. 16–17)

Within this context, we consider primary prevention efforts to be *aimed at the total school population prior to any suicidal threats or behaviors* with the goal of reducing the incidence of suicidal behaviors. We consider secondary prevention efforts to be those interventions *aimed at the suicidal individual and the subpopulation of the total school population who have had contact with the youth who has attempted or completed suicide*. The goal of these efforts is to reduce the immediate damage caused by suicidal thoughts and behaviors. This includes suicide intervention (with the suicidal individual) and postvention (with those who have had contact with the individual who attempted or committed suicide). Finally, we consider tertiary prevention efforts to be *aimed at the individual who attempted suicide and/or the family and close friends of the person who has committed suicide*. The goal of these efforts is to reduce the long-term impairment caused by suicidal behavior.

## PRIMARY PREVENTION: SUICIDE PREVENTION

Looking toward the future, Berman and Jobes (1995) proposed a "second generation" for youth suicide prevention programs. Their proposal seeks to expand and refine earlier efforts (i.e., Centers for Disease Control, 1992). They suggest that primary prevention programs that appear to have the greatest potential are those that "... focus on reducing the likelihood of antecedent conditions (e.g., mental disorders, comorbidity) and, alternatively, to strengthen protective factors (e.g., attachments, family cohesion, help seeking, etc.)" (p. 148). Berman and Jobes offer three specific focuses for primary prevention program components: (a) individual predispositions, (b) social milieu, and (c) proximal causes. In addition to these program focuses, the authors also include in this discussion suicide awareness and crisis preparedness programs.

### Individual Predispositions

The first component of the Berman and Jobes (1995) model focused on skill-based training for youth to decrease individual predispositions to suicide. Specific program types are the following: (a) depression management skills, (b) anger and aggression management, (c) loneliness prevention, (d) interpersonal problem-solving skills, (e) competency enhancement skills, (f) critical viewing skills, and (g) help-seeking behavior skills.

### Social Milieu

The second component of the Berman and Jobes (1995) primary prevention program focuses on the social milieu by providing community based health education, promotion, and protection. Specific program types proposed are the following: (a) school dropout prevention and school enhancement programs, (b) early detection and referral of parental pathology, (c) surrogate role model programs, and (d) media guidelines for reporting suicide stories.

### Proximal Causes

The third component of the Berman and Jobes (1995) primary prevention program focused on the proximal causes of suicide by providing education and training about potentially lethal suicide methods. Specific program types include the following: (a) gun safety training for parents, (b) pediatrician gun education, (c) suicide awareness among health care providers, and (d) long-term federal firearms prevention education. For additional information about each of the just mentioned program types, the reader is encouraged to refer to Berman and Jobes.

### Awareness Programs

General suicide education programs are another commonly used primary prevention strategy. These programs, often referred to as "awareness programs" attempt to give an entire student body information about suicide risk factors and how to seek help for themselves and others (Sandoval & Brock, 1996). A number of different curricula have been developed. An example of a curriculum-base preventive program strategy is California's *Youth Suicide School Prevention Program* (California State Department of Education, School Climate Unit, 1986). This approach includes activities designed (a) to increase student awareness of the relationship between drug and alcohol use and youth suicide, (b) to teach students to recognize signs of suicidal tendencies in self and others and other facts about youth suicide, and (c) to inform students of available community youth suicide prevention services.

It is important to note that concerns have been raised regarding these school-based awareness programs (Brock & Sandoval, 1996). Specifically, it has been noted that among most education programs there is a tendency to normalize suicidal behavior. In an apparent attempt to make it more palatable to seek help for suicidal thoughts, these programs present suicide as a response to stress that could happen to anyone. It has been argued that this approach may result in suicide being viewed as a "mainstream" solution to problems (Garland, Shaffer, & Whittle, 1989; Garland & Zigler, 1993; Shaffer & Bacon, 1989). Also, the effect of such programs on students who have attempted suicide is of concern. It has been reported that these individuals may react more negatively to this type of curriculum than those who have not made a suicide attempt (Garland et al., 1989; Shaffer et al., 1990).

### Crisis Preparedness

The final primary prevention strategy discussed includes procedures designed to ensure that school personnel are prepared to deal with crisis events that might lead to suicidal ideation and behaviors. By making sure that a school is ready to provide crisis intervention services to students following crises, such as a completed suicide, the chances that adaptive coping will occur are increased. An example of crisis preparedness procedures can be found in the book *Preparing for Crises in the Schools* (Brock, Sandoval, & Lewis, 2001).

The specific school-based response to the crisis generated by the suicidal behavior of a significant other is referred to as suicide postvention. Following such a sudden and unexpected death it is not unusual for some to enter into the crisis state. Postvention identifies and assists these individuals to cope more adaptively with the problems generated by the suicide. Simultaneously, postvention also addresses the issue of contagion (i.e., that others will be "given permission" or encouragement to copy such behavior). As such, postvention is also considered a form of suicide prevention. Although such copy-cat behaviors are unusual, the potential for suicide contagion appears to be a unique issue for adolescents (Davidson, 1989). An effective postvention will require preparation and preparedness (Brock, Sandoval, & Lewis, 2001). Specific postvention activities proposed by Brock and Sandoval (1996) are provided in Table 13.4.

## SECONDARY PREVENTION: SUICIDE IDENTIFICATION, INTERVENTION, AND REFERRAL

Secondary prevention activities take place after suicidal behaviors or ideation have occurred. They are designed to minimize the duration and harm that can result from these behaviors and thoughts. Specific activities to be discussed include identification of the suicidal youth, intervention with those judged to be at risk for suicidal behavior, and a review of referral options. It should be noted that while the actual implementation of

TABLE 13.4
Recommended Suicide Postvention Activities

| | |
|---|---|
| 1. | Verify that the death was, in fact, a suicide. Do not label even what appear to be obvious suicides as such until suicide has been officially identified as the cause of death. |
| 2. | Assess the impact of the suicide on the school and determine the level of the postvention response. |
| 3. | Notify the school district office and other sites that could be affected. |
| 4. | Contact the family of the deceased to express sympathy and, if appropriate, provide information about community supports. |
| 5. | Determine what information should be shared about the death. Ensure that rights to confidentiality are respected and avoid describing details about the method of suicide. |
| 6. | Determine how the information is to be shared. Avoid strategies that might glorify or sensationalize the death (e.g., all-school assemblies). |
| 7. | Identify high risk students and plan interventions. High risk students would include students who facilitated the suicide, failed to recognize the suicidal intent of behaviors, believed they caused the suicide, had a close relationship and/or identify with the decedent, have a history of suicidal behavior and/or mental illness. Interventions may include individual, small group and classroom crisis intervention sessions. |
| 8. | Keep the school staff informed of all postvention activities. |
| 9. | Hold a debriefing for all caregivers involved in the postvention. |
| 10. | Carefully weight the benefits and liabilities of memorials. Make sure that, if memorials are employed, they do not glorify the suicide victim. |

*Note.* Adapted from "Suicidal Ideation and Behaviors," by S. E. Brock & J. Sandoval, 1996. In G. G. Bear, K. M. Minke, & A. Thomas (Eds.),*Children's Needs II: Development, Problems and Alternatives*, Bethesda, MD: National Association of School Psychologists, pp. 368-372.

these activities is clearly secondary prevention, preparing a school to provide these services could be classified as primary prevention.

## Identifying Suicidal Youth

***Indicators of Suicidal Behavior.*** The first step in the identification of suicidal youth is knowing the indicators of potential suicidal behavior. The American Association of Suicidology (1999) lists six "danger signs" as follows: (a) a suicide threat, (b) statements indicating a desire or intention to die, (c) a previous suicide attempt, (d) marked changes in behaviors or personality, (e) depression, and (f) making final arrangements. Table 13.5 provides a further discussion of these behaviors and examines if or how they would become manifest at different developmental stages.

***Direct Approaches to Identification.*** With the indicators of suicidal behavior in mind, options for identifying the suicidal youth include both direct and indirect approaches (Centers for Disease Control, 1992). The former would include screening programs that make use of questionnaires. Sandoval and Brock (1996) indicated that such psychometric screening for

TABLE 13.5
Indicators of Potential Suicidal Behavior

| |
|---|
| *A suicide threat and/or statements revealing a desire to die.* People who are thinking about suicide often tell others. It has been estimated that up to 80% all suicide victims had given clues about their intentions (Maris, 1992b). These clues may be direct or, unfortunately, indirect. In adolescence, indirect clues could be offered through joking or through references in school assignments, particularly creative writing or art pieces. In concrete and preoperational children, indirect clues may come in the form of acting-out, violent behavior often accompanied by suicidal and/or homicidal threats. In discussing latency-aged children, Pfeffer, Conte, Plutchik, and Jerrett (1980) found that the "specific high-risk factors of childhood suicidal behavior are the wish to die (often verbalized), intense preoccupations with death, and suicidal behavior in the parents" (p. 708). To identify the possible presence of a threat or desire to die, Maris offers that asking "people whether they are thinking about killing themselves" is often "the best predictor of suicide" (p. 11). |
| *A previous attempt.* It is important not to dismiss previous attempts, even if they seemed superficial or attention-getting. This check is a critical part of a suicide evaluation, for whereas only .001% of the general population commits suicide, 15% of individuals with a history of one or more suicide attempts will go on to kill themselves (Maris, 1992b). Suicide attempts and/or ideation in the parents need to be explored, as well as whether family abuse (Cohen-Sandler, Berman, & King, 1982) or "death wishes" (Rosenbaum & Richman, 1970) on the part of parents exist.<br>Specific methods to achieve suicide do not seem to be tied to age. Pills, guns, hanging and leaping to one's death span all ages. However, there are some obvious differences (e.g., suicide by automobile is more common among adolescents). Something somewhat comparable in middle and early childhood is jumping out of moving vehicles and dashing into traffic. While these kinds of attempts are often not viewed as suicidal behavior, they are often intended as such. |
| *Depression and marked changes in behavior.* It has been estimated that 15% of persons with depression eventually commit suicide (Maris, 1992b). However, hopelessness has been found to be an even better predictor of suicidal ideation and behavior than depression (Beck, 1986). Common thoughts are that things are awful, will never get better, and no one can help; there is little interest or pleasure in formerly enjoyable endeavors. A move toward social isolation is also a key indicator. Maris (1981) reported that 50% of completed suicides had no close friends, whereas 20% of nonfatal suicide attempts were similarly isolated.<br>Other symptoms that often emerge are changes in eating and sleeping habits, sudden and quite noticeable changes in behavior and/or personality, acting-out behavior, hyperactivity (an agitated depression), school problems, substance abuse, psychosomatic ailments, high risk-taking behavior, and constant accidents or other forms of self-destructive behavior. |
| *Final arrangements.* This behavior may take many forms. In adolescents, it might be giving away prized possessions (e.g., jewelry, skis, books, etc.). Although no mention of this behavior appears in the research literature, it seems likely that preoperational children lack the cognitive skills necessary to plan for making final arrangements. Concrete operational children are more capable of planning, but whether they do so as often as their formal operational counterparts is open to research and speculation. |

suicidal behavior is a two-stage process. The first stage involves the administration of a questionnaire designed to identify suicidal ideation. An example of such a questionnaire is the *Suicidal Ideation Questionnaire* (Reynolds, 1988). The second stage involves a thorough clinical evaluation of students identified by the screening as being suicidal.

***Indirect Approaches to Identification.*** Indirect approaches for identifying suicidal youth include gatekeeper training and general suicide education. Gatekeeper trainings are designed to give those who are in youth caregiver roles the knowledge and skill needed to identify, intervene, and refer the suicidal youth. Increasingly, peers caregivers (e.g., conflict managers, peer helpers, etc.) are included in these trainings (Brock & Sandoval, 1996). An example of such a training program is the *Suicide Intervention Workshop* (Ramsay et al., 1996).

## Suicide Evaluation

Once the potential for suicidal ideation and behaviors has been identified, the next step is to evaluate the risk for engaging in suicidal behaviors. The following nine areas need to be addressed so that decisions regarding the child or adolescent can be made. Examples of the kinds of questions found useful for interviewing children and parents are provided in Table 13.6. It is assumed that a positive rapport has been established before questioning. If rapport has not been established, it is then safest to hospitalize, given the hospital staff will have more time to develop a rapport and to insure closer monitoring until needed information is obtained.

***Suicide Potential.*** Pfeffer, Conte, Plutchik, and Jerrett (1979) proposed a 5-point spectrum of suicidal potential ranging from "nonsuicidal" to "serious attempt." The 5-point spectrum of suicidal potential is as follows: (a) nonsuicidal; (b) suicidal ideation (including controlled thoughts and uncontrolled thoughts such as hallucinations or delusions); (c) suicidal threat (e.g., "I'm going to jump off the roof, out of the car, hang myself," etc.): (d) mild attempt (a self-destructive act that the youth *believes* would not have killed him or her); (e) serious attempt (any attempt which obviously would have killed the youth, and which the youth *genuinely believed* would have been fatal).

***Suicide Plan.*** As Beebe (1975) cautioned, suicidal thoughts must be distinguished from actual planning. In evaluating the suicidal potential of a person, the lethal potential of his or her plan, the availability of the means, and the level of sophistication of the plan (including the developmental level of the interviewee) must be taken into account. When assessing the suicidal plan, Ramsay et al. (1996) recommended asking "how," "how prepared," and "how soon." Generally speaking, the greater the planning, the greater the suicide risk.

There are developmental differences here in that planning is relatively nonexistent in a preoperational child but increases with developmental level. However, there is no guarantee that formal operational adolescents

TABLE 13.6
Examples of Evaluation Questions for Children and Parents

| Child Questions | Parent Questions |
| --- | --- |
| • It seems things haven't been going so well for you lately. Your parents and/or teachers have said _____. Most children your age would feel upset about that.<br>• Have you felt upset, maybe some sad or angry feelings you've had trouble talking about? Maybe I could help you talk about these feelings and thoughts<br>• Do you feel like things can get better or are you worried (afraid, concerned) things will just stay the same or get worse?<br>• Other children I've talked to have said that when they feel that sad and/or angry they thought for a while that things would be better if they were dead. Have you ever thought that? What were your thoughts?<br>• What do you think it would feel like to be dead?<br>• How do you think your father and mother would feel? What do you think would happen with them if you were dead?<br>• Has anyone that you know of attempted to kill themselves? Do you know why?<br>• Have you thought about how you might make yourself die? Do you have a plan?<br>• Do you have (the means) at home (available)?<br>• Have you ever tried to kill yourself before?<br>• What has made you feel so awful? | • Has any serious change occurred in your child's or your family's life recently (within the past year)?<br>• How did your child respond?<br>• Has your child had any accidents or illnesses without a recognizable physical basis?<br>• Has your child experienced a loss recently?<br>• Has your child experienced difficulty in any areas of his/her life?<br>• Has your child been very self-critical or have you or his/her teachers been very critical lately?<br>• Has your child make any unusual statements to you or others about death or dying? Any unusual questions or jokes about death or dying?<br>• Have there been any changes you've noticed in your child's mood or behavior over the last few months?<br>• Has your child ever threatened or attempted suicide before?<br>• Have any of his friends or family, including yourselves, ever threatened or attempted suicide?<br>• How have these last few months been for you? How have you reacted to your child (anger, despair, empathy, etc.)? |

*Note.* Words and phrasings should be changed to better fit the child and/or interviewer. Two things need to be accomplished during this questioning: (1) to gather more information about the child, and (2) to try to evaluate the parents in terms of their understanding, cooperation, quality of connection with their child, energy to be available to a child in crisis.

are going to formulate a plan rather than act impulsively; and, if they do, there is no guarantee that they will directly communicate it.

***Past Suicide Attempts.*** This includes both the child's past attempts and any significant others' past attempts (Ramsay et al., 1996). The latter is often overlooked but is of important, because of the profound influence of the child's family and the possibility of covert messages.

***Affects and Behaviors.*** Pfeffer et al. (1979) found a variety of feelings and behaviors to be associated with suicidal children. They included the following: anxiety, anger, sadness, hopeless resignation, temper tantrums, psychomotor retardation or increased activity level, defiance, trouble sleeping, social withdrawal, weight loss, alcoholism, drug addiction, running away, firesetting, or other evidence of transformed rage or masked depression.

***Family Background.*** Is there any drug, alcohol, or child abuse? Are there recent separations or deaths? What is the level of parental depression or other psychopathology? What types of discipline or punishment are used, and do the parents have any plan or course of action to deal with the crisis? As was mentioned earlier, familial characteristics that increase suicide risk include a family history of suicide, medical and psychiatric illness, economic stress, significant family strife, and family loss. Suicidal children experience more parental separations, divorces, and remarriages. Suicide attempters often view their parents as indifferent, rejecting, and unsupportive (Davis & Sandoval, 1991; Moscicki, 1995; Pfeffer, 1989).

***Precipitating Events.*** Perhaps the most common antecedent is some loss or threat of loss. Other possibilities are health or medication problems, social disgrace, school problems, or loss of the reason to live. Seldom is suicide attempted due to only one event; rather, the precipitating event is more akin to the straw that broke the camel's back (Moscicki, 1995).

***Response From the Support Network.*** Under this heading comes Beebe's (1975) notion of a lifeline: "A lifeline is one or more interested persons who want the patient to stay alive. An immobilized other, no matter how significant, is not a lifeline. In fact, if he is immobilized enough, he may unconsciously drive the patient to suicide" (p. 38). It may be that a temporary hospitalization or out-of-home care or placement is necessary until an "immobilized other" (an exhausted single parent would be a good candidate) can regain adequate functioning.

***Concept of Death.*** The evaluation of the child's understanding of death is important. Knowledge of such understanding will suggest how to reason with the child during counseling as well as to predict how potentially lethal the situation is.

***Ego Functions.*** Ego functions (e.g., reality testing, intelligence, impulse control, and regulation of affect) and defenses need to be assessed. The more disturbed the ego functions and the more primitive the defenses, the

TABLE 13.7
Recommended School Suicide Intervention Procedures

1. A student who has threatened suicide must be constantly observed.
2. Under no circumstances should a suicidal student be allowed to leave school.
3. Helpers to a suicidal student must not agree to keep suicidal intentions a secret.
4. If the means of the threatened suicide are present determine if they can be voluntarily relinquished.
5. Take the suicidal student to a prearranged room.
6. Notify the "designated reporter" immediately. Schools should identify one or more individuals who receive and act upon all reports from teachers and others about students who may be suicidal (Davis & Sandoval, 1991).
7. Inform the suicidal youth that outside help has been called and describe what the next steps will be.

*Note.* Adapted from "Suicidal Ideation and Behaviors," by S. E. Brock & J. Sandoval, 1996. In G. G. Bear, K. M. Minke, & A. Thomas (Eds.), *Children's Needs II: Development, Problems and Alternatives*, Bethesda, MD: National Association of School Psychologists, p. 369.

less hopeful the prognosis and the more cautious and conservative the interventions.

## Suicide Intervention and Referral

The two primary questions that need to be answered by the suicide evaluation are: (a) In your professional opinion, is the child or adolescent at risk for attempting suicide?; and (b) What interventions are necessary given the answer to the first question? Specific school-based suicide intervention procedures developed by Brock and Sandoval (1996) are offered in Table 13.7. The following reviews some basic suicide intervention options.

***Hospitalization.*** If the child or adolescent is assessed to be in imminent danger and needs constant monitoring, hospitalization is required. If the danger is not imminent, a halfway house, crisis intervention, or outpatient psychotherapy are alternatives. The choice depends on a combination of three factors: (a) suicidal risk, (b) family strengths and dynamics, and (c) community resources.

If danger is imminent and legal guardians agree and are cooperative, hospitalization can move smoothly as long as the evaluator is aware of the local resources. If the legal guardians disagree or are uncooperative, the evaluator may need to initiate the state "involuntary hold"[2] code. Such a procedure usually entails calling the police or sheriff's department and hav-

[2]In California this is referred to by State Law 5150, which enables authorized personnel, usually the police or an emergency or crisis center, to hospitalize patients without consent for 72 hours for further evaluation if they are suicidal, homicidal, or gravely disturbed. In California, if at the end of 72 hours more evaluation is needed, a 5151 or 14-day hold can be invoked.

ing the child or adolescent taken to the emergency/crisis clinic or a psychiatric clinic or hospital.

When dealing with minors, especially adolescent minors, there is sometimes a gray area when the legal guardians agree to the hospitalization but the child or adolescent does not. If the guardians cannot control the child or adolescent and facilitate the hospitalization, the law enforcement authorities should be summoned. Should this occur, it is very important that the guardians be informed about what will happen (e.g., their child may be handcuffed and taken away in a police vehicle).

After hospitalization, when it is deemed safe for the child or adolescent to leave the protection of the hospital, the decision as to whether the child returns to home and school, to a half way house, or to a foster home needs to be made. This decision is most often made by the hospital staff after an extended evaluation.

***Outpatient Treatment.*** If the youth is assessed as being suicidal, but the danger is not imminent, then immediate outpatient treatment may be appropriate. As has already been mentioned, such options might include a halfway house, crisis intervention, or outpatient psychotherapy.

***Contracting.*** In cases where the suicide risk is judged to be low enough not to require an immediate treatment (e.g., there is only ideation and no suicide plan), then a "no-suicide" contract may be an appropriate option. Such a contract is a personal agreement to postpone suicidal behaviors until help can be obtained. Poland (1989) suggested that "each contract be tailor made for the student. The most official-looking school stationery should be used. The contract should be signed by the student and the counselor, and the student should be given a copy" (p. 82).

## TERTIARY PREVENTION: LONG-TERM AFTER-CARE

This area is not generally in the domain of the school personnel. One form of intervention can be therapy for the family and close friends who survive a completed suicide so they do not decompensate or become symptomatic. Another form is working with the family and the victim of a suicide attempt who has survived but has incurred some permanent disability (e.g., paralysis) from the attempt. In the latter situation, the school mental health professionals can help in the evaluation and planning of a continuing educational plan for the now handicapped student. The school psychologist or counselor may also be called upon to collaborate or consult with staff and family around issues that arise during the planning.

The treatment of the individual who has displayed suicidal behavior is also a tertiary prevention issue. Regarding such treatment, most experts (e.g., Pfeffer, 1984; Toolan, 1975) agree that long-term (usually more than a year) psychotherapy is necessary and few school mental health professionals have the time or training to do this. But, the issues that first need to be addressed in therapy are frequency of sessions, medication, and modality of treatment. The actual treatment, as summarized by Pfeffer (1984), "should focus on helping the child (1) alter his expectation of abandonment and punishment, (2) decrease emphasis on a ideal self, (3) develop healthier identifications, and (4) modify aggressive responses to frustrations and disappointments and reduce depression and hopelessness with increasing self-esteem" (p. 367). Modifications within the family structure and communication system need to be addressed, as might parental psychopathology.

Perhaps the most important tertiary prevention role for the schools involves monitoring the status of the student who has returned to school following a suicide attempt. The importance of this monitoring can be found in the observation that less severe forms of behaviors can evolve into more severe forms (Diekstra & Garnefski, 1995). How these transformations take place is unclear. However, it is clear that persons who have attempted suicide have a 35 times greater risk of committing suicide than do people without such a history (Tanney & Motto, 1990). Thus, following the return to school of a student who had attempted suicide, it would be critical for schools to be especially alert to the warning signs of suicide and to ensure that appropriate mental health services have been provided.

## CONCLUSION

As clinicians, even though we have learned much since the 1990s of studying child and adolescent suicide, we continue to be confronted by both how much more we need to learn and how little of the important data we actually have available to us in the moment of a suicidal crisis. This is not meant as a discouragement, but rather as an appreciation of the complexity of how much we need to know about the concept of suicide juxtaposed with the dynamic moments in the evaluative process with a client.

For these reasons, perhaps the most important concepts to take from this chapter are:

1. that there is an important body of knowledge about which we need to know regarding child and adolescent suicide,
2. that school systems need to incorporate this knowledge into a *plan of action* or preparedness plan which includes specific persons from

within the school community and from the broader community (e.g., other districts, community mental health, clergy, etc.),

3. that *time* needs to be made to develop a level of expertise and of collaboration necessary to implement a preparedness plan, and
4. that there needs to be postvention for the postventioners. The postvention aspect of the plan needs to address the fears, anxieties, and emotional reactions of the care givers as well as the care receivers.

## REFERENCES


Anthony, S. (1971). *The discovery of death in childhood and after.* New York: Basic Books.

American Association of Suicidology. (1999). *Suicide in youth: What you can do about it.* Available from American Association of Suicidology: *http://www.suicidology.org*

Beebe, J. E. (1975). Evaluation of the suicidal patient. In C. P. Rosenbaum & J. E. Beebe, III (Eds.), *Psychiatric treatment: Crisis, clinic and consultation.* New York: Basic Books.

Berman, A. L., & Jobes, D. A. (1995). Suicide prevention in adolescents (Age 12–18). *Suicide and Life-Threatening Behavior, 25,* 143–154.

Brent, D. A., Perper, J. A., Allman, C. J., Moritz, G. M., Wartella, M. E., & Zelenak, J. P. (1991). The presence and accessibility of firearms in the home of adolescent suicides: A case-control study. *Journal of the American Medical Association, 266,* 2989–2995.

Brock, S. E., & Sandoval, J. (1996). Suicidal ideation and behaviors. In G. G. Bear, K. M. Minke, & A. Thomas (Eds.), *Children's needs II: Development, problems and alternatives* (pp. 361–374). Bethesda, MD: National Association of School Psychologists.

Brock, S. E., Sandoval, J., & Lewis, S. (2001). *Preparing for crises in the schools: A manual for building school crisis response teams* (2nd ed.). New York: Wiley.

Brown, G. L., & Goodwin, F. K. (1986). Cerebrospinal fluid correlates of suicide attempters and aggression. *Annals of the New York Academy of Science, 487,* 175–188.

California State Department of Education, School Climate Unit. (1986). *Implementation guide to the youth suicide school prevention program.* Sacramento, CA: California State Department of Education.

Caplan, G. (1964). *Principles of preventive psychiatry.* New York: Basic Books.

Centers for Disease Control. (1992). *Youth suicide prevention programs: A resource guide.* Atlanta, GA: US Department of Health and Human Services, Public Health Service, Centers for Disease Control.

Centers for Disease Control. (1995). Suicide among children, adolescents, and young adults—United States, 1980–1992. *Morbidity and Mortality Weekly Report, 44,* 289–291.

Clark, D. A. (1992). Understanding the development of the concept of suicide though the use of early memory technique. *Death Studies, 16,* 299–316.

Davidson, L. E. (1989). Suicide clusters and youth. In C. R. Pfeffer (Ed.), *Suicide among youth: Perspectives on risk and prevention* (pp. 83–99). Washington, DC: American Psychiatric Press.

Davis, J. M. (1988). Suicide and the schools: Intervention and prevention. In J. Sandoval (Ed.), *Crisis counseling, intervention and prevention in the schools* (pp. 187–203). Hillsdale, NJ: Lawrence Erlbaum Associates.

Davis, J. M., & Sandoval, J. (1991). *Suicidal youth: School-based intervention and prevention.* San Francisco: Jossey-Bass.

Diekstra, R. F. W., & Garnefski, N. (1995). On the nature, magnitude and causality of suicidal behaviors: An international perspective. *Suicide and Life-Threatening Behavior, 25,* 36–57.

Elkind, D. (1978). *The child's reality: Three developmental themes.* New York: Wiley.

Everstine, D. S., & Everstine, L. E. (1983). *People in crisis: Strategic therapeutic interventions*. New York: Brunner/Mazel.

Garland, A. F., Shaffer, D., & Whittle, B. (1989). An national survey of school-based adolescent suicide prevention programs. *Journal of the American Academy of Child and Adolescent Psychiatry, 28*, 931–934.

Garland, A. F., & Zigler, E. (1993). Adolescent suicide prevention: Current research and social policy implications. *American Psychologist, 48*, 169–182.

Gould, R. E. (1965). Suicide problems in children and adolescents. *American Journal of Psychotherapy, 19*, 228–246.

Jobes, D. A., Berman, A. L., & Josselsen, A. R. (1986). The impact of psychological autopsies on medical examiners' determination of manner of death. *Journal of Forensic Science, 31*, 117–189.

Jobes, D. A., Berman, A. L., & Josselsen, A. R. (1987). Improving the validity and reliability of medical-legal certifications of suicide. *Suicide and Life-Threatening Behavior, 17*, 310–325.

Kann, L., Kinchen, S. A., Williams, B. I., Ross, J. G., Lowry, R., Hill, C. V., Grunbaum, J., Blumson, D. S., Collins, J. L., & Kolbe, L. J. (1998). Youth risk behavior surveillance—United States, 1997. *Morbidity and Mortality Weekly Report, 47*, 1–89.

Koocher, G. P. (1973). Childhood, death and cognitive development. *Developmental Psychology, 9*, 369–375.

Koocher, G. P. (1974). Talking with children about death. *American Journal of Orthopsychiatry, 44*, 404–411.

Maris, R. W. (1992). How are suicides different? In R. W. Maris, A. L. Berman, J. T. Maltsberger, & R. I. Yufit (Eds.), *Assessment and prediction of suicide* (pp. 65–87). New York: Guilford Press.

Mishara, B. L. (1999). Concepts of death and suicide in children ages 6–12 and their implications for suicide prevention. *Suicide and Life-Threatening Behavior, 29*, 105–118.

Moscicki, E. K. (1995). Epidemiology of suicidal behavior. *Suicide and Life-Threatening Behavior, 25*, 22–35.

Nagy, M. (1959). The child's view of death. In H. Feifel (Ed.), *The meaning of death* (pp. 79–98). New York: McGraw-Hill.

National Center for Injury Prevention and Control. (1998). *Scientific data, surveillance and injury statistics*. Atlanta, GA: Centers for Disease Control and Prevention. Available from *http://www.cdc.gov/ncipc/osp/mortdata.htm*

Normand, C. L., & Mishara, B. L. (1992). The development of the concept of suicide in children. *Omega: Journal of Death and Dying, 25*, 183–203.

O'Carroll, P. W., Berman, A. L., Maris, R. W., Moscicki, E. K., Tanney, B. L., & Silverman, M. M. (1996). Beyond the Tower of Babel: A nomenclature for suicidology. *Suicide and Life-Threatening Behavior, 26*, 237–252.

O'Carroll, P. W., Potter, L. B., & Mercy, J. A. (1994). Programs for the prevention of suicide among adolescents and young adults. *Morbidity and Mortality Weekly Report, 43*, 1–7.

Orbach, I., & Glaubman, H. (1979). the concept of death and suicidal behavior in young children. *Journal of the American Academy of Child Psychiatry, 18*, 668–678.

Peters, K. D., Kochanek, K. D., & Murphy, S. L. (1998). *Deaths: Final data, 1996. National vital statistics Report, 47*, Hyattsville, MD: National Center for Health Statistics. [DHHA Publication No. (PHS) 99-1120.]

Pfeffer, C. R. (1984). Modalities of treatment of suicidal children: An overview of the literature on current practice. *American Journal of Psychotherapy, 38*, 364–372.

Pfeffer, C. R. (1989). Life stress and family risk factors for youth fatal and nonfatal suicidal behavior. In C. R. Pfeffer (Ed.), *Suicide among youth: Perspectives on risk and prevention* (pp. 143–164). Washington, DC: American Psychiatric Press.

Pfeffer, C. R., Conte, H., Plutchik, R., & Jerrett, I. (1979). Suicidal behavior in latency age children: An empirical study. *Journal of the American Academy of Child Psychiatry, 18*, 679–692.

Poland, S. (1989). *Suicide intervention in the schools*. New York: Guilford Press.

Potter, L. B., Powell, K. E., & Kachur, S. P. (1995). Suicide prevention from a public health perspective. *Suicide and Life-Threatening Behavior, 25*, 82–91.

Ramsay, R. F., Tanney, B. L., Tierney, R. J., & Lang, W. A. (1996). *Suicide intervention workshop* (6th ed.). Calgary, AB: LivingWorks.

Reynolds, W. M. (1988). *The suicidal ideation questionnaire: Professional manual.* Odessa, FL: Psychological Assessment Resources.

Roberts, R. E., Chen, Y. R., & Roberts, C. R. (1997). Ethnocultural differences in prevalence of adolescent suicidal behaviors. *Suicide and Life-Threatening Behavior, 27*, 208–217.

Ross, C. (1985, March). *A survey of high-school seniors.* Reported at presentation of The Youthful Suicide Epidemic, Berkeley, CA.

Safier, G. (1964). A study in relationships between life and death concepts in children. *Journal of Genetic Psychology, 105*, 282–294.

Sandoval, J., & Brock, S. E. (1996). The school psychologist's role in suicide prevention. *School Psychology Quarterly, 11*, 169–185.

Shaffer, D. (1974). Suicide in childhood and early adolescence. *Journal of Child Psychology and Psychiatry, 15*, 275–291.

Shaffer, D., & Bacon, K. (1989). A critical review of preventive intervention efforts in suicide, with particular reference to youth suicide. In Alcohol, Drug Abuse, and Mental Health Administration, *Report of the secretary's task force on youth suicide: Vol. 3. Prevention and interventions in youth suicide* (DHHS Publication No. ADM 89-1623, pp. 31–61). Washington, DC: US Government Printing Office.

Shaffer, D., Vieland, V., Garland, A., Rojas, M., Underwood, M., & Busner, C. (1990). Adolescent suicide attempts: Response to suicide prevention programs. *Journal of the American Medical Association, 264*, 3151–3155.

Spirito, A., Overholser, J., & Stark, L. J. (1989). Common problems and coping strategies: II. Findings with adolescent suicide attempters. *Journal of Abnormal Child PsycPhology, 17*, 213–221.

Tanney, B. L., & Motto, J. (1990). Long-term follow up of 1570 attempted suicides. *Proceedings of the 23rd Annual Conference of the American association of Suicidology*, New Orleans: American Association of Suicidology.

Toolan, J. M. (1975). Suicide in children and adolescents. *American Journal of Psychotherapy, 29*, 339–344.

Wass, H. (1982). Parents, teachers and health professionals as helpers. In H. Wass & C. A. Corr (Eds.), *Helping children cope with death: Guidelines and resources.* Washington, DC: Hemisphere.

CHAPTER

# 14

# Gay, Lesbian, Bisexual, and Questioning Youth

Suzy R. Thomas
Timothy G. Larrabee
University of California, Davis

Gay, lesbian, and bisexual youth are a largely invisible minority group at serious risk for a variety of physical, emotional, and social problems. Because of widespread societal prejudice and lack of awareness, school counselors and other school personnel have, in general, failed to protect or serve this vulnerable group. The estimate that 10% of the general population has a same-sex or bisexual orientation (Bass & Kaufman, 1996; Buhrke, 1989; Kinsey, Pomeroy, & Martin, 1948; Kinsey, Pomeroy, Martin, & Gebhard, 1953) means that there may be up to three million gay, lesbian, and bisexual teenagers in the world (Herdt, 1989; Price & Telljohann, 1991). Although these figures have been disputed, it is safe to assume that there are gay, lesbian, and bisexual students in every school.

Many gay[1] adolescents experience isolation, rejection, and internalized lack of self-acceptance. Gay people of all ages face discrimination, harassment, and violence, much like any other minority group. Unlike other minorities, however, gays, lesbians, and bisexuals commonly do not have the support of or solidarity with their families (Telljohann & Price, 1993). An African American, Jewish, or Latino/Latina youth will not be expelled from his or her home for being African American, Jewish, or Latino/Latina, whereas a gay or lesbian youth might be (Martin & Hetrick, 1988).

[1]Throughout the chapter, we often use the word *gay* to refer to gay males, lesbians, bisexuals, and questioning (those who are uncertain as to their sexual identity) youth. The word *gay* is used for purposes of simplicity, and is meant to be inclusive of all of the above categories. We also use the term *sexual minority youth*, in response to its current popularity in the literature.

To date, there has been a paucity of research specifically aimed at the issues related to gay and lesbian adolescents (Fontaine, 1998; Fontaine & Hammond, 1996). For the most part, schools have continued to be unresponsive to the needs and issues of gay, lesbian, and bisexual students (Savin-Williams, 1994). Stigmatization of homosexuality and bisexuality is still institutionalized in laws and churches; and, until recently, the helping professions saw homosexuality as a pathological and treatable condition (Dworkin & Gutierrez, 1989). Until the early 1970s, the traditional approach in the psychological and psychiatric communities was to view homosexuality as an illness, despite research that demonstrated the psychological health of gay people (Hooker, 1957). Treatment involved attempting to change the gay, lesbian, or bisexual person's orientation by causing a "heterosexual shift" (Coleman, 1978).

Slowly, the field of psychology has moved toward a model that views homosexuality and bisexuality as normal variations of sexual orientation. In 1973, "homosexuality" was removed from the classification of mental disorders in the *Diagnostic and Statistical Manual of Mental Disorders* (DSM-II) (American Psychiatric Association, 1968). The Gay Rights Movement of the 1960s and 1970s and the removal of homosexuality from the DSM-II forced the mental health field to re-evaluate its understanding of and attitude toward homosexuality (Iasenza, 1989).

Many of the myths concerning homosexuality have been dispelled, or at least modified, in recent years. However, some of these myths continue to influence the thinking of many adults who work directly and indirectly with children and adolescents, including psychologists, counselors, social workers, and educators (Durby, 1994; Slater, 1988). Gay youth need supportive school counselors and a supportive school environment (Bass & Kaufman, 1996; Omizo, Omizo, & Okamoto, 1998).

## A SYSTEMS PERSPECTIVE

From a family systems point of view, the family of the adolescent is in a time of intergenerational change, as several members typically enter a new life cycle at the same time. As children become adolescents, parents are often entering middle age, while grandparents reach retirement age. The conflicting demands caused by these changes can make adolescence a difficult time not only for young people but also for all members of the family system (Garcia Preto, 1989). Family systems theory (similar to developmental theory, discussed next) holds that individuals do not act in a vacuum, but rather as the result of interacting with the environment. Each member subscribes to a set of rules, roles, and scripts, which can be rigid or healthy. When one member of the system changes, the entire system is dynamically altered (Blevins, 1994).

The school is also a system with subsystems, including students, teachers, counselors, administrators, and parents, each of which interacts with and influences the others. With regard to gay youth in a school setting, each subsystem has adopted similar roles and rules, some of which must be changed if gay youth are to survive and be given the opportunity to have a safe and affirming school experience. For example, adults often ignore the existence of gay youth, and tend to omit or devalue the historical and present-day contributions of gays and lesbians. Students have been allowed to tease and harass gays, lesbians, and any individuals who do not conform to traditional sex-role expectations.

Two reports from the Safe Schools Coalition of Washington (Reis, 1999; Reis & Saewyc, 1999) found that sexual minority students who were harassed because of their perceived sexual orientation were twice as likely as their nonharassed sexual minority peers to have missed at least one day of school per month out of fear for their safety. Heterosexual students who were harassed because they were perceived to be gay were three times as likely to miss one or more days of school as their nonharassed heterosexual counterparts. Several students changed schools (sometimes more than once) or dropped out of school altogether to avoid harassment. Prejudice negatively affects all members of the entire system and the larger system of the surrounding community.

## DEVELOPMENTAL THEORIES AND ADOLESCENT DEVELOPMENT

According to several developmental theories, identity is acquired through the dynamic interaction between individual and environment. Some developmental theorists conceptualize life as a series of identifiable stages, which progress in a logical, interrelated sequence as the individual ages (Fuhrmann, 1990). Erikson (1963), for example, considered the individual from a psychosocial perspective, and described each stage of life as involving a "normative crisis," or primary conflict that must be resolved in order for healthy progression to the next stage to occur. The crisis of adolescence is one of "identity versus role confusion" (Erikson, 1963). Individuals who manage this stage well enter adulthood with a solid sense of values and peace with who they are and an ability to deal with conflict, diversity, and difficulties. Those who do not handle the identity crisis of adolescence well are likely to develop poor habits, become withdrawn, or engage in self-destructive or delinquent behavior (Fuhrmann, 1990).

Developmental tasks are challenges in the life of an individual that lead to happiness and future success if satisfactorily completed, versus unhappiness and difficulty with later tasks if not successfully achieved (Erikson, 1963; Fuhrmann, 1990). The tasks of adolescence involve coping with a sudden and dramatic transformation of identity in all areas, including bodily changes, an increase in sexual thoughts, emotional changes, the achievement of new cognitive abilities, and a pronounced focus on social issues outside the home (Garcia Preto, 1989). Gay adolescents face these tasks as adolescents, as well as additional issues associated with the emergence of their sexual orientation (Mallon, 1994).

Adolescence implies the task of turning away from childhood and the total dependence on parents that was necessary during childhood. In some cultures, the adolescent is compelled to move toward independence and separation from the family (Wolf, 1991). The family, as a system, must prepare for qualitative changes in all relationships (McGoldrick & Gerson, 1989). The adolescent individual is in the process of solidifying her or his identity, which involves shifts in family structure and the renegotiation of roles. This process can be disruptive and confusing to the entire family (Garcia Preto, 1989). Sexual orientation issues further complicate this time for adolescents and their families.

## Development of Sexual Orientation

Acquisition of sexual orientation has been described in biological, psychological, and cultural terms. Cass (1979) saw gay identity development as similar to other identity formation theories, and underscored the importance of recognizing the significance of both psychological and social factors. She conceptualized homosexual identity development as a process in which the individual is actively involved in the acquisition of a gay identity. At every developmental stage an alternate path is presented, and the individual is able to choose whether to interrupt and suppress the continued development of a gay identity. The gay individual can achieve sufficient levels of congruency or integration, although complete congruency is an impossibility because of the effects of societal prejudice.

Cass (1979) proposed a linear developmental model, with delineated places of beginning and end (see Fig. 14.1). She also posited, however, that identity is a cognitive construct, in a constant state of change. Cass described increasing identity development as the result of increasing congruency between the private and public aspects of a person's identity. Her model is the most widely used gay identity development model in the psychological literature (Eliason, 1996).

Linear models of identity development, however, have been criticized in recent years. The most current trend regarding gay, lesbian, and bisexual identity is to consider its development in terms of the interactions with or influences of racial, ethnic, sociopolitical, and historical contexts, and to use or create models that view development in fluid, comprehensive, interdisciplinary terms (Eliason, 1996; Russell, 1989).

***Adolescent Gay Identity Development.*** Mental health professionals only recently began to allow for the possibility that an adolescent could have an established gay, lesbian, or bisexual identity (Coleman & Remafedi, 1989).

| | | |
|---|---|---|
| Identity Confusion<br>*(conflict due to realization of same-sex feelings) identity)* | Identity Comparison<br>*(feeling different; loss of belonging)* | Identity Tolerance<br>*(exploring gay community; greater commitment to gay* |
| Identity Acceptance<br>*(increased contact with gay community; attempts to normalize identity)* | Identity Pride<br>*(devaluing of dominant society and heterosexuality; expression of pride in being gay)* | Identity Synthesis<br>*(integration of gay identity; end of process)* |

FIG. 14.1. Cass' model of homosexual identity formation (1979).

Although early homosexual experiences may not predict a same-sex orientation, it is also true that a same-sex orientation may be well-established by adolescence (Slater, 1988). Gay identity often begins in childhood, with a generally unidentifiable feeling of being different, and presents an added developmental task for the adolescent at an already difficult time (Mallon, 1994; Telljohann & Price, 1993).

Transformation such as that which occurs during adolescence implies loss of previous attachments. Separation becomes more difficult if the support system provided by the parents is not functional or available (Garcia Preto, 1989). Although this breakdown can occur in any family, it is common in families with a gay adolescent. The ability to develop a positive sexual self-concept is restricted in families in which the adolescent's emerging sexuality is ignored, denied, or rejected (Garcia Preto, 1989). Again, although this possibility exists in the family of any adolescent, rejection is far likelier in the family of a gay adolescent (Russell, 1989; Savin-Williams, 1989).

## COMMON PROBLEMS EXPERIENCED BY GAY YOUTH

An essential limitation in much of the research on adolescent homosexuality and bisexuality is that many studies are retrospective in nature, relying on the memory of gay and lesbian adults to describe the adolescent experience. The results of retrospective studies can be influenced by current bias and distortion of the past. In addition, most of the early studies about gay youth used samples from bars, prisons, and psychiatric wards, rather than attempting to obtain a more representative sample pool (Herdt, 1989). In recent years, however, attempts have been made to study gay adolescents themselves. However, many of these studies rely on samples from community centers serving gay adolescents, which affects the generalizability of their data (Savin-Williams, 1994). It is difficult, therefore, to study the gay adolescent population at large, because many of its members have not yet recognized their same-sex attractions, or felt safe to share their feelings with others.

Gay adolescents are vulnerable in a variety of physical, emotional, and social ways. Common problems of sexual minority youth include: dropping out of school, running away from home, homelessness, sexual abuse, prostitution, AIDS, sexually transmitted diseases, substance abuse, suicide, violence, harassment, discrimination, and lack of support from family, peers, and school personnel (Coleman & Remafedi, 1989; Cooley, 1998; Cranston, 1992; D'Augelli, Hershberger, & Pilkington, 1998; Durby, 1994; Fontaine, 1998; Martin & Hetrick, 1988; McFarland, 1998; Muller & Hartman, 1998; Popenhagen & Qualley, 1998; Remafedi, Farrow, & Deisher, 1991; Rotheram-Borus, Koopman, & Ehrhardt, 1991; Savin-Williams, 1994; Telljohann & Price, 1993). The problems experienced by gay youth arise from the hostile attitudes, discrimination, and stigmatization that they experience from others, not as a result of their sexual orientation (Gonsiorek, 1988; Martin & Hetrick, 1988; Slater, 1988). In the following sections, we discuss the problems of isolation, "passing" versus coming out, violence, suicide, HIV, the additional complications for gay youth of color, and prejudice within the school system.

## Isolation

Isolation is commonly referred to as the number one problem faced by gay youth (Gover, 1994; McFarland, 1998; Sears, 1992; Strommen, 1989; Telljohann & Price, 1993). Martin and Hetrick (1988), the cofounders of The Institute for the Protection of Lesbian and Gay Youth (IPLGY) in New York, reported the presenting problems among the gay, lesbian, and bisexual youth who sought services at their agency to be the following: (a) cognitive (lack of information), social (stigmatization), and emotional (feeling alone and unique) isolation; (b) family problems, ranging from isolation to expulsion from the home; and (c) violence, about half of which occurs in the home.

## "Passing"

Many gay, lesbian, and bisexual adolescents are aware of the lack of social acceptance of, and hatred toward, homosexuality. They often attempt to hide their homosexuality, to monitor their behavior and appearance in order to "pass" as heterosexual (Rofes, 1989). Gay youth try to avoid possible rejection from family, peers, and school personnel by not revealing or discussing their sexual orientation (Telljohann & Price, 1993). However, not all adolescents are able to "pass" as heterosexual, and those who do still belong to a minority group. Whether a gay youth is able to pass or not, he or she may act out in dangerous or destructive ways as a result of the pressures of being gay in a prejudiced society (Martin & Hetrick, 1988). Those who do not reveal their same-sex orientation witness what happens–both the positive and the negative–to those who do (Savin-Williams, 1989).

## Coming Out

Coming out has been described as the process or series of stages in which individuals recognize their sexual identity and integrate this knowledge into their lives (Kahn, 1991; Strommen, 1989; Zemsky, 1991). Coming out begins with feelings of incongruency, internal dissonance, and "differentness" that impel the person to "push and pull" internally, in an effort to resolve these inconsistencies. The process of coming out often involves a combination of complex internal shifts accompanied by the risks of sharing one's identity with family and community (Newman & Muzzonigro; 1993; Telljohann & Price, 1993; Zemsky, 1991).

Coming out is particularly troublesome for gay adolescents, who must choose between possible rejection by their families and peers at a critical developmental time, or the isolation and invisibility of attempting to pass as heterosexual. As minors, adolescents are dependent on their families, and have limited rights, mobility, and access to information (Krysiak, 1987). The reaction of parents to a child's disclosure of homosexuality seems generally negative. Disclosure tends to precipitate a family crisis, which may or may not be resolved eventually. Disclosure involves the loss of a previous role, and all of the expectations that accompanied that role. Parents tend to apply their misconceptions and negative values about homosexuality to their child, whom they begin to perceive and experience as a stranger. Parents also frequently experience a sense of responsibility, guilt, and failure, as if they somehow caused the "problem" (Strommen, 1989).

Coming out seems to be psychologically beneficial, and contributes to healthy self-esteem (Savin-Williams, 1989). Coming out to others can also decrease one's sense of isolation, help with identity integration, and increase the intimacy of relationships (Lipkin, 1999). However, disclosure may result in painful experiences, ranging from a period of difficult adjustment with eventual acceptance to complete rejection and isolation for the gay person (D'Augelli et al., 1998; Martin & Hetrick, 1988; Russell, 1989; Telljohann & Price, 1993). Strommen (1989) saw the family's reaction as a process that *can* be worked through to the achievement of integration, although this is not always the case. Telljohann and Price (1993) warned that many gay adolescents suffer as a result of coming out to their parents. For teenagers, then, the risks of disclosure are at times as serious as those of staying "in the closet."

## Violence

If gay teenagers are not invisible, they are often attacked. A 1984 survey of 2,074 gay men and lesbians revealed that one fifth of the women and one half of the men had been harassed, threatened, or assaulted during high school for being perceived or assumed to be gay (Gover, 1994). In another study, nearly two thirds of gay males and one third of lesbians reported experiencing verbal or physical harassment in junior high school, senior high school, or college (Gross & Aurand, as cited in Bass & Kaufman, 1996). More than one fourth of bisexual and gay male teenagers are forced to drop out of school because of these attacks (Remafedi, as cited in Bass & Kaufman, 1996). Gonsiorek (1988) noted that one of the most apparent sources of stress for gay adolescents is verbal and physical abuse from their peers. With regard to violence at school, dropping out is often seen as the only solution because of the common refusal in most school settings to address homosexuality (Martin & Hetrick, 1988).

## Suicide

The combination of being unseen and unaccepted can lead gay teenagers to suicide. Many authors have noted a disproportionately high risk of suicide among gay youth (Cooley, 1998; Fontaine, 1998; McFarland, 1998; Muller & Hartman, 1998; Popenhagen & Qualley, 1998; Remafedi et al., 1991; Savin-Williams, 1994). Remafedi et al. (1991) found that suicide among gay and bisexual male adolescents was related not to sexual orientation per se, but to personal or interpersonal difficulties regarding sexual orientation. A recent study by D'Augelli et al. (1998) found higher rates of suicide attempts among youths who had disclosed their sexual orientation to a family member than among those who were not yet out to their families. Shaffer, Fisher, Parides, and Gould (1995), however, found that gay adolescents were only slightly, not significantly, at greater risk of suicide than their straight counterparts. They concluded that the reported connections between homosexuality and suicide may detract from other important issues of possible study regarding gay adolescents, including AIDS/HIV.

## HIV/AIDS

Gay youth are also at risk of contracting HIV because they are less likely to practice safer sex and more likely to be in situations in which they are victimized (Cooley, 1998; Cranston, 1992; Rofes, 1989; Rotheram-Borus, Gillis, Reid, Fernandez, & Gwadz, 1997; Rotheram-Borus, Koopman, & Ehrhardt, 1991; Rotheram-Borus, Mahler, & Rosario, 1995). Many AIDS experts see young people as the next group to be affected by the disease. According to the Centers for Disease Control and Prevention (1997), as of June 30, 1997, there were 2,953 reported cases of AIDS in the United States among adolescents ages 13 to 19. There were 22,070 cases of AIDS reported among people between the ages of 20 to 24, and it is suspected that many of these individuals may have become infected during adolescence (Centers for Disease Control and Prevention, 1997).

All adolescents face major changes in terms of their physical, sexual, emotional, cognitive, and social development. For adolescents with issues concerning sexual orientation, those changes are often doubly difficult and painful.

## Multicultural Issues

Gay youth of color face additional challenges as members of two minority groups (Chung & Katayama, 1998; Savin-Williams, 1994). They may feel pressured to choose between these two groups. Once they become aware of their sexual orientation, gay youth of color may not feel at home in either group. Homosexuality is widely perceived by people of color to be caused by the decadence of White, urban society (Tremble, Schneider, & Appathurai, 1989). Gay youth of color risk rejection within their racial or ethnic communities because of their sexual orientation. Furthermore, there is a myth that the gay community is open and accepting because of its oppression by the majority. Yet many non-White gays and lesbians experience discrimination and lack of acceptance within the gay community (Tremble et al., 1989). The gay community parallels the general population in many ways, including that White men have social and economic advantages over people of color and women (Herdt, 1989).

Gay adolescents are assumed to be homogeneous (Herdt, 1989). In reality, cultural differences affect the definition and expression of homosexuality and the values associated with it. It is crucial to understand the different meanings assigned to homosexuality and coming out in cross-cultural contexts. For example, gay youth of color do not necessarily share the value of disclosure or "coming out" commonly espoused by White gay men and lesbians (Herdt, 1989).

Tremble et al. (1989) noted that ethnic minorities faced unique difficulties in (a) coming out to their families, (b) finding a place within the gay community, and (c) synthesizing their sexual and ethnic identities. For an adolescent from an ethnic minority, coming out occurs in the contexts of ethnic traditions, family values, and social networks, and poses additional pressures and conflicts for the youth at an already difficult time. Gay youths who are immigrants must deal with the forces and influences of two distinct cultures, in addition to issues of sexual orientation.

## Prejudice Within the School System

The healthy psychological and emotional development of gay, lesbian, and bisexual students is threatened because of the isolation and harassment they face when their sexuality is recognized. As a result, many gay adolescents experience the school environment as hostile and rejecting (Reynolds & Koski, 1995). Some school counselors are unable or unwilling to work with gay students, or on their behalf, because of prejudice. Some counselors who do work with gay and lesbian clients and students do not believe they have received adequate training (Dworkin & Gutierrez, 1989).

In a study by Telljohann and Price (1993), only 16% of the lesbians surveyed and 20% of the gay males could identify someone at school who had been helpful to them. Sears (1992) found that adolescents were aware that most teachers responded to racial slurs in the classroom, but took no action with regard to prejudiced remarks made by other students when those remarks related to homosexuality. His study also indicated negative attitudes and feelings among both school counselors and prospective teachers regarding homosexuality. Most of the participants did not believe that gay youth constituted a group in need of special services. Sears concluded that personal feelings and negative attitudes interfere with professional service delivery to gay, lesbian, and bisexual youth in the school setting, even if only through the "benign neglect" that reinforces heterosexism in school curricula and classrooms.

Price and Telljohann (1991) also found that counselors underestimated the presence of gay students in their schools, as well as their high level of risk for suicide and substance abuse. Their recommendations included (a) inservice training for teachers and counselors; (b) support groups for gay, lesbian, and bisexual students; (c) information about homosexuality in health classes; and (d) similar studies of administrators, teachers, and nurses.

## THE ROLE OF THE CRISIS COUNSELOR

The crisis counselor is in a unique position to assist gay youths in (a) developing a healthy gay identity, (b) adjusting to their sexual orientation, (c) coping with prejudice, and (d) deciding how and to whom to disclose their sexual orientation (Krysiak, 1987). School guidance workers who address this issue in their schools must be both creative and courageous in developing programs and interventions that fit the needs of their schools. Working with gay youth is a new frontier in school counseling. However, a 1989 resolution passed by the National Education Association stated that, "Every school district should provide counseling by trained personnel for students struggling with their sexual/gender orientation" (Flax, 1990). Counselors can have a positive impact on the lives of all students, by working directly with the gay student population and by fostering awareness, understanding, and acceptance among all members of the school community.

### Self-Awareness for Counselors

In order to be effective, school counselors must be aware of their own attitudes, informed about referral sources, and accepting of gay students (Coleman & Remafedi, 1989; Logan, 1996; Russell, 1989). Without education and awareness, school counselors are likely to remain inattentive to the gay, lesbian, and bisexual student population in their schools. School counselors who attempt to address the needs of gay students must deal with and heal from their own prejudice or ignorance through self-assessment, which can take the form of values clarification exercises, talking with others, and similar activities (Black & Underwood, 1998; Iasenza, 1989). Self-education can also include reading books and articles or watching movies with gay characters or themes (Besner & Spungin, 1995).

### Strategies for Working With Gay Youth: Direct Services

Secondary prevention efforts address problems in groups of people who have been identified as vulnerable (Bower, 1965). The direct service counseling suggestions described next serve as secondary prevention tools because they aim to protect gay students and to prevent or reduce the development of the physical, social, and emotional problems to which they are vulnerable.

***Individual Counseling Suggestions.*** School counselors must be viewed by students and adults as approachable regarding the topic of sexual orientation (Krysiak, 1987). When discussing sexuality and relationships with a student, they should use gender-neutral language, and not assume that the student is heterosexual (Krysiak, 1987). School counselors should also pay attention to the specific needs of gay and lesbian students from ethnic minorities, as these students face a variety of issues associated with the interactions between their ethnic and sexual identities (Chung & Katayama, 1998).

School counselors can work with gay students in the following areas:

1. *Personal Issues.* Counselors can assist gay students with identity development, self-esteem, and self-acceptance. They can help gay students to work through social, emotional, and physical problems by counseling them individually or in groups, and by providing useful community counseling resources. Counselors can do a lot for gay youth by protecting them from harassment and harm, and by being a consistent and supportive presence in their lives.

2. *Academic Issues.* The academic counseling needs of gay students are in many ways the same as those of any student. However, gay students are disproportionately more likely to consider dropping out of school because of harassment or abuse (Martin & Hetrick, 1988). Therefore, counselors working with gay students should assess for risk of drop out, and should work to address harassment within the school community. Gay students have special safety needs that must be addressed at school in order for them to be able to achieve academically and grow personally.

3. *Relationship Issues*. Gay students may need support and assistance with relationships. For example, these students need to find safe ways to socialize with other gay students. In addition, gay students may benefit from counseling in terms of friends and families. They may want to come out to their straight friends or families, and they may or may not experience acceptance within these important relationships. Counselors can help gay students to explore the possible consequences of coming out, and can give these students resources and referrals to community agencies where they can find additional support. Counselors should not encourage students to come out to their families or friends without having a clear sense that they will be accepted and that they will be able to deal with the emotional repercussions in a healthy way. Some students may place themselves in danger by coming out, and the counselor's primary focus should always be the safety of the student. By working to create an affirming school environment, counselors can be assured that there is at least one safe and supportive place for these students.

Specific counseling strategies when working with gay youth are in some ways no different than those used with any student. The following skills are useful in counseling gay youth: (a) accurate, empathic listening; (b) conveying acceptance and respect; (c) providing a safe, confidential environment; (d) assisting with developmental, interpersonal, and adjustment issues; (e) assessing for problems and stressors; (f) identifying and mobilizing resources; (g) exploring and promoting coping tools; and (h) offering accurate educational information about sexual orientation, HIV, and support services and other resources for gay adolescents. Mallon (1994) offered the reminder that the overarching goal of counseling is to "help the client function more fully as a human being" (p. 86). A primary goal when working with gay youth is to ensure their safety within their families as well as within the school and community at large.

When working with a student whom you know or suspect to be gay, there are some specific issues to be aware of. For example, some students may be unaware of their sexual orientation, and it is critical not to directly address sexual orientation before they do. It is important for gay, lesbian, bisexual, and questioning students to be "met" by a counselor wherever they are in their understanding and expression of their sexual orientation, and not to feel pressured to label themselves prematurely. There should be room for exploration and openness, and interventions should be individually designed to meet the specific needs of each student (Fontaine & Hammond, 1996; Gonsiorek, 1988; Mallon, 1994).

***Group Counseling Suggestions.*** Given that group counseling can be an effective intervention for students and an efficient use of counselor time, school counselors can develop and facilitate a group for gay and lesbian adolescents (Muller & Hartman, 1998). School counselors can also initiate a support group on campus for gay students. (See the Appendix for resources that provide guidelines for establishing and conducting support groups.)

It is crucial for young gay people to find safe ways to spend time with each other. Inappropriate sexual or personal relationships with gay adults are frequently the only avenue available to gay adolescents to explore their emerging sexuality, or to find companionship. The school counselor who organizes a support group or counseling group for gay students can help to encourage these students to build age-appropriate social networks. Support groups can assist students to overcome their sense of isolation and decrease the likelihood of health compromising behavior (Rienzo, Button, & Wald, 1997). Counselors can also provide support and information for the families of gay students who are out or coming out, and assist these families with adjustment and acceptance (Cooley, 1998).

***Crisis Counseling Suggestions.*** Because of the serious nature of some of the problems commonly experienced by sexual minority youth, counselors must assess for (a) depression and suicidal ideation, (b) substance abuse, (c) school failure and risk of dropping out of school, and (d) abuse or harassment inside or outside the home. Counselors may be called upon to engage in crisis counseling with gay students. In situations where the student's immediate safety is paramount, counselors must be able to take appropriate action and focus on short-term outcomes. Some general principles of crisis counseling (chap. 1) include: (a) taking action and intervening immediately, (b) expressing concern and displaying competence, (c) listening carefully and reflecting the student's feelings, (d) widening the circle of support and providing resources, (e) helping the student accept that the crisis has occurred, (f) discouraging blaming and avoiding false reassurance, (g) engaging in focused problem-solving, and (h) making appropriate reports as well as referrals when the issue is beyond the counselor's scope of practice.

When the issue does not involve a crisis, the counselor can work with the student to improve the student's self-esteem and self-acceptance, and help the student to find other useful resources. School counselors can alleviate some of the isolation experienced by sexual minority youth and provide much-needed support by working directly with these students in a positive, open, informed, and accepting manner.

***Finding and Displaying Resources.*** Counselors can make their offices gay-friendly by displaying gay-related books and posters. They can place fliers with local resources for gay, lesbian, and bisexual people in hallways or other places where students can pick them up anonymously (Street, 1994). School libraries can be an excellent source of information that gay students can access privately to reduce their sense of cognitive isolation. Straight students with gay friends or family members may also access this information. Additionally, educators will likely seek out this information if they are aware they are working with gay adolescents (Fischer, 1995; Gough & Greenblatt, 1992; Jenkins, 1990).

Counselors should become aware of gay-friendly colleges and universities (Krysiak, 1987), and provide information about same-sex relationships and about local resources for gays, lesbians, and bisexuals (Besner & Spungin, 1995; Robinson, 1994). It is a good idea for counselors to visit these places personally or call them in order to gain familiarity with the services they offer. School counselors who are too uncomfortable with the issue of sexual orientation to work directly with gay, lesbian, and bisexual students or to provide them with direct services should have an accurate referral and resource list as a minimum effort to serve these students (Black & Underwood, 1998; Slater, 1988).

## Strategies for Working With Gay Youth: Interventions at Various School Levels

Most of the interventions and strategies discussed in this chapter would be primarily applicable at the secondary and, possibly, middle-school levels. Many of the problems faced by gay youth, such as suicidal ideation and substance abuse, would not, in many cases, appear until then. In addition, gay adolescents are more likely to be able see the connections between their experiences and their emerging sexuality than younger children. Adolescents, in general, are dealing with the onset of puberty and all of the accompanying changes; as such, they are more likely to be capable of and interested in talking about sexual orientation.

However, given that gay identity often begins in early childhood, it is possible for younger children to have an awareness of sexual orientation. They may have parents or other family members who are gay or lesbian which would also raise their awareness of sexual orientation. Elementary-age children who display gender atypical behavior need support and acceptance within the school setting, and counselors can help to ensure that such support is available. Age-appropriate counseling strategies and interventions for these children could also be used. For example, although a list of community resources might be handed out to high school students who are questioning their sexuality, a more appropriate intervention at the elementary school level might be a classroom discussion about different kinds of families (i.e., those with a mom and a dad, or with two moms or two dads, or just a mom or a grandmother, and so on).

Some states, such as California, have passed laws prohibiting any direct discussions of homosexuality in elementary school. These laws pose an additional barrier to those who seek to find creative ways to work with younger children on the issue of sexual orientation. Counselors who work in an informed and accepting way with younger children who may be gay may help prevent some of the problems typically experienced by these students by the time they reach secondary school.

### Strategies for Working With Gay Youth: Indirect Services

School counselors can also work to educate other staff members and students about working with gay, lesbian, and bisexual youth by conducting or arranging for in-service training for teachers and administrators on gay, lesbian, and bisexual issues (Robinson, 1994). They can help teachers learn how to handle name calling in class. They can offer suggestions for curricular reform (Krysiak, 1987). The inclusion of gay and lesbian issues in curriculum will help alleviate the sense of cognitive isolation felt by many gay and lesbian adolescents (Lipkin, 1994). Additionally, "the majority of high school students need guidance and an ongoing class to discuss and learn about various forms of sexuality and gender" (Elia, 1994, p. 183).

Counselors can help develop and enforce school policies that protect, support, and affirm gay, lesbian, and bisexual students, staff, and parents (Bass & Kaufman, 1996). Establishing and enforcing policies that prohibit harassment of gay youth is the least controversial but the most fundamental action needed to make schools conducive to learning for gay and lesbian students (Rienzo et al., 1997).

Counselors can also run educational groups, make classroom and schoolwide presentations, including a diversity day or week at school with presentations, videos, speakers, discussion, and exercises (Bass & Kaufman, 1996; Croteau & Kusek, 1992). Alternative activities that deal with prejudice in a more general way can be provided as an alternative for students who do not wish to participate, or whose parents do not permit their participation (Bauman & Sachs-Kapp, 1998).

It is not necessary for a counselor to be gay, lesbian, or bisexual in order to work effectively with gay youth (Mallon, 1994). Whether gay or straight, school counselors can provide a visible presence in support of gay, lesbian, and bisexual people. (See Appendix for a list of curriculum guides that provide materials for staff development and curriculum.)

## IMPLEMENTING PREVENTION AND INTERVENTION PROGRAMS

Gay adolescents are a minority group vulnerable to various physical, emotional, and social problems. They need supportive, informed school counselors and a safe, affirming school environment. Although there are various programs throughout the United States that serve gay, lesbian, and bisexual youth, most school districts have not implemented such programs. The school is an ideal and appropriate setting for addressing the needs of gay students, and for educating all students and adults about sexual orientation and prejudice. School systems have traditionally assisted students in their academic, emotional, social, and physical development and adjustment.

Given that sexuality and identity formation are also developmental processes, it is reasonable to urge school personnel to take an active role in helping students with these issues as well (Besner & Spungin, 1995).

McFarland (1998) noted that developmental guidance programs should serve all students and should aim to prevent, as well as remediate, problems. Developmental programs tend to include the following components: (a) guidance curriculum, including classroom presentations and curriculum materials; (b) responsive services, such as individual and group counseling; (c) individual planning regarding academic and career goals; and (d) program management, which refers to the support needed from the larger school system, and also includes professional development for counselors.

Marinoble (1998) argued that a successful school program for gay youth should address policy and curriculum, as well as provide support services for students and staff development activities within the school system. Bauman and Sachs-Kapp (1998) support the implementation of school-wide programs addressing sexual orientation issues. They demonstrated the effectiveness of active student participation and leadership in the design, implementation, and evaluation of the program. Key components of their program included using the theme "Hate hurts" to guide the activities, and having a series of guest speakers, panel discussions, and small group discussions over the course of a day. Posters reflecting "key learnings" from the small discussion groups were displayed on the school campus to serve as ongoing reminders of the experience.

Successful AIDS-prevention programs have clearly articulated goals which relate to specific behavioral outcomes, an effective context (such as small group work) in which to deliver the intervention, and a strong theoretical base or model underlying the program (Rotheram-Borus, Mahler, & Rosario, 1995). Finally, James (1998) identified common elements of successful community-based programs for gay youth, including (a) identifying local issues related to the struggles of gay youth, (b) building coalitions of people interested in working on the issue, (c) gathering information about issues and needs, (d) taking action based on the information gathered, and (e) regularly evaluating the actions taken.

Comprehensive, school-based programs involve all members of the school community in an effort to address the needs of gay youth and to promote education, awareness, and tolerance. The purposes of such programs should be: (a) to make the school a safe place for gay, lesbian, and bisexual students; (b) to address the needs of gay students as a vulnerable population; and (c) to provide education about homosexuality, bisexuality, and prejudice to students, teachers, counselors, parents, and administrators. Specific suggestions regarding what should be included in school-based programs are outlined as follows:

- *Needs assessment* and identification of goals.

- *School-wide involvement*, including student participation and leadership.
- *Direct services*, including crisis counseling, individual and group counseling, and support groups for students.
- *Educational and prevention activities*, including classroom presentations, school-wide assemblies and workshops, written pamphlets, and other materials.
- *Curriculum materials and curricular reform* with regard to the inclusion of gay people and specific educational components on related topics.
- *Professional development*, such as in-service training for staff, attendance at outside workshops, and ongoing self-awareness activities.
- *Policy changes*, such as changes in school codes and a school-wide focus on safety.
- *Connection to the wider community* through resources, referrals, and guest speakers.
- *Ongoing, formal evaluation* of the program.

This suggested outline combines primary and secondary prevention methods in a comprehensive effort to address prejudice within a school system, as well as to protect vulnerable populations such as gay members within the school community. Primary prevention is defined by Bloom (1996) as: "coordinated actions seeking to prevent predictable problems, to protect existing states of health and healthy functioning, and to promote desired potentialities in individuals and groups in their physical and sociocultural settings over time" (p. 2). Primary prevention programs aim to prevent the development of mental health problems and to promote "mental and emotional robustness" in entire populations (Bower, 1965).

Meyers and Parsons (1987) identified two types of primary prevention programs. One approach involves the development of competence through the building of interpersonal skills and self-esteem, and the other involves modification of the environment and stress reduction in an effort to eliminate those factors associated with maladjustment. The foregoing outline combines these two strategies in a comprehensive effort to reduce the levels and harmful effects of prejudice.

Strengths of the suggested program include: (a) clearly articulated goals, (b) the combination of direct and indirect services, (c) the active participation of students, (d) an emphasis on ongoing professional development, and (e) a formal evaluation process. All of these suggestions are supported by recommendations from successful programs. The suggested outline also recognizes the effectiveness of combining policy and curricular changes with attempts to improve self-awareness and to alter individual attitudes and beliefs. A program such as the one described above should be a flexible tool for system-wide change that can be adapted according to the specific needs of each school environment.

## ANTICIPATED SOURCES OF RESISTANCE

Given widespread societal prejudice and the controversial nature of the topic of sexual orientation—especially in the school setting—resistance to addressing the issue can be expected. School communities, like any other system, tend to resist change in favor of the status quo (Meyers & Parsons, 1987). Meyers and Parsons (1987) outlined nine factors that help to minimize resistance, including (a) knowledge of the problem, (b) understanding the specific culture of the school, (c) a clear focus, (d) direct involvement with members of the school administration, (e) an effort to ensure that all involved parties understand the program, (f) adequate time for implementation without haste or rush, (g) active involvement of school staff, (h) willingness to begin by addressing secondary and tertiary prevention projects first if necessary, and (i) an effort to reduce resistance before implementing major change. Counselors can also present the disturbing statistics regarding common problems faced by gay youth in order to justify the need for working with gay youth and to gain the support of administrators and other members of the school system (Muller & Hartman, 1998).

## CONCLUSIONS

Regardless of societal recognition or acceptance of homosexuality, a percentage of children will grow up to be gay, lesbian, or bisexual (Coleman & Remafedi, 1989). The problems experienced by gay youth correlate to the areas of development they are experiencing as adolescents. Gay youth are in the midst of physical, sexual, emotional, cognitive, and social development. They are vulnerable in all of these areas. The problems of sexual minority youth do not result directly from the emergence of a gay, lesbian, or bisexual identity. Rather, they are caused by widespread societal prejudice and heterosexism—the negative attitudes, feelings, and beliefs that people hold and express towards gays, lesbians, and bisexuals (Martin & Hetrick, 1988; Slater, 1988).

Gay youth will continue to suffer in physical, emotional, and social ways unless something is done on their behalf. Most school communities, however, can be characterized as unsupportive in nature (Savin-Williams, 1994; Slater, 1988). Many students do not believe they will receive help or acceptance regarding sexual orientation issues from adults in their schools (Street, 1994; Telljohann & Price, 1993). We see it as the responsibility of school counselors and other educators to work with gay youth in an informed and accepting manner and to play a role in implementing changes on their behalf, in order to ensure the safety of all students and the promotion of a healthier, more tolerant society.

## REFERENCES


American Psychiatric Association. (1968). *Diagnostic and statistical manual of mental disorders* (2nd ed.). Washington, DC: Author.

Bass, E., & Kaufman, K. (1996). *Free your mind: The book for gay, lesbian, and bisexual youth—and their allies*. New York: HarperCollins.

Bauman, S., & Sachs-Kapp, P. (1998). A school takes a stand: Promotion of sexual orientation workshops by counselors. *Professional School Counseling, 1*(3), 42–45.

Besner, H. F., & Spungin, C. I. (1995). *Gay and lesbian students: Understanding their needs*. Washington, DC: Taylor & Francis.

Black, J., & Underwood, J. (1998). Young, female, and gay: Lesbian students and the school environment. *Professional School Counseling, 1*(3), 15–20.

Blevins, W. (1994). *Your family your self*. Oakland, CA: New Harbinger.

Bloom, M. (1996). *Primary prevention practices* (Vol. 5). Thousand Oaks, CA: Sage.

Bower, E. M. (1965). Primary prevention of mental and emotional disorders: A frame of reference. In N. Lambert (Ed.), *The protection and promotion of mental health in schools* (pp. 1–9). Bethesda, MD: United States Department of Health, Education, and Welfare Public Health Services.

Buhrke, R. A. (1989). Incorporating lesbian and gay issues into counselor training: A resource guide. *Journal of Counseling and Development, 68*, 77–80.

Cass, V. C. (1979). Homosexual identity formation: A theoretical model. *Journal of Homosexuality, 4*(3), 219–235.

Centers for Disease Control and Prevention. (1997). *HIV–AIDS Surveillance Report, Mid-Year, 9*(1).

Chung, Y. B., & Katayama, M. (1998). Ethnic and sexual identity development of Asian-American lesbian and gay adolescents. *Professional School Counseling, 1*(3), 21–25.

Coleman, E. (1978). Toward a new model of treatment of homosexuality: A review. *Journal of Homosexuality, 3*(4), 345–359.

Coleman, E., & Remafedi, G. (1989). Gay, lesbian, and bisexual adolescents: A critical challenge to counselors. *Journal of Counseling and Development, 68*, 36–40.

Cooley, J. J. (1998). Gay and lesbian adolescents: Presenting problems and the counselor's role. *Professional School Counseling, 1*(3), 30–34.

Cranston, K. (1992). HIV education for gay, lesbian, and bisexual youth: Personal risk, personal power, and the community of conscience. *Journal of Homosexuality, 22*(304), 247–259.

Croteau, J. M., & Kusek, M. T. (1992). Gay and lesbian speaker panels: Implementation and research. *Journal of Counseling and Development, 70*, 396–401.

D'Augelli, A. R., Hershberger, S. L., & Pilkington, N. W. (1998). Lesbian, gay, and bisexual youth and their families: Disclosure of sexual orientation and its consequences. *American Journal of Orthopsychiatry, 68*(3), 361–371.

Durby, D. D. (1994). Gay, lesbian, and bisexual youth. In T. DeCrescenzo (Ed.), *Helping gay and lesbian youth: New policies, new programs, new practice* (pp. 1–37). New York: The Haworth Press.

Dworkin, S. H., & Gutierrez, F. (1989). Counselors be aware: Clients come in every size, shape, color, and sexual orientation. *Journal of Counseling and Development, 68*, 6–8.

Elia, J. P. (1994). Homophobia in the high school: A problem in need of a resolution. *The High School Journal, 77*(1–2), 177–185.

Eliason, M. J. (1996). Identity formation for lesbian, bisexual, and gay persons: Beyond a "minoritizing" view. *Journal of Homosexuality, 30*(3), 31–58.

Erikson, E. (1963). *Childhood and society* (2nd ed.). New York: Norton Press.

Fischer, D. (1995). Young, gay . . . ignored? *Orana, 31*(4), 220–232.

Flax, E. (1990). Special problems of homosexual students need special attention, advocates urge. [Online] Available *http://www.edweek.org/htbin/fastweb?getdoc+view4+ew*, February 7, 1990

Fontaine, J. H. (1998). Evidencing a need: School counselors' experiences with gay and lesbian students. *Professional School Counseling, 1*(3), 8–14.

Fontaine, J. H., & Hammond, N. L. (1996). Counseling issues with gay and lesbian adolescents. *Adolescence, 31*(124), 817–830.

Fuhrmann, B. S. (1990). *Adolescence, adolescents* (2nd ed.). Glenview, IL: HarperCollins.

Garcia Preto, N. (1989). Transformation of the family system in adolescence. In B. Carter & M. McGoldrick (Eds.), *The changing family life cycle: A framework for family therapy* (2nd ed.; pp. 255–283). Boston: Allyn & Bacon.

Gonsiorek, J. C. (1988). Mental health issues of gay and lesbian adolescents. *Journal of Adolescent Health Care, 9*, 114–122.

Gough, C., & Greenblatt, E. (1992). Services to gay and lesbian patrons: Examining the myths. *Library Journal, 117*(1), 59–63.

Gover, J. (1994). Gay youth: A suicide risk. *Student Assistance Journal, Sept./Oct.*, 29–31, 37.

Herdt, G. (1989). Introduction: Gay and lesbian youth, emergent identities, and cultural scenes at home and abroad. *Journal of Homosexuality, 17*(1–2), 1–41.

Hooker, E. A. (1957). The adjustment of the male overt homosexual. *Journal of Projective Techniques, 21*, 18–21.

Iasenza, S. (1989). Some challenges of integrating sexual orientations into counselor training and research. *Journal of Counseling and Development, 68*, 73–76.

James, S. E. (1998). Fulfilling the promise: Community response to the needs of sexual minority youth and families. *American Journal of Orthopsychiatry, 68*(3), 447–454.

Jenkins, C. (1990). Gay and lesbian issues for school libraries and librarians. In C. Gough & E. Greenblatt (Eds.), *Gay and lesbian library service* (pp. 11–23). Jefferson, NC: McFarland.

Kahn, M. J. (1991). Factors affecting the coming out process for lesbians. *Journal of Homosexuality, 21*(3), 47–70.

Kinsey, A. C., Pomeroy, W. B., & Martin, C. E. (1948). *Sexual behavior in the human male*. Philadelphia: Saunders.

Kinsey, A. C., Pomeroy, W. B., Martin, C. E., & Gebhard, P. H. (1953). *Sexual behavior in the human female*. Philadelphia: Saunders.

Krysiak, G. J. (1987). A very silent and gay minority. *The School Counselor, 34*(4), 304–307.

Lipkin, A. (1994). The case for a gay and lesbian curriculum. *The High School Journal, 77*(1–2), 95–107.

Lipkin, A. (1999). *Understanding homosexuality, changing schools: A text for teachers, counselors and administrators*. Boulder, CO: Westview Press.

Logan, C. L. (1996). Homophobia? No, homoprejudice. *Journal of Homosexuality, 31*(3), 31–53.

Mallon, G. P. (1994). Counseling strategies with gay and lesbian youth. In T. DeCrescenzo (Ed.), *Helping gay and lesbian youth: New policies, new programs, new practice* (pp. 75–91). New York: Haworth.

Marinoble, R. M. (1998). Homosexuality: A blind spot in the school mirror. *Professional School Counseling, 1*(3), 4–7.

Martin, A. D., & Hetrick, E. S. (1988). The stigmatization of the gay and lesbian adolescent. *Journal of Homosexuality, 15*, 163–183.

McFarland, W. P. (1998). Gay, lesbian, and bisexual student suicide. *Professional School Counseling, 1*(3), 26–29.

McGoldrick, M., & Gerson, R. (1989). Genograms and the family life cycle. In B. Carter & M. McGoldrick (Eds.), *The changing family life cycle: A framework for family therapy* (2nd ed., pp. 164–189). Boston: Allyn & Bacon.

Meyers, J., & Parsons, R. D. (1987). Prevention planning in the school system. In J. Hermalin & J. A. Morrell (Eds.), *Primary prevention in mental health* (Vol. 9, pp. 111–150). Newbury Park, CA: Sage.

Muller, L. E., & Hartman, J. (1998). Group counseling for sexual minority youth. *Professional School Counseling, 1*(3), 38–41.

Newman, B. S., & Muzzonigro, P. G. (1993). The effects of traditional family values on the coming out process of gay male adolescents. *Adolescence, 28*(109), 213–226.

Omizo, M. M., Omizo, S. A., & Okamoto, C. M. (1998). Gay and lesbian adolescents: A phenomenological study. *Professional School Counseling, 1*(3), 35–37.

Popenhagen, M. P., & Qualley, R. M. (1998). Adolescent suicide: Detection, intervention, and prevention. *Professional School Counseling, 1*(4), 30–35.

Price, J. H., & Telljohann, S. K. (1991). School counselors' perceptions of adolescent homosexuals. *Journal of School Health, 61*, 433–438.

Reis, B. (1999). *They don't even know me! Understanding anti-gay harassment and violence in schools: A report on the five year anti-violence research project of the Safe Schools Coalition of Washington State*. Washington: Safe Schools Coalition of Washington.

Reis, B., & Saewyc, E. (1999). *Eighty-three thousand youth: Selected findings of eight population-based studies as they pertain to anti-gay harassment and the safety and well-being of sexual minority students*. Washington: Safe Schools Coalition of Washington.

Remafedi, G., Farrow, J. A., & Deisher, R. W. (1991). Risk factors for attempted suicide in gay and bisexual youth. *Pediatrics, 87*(6), 869–876.

Reynolds, A. L., & Koski, M. J. (1995). Lesbian, gay, and bisexual teens and the school counselor: Building alliances. In G. Unks (Ed.), *The gay teen: Educational practice and theory for lesbian, gay, and bisexual adolescents* (pp. 85–93). New York: Routledge.

Rienzo, B. A., Button, J. W., & Wald, K. D. (1997). School based programs addressing gay/lesbian/bisexual youth issues. *Journal of the International Council for Health, Physical Education, Recreation, Sport and Dance, 33*(2), 21–25.

Robinson, K. E. (1994). Addressing the needs of gay and lesbian students: The school counselor's role. *School Counselor, 41*, 326–332.

Rofes, E. (1989). Opening up the classroom closet: Responding to the educational needs of gay and lesbian youth. *Harvard Educational Review, 59*(4), 444–453.

Rotheram-Borus, M. J., Gillis, J. R., Reid, H. M., Fernandez, M. I., & Gwadz, M. (1997). HIV testing, behaviors, and knowledge among adolescents at high risk. *Journal of Adolescent Health, 20*(3), 216–225.

Rotheram-Borus, M. J., Koopman, C., & Ehrhardt, A. A. (1991). Homeless youths and HIV infection. *American Psychologist, 46*(11), 1188–1197.

Rotheram-Borus, M. J., Mahler, K. A., & Rosario, M. (1995). AIDS prevention with adolescents. *AIDS Education & Prevention, 7*(4), 320–336.

Russell, T. G. (1989). AIDS, education, homosexuality, and the counselor's role. *The School Counselor, 36*, 333–337.

Savin-Williams, R. (1989). Coming out to parents and self-esteem among gay and lesbian youths. *Journal of Homosexuality, 18*(1–2), 1–35.

Savin-Williams, R. C. (1994). Verbal and physical abuse as stressors in the lives of lesbian, gay male, and bisexual youths: Associations with school problems, running away, substance abuse, prostitution, and suicide. *Journal of Consulting & Clinical Psychology, 62*(2), 261–269.

Sears, J. T. (1992). Educators, homosexuality, and homosexual students: Are personal feelings related to professional beliefs? *Journal of Homosexuality, 22*(3–4), 29–79.

Shaffer, D., Fisher, P., Parides, M., & Gould, M. (1995). Sexual orientation in adolescents who commit suicide. *Suicide & Life-Threatening Behavior, 25*(Suppl.), 64–71.

Slater, B. R. (1988). Essential issues in working with lesbian and gay male youths. *Professional Psychology Research and Practice, 19*(2), 226–235.

Street, S. (1994). Adolescent male sexuality issues. *The School Counselor, 41*, 319–325.

Strommen, E. F. (1989). "You're what?": Family member reactions to the disclosure of homosexuality. *Journal of Homosexuality, 18*(1–2), 37–56.

Telljohann, S. K., & Price, J. H. (1993). A qualitative examination of adolescent homosexuals' life experiences: Ramifications for secondary school personnel. *Journal of Homosexuality, 26*(1), 41–56.

Tremble, B., Schneider, M., & Appathurai, C. (1989). Growing up gay or lesbian in a multicultural context. *Journal of Homosexuality, 17*(3–4), 253–267.

Wolf, A. E. (1991). *Get out of my life, but first could you drive me and Cheryl to the mall?* New York: The Noonday Press.

Zemsky, B. (1991). Coming out against all odds: Resistance in the life of a young lesbian. In C. Gilligan, A. G. Rogers, & D. L. Tolman (Eds.), *Women, girls & psychotherapy* (pp. 185–200). New York: Harrington Park Press.

# APPENDIX

| *Resource* | *Contact Information* | *A* | *B/V* | *C* | *Pol* | *Gl* | *LI* | *M/P* | *SD* | *SG* |
|---|---|---|---|---|---|---|---|---|---|---|
| Inclusive Curriculum: The Silent Minority Comes to the Classroom | Gay, Lesbian, Straight Education Network of Los Angeles (GLSEN/LA)<br>1125 McCadden Place, Suite 150<br>Los Angeles, CA 90038<br>(323) 460-4573<br>www.glsen.org | • | • | • | • | • | • | • | • | |
| Meeting the Needs of Sexual Minority Youth and Families | School Health Programs Department<br>San Francisco Unified School District<br>1512 Golden Gate Ave.<br>San Francisco, CA 94115<br>(415) 749-3400 | | • | | | • | • | • | • | |
| Project 10 | Gail Rolf,<br>Hamilton High School<br>Los Angeles Unified School District<br>2955 S. Robertson Blvd.<br>Los Angeles, CA 90034 | | | | | | | • | | • |
| The Safe Schools Resource Guide | Northwest Coalition Against Malicious Harassment<br>P.O. Box 16776<br>Seattle, WA 98116<br>(206) 233-9136<br>http://www.safeschools-wa.org/ | • | • | • | • | | | • | • | • |
| Strengthening the Learning Environment: A School Employees's Guide to Gay and Lesbian Issues | National Education Association<br>1201 16th Street, NW<br>Washington, DC 20036-3290<br>(202) 822-7700 | • | • | • | | | • | • | • | • |
| Tackling Gay Issues In School: A Resource Module | Planned Parenthood of Connecticut<br>129 Whitney Avenue<br>New Haven, CT 066<br>(203) 865-5158<br>PPCTLeif@aol.com | • | • | • | • | • | • | • | • | • |
| Working with Gay, Lesbian, and Bisexual Youth: A Resource Packet for Counselors and Educators | Suzy R. Thomas, M.A., P.P.S.<br>Division of Education<br>University of California, Davis<br>Davis, CA 95616 | • | • | | • | • | • | • | • | |

Key: A = Agencies, B/V = Books & Videos, C = Curriculum, Pol = Policy, Gl = Glossary, LI = Legal Issues, M/P = Mental & Physical Health, SD = Staff Development, SG = Support Groups.

CHAPTER

# 15

# Adolescent Parenthood: A Crisis for Males and Females

Barbara S. Hardy
Clark County School District, Henderson, NV

Adolescence is a period marked by rapid physical growth and social challenge of numerous complicated developmental tasks, and the need to adjust to physical, intellectual, social, and emotional changes. Today's adolescents' behavior is greatly influenced by various social variables at a younger age than those of past generations (National Research Council, 1987). In achieving an appropriate sense of identity, the adolescent must confront issues of anticipated future achievement, self-concept, relations with authority, and peer acceptance. Personal relationships become important and meaningful during this period, not only because of peer acceptance but also because of the need for intimacy with others, particularly with the opposite gender.

Since the earliest studies concerning sexual behavior between unmarried young people (Bromley & Britten, 1938; Davis, 1929; Hamilton, 1929) societal attitudes concerning sexual behavior have been gradually changing toward more tolerance of sexual expression of feelings (Dryer, 1982). The implications of society's increasingly tolerant attitudes and the adolescents' management of their sexual behavior should be areas of concern to the adolescent, parent, and educator. Knowing the needs of today's adolescents and the resulting behavior may help to provide proper guidance and direction for adolescents.

## SCOPE OF THE PROBLEM

### Adolescent Sexuality

Adolescent sexual behavior has increased markedly over the past two decades (Hofferth, Khan, & Baldwin, 1987). Although it is difficult to determine the reason for the rise in sexual activity among teenagers and college youth, some of the contributing factors include family structure, family relationships, physical maturation, behavior and personality characteristics, socioeconomic status, religion, sexual offense, use of drugs and alcohol, limited problem-solving strategies, and the lack of emphasis the educational system places on sex education (Boyer & Fine, 1992; DeRidder, 1993; Ohannessian & Crockett, 1993). The increase in sexual activity among adolescents began with the sexual revolution of the late 1960s, which was characterized by a sharp increase in premarital intercourse among adolescents. Trends that began in the late 1960s and 1970s that contributed to adolescent pregnancy include a rise in divorce rates, a more accepting attitude by society toward sexual behavior and "alternative" lifestyles, and the rise of the feminist movement. The lack of parental supervision has also contributed to the influx of sexual activity among adolescents (Olson, Huszti, & Youll, 1995). Research has shown that adolescents who lived with a single parent, lacked parental supervision, had poor relationships with their parents, or poor communication with their parent(s) were more likely to engage in sexual intercourse at a younger age (Olson et al., 1995). The availability of reliable birth control in the form of the pill, the birth control patch, birth control shot, and Norplant's have also contributed to the increase in sexual activity among adolescents (Corcoran, Franklin, & Bell, 1997). Today, one fourth of all 15 year-old girls are sexually active, one half by age 17, and three fourths by age 19. A survey of adolescents reported 73% of males and 65% of females in the United States have had sexual intercourse by age 18 (Alan Guttmacher Institute, 1994). Studies estimate that approximately 70% of all high school and college students are currently sexually active, and one third of these sexually active adolescents have had at least four sexual partners (DiClemente, 1990; Hein, 1992).

Between 1970 and 1992, the proportion of births to unwed teen mothers increased from 29% to 70% (National Center for Health Statistics, 1996). Although the number of sexually active teenagers has increased, the number of teenage marriages continues to decline. This decline in marriage may be attributed in part to the decreasing concern of teenagers to marry in order to legitimize a premaritally conceived child (Besharov & Gardiner, 1997).

### Prevalence of Pregnancy Among Adolescents

The teen birth rate has declined slowly from 1991 to 1996 with an overall drop of 12% for females ages 15 to 19. The birth rate for females 15 years of age is approximately 35% and for females 18 and 19 years old is 62% (Roditti, 1997). The rate of illegitimate births for females has increased dramatically since 1965 (Roditti, 1997). Most of these pregnancies are unintended. However, more than half of these females choose to bear their children (Roditti, 1997). More than one-half million children are born to teenagers in the United States annually, with most of these teenage mothers opting to raise their children (Alan Guttmacher Institute, 1994). Research indicates ethnic differences in birth rate among adolescents with the rate for Blacks being highest. Just as there are differences in birth rate, there are also ethnic differences in pregnancy management, with Black teens more likely than other teens to oppose abortion and choose to raise their child. White teenagers are more likely to marry before the birth of their child, to have an abortion, or to choose adoption (Roditti, 1997).

### Gender and Ethnic Differences in Sexuality and Attitudes Toward Pregnancy

Traditionally, permissiveness has been associated with higher educational levels, lower socioeconomic status (SES), greater sexual experience, greater age, being male, and being Black. Research consistently reports that males have engaged in sexual intercourse earlier than females and have had more sexual partners (Hofferth & Hayes, 1987).

Blacks have had and continue to have more permissive sexual attitudes than do Whites (Hofferth & Hayes, 1987). Although the proportion of sexually active Black teenagers tends to be higher than that of Whites, the increase in sexual activity among Whites has narrowed the gap (Hofferth & Hayes, 1987). Overall, approximately 40% of 18-year-old females in 1970 reported being sexually active (Besharov & Gardiner, 1997). In 1988, a survey revealed that the proportion of sexually active females age 18 or younger had increased to 70% (Besharov & Gardiner, 1997).

## CONTRIBUTIONS TO ADOLESCENT PREGNANCY

The explanations for adolescent pregnancy have varied since the 1920s. During the 1920s, bad peer associations and mental deficiency were considered to lead to adolescent pregnancy, whereas in the 1930s broken homes and poverty were associated with unwed motherhood. Psychological factors such as low educational goals and poor parent relationships were associated with pregnancy of the 1940s and there was a shift back to the sociological perspective of delinquent behavior in the 1950s (Foster & Miller, 1980). Since the 1960s, however, it has become apparent that there is no single cause of adolescent pregnancy, but many factors that interact (Ohannesian & Crockett, 1993; Roditti, 1997).

## Factors Associated With Adolescent Sexual Attitudes

***Sociological.*** Studies of factors associated with adolescent sexual attitudes have primarily focused on the sociological variables of race, educational level, nationality, and region of the United States (Dreyer, 1982). Although these factors remain important, there exist other sociological factors, as well as psychological and biological factors, that also contribute to adolescent sexual attitudes. In today's society our teenagers have greater exposure, via mass media such as television, movies, and magazines, to permissive sexual norms and explicit sexual activity.

There is probably no period in life when peer pressure is more influential than in adolescence. This pressure often leads to adolescents engaging in coitus with little or no consideration of the risks involved. If today's youth associate with peers who either have sexually permissive attitudes or are sexually active, they themselves tend to feel pressure to also become sexually active. In addition, many of today's teenagers are subjected to peer pressure both to be attractive to and to please the opposite sex (Corcoran et al., 1997; Olson et al., 1995, Roditti, 1997). The most important sociological factor contributing to adolescent pregnancy concerns societal standards regarding sex education. Teenagers risk pregnancy by being misinformed, not being informed early enough, or being ill-informed on sexuality, sexual relationships, and contraception because sex education is not taught well or at all in the schools. As a result, the burden rests on the parents to educate their adolescents about these topics. Unfortunately, parents have not accepted this challenge, with the result that today's youth are never properly exposed to this information (Corcoran et al., 1997; Olson et al., 1995).

***Psychological.*** Psychological factors are also contributors to adolescent coitus (Roditti, 1997). Low educational aspirations, an unhappy home life, beliefs in commitment to a partner, and lack of self-control have been associated with early sexual activity, particularly in teenagers from low socioeconomic backgrounds. These factors lead to a sense of hopelessness and helplessness where sexuality is the only arena for achievement and the source of gratification. Limited communication between parents and youth and poor relationships with one's parents are additional factors contributing to adolescent coitus. Because of a poor relationship with one's parents, teenagers tend to reject parental standards, thus leading them to engage in sexual relationships to escape the home environment. The need for the affection that youth have not been and are not receiving from their parents often encourages the teenager to engage in a relationship to meet this need (Roditti, 1997). Some adolescent females believe that a baby and/or a commitment from a partner will address the emptiness in their life. They believe that a baby will fill the void of love and affection not received during childhood from their parents. Additionally, as a consequence of possessing strong feelings for a male, some adolescent females engage in coitus, which may result in pregnancy and possibly a commitment by the child's father (Roditti, 1997).

In younger adolescents, self-control is not as well developed as it is in older adolescents. This lack of self-control increases the desire for affection, dependency, and self-esteem among adolescents, making the adolescent more vulnerable psychologically and leading to early participation in coitus (Roditti, 1997).

***Biological.*** The biological factors associated with adolescent coitus are limited. As a result of the baby boom following World War II there are more adolescents today. There are more women between the ages of 15 and 19 than there were in 1950. Today's youth also reach puberty at an earlier age. Peer pressure strongly influences an adolescent's sexual behavior, and may influence younger adolescents more because they are more vulnerable (Olson et al., 1995).

### Factors Associated With Use of Contraception

Researchers have found that cognitive ability is a significant predictor of decision making regarding the use of contraceptives (Green & Johnson, 1993). Knowledge about contraception and the use of contraceptives has not kept up with the increase of sexual activity among adolescents (Corcoran et al., 1997; DeRidder, 1993; Olson et al., 1995; Roditti, 1997). The sexually active female now has birth control options to explore. The birth control pill continues to be an option for sexually active females. Alternatively, the adolescent female may choose a birth control shot that is effective for a 3-month period, or norplants, which are implants that the female puts under her skin. Norplants are similar to the birth control pill but work in a time release fashion. National surveys from 1979 to 1988 reported an increase in condom use for adolescent males (Ku, Sonenstein, & Pleck, 1992; Pleck, Sonenstein, & Ku, 1993). Data from studies (Besharov & Gardiner, 1997) show that only 31% of White female teens and 41% of Black female teens used contraceptives at the time of their first intercourse. Condom use increased during the 1990s. According to Abma, Chandra, Nosher, Peterson, and Piccinino, (1997), 77% of teenage females were using contraceptives in 1995. This increase may be attributed to the adolescent being able to obtain condoms without the consent of their parents. However, research has reported that approximately 90% of Blacks and 70% of Whites who were sexually active in high school had unprotected intercourse at least once, and the number of adolescents engaging in unprotected sexual activity continues to be of concern (Olson et al., 1995).

Teenagers risk pregnancy by not being properly informed about contraception (DeRidder, 1993). Even following instruction on contraceptive methods, they continue to believe that contraception limits the naturalness of sexual relations, that contraceptives may be physically harmful, or that contraceptives are not necessary because pregnancy could never happen to them (Foster & Miller, 1980). The longer an adolescent female is involved in a relationship, however, the more likely she is to use contraceptives and to use them effectively.

A lack of contraceptive use may be attributed to several factors. In some instances, there is a reliance of adolescent women upon men for contraceptive use. National surveys between 1979 and 1988 reported an increase in condom use among males between the ages of 17 and 19 from 21% in 1979 to 58% in 1988 (Forest & Singh, 1990; Pleck, Sonenstein, & Ku, 1990; Sonenstein, Pleck, & Ku, 1991). A contributing factor to a female adolescent's poor use of contraceptives may be associated with the fact that many teenage females are ambivalent about getting pregnant and do not fear pregnancy (Corcoran et al., 1997).

Because many adolescent females have difficulty accepting their sexual activity, they ignore the use of contraceptives. However, this concept does not appear to be true of females over age 18. These older adolescents are more likely to accept their sexual activity, choose to use contraceptives, and use contraceptives effectively. Characteristics of females using contraceptives include involvement with one man over an extended period of time or engagement in intercourse regularly, which leads to planning for sexual activity. Adolescent females from middle and upper socioeconomic classes are more likely to use contraceptive methods than are females from low socioeconomic backgrounds. Previous experience of having an abortion or a baby as well as the fear of pregnancy are other factors influencing the use of contraceptive methods (Corcoran et al., 1997).

## PRIMARY PREVENTION OF PREGNANCY

Both state and federal programs continue to be conservative in their allotment of money toward pregnancy prevention (Olson et al., 1995). Thus, there is a strong need for sex education in the schools. Rather than wait until adolescence, this education should begin in the elementary years. Emphasis upon reproduction, methods of contraception by males and females, and instruction on sexuality should be stressed. It is increasingly important that schools incorporate sex education into their curricula. Although sex education is provided and attempts are being made to focus on sexual activity of today's adolescents, research indicates that more comprehensive programs are needed (Hardy & Zabin, 1991). Today's sex education programs fail to address interpersonal skills, which are needed for the adolescent in order to develop appropriate alternative relationships in line with society's expectations (Olson et al., 1995). Sex education programs should also include topics such as decision making, peer counseling, peer resistance training, behavioral skills training, and decreasing risk-taking behavior (Brooks-Gunn & Furstenberg, 1989). The reluctance to provide education in birth control is consistent with the approach of federal agencies that currently promote sexual abstinence as the most effective method of contraception (Everett, 1984).

School psychologists advocating education on contraception should, therefore, be aware of the possible controversy such a position may provoke. Schools should provide programs designed to emphasize parenting skills, child development, and awareness of community resources (Roditti, 1997). With schools reluctant to educate youth regarding family planning, community-based services designed to meet the special needs of adolescents are a necessity, and practitioners might consider coordinating services with agencies such as Planned Parenthood, Maternal and Infant Care Projects, Pregnancy Prevention Programs, and Teenage Pregnancy and Parenting Projects. Despite controversy about the success of such programs, research indicates that family planning programs and pregnancy prevention programs are successful (Roditti, 1997).

Although schools may provide sex education for the adolescent, more informative instruction on sexuality and contraception is imperative at an earlier age. Programs for upper elementary school children designed to help them understand the physical changes they are to encounter should be incorporated into the curriculum. Junior high and high school programs should de-emphasize instruction of human physiology and examine such topics as dating, premarital relationships, and various aspects of marriage and family life (Corcoran et al., 1997). Programs that discuss an individual's rights, needs, and desires in a relationship may help adolescents decide whether to involve themselves in a sexual commitment (Corcoran et al., 1997). The education of school personnel by professionals who, themselves, have been trained to deal with adolescent sexual dilemmas may foster more effective school programs (Brooks-Gunn & Furstenberg, 1989; Corcoran et al., 1997). With the high rate of adolescent pregnancy it is crucial that schools incorporate sex education into their curricula. Besides improving awareness of contraceptives, counseling goals should be to develop responsibility, socialization skills, personal efficacy, and a positive orientation to future goals. The school psychologist or other guidance personnel should encourage the adolescent to accept his or her sexuality and the adult responsibility that sexual activity connotes. These individuals must learn to accept the conventions of society, take responsibility for their actions, develop a feeling of competency, and establish an internal locus of control of reinforcement. The school psychologist should help each teenager to develop coping and problem-solving skills relating to sexuality, which include knowledge of birth control and reproduction. The school psychologist should help teenagers to plan for their future by emphasizing the importance of future goals.

Programs designed to further the education and counseling of adolescents' parents regarding sexuality and birth control may also be warranted. Increasing parent knowledge of adolescent concerns can help them to better guide their teenagers through difficult decisions regarding intimate relationships during adolescence (Corcoran et al., 1997).

School psychologists can play a variety of roles in these primary prevention activities thereby increasing school personnel and adolescents' awareness of the psychologist as someone both interested in and capable of providing services to adolescent parents. As experts in psychosexual development, they may effectively provide teacher training in skills needed to counsel adolescents concerning sexual issues. They might also serve as guest instructors for sex education classes focusing on personal values and relationship responsibilities. As a liaison between the school, adolescents, and their parents, psychologists may actively coordinate parent groups, the goal of which is to empower parents to open communication regarding sexual matters. Primary prevention programs should begin in elementary school and extend through high school.

## SECONDARY PREVENTION

Teenage pregnancy results in risks to both the adolescent parents and the child. The adolescent parents are faced with social and emotional issues. The child is at multiple risks physically, socially, and cognitively (Corcoran et al., 1997). The child may suffer medical complications resulting from prematurity, inadequate prenatal care by the mother, and a marginal nutritional status of the mother during pregnancy. Thus, the role of the psychologist in counseling the adolescent parents should be twofold. First, the practitioner must increase the adolescent female's awareness of the importance of good health and regular visits to the physician during the pregnancy. Second, the psychologist must provide to the adolescent parents information regarding the risks involved to both of them as well as the child.

The emphasis of secondary prevention programs should be on identifying and serving those adolescent females who have a possibility of becoming pregnant and who would be excellent candidates for special counseling programs. Although some aspects of these programs may be similar to primary prevention programs, the population served and the counseling goals differ slightly.

There are many demographic, situational, and psychological characteristics of women less likely to use contraceptives or to use them effectively. Demographic variables include being less than 18 years of age, being single, having a low SES, being a minority, and religious beliefs. Situationally, the female at risk is usually not in a steady relationship, has never been pregnant, has infrequent intercourse, and has a lack of family planning services, parental guidance, and friends using contraceptives. Psychologically, the female may have a desire for pregnancy, or have an ignorance of family planning or risk of pregnancy. The adolescent female may possess a risk-taking or pleasure-seeking attitude, have an unrealistic view of sexual behavior, be highly anxious, and fear side effects and infertility from the use of contraceptives. These females, along with academically low-achieving females, lonely sexually active females, and females who have been pregnant before are excellent candidates for special preventive programs. Because today's youth are given little consistent guidance for their sexual attitudes and behaviors, adolescents usually are ambivalent about their own sexual attitudes and behaviors and are good candidates for counseling (Roditti, 1997).

There are several aspects that such a program should address with sexually active females. First might be a focus on relationships and why the teenage female wants to or feels the need to engage in a sexual relationship. Various contraceptive measures and consequences for engaging in coitus without the use of contraceptives should be emphasized. During the program, the female should receive assistance in seriously examining her future goals and how she might pursue them. The guidance counselor or psychologist should try to help the adolescent imagine how achievement of these goals may be more difficult should she have a child to raise. It is imperative that the psychologist or guidance counselor promotes an open-door policy that encourages teenagers to come and discuss personal situations without feeling embarrassed or threatened. In a school setting, the psychologist or guidance counselor may hear of females who may benefit from this program. When this occurs the counselor should seek out these females and encourage them to share problems. The counselor should provide information about adolescence and sexuality. Literature should be made available on contraceptives to enhance female awareness. Literature on outside agencies may also prove useful. To insure the continuation of these teenagers returning for advice or support, confidentiality must be established early.

## CRISIS INTERVENTION

The adolescent involved in teen pregnancy confronts two maturational crises in addition to those arising from adolescence—the challenges of adulthood, and the acceptance of parenthood. At a time when support systems are needed, the adolescent discovers there are few resources available for either help or support. Crisis counseling by school psychologists can be beneficial in filling this void. The psychologist can serve both the male and female adolescent involved in pregnancy by offering support and a non-judgmental attitude, serving as confidant, informing the adolescent of alternatives and resources, and assisting with decision making. Crisis counseling should be directed toward helping individuals accept responsibility for their situation and developing strategies for coping with the pregnancy.

## The Adolescent Female

During counseling the practitioner must not only provide information, but also carefully listen to and assess the individual's reasoning and logic to ensure that alternatives have been thoroughly examined before decisions are reached (Resnick, 1984). In counseling the female adolescent, the school psychologist should prepare her for emotional crisis that may be precipitated by: (a) discovering and confirming the pregnancy; (b) disclosing the pregnancy to others; (c) having to make decisions regarding pregnancy alternatives; (d) experiencing labor and delivery; (e) confronting alternatives for raising the child; and (f) having to reassess educational goals.

During the discovery and confirmation period, the psychologist should explore the teenager's feelings and fears about the possible pregnancy. During this time the teenager expresses guilt, hostility, and anger. Should the adolescent find she is not pregnant, family planning, as well as referring the individual to information on sexuality may be recommended. Should the diagnosis of pregnancy by the physician be positive, the psychologist must establish a support system and a trusting relationship with the adolescent. Disclosing the pregnancy to others is one of the most difficult tasks for the adolescent. The psychologist can ameliorate anxiety through positive approaches such as role plays to help prepare the person for others' reactions, or being present to offer support and guidance when the female informs others (Roditti, 1997).

One of the greatest problems for the pregnant adolescent is maintaining a relationship with her own parents. Depending on the age of the minor, in some states the parents will have some say about the decisions that will be made. In any case, they will need to be informed about the pregnancy at some point. The issue of communication with parents must be dealt with squarely and techniques to help the pregnant teenager prepare for the reactions of her parents must be included in counseling.

The practitioner must be prepared to assist teenagers in deciding whether or not to maintain the pregnancy, and if deciding to bear the child, whether to release the child for adoption. Over the last few years, the decision for adoption has decreased among adolescents (Roditti, 1997). The decision to relinquish a child for adoption has been guided to cultural beliefs or the ability to financially care for a child (Musick, 1993). It is common among African American and Latino families to have the child raised by a family member rather than place the child up for adoption; however, Caucasian families are more likely to relinquish their child (Musick, 1993). Regardless of whether the adolescent chooses to abort, adopt, or keep the child, counseling should continue beyond the point of decision. Depending on the adolescent's choice, the practitioner should assist in contacting appropriate agencies or in enrolling the young parent in classes that offer support and skills necessary for child rearing (Roditti, 1997). Anticipatory guidance will prove useful as well as an examination of postchoice emotions such as guilt and depression.

The psychologist should reinforce the importance of education and encourage its continuation during and after the pregnancy. The greatest difficulty the adolescent will face will be the ability to cope with the reactions of peers and teachers. The adolescent will probably feel singled out, alienated, and different from her peers. Thus, it is incumbent upon the psychologist to prepare the individual for these reactions and to explore alternative educational experiences such as homebound programs and adult education.

During the pregnancy, the teenager will have fears about labor and delivery. The Psychologist must help the adolescent develop adaptive strategies for coping with childbirth. Attendance at childbirth classes should be recommended. The psychologist may assume the role of explaining and discussing labor and delivery to the adolescent (Foster & Miller, 1980).

### The Adolescent Male

Little attention or support has been given to the adolescent male in programs or literature involving teenage parenthood; yet adolescent fathers are also in need of guidance and counseling. Research indicates that they are willing to participate in counseling, particularly when there is a lack of friends with whom to share their feelings, fears, and concerns (Barret & Robinson, 1981). Participation of the adolescent father, however, rests on his awareness of the programs and the individuals that can assist him. The psychologist might seek out adolescent fathers in neighborhoods or in schools rather than wait for them to come for help, but how and if this is done depends on rights of privacy and confidentiality. In order to make services less threatening and woman-oriented, male psychologists should be available. Expectant father support groups can be formed to provide youths the opportunity to share feelings, fears, concerns, and solutions, and reduce the social isolation common to adolescent fatherhood. Finally, the psychologist can assist in locating teen-parent programs that teach parenting and coping skills.

Adolescent fathers have a variety of needs and concerns. In crisis counseling, the school psychologist should prepare the male for emotional upheaval that may be initiated by (a) a lack of involvement or control in the pregnancy decision and later child care; (b) communication problems with the mother; (c) a lack of communication with members of the mother's family; (d) a reexamination of educational goals; (e) financial obligations to the child and mother; (f) the restriction of freedom concomitant with fatherhood; and (g) the minimal visitation rights with the child after birth. Because of his young age, the adolescent father is typically ill-prepared psychologically for the demands posed by these issues (Barret & Robinson, 1981).

Because the adolescent father may be ambivalent regarding the pregnancy, the school psychologist should inform him of the alternatives and encourage him to discuss these with the mother. The practitioner may assist in the couple's decision-making process by facilitating communication during the couple's discussion of alternatives. The adolescent father is usually not cognizant of his role as caretaker and provider (Roditti, 1997). Because this role may interfere with attainment of educational goals, the psychologist should reiterate the importance of education, assist in the adolescent's re-examination of these goals, and provide alternatives to the male for achieving these goals when faced with financial obligations.

Paternal involvement with the mother and child following pregnancy can be problematic. Cattanach (1976) reported only 29% of unmarried mothers continued seeing the father one or more times per week following pregnancy. Although the majority of adolescent fathers maintain contact with their children for up to 5 years after birth, visitation frequency declines. Explanations for the decline in involvement by adolescent fathers with their child include lack of employment, substance abuse, incarceration, and poor quality education (Roditti, 1997). Given that paternal involvement contributes to the cognitive and social development of a child, the psychologist should encourage the adolescent to maintain the contact important for the child's development.

Accepting responsibility in the pregnancy, overcoming feelings of guilt, depression, and adjusting to the social isolation often accompanying fatherhood are issues to be confronted during counseling (Barret & Robinson, 1981). As for the adolescent mother, services for the father should be provided not only during the pregnancy, but should continue into the postpartum period as the father copes with his paternal role and responsibilities.

## The Adolescent Couple

Within the first 12 weeks, the adolescent parents must make a decision about the pregnancy. The adolescents are faced with two alternatives: to terminate or to continue the pregnancy. If the second alternative is chosen, the parents must decide between keeping the baby or giving it up for adoption. The psychologist's responsibility is to present both alternatives and to provide the adolescent parents with the opportunity to explore each. The psychologist should aid in the discussion of each alternative. If the parents choose to terminate the pregnancy, they will need support and counseling before and following the abortion to resolve any feelings of guilt.

Should the parents opt to keep the baby, the psychologist should provide a support system. The psychologist will need to assist the adolescent parents in coping with the frustration of pregnancy and the attitudes significant others may have of them during the pregnancy. During the postpartum period the psychologist should continue to offer support and serve as a resource to assist in teaching parenting skills and in identifying vulnerable areas in the bond that exists between the mother and child. Should adolescent parents choose adoption, they must first accept the reality of the baby's existence. Although in the past mothers were not allowed to see their baby before giving it up, today professionals believe differently. Today it is felt that the mother should be allowed to see her child before giving it up for adoption. The psychologist's role proves to be invaluable to the adolescent mother and father during this period. Because the adolescent parents may feel grief over their decision, it is imperative that the psychologist serve as a support and a resource of reinforcement in helping the parents in accepting their decision of adoption (Roditti, 1997).

## SUMMARY

Adolescence is a time for many changes for both the adolescent male and female. These individuals experience cognitive, physical, and emotional changes that significantly impact their lives. Data has shown that an increasing number of adolescents are becoming sexually active at earlier ages. The most vulnerable teenagers are those that are coming from a home characterized by a lack of family structure, sexual abuse, and low SES. The alienation from the use of drugs and alcohol also contribute to teen pregnancy. These factors lead to low self-esteem among adolescents, vulnerability to pressure from peers, and poor educational goals by the adolescent. However, it is difficult for the practitioner to provide the range of services essential in a program to help adolescents involved in teen pregnancy. Not only should the school psychologist assist in providing programs that emphasize decision making, peer counseling, contraception, and strategies to deal with peer pressure, he or she should also provide the adolescent parents with information about community services and resources. The school psychologist should also help the teenage parents feel better about themselves, accept their sexuality, and develop coping strategies to adjust psychologically to their new role as parents. The key to developing a better self-concept during this trying period is through an active and continuous counseling program.

The role of the school psychologist should be to provide services to both parents. Although it is more difficult to engage the teenage father in a counseling program, the psychologist should seek out these males, provide male practitioners to them for counseling, and encourage them to actively participate in the pregnancy as well as the decision-making process. Just as with female youth, counseling with males should continue beyond the postpartum period.

During the provision of services, the school psychologist must be accepting of the adolescents confronting this crisis by maintaining a nonjudgmental attitude. The practitioner must also provide an environment in which the adolescents feel safe to discuss their feelings and concerns. In addition, the school psychologist plays a vital role in offering pregnancy alternatives and facilitating problem-solving strategies. The psychologist should continue to reinforce the importance of education by offering educational alternatives and assist in developing ways to maintain the adolescent parents' interest in the continuation of their education.

## REFERENCES


Abma, J. C., Chandra, A., Nosher, W., Peterson, L., & Piccinino, L. (1997). Fertility, family planning and women's health: New data from the 1995 National Survey of Family Growth. *National Center for Health Statistics Vital Health Statistics, 23*(9).

Alan Guttmacher Institute. (1994). *Sex and America's teenagers.* New York: Author.

Barret, R. L., & Robinson, B. E. (1981). Teenage fathers: A profile. *Personnel and Family Journal, 60,* 226–228.

Besharov, D. J., & Gardiner, K. N. (1997). Trends in teen sexual behavior. *Children and Youth Services Review, 19*(5/6) 341–367.

Bromley, D., & Britten, F. (1938). *Youth and sex.* New York: Harper & Row.

Brooks-Gunn, J., & Furstenberg, F., Jr. (1989). Adolescent sexual behavior. *American Psychologist, 44,* 249–257.

Boyer, D., & Fine, D. (1992). Sexual abuse as a factor in adolescent pregnancy and child maltreatment. *Family Planning Perspectives, 24,* 4–11.

Cattanach, T. J. (1976). Coping with intentional pregnancies among unmarried teenagers. *The School Counselor, 23,* 211–215.

Corcoran, J., Franklin, C., & Bell, H. (1997). Pregnancy prevention from the teen perspective. *Child and Adolescent Social Work Journal, 14*(5), 365–382.

Davis, K. (1929). *Factors in the sex life of twenty-two hundred women.* New York: Harper & Row.

DeRidder, L. M. (1993). Teenage pregnancy. Etiology and educational interventions. *Educational Psychology Review, 5*(1), 87–107.

DiClemente, R. J. (1990). The emergence of adolescents as a risk group of human inmmunodeficiency virus infection. *Journal of Adolescent Research, 5,* 7–17.

Dreyer, P. H. (1982). Sexuality during adolescence. In B. B. Wolman (Ed.), *Handbook of developmental psychology* (pp. 559–601). Englewood Cliffs, NJ: Prentice-Hall.

Everett, B. A. (1984, October). Adolescent pregnancy. *Washington report, 1.* Washington, DC: Society for Research in Child Development.

Forrest, J. D., & Singh, S. (1990). The sexual and reproductive behavior of American women, 1982–1988. *Family Planning Perspectives, 22,* 206–214.

Foster, C. D., & Miller, G. M. (1980). Adolescent pregnancy: A challenge for counselors. *Personnel and Guidance Journal, 58,* 236–240.

Green, V., & Johnson, S. (1993). Female adolescent contraceptive decision-making regarding contraceptive usage. *Adolescence, 27,* 613–632.

Hamilton, G. (1929). *A research in marriage.* New York: A. & C. Boni.

Hardy, J. B., & Zabin, L. S. (1991). *Adolescent pregnancy in an urban environment.* Washington, DC: Urban Institute Press.

Hein, K. (1992). Adolescents at risk for HIV infection. *Adolescent Medicine, 14,* 101–121.

Hofferth, S. L., & Hayes, C. D. (Eds.). (1987). *Risking the future: Adolescent sexuality, pregnancy, and childbearing* (Vol. 2). Washington, DC: National Academy Press.

Hofferth, S. L., Khan, J. R., & Baldwin, W. (1987). Premarital sexual activity among U.S. teenage women over the past three decades. *Family Planning Perspectives, 19,* 46–53.

Ku, L. C., Sonenstein, F. L., & Pleck, J. H. (1992). The association of AIDS education and sex education with sexual behavior and condom use among teenage men. *Family Planning Perspectives, 24,* 100–106.

Musick, J. S. (1993). *Young, poor and pregnant: The psychology of teenage motherhood.* New Haven, CT: Yale University Press.

National Center for Health Statistics. (1996). Advance report on final natality statistics, 1994. *Monthly Vital Statistics Report, 44*(11), 1–88.

National Research Council. (1987). *Risking the future: Adolescent sexuality, pregnancy, and childbearing* (Vol. 1). Washington, DC: National Academy Press.

Ohannessian, C., & Crockett, L. (1993). A longitudinal investigation of the relationship between educational investment and adolescent sexual activity. *Journal of Adolescent Research, 8,* 167–182.

Olson, R., Huszti, H., & Youll, L. K. (1995). Sexual behaviors and problems of adolescents. In M. C. Roberts (Ed.), *Handbook of pediatric psychology* (pp. 327–341). New York: Guilford Press.

Pleck, J. H., Sonenstein, F. L., & Ku, L. C. (1990). Contraceptive attitudes and intention to use condoms in sexually experienced and inexperienced adolescent males. *Journal of Family Issues, 11,* 294–299.

Pleck, J. H., Sonenstein, F. L., & Ku, L. C. (1993). Changes in adolescent males' use of and attitudes toward condoms, 1988–1991. *Family Planning Perspectives, 25,* 106–117.

Resnick, M. D. (1984). Studying adolescent mothers' decision making about adoption and parenting. *Social Work, 29,* 5–10.

Roditti, M. (1997). Urban teen parents. In N. K. Phillips & S. L. A. Straussner (Eds.), *Children in the urban environment: Linking social policy and clinical practice* (pp. 93–112). Springfield, IL: Thomas.

Sonenstein, F. L., Pleck, J. H., & Ku, L. C. (1991). *Levels of sexual activity among adolescent males in the United States.* Unpublished paper, Wellesley College, Center for Research on Women, Wellesley, MA.

CHAPTER

# 16

# Parent–Adolescent Crises

**Marvin J. Fine**
University of Kansas

**Linda D. Robert**
Kansas City, Kansas Public Schools

**Jonathan Sandoval**
University of California, Davis

A number of experts writing on adolescence have emphasized the increased stress on the adolescent brought about by significant societal changes. Many of these changes relate to the home and include economic stress, divorce, and the need for both parents to be employed. There are also "culture shock" changes regarding music, clothing, hair styles, and body "ornamentation" that can create an even greater gap between the growing up experiences of parents and their children (Elkind, 1984, 1994; Preto & Travis, 1985; Youniss & Smollar, 1985).

Parent–adolescent crises often occur within the context of the adolescent's striving for independence. The crisis may revolve around some specific concern ranging from choice of friends, curfew, clothing styles, and the use of the family car, through school performance and grades, to drug and alcohol use, sexual behavior, depression, and threats of suicide. But the underlying issue is frequently that of the adolescent's move toward a more equal position vis-à-vis the parents. It is also important to note that the characterization of adolescence as a period of great stress and conflict appears to be an overgeneralization when applied to virtually all persons between 13 and 19 years of age. Although it can be a time of remarkable turbulence and change, most adolescents weather this period well and get on with their lives. The popular literature dramatizes the problems of adolescents rather than their successes and positive contributions.

And yet the information available on the problems adolescents experience does underscore the potential for numerous crises during this period. A recent review by Arnett (1999) of adolescent "storm and stress" highlighted that this is a period of risk-taking (including injury to self and others), with rates of crime rising along with rates of substance abuse rising until the late teens. As many counselors will testify, adolescents who violate legal boundaries such as drug use will often speak of their intention to control these behaviors once they become 18 years old and will be treated as an adult by the legal system. Teenagers also view adolescence as a time of rebellion against authority during which they are immune to consequences.

When a crisis occurs there are several avenues of intervention available to school mental health professionals within the short-term and action-oriented parameters of crisis intervention. Crisis intervention focuses initially on the present situation with a problem-solving orientation. The immediate goal is typically to restabilize a situation before moving into a more proactive and ameliorative stance. Although a family orientation would encourage the mental health professional to include concurrently student and parent, this may not always be feasible or even desirable. Specific interventions to handle the crisis could focus on the student or on the parents alone. In other situations the parent and student may need to acquire more effective communication and problem-solving skills through separate sessions before coming together. It may also be appropriate to include others in the intervention plan such as teachers whose actions or reactions are connected to the crisis event. These are judgments that the involved school mental health person will need to make.

This chapter examines parent–adolescent crises against the background of the child growing up within a healthy family system. Characteristics of healthy families include clear generational boundaries, support within the family for changing roles and expectations of children as they mature, and constructive communication patterns. The "normal" crises of adolescence can become exacerbated when nested within a dysfunctional family. The kinds of behavior that get defined as a crisis, who gets involved and how they respond, and traditional patterns of crisis resolution emerge in part out of the family background with its history of parent–child relationships. New potential for easing parent–adolescent crises lies in the presence of a school-based mental health professional; the school psychologist, counselor, or social worker. This person can assume leadership in (a) anticipating a crisis and behaving proactively, (b) responding at the time of crisis, and (c) helping the involved parties to exploit the opportunities inherent in a crisis situation toward the modification of crisis-precipitating factors.

## A VIEW OF CRISIS INTERVENTION

The ensuing discussion draws on the general crisis intervention literature, much of which has already been presented in earlier chapters, but will underscore specific aspects of crisis intervention germane to parent–adolescent crises.

In recent years there has been an increase in both quantity of literature on crisis intervention in the schools and on the quality of conceptualization and theory building around crisis intervention (Pitcher & Poland, 1992; Steele & Raider, 1991). Most persons would agree with Aguilera and Messick (1978) that "The goal of crisis intervention is the resolution of an immediate crisis. Its focus is on the generic present, with the restoration of the individual to his precrisis level of functioning or probably to a higher level of functioning" (p. 26).

But what is an "immediate crisis," and how is this concept useful in relation to parent–adolescent crises? Certainly, the sudden precipitation of an event such as the student verbally threatening or physically attacking a teacher, or the school contacting the parents to report that their teenager passed out intoxicated at a school dance, would be generally classified as a crisis. Both of these events are likely to energize concerned persons such as school officials and parents, into an active role. It is a crisis for these adults, but one must ask, is it a crisis for the adolescent?

Even though there is evidence of a precipitating event, the awareness and involvement of persons may differ. For example, in one situation, a student may appear to others to be getting along well, but in another situation may act strangely enough to concern family members, teachers, or friends. Although often in retrospect people can identify some indicators that sensitive observers, parents, friends, and others should have noticed, at the time, the behaviors were cloaked enough to cover up their crisis nature. As another example of how an event can become a crisis, consider the instance of a student deciding to quit school. This declaration by the student might provoke a strong, angry parental reaction and create a great deal of turmoil in the family. But the student may have experienced a long history of school failure with continuing parent–adolescent bickering over grades, homework, and study time. Although these problems were annoying and troublesome, it was only the decision of the student actually to drop out of school that precipitated a "crisis."

Much of the literature on crisis intervention deals with life-threatening, desperate kinds of situations, with suicide and homicide being prime examples. The prospect of adolescent suicide has historically been of great concern to the professional community and families (Grob, Klein, & Eisen, 1983; Jacobs, 1980). The horrifying school shootings over the last several years have alarmed the nation and generated much activity in schools regarding detection of individuals-at-risk, prevention and crisis response programs. But the preponderance of involvement by school mental health professionals is much broader and often less dramatic in focus. Admittedly, crisis issues will vary from one situation to another but the greater frequency of adolescent crises are issues such as school failure, dropping-out, visible depression, drug and alcohol abuse, aggressive and assaultive acts, pregnancy and the discovery of alternative sexual orientations, and thefts and vandalism. Additionally, one can envision home-based conflicts between parent and adolescent that are at an impasse, spilling over into the school setting and correspondingly involving school-based personnel.

The question of "who has the problem?" can present a dilemma to the school mental health professional. Although society, in the form of teachers, parents, policemen, or the courts, may perceive the adolescent as being in crisis, the young person may insist he or she can manage without outside help. Sometimes the adolescent is seeing a situation clearly and has good coping skills; the problem is in the adults.

However, an adolescent may voluntarily seek out the mental health professional or may confide in a teacher that he or she is experiencing a high stress situation and is having difficulty coping. The student may indeed be in crisis although no one has noticed. A third possibility is that persons familiar with the adolescent and who learn about mental health crisis indicators (e.g., moodiness, irritability, reclusiveness, breaking relationships, changes in sleeping or eating habits, sudden drop in grades, and so on), now become concerned. They view the adolescent as one who is in crisis and who needs help, even though the adolescent is unconcerned as are his or her family and school authorities.

These multiple possibilities for a student coming to the attention of the school mental health professional raise the question of whether the professional should initiate contact with an "involuntary" client. Contact places the student in the position to refuse involvement and to tell the professional that someone else (i.e., the concerned other) has the problem. Connected to the voluntarism issue is the important question of when should parents be involved? Fine (1982) spoke to that question in relation to counseling adolescents:

> A number of adolescents have conflict around gaining independence and autonomy, and the involvement of their parents may escalate the adolescent's anger . . . it may be judicious in some cases to keep the parents out, until the adolescent feels more comfortable and prepared to deal with them in a counseling situation. (pp. 396–397)

Such judgments may be inappropriate in crisis situations where legal considerations or the nature of the crisis may prompt the mental health professional to contact and involve parents. Concerns with the adolescent's potential for suicide or self-injurious behavior or injurious behavior to others are common examples of where the mental health professional will notify parents and other authorities.

## THE FAMILY CONTEXT OF ADOLESCENCE

Erikson's (1968) writings on the identity issues of adolescence helped professionals and indeed parents to better understand what adolescents might be experiencing. The adolescent's questioning of family values, stronger peer-group identification, and emotional reactivity were seen as the adolescent's struggle to establish a sense of personal identity. The adolescent's need to experience competence and power also become moving forces in terms of the adolescent forming new relationships, seeking new experiences, and asserting him or herself more within the family. Jones (1980) described how adolescents who are unable to achieve a sense of personal significance, competence, and power tend to exhibit behavior problems.

Many experts (Ames, 1988; Barkley, Edwards, & Robin, 1999; Dinkmeyer, McKay, McKay, & Dinkmeyer, 1998; Elium & Elium, 1999; Elkind, 1993; Ginott, 1969; Gordon, 1989) have presented useful information to parents on how to set limits, discipline, communicate, and negotiate differences, as well as how to separate their concern for the child's behavior from their continuing love and support of the child. What has been missing from some of the popular books and texts on adolescent development is a picture of the family as an organized entity, and how adolescents develop and interact within the family. It is a complex picture because it is within the family context that the adolescent is experiencing physical, cognitive, and emotional changes. The readily observable physical changes of adolescence can obfuscate the fact that important internal cognitive changes are also occurring (Elkind, 1984; Youniss & Smollar, 1985). The adolescent reasons at a higher level than the younger child and is better able to reflect on issues and indeed on thought, and can comprehend "gray areas." Simultaneously, however, there is a greater emotional investment in friends and the potential for highly moralistic stances. The parents' apparent hypocrisies are revealed and played back. "Well, you drink hard liquor while all I do is have a few beers"; "Your constant cigarette smoking is worse than my occasional pot smoking."

The literature focusing narrowly on the adolescent, his or her response to pubescence, and the personal identity issues, has not paid enough attention to the overall family development picture, parental changes and stress, and the interaction effects of parent–adolescent and family–adolescent relationships (Leigh & Peterson, 1986). Parents can differ markedly in their parenting styles and in their readiness to cope with the challenges presented by adolescents. Arnett's recent excellent review while devoting a section to "conflict with parents" did not deal with the bidirectionality and systemic nature of the parent–adolescent relationship (Arnett, 1999). In contrast, Hughes and Noppe (1991) expressed an appreciation for the stress that families with an adolescent may be experiencing in terms of the multiple demands on the parents to meet their own needs, possibly be dealing with their aged parents, and also attempting to cope with an adolescent.

This point is underscored by Kidwell, Fischer, Dunham, and Baranowski's (1983) observation that "much of the stress expressed by families during the adolescent years arises out of normative life stage developmental events, experienced to varying degrees in all families in which there is an adolescent" (p. 75). But families by their history, parenting, and interactive styles will cope differentially with a crisis event.

## DYNAMICS OF PARENT ADOLESCENT CRISES

The earlier protective and controlling functions of the family for its child members need to change as children mature into adolescence (Elkind, 1984, 1994; Leigh & Peterson, 1986; Preto & Travis, 1985; Youniss & Smollar, 1985). The child is now more likely to challenge the existing family boundaries in terms of values and behaviors, sometimes as mentioned earlier with a highly moralistic logic, or with individualizing statements such as "I'm me, not you," and "I need to decide what's right for me." If the parents prevail in the ensuing struggle, then the adolescent's emotional growth may be restricted. If the adolescent wins the struggle, then key family values may be rejected on a wholesale basis, leaving the adolescent even more anxious and unsure in terms of personal values. When parent–child (really family–child) conflict escalates to where indelible lines are drawn, for example, on the order of "If you do ____, you're no longer a member of our family," then, the involved persons become resistive and the issues can get polarized forcing the parties into rigid stances.

The boundaries of the family need to become more permeable to allow for a healthy in-and-out flow of new ideas as the adolescent brings back to the family his or her new ways of viewing the world and modified values. The stands the adolescent takes can challenge key aspects of the family structure such as the authority position of the parents, and in the adolescent's attempt to debate issues, (as if he or she had the right to do so) some cherished family values may be breached. From a more rigid parental stand, the adolescent is being a "smart ass," trying to be in charge, or disrespectful. Under these conditions, tension and conflict grow, and crises are predictable. A common adolescent response to perceived closedness and rigidity of the family system is active rebellion, be it in terms of rejecting school, engaging in sexual activity, drug or alcohol usage, violating family rules, increasing defiance, and even physically assaulting encounters with parents.

Added to these dynamics is the phenomenon of adolescent egocentrism (Elkind, 1993). With adolescence there is a re-emergence of extreme egocentrism. This egocentrism has positive qualities in that it allows the teen to experiment with new roles and identities (the personal fable), but it also has negative features in that it makes the child extremely self-conscious (the imaginary audience) and reclusive. The general self-absorption, selfishness, and inability to see things from another (adult's) point of view leads to a new level of inconsiderate behavior. Because they believe themselves to be unique and invulnerable to negative consequences of risky behavior, they do not worry about themselves, and do not understand why others do worry. Parents are constantly confronted with self-centered responses from their children who had been "reasonable" at an earlier age.

### Crises and Family Histories

One also needs to consider some historical family patterns and dynamics that might have either precipitated or exacerbated the crisis and will eventually need to be addressed in the process of crisis resolution. For example, has the family been relatively disengaged in terms of emotional relationships? Has the adolescent grown up perceiving him or herself as "alone against the world"? Has this been a family that has historically been very supportive of each other with a positive history of family relationships to fall back upon in times of crisis? Some families are so emotionally enmeshed that any move toward individual thinking or value exploration precipitates a family crisis with the adolescent being seen as rejecting the cherished family values and likely to do something "wrong." In the latter case, it is clear that the resolution of the crisis will eventually require some fairly major shifts in the family orientation toward individual behavior.

One aspect of family structure that therapists frequently look to in their attempts to understand family dynamics is the concept of generational boundaries. In some families, if one were just to read a transcript of family interaction, it would be difficult to determine who were the parents and who were the children. One finds examples of this in families of gifted children where verbal precocity sometimes moves the child into a pseudoparenting role. There are also some families in which a child becomes the "parental child" and somehow, possibly through underfunctioning parents, has been allowed or encouraged over the years to assume a more parental role in relation to other family members. Here generational boundaries have become blurred and disrupted. Often in immigrant families, children who learn English more rapidly than their parents assume adult roles when dealing with the outside world. They are expected to shift back to a child's role when they return to the home.

Another window into family dynamics is through understanding the historic alliances and collusions that have been created. In one Caucasian family the father and daughter had maintained a supportive relationship over the years and they considered themselves to have a very special understanding. The mother correspondingly often found herself on the outside of their discussions and in instances where there were parent–child disagreements it was typically the mother trying to exercise some restriction on the daughter. The usual family pattern involved the daughter pulling the father into a rescuer role with him often softening whatever limits were placed on the daughter by her mother. It was against this background that the family found itself in conflict over the daughter's intentions to date an African-American classmate. Although both parents shared in their strong feelings against the dating, the mother was especially hostile toward the father. She maintained that it was his permissiveness that allowed the daughter to reach this point in her dating relationships. The daughter's anger at both parents over what she saw as their bigotry was particularly hurtful to the father who was experiencing the destruction of what to him had been a very special relationship with his daughter. The effects of the conflict eventually moved into the school setting. Teachers commented on the girl's moodiness and her friends became very concerned by what they saw as depression and even possible suicidal thinking.

The counselor scheduled a session with the parents and the daughter to find out what was happening and to see what kind of intervention was appropriate. The first such session produced an immediate surfacing of each family member's anger and frustration with the other. It was apparent that neither mother nor father was equipped by the history of family relationships to discuss the issue in a reasonable fashion. Their attempts at trying to make sense out of what was happening quickly deteriorated into accusations and defensive responses. This event was exceedingly painful to the teenager who, although initially caught up in anger at her parents' reactions, now saw herself as the main cause of this horrible discord. The crisis dimension of the situation expanded rapidly in the counselor's office as his initial interest in gathering some information moved the family into a reenactment of the conflict.

This example illustrates how virtually impossible it is for the crisis counselor to not be confronted with some of the historical family conflicts and therefore the need to deal to some extent with the family history at the time of crisis intervention. The crisis counselor will have to decide whether the extent of historic family discord and dysfunctionality is so great that, rather than attempting a school-based crisis intervention, an immediate referral to an agency that is better able to offer comprehensive family counseling services might be appropriate.

### Parental Change and Adolescent Crisis

Another way of viewing parent–adolescent tensions is to consider that not only is the adolescent going through some major personal changes, but the parents are as well (Kidwell et al., 1983). The parents, typically in their late 30s to 40s, may be going through crises related to life goals, job satisfaction, changes in marital relationship, and personal physical changes. A number of unresolved parental issues may interfere with, or be provoked by the adolescent's behavior (Fine, 1982; Kidwell et al., 1983; Preto & Travis, 1985). As Kidwell et al. (1983) observed:

> Stress theory would suggest that when the parents' transition periods coincide with the offspring's transitions, the family system will undergo greater strain than when the parents' transition periods occur before or after the adolescence of their children. The presence in the home of an adolescent who questions parental values and customs may exacerbate the parents' own inner turmoil. (pp. 81–82)

The parents preoccupation with their own issues and their sense of vulnerability as they face life-transition decisions, may undermine the kinds of understanding, tolerance, and good humor, needed by parents to cope with changing adolescent behavior.

## PREVENTION STRATEGIES

### Prevention Aimed at Adolescents

As mentioned, there is also a role for the schools in anticipating a crisis and taking the initiative. This stance is clearly different from the crisis "hot line" approach of waiting until someone calls for help. School personnel may offer programs aimed at giving teens improved communication skills and by presenting family life education courses, which teach adolescents themselves to be more effective parents.

***Skill-Building.*** A number of programs have been implemented in secondary schools to help adolescents understand themselves in their relationship with their parents and to develop more effective means of communicating and problem solving.

Many of the programs described in the literature tend to be time-limited programs focusing on teaching the adolescent specific communication, interpersonal, or problem-solving skills. For example, Trower (1978) described a program that teaches adolescents to deal with their parents in a more adult way in terms of specific verbal skills including how to argue, console, advise, and criticize. He was also concerned with appropriate body language as a part of the message.

Brion-Meisels has published several papers describing adolescent social competency and in particular, interpersonal negotiation strategies (Brion-Meisels, Rendeiro, & Lowenheim 1984; Brion-Meisels & Selman, 1984, 1996). His work derives in part from the earlier publications on problem solving by Spivack and Shure (1974, 1989) and Spivack, Platt, and Shure (1976). The proposed interpersonal negotiation model involves four social-cognitive skills: (a) labeling the problem, (b) generating alternative solutions, (c) anticipating consequences for self and other, and (d) evaluating results. These four skills interact with four levels of interpersonal negotiation strategies. The model and curriculum seem to hold a great deal of promise for training adolescents, and although not specifically focused on parent–adolescent crises, it does interface with that area.

A program entitled Skills for Adolescence is described by Gerler (1986) and Crisci (1986). It involves a semester-long curriculum dealing with 10 adolescent concerns. "Two of the units one dealing with friends and the other dealing with family focus on ways of appreciating and enhancing relationships and dealing effectively with problems and conflicts when they do occur" (Gerler, 1986, p. 438). More than 500 schools have adopted the curriculum and some positive outcomes have been reported from evaluation studies.

A number of other programs have been described in the literature with different populations of children, focusing on problem solving and communication skills (Barkley et al., 1999; Goldstein, Sprafkin, Gershaw, & Klein, 1980; Ollendick & Hersen, 1979; Sarason & Sarason, 1981). These represent program prototypes and models that can be modified and implemented with adolescents in schools around parent–adolescent conflicts.

***Family Life Education.*** Many schools offer family life education courses, either as part of the social studies curriculum or as part of health education. The intent of these courses, which include simulation activities such as forming pairs as couples, and charging them with the care of an egg, is to give them some insight into the responsibilities and skills necessary to be an effective parent. The hope of these programs is to forestall teen pregnancy (Nitz, 1999). Often the focus is on parenting young children and infants, but courses may include dilemmas related to parenting adolescents.

## Prevention Aimed at Parents

In consultation with a mental health professional, one can envision the parents presenting specific incidents and utilizing the mental health professional as a sounding board, helping them to reflect on their thinking and behaviors and also as a source of some skill development. Those initially limited contacts with the parents can easily extend into a referral to a parent training group. In many communities there are ongoing parent education groups such as Parent Effectiveness Training (Gordon, 1975), Systematic Training for Effective Parenting (STEP) programs (Dinkmeyer & McKay, 1976; Dinkmeyer, McKay, McKay, & Dinkmeyer, 1998), and Active Parenting (Popkin, 1983). These programs assist parents in understanding the complexities of parent–child relationships and support them in developing a sympathetic view toward the child and themselves in the parenting role; in addition, parents are typically offered specific communication and intervention skills. For example, Gordon's program provides a model for effective parent–child relationships in which the emphasis is on recognizing faulty communication patterns, developing effective listening skills, and managing conflict by mutually exploring and agreeing on a solution. Moving to workable solutions characterizes recently developed programs (Metcalf, 1996; Todd, 2000).

The Adlerian based STEP program (Dinkmeyer et al., 1998) is one the most widely used and evaluated parent education programs used in schools as well as other institutions (Burnett, 1988). STEP is a lecture-and-discussion based systematic training program focusing on the purposive nature of the child's behavior and its social consequences. In nine sessions, it attempts to instill in parents a sense of greater self-confidence as parents by giving them a framework to understand their child and tools to communicate with them more effectively. It seeks to create a democratic child rearing approach where power struggles are avoided and communications skills result in workable solutions to problems.

The time the mental health professional spends with the parents may also reveal some family problems that go beyond just communication difficulties with their adolescent. For example, some marital difficulties may be revealed along with other family happenings of a historical or contemporary nature such as abuse situations. A referral may be deemed appropriate to treatment or intervention sources that are better equipped to deal with more deep-seated, chronic family issues.

## INTERVENTION STRATEGIES

As discussed earlier, the school mental health professional may have several entrees into a crisis situation. The adolescent may approach the professional with a problem, or the parents may contact the school expressing concern about what they are experiencing with the adolescent, or even third parties such as a friend of the student may contact the professional. The initial concerns of the mental health professional have to do with the urgency and potentially life-threatening nature of the situation and concomitantly the rights of the parent and adolescent (Fine, 1982; Grob et al., 1983). Certainly some behaviors exhibited by the adolescent such as physical aggression, drug or alcohol abuse, visible depression, and suicidal indications need to be responded to immediately and with parental involvement.

In instances where the adolescent shares an ideation or intention that would be harmful to him or herself, or others, the professional's obligations to involve others should be communicated to the student as well as the desirability of involving other people, mainly the parents. One way of conceptualizing the expression of such a crisis is that it is simultaneously a call for help. The crisis may reflect the unbalancing of the family homeostatic system and can represent a quest for someone or something to help put things back in order. Counselors and psychologists in the schools who deal with adolescents manifesting or expressing acute behaviors or thoughts find that the adolescent and parent will focus very quickly on some family relationship issues once they are brought together. Decisions will usually be made fairly early in the intervention process as to how to proceed, whether hospitalization is needed for the adolescent or whether the parents and adolescent can contract together to work on "their" problem.

### School-Based Intervention

***Group Interventions.*** Support groups are useful tools for helping adolescents with common problems express feelings, explore thoughts, generate alternative solutions, and gain a sense of control over their lives. Support groups may be formed for students experiencing conflict with parents. If such a group exists in the high school as an ongoing group, then it becomes a convenient referral source for the student. It may require a few sessions with the mental health professional to prepare the student to benefit from a group process. The ongoing nature of the group means that there will be some students who have been in it for several weeks along with students who are just entering. Students who have been in the group for a while have had the opportunity to test their new skills with their parents. The kinds of discussion and feedback opportunities that this group presents for an adolescent can break through adolescent egocentrism and promote reality testing. Peers are usually accorded more credibility than adults are, and a well structured group provides opportunities for adolescents to hear messages from peers that would be ignored coming from adults. This contact with reality may be especially valuable for the adolescent who feels that no one else has had this kind of problem or that his or her parents are the "worst" parents or are unapproachable. Being in a group with other adolescents who are also experiencing difficulties with their parents and who are perhaps farther down the road in coming to terms with their own inputs to the parent–adolescent problem can be extremely educative to the new group member.

***Individual Interventions.*** Families who have a history of healthy family interaction and communication are able to deal with crises as they arise, occasionally seeking some outside help. Many of the crises that come to the attention of school personnel are at a point where perhaps the history of ineffective communication patterns have rendered the involved parties relatively helpless in working toward resolution without the participation of an outsider. One can anticipate that as persons contact the school mental health professional and express their concerns about some parent–adolescent issue, that the parties experiencing the crisis are implicitly or explicitly seeking some direction and support. In the case of parents, they may be looking to the school mental health professional to do what they feel they have not been able to do, which is to correct and influence the "wayward adolescent." This temporary abdication of parental authority speaks to the frustration that the parents have experienced in their own attempts to cope with the adolescent's behavior and reactions. There is an obvious danger in taking sides that requires sensitivity by the mental health professional. Because the ultimate goal is to assist the involved parties in resolving their crisis, the mental health professional needs to assume both an empathetic and caring stance and simultaneously an objective and neutral stance. The emphasis should be on finding solutions rather than making judgments.

***A Mediator Role.*** Common complaints of adolescents about their parents included the perception that the parent does not listen, does not understand, is not sympathetic to what the adolescent is experiencing, is judgmental, and is not willing to give time to the adolescent. Without exactly sitting on the edge of his or her seat expressing an inordinate intensity of focus, the school mental health professional needs to convey the message of "I am here, I am interested in hearing and understanding what is happening with you, and I am available to be involved in a potentially helpful way in your situation."

When we are focusing on problems that a parent or adolescent is experiencing in relation to the other the eventual bringing together of the conflicting parties is extremely important. The conflict resolution literature (Bach & Wyden, 1968; Deutsch, 1973; Gordon, 1975) speaks to how persons in conflict tend to polarize issues, draw position lines in an indelible fashion, think in terms of we–they or I–you, and engage in projection around the other persons position. A function of a mediator is to assist the parties in obtaining a clearer understanding of each other's position, a more objective view of the respective concerns and issues, a careful examination of impasses, and consideration of new options. The mediator sets important ground rules, such as making no interruptions, taking turns in presenting points of view, and searching for "win–win" solutions. The perceived authority, knowledge, skill, and fairness of the mediator plays a very important role in the response of the "opposing" parties to conflict resolution procedures.

The mediator in the aforementioned context needs to establish his or her authority and psychological position in the conflict–mediation situation. The mediator is neutral but respects both parties, is skilled in the process of mediation, and is dedicated to resolving the conflict. These qualities appear to hold especially true for the mental health professional involved with parents and adolescents at a time of crisis. Their crisis is real and needs to be responded to with care and respect by the mental health professional. Both parties, parents and adolescent, typically feel vulnerable and defensive about their stance and need to receive a message from the professional that the issues and their thoughts and feelings are valid.

***Specific Interventions.*** The intent of crisis intervention is to restabilize a system and to reduce the crisis nature of the situation. Following that, other decisions have to be made in relation to establishing a counseling program with the individuals involved, terminating contacts, referring to another agency, or acting out some other option.

The nature and extent of the counseling that school mental health professionals should engage in is subject to some debate based on questions of competency and of the roles and function of school mental health professionals. Because the view of crisis intervention with parent–adolescent problems presented here has a family orientation, we are concerned with ways that the student and parents can be productively involved not only to cope with the immediate crisis but also to develop a better mutual understanding and more effective ways of dealing with future issues.

It is not the intent to present the school mental health professional as someone for whom the practice of family therapy per se is appropriate. But within the context of crisis intervention, several sessions might occur involving the respective family members, sometimes with the student and parents meeting together and other times with the student or the parents involved separately. These sessions fall short of being family therapy but can benefit from the professional's familiarity with concepts and techniques of family therapy (Fine, 1995; Fine & Holt, 1983; Green, 1985). Another option is that as student and parent meet together the mental health professional may choose to have one of the other parties leave the room. The professional then attempts to negotiate some aspect of the situation with the remaining person(s) following which the professional may meet with the other person(s). At some point all parties will meet together.

## Contact With the Adolescent

Some of the basic skills and activities in the initial crisis intervention have been discussed elsewhere in this text. It would be expected that in the early course of listening to the adolescent-in-crisis that the mental health professional would inquire as to who else is involved or who else is aware of what is happening and, in particular, how aware and involved are the parents. The challenge for the crisis counselor is to continue to be supportive and sympathetic to the student in what he or she is experiencing while at the same time not actively siding with the student against the parent. The other side of the coin, of course, is that the professional on hearing what sounds like distortion, overreactions, misperceptions, or inappropriate thinking by the adolescent, may be pulled into speaking from the parents' point of view. However objectively the mental health professional has attempted to respond, there is a good likelihood that the adolescent will view the professional as taking the parents' side and probably not being adequately sympathetic to the student's position. Only by acting consistently with integrity over time, can trust in the helper be established.

Because a key element of a person experiencing a crisis is the lack of awareness of options or the sense that one can act on those options, a function of the professional at an appropriate time is to begin helping the adolescent consider available options. An important option especially in light of conflict between parent and adolescent is to encourage the adolescent toward an involvement in a process that can generate options rather than necessarily coming up with concrete solutions in the crisis counseling session. It is understandable that the adolescent once having invested some trust in the mental health professional may respond in a dependent way seeking some concrete direction. Although the professional may see a role as an information giver, it may be more useful ultimately to have the student focus on ways that he or she can move into a problem solving posture with parents. To that end, the professional may need to work with the student in terms of some specific communication and conflict resolution skills and strategies that the student might venture to try with parents, continuing to use the professional as a support person.

## Contact With Parents

It is important to remember that when an adolescent is experiencing a crisis involving his or her parents, that the parents also are experiencing a crisis. The decision of the mental health professional to meet once or even have several sessions with the parents should be based on the parents' needs to ventilate, to develop a more positive perspective on the situation, and to think through more effective ways of communicating with the adolescent. The recommendations for the parents to be involved in sessions with the mental health professional without the adolescent present will also be predicated on the belief that the nature of the relationship at that time could not be usefully affected through having the parent and adolescent meeting together. The adolescent may be receiving some individual or group help in developing more effective communication and problem-solving skills or perhaps the adolescent has even refused any involvement. The parents can still be helped to increase their capability of negotiating differences with the adolescent and being appropriately supportive at the time of the crisis.

### Conjoint Contacts With Parents and Adolescents

When the mental health professional schedules sessions that involve both parent and adolescent, the professional must have some appreciation for group process and the importance of his or her leadership role. These meetings of parent, adolescent, and professional should allow for ventilation, should encourage interaction between parent and adolescent, and should also present the mental health professional in a leadership–control role. The professional posture and exhibited leadership competencies of the mental health professional can go a long way toward reducing the anxiety level of the participants and in helping them to see themselves in a process that can lead to some resolution. At times, the professional may need to play a "traffic cop" role in directing people who are going off tangentially or speaking in a destructive way and in making sure that everyone's position is heard and respected. The neutrality image needs to be strongly maintained. The respective family members are likely to feel some vulnerability in the conjoint session and may tend to experience any disagreement with them or support of the other person by the professional as side-taking or not understanding their point of view. The mental health professional needs to be very sensitive to this phenomenon and to do what is necessary to anticipate misperceptions and to support the image of neutrality.

There are a number of techniques and strategies that derive from family therapy that can be useful in the short-term crisis intervention sessions. As the mental health professional explores each side's point of view on events that occurred, it might be more useful to avoid "why" questions and to ask instead "what happens when" questions. Such questioning can do much to reveal some of the communication and behavior patterns in the family that precipitate conflict. Such circular questioning also avoids a blaming and a "who's right" stance and aids the family members to see and better understand dysfunctional patterns. The professional can also use the technique of reframing to present a more positive and sympathetic interpretation to someone's behavior. For example, when a parent talks about how angry he or she becomes when the adolescent does a certain thing, the positive reframing could be in terms of "I can see how much you care for your child and how frightened and frustrated you get when you believe he is setting himself up to get hurt."

The sense of crisis should reduce somewhat on the part of the family members just as a function of knowing that they are in a potentially helpful process. Also, the revealing of dysfunctional patterns of communication can begin to suggest ways that the parents and adolescent can shift to a more mutually respectful, problem solving and less combative stance. The modeling influence of the mental health professional cannot be overstressed. As a reasonable, rational, caring person who evidences logical problem-solving skills, the professional is implicitly teaching parents and the adolescent how to listen, think, and be appropriately assertive.

At some point in the conjoint session(s), it may be useful to negotiate a contract that spells out both parental and adolescent future behaviors. The preparation of the contract is a strategic device to make explicit the concerns of the respective parties. It also requires thinking and planning by the participants that at that point in the crisis intervention process can help to move them away from an excessively emotional mode into a thinking mode. Because a contract typically involves commitments by both parties, it can be "face saving" in that it is not just one party who is giving in.

An exciting approach to working with the whole family at time of parent–adolescent crisis is described by Robin and Foster (1989). The program is a behavioral-family systems approach that addresses skill deficits, cognitive distortions, structural difficulties, and functional interaction patterns. The intervention includes training in problem-solving strategies, targeting and transforming ineffectual communication habits, recognizing and restructuring cognitive sets that contribute to conflict (e.g., overgeneralization, arbitrary inference, dichotomous reasoning), and targeting and modifying family structural and functional patterns that may be maintaining maladaptive interactions. A range of "teaching" techniques is used including modeling, behavior rehearsal, and corrective feedback. Homework is utilized to encourage generalization. The program involves 7 to 15, one-hour sessions.

It would be unrealistic to believe that one or even several sessions at the time of crisis will completely resolve what may be a history of significant family dysfunction. There will be the tendency, even though important gains may have been made within the context of the crisis counseling sessions, for the family to revert back to old patterns. Therefore, in order to capitalize on the gains that may have been made, referral to another agency or resource that can work with the family on an ongoing basis may be appropriate. Examples of such services may be an ongoing family therapy program at a local mental health clinic or perhaps a family-life education program as offered through a local church or other agency.

It is important to remember, however, that the family may decide to terminate professional contacts once the crisis has abated. The family and its respective members may not want to work on improving relationships to a more idealized level. There may be an acceptable "discomfort level" that the family can tolerate, and only when the discomfort exceeds that level is motivation for professional involvement expressed. Szasz's (1961) view of people not experiencing mental illness as a "disease," but rather experiencing difficulties in coping with problems of daily living is a relevant consideration. Once people have improved their capacity to cope to their satisfaction with a formerly problematic situation they are often ready to terminate the help process.

## SUMMARY

This chapter has examined parent–adolescent crises against the background of the child growing up within a family system. Areas such as family histories, family dynamics, intervention strategies, and prevention programs were discussed with a view toward the relationship of these areas to crisis intervention. As the school-based mental health professional becomes increasingly involved in working with parent–adolescent crisis situations, they must be cognizant of how the family system operates, its relationship to the crisis, and how it influences the choice of intervention.

Although the "normal crises" of adolescence can be problematic for any family, they can be extremely stressful for the dysfunctional family unit. This type of family unit, with the history of ineffectual patterns of responding to normative changes, can intensify situations so that they escalate to a crisis level. It is at this point of crisis that the school-based mental health professional may become actively involved through counseling, mediating, or referring to another appropriate agency, so that the system can restabilize and the crisis nature of the situation can be reduced. How well the school-based mental health professional deals with parent–adolescent crisis will depend on the professional's level of flexibility, degree of decisiveness, awareness of options, knowledge of family patterns and dynamics, and how realistic his or her expectations are of respective family members' commitment to change.

## REFERENCES

Aguilera, D. C., & Messick, J. N. (1978). *Crisis intervention: Theory and methodology*. St Louis, MO: Mosby.

Ames, L. B. (1988). *Questions parents ask*. New York: Delta Books.

Arnett, J. J. (1999). Adolescent storm and stress, reconsidered. *American Psychologist, 54,* 317–326.

Bach, G. R., & Wyden, P. (1968). *The intimate enemy.* New York: Aron.

Barkley, R. A., Edwards, G. H., & Robin, A. L. (1999). *Defiant teens: A clinician's manual for assessment and family intervention.* New York: Guilford Press.

Brion-Meisels, S., Rendeiro, B., & Lowenheim, G. (1984). Student decision-making: Improving the school climate for all students. In S. Braaten, R. Rutherford, Jr., & C. Kardash (Eds.), *Programming for adolescents with behavioral disorders* (pp. 117–130). Reston, VA: Council for Exceptional Children.

Brion-Meisels, S., & Selman, R. L. (1984). Early adolescent development of new interpersonal strategies: Understanding and intervention. *School Psychology Review, 13,* 278–291.

Brion-Meisels, S., & Selman, R. L. (1996). From fight or flight to collaboration: A framework for understanding individual and institutional development in the school. In A. M. Hoffman (Ed.), *Schools, violence, and society* (pp. 163–184). Westport, CT: Praeger/Greenwood.

Burnett, P. C. (1988). Evaluation of Adlerian parenting programs. *Individual Psychology: Journal of Adlerian Theory, Research & Practice, 44,* 63–76.

Crisci, P. E. (1986). The Quest National Center: A focus on prevention of alienation. *Phi Delta Kappan,* 67, 442–446.

Deutsch, M. (1973). *The resolution of conflict: Constructive and destructive processes.* New Haven, CT: Yale University Press.

Dinkmeyer, D., & McKay, G. (1976). *STEP-TEEN.* Circle Pines, MN: American Guidance Service.

Dinkmeyer D., Sr., McKay, G. D., McKay, J. L., & Dinkmeyer, D., Jr. (1998). *Parenting teenagers: Systematic training for effective parenting of teens.* Circle Pines, MN: American Guidance Services.

Elium, J., & Elium, D. (1999). *Parenting a teenager: The nurturing of a responsible teen.* Berkeley, CA: Celestial Arts.

Elkind, D. (1984). *All grown up and no place to go.* Menlo Park, CA: Addison-Wesley.

Elkind, D. (1993). *Parenting your teenager.* New York: Ballantine.

Elkind, D. (1994). *Ties that stress: The new family imbalance.* Cambridge, MA: Harvard University Press.

Erikson, E. H. (1968). *Identity: Youth and crisis.* New York: Norton.

Fine, M. J. (1982). Issues in adolescent counseling. *School Psychology Review, 11,* 391–398.

Fine, M. J. (1995). Family-school intervention. In R. H. Miksell, D. D. Lusterman, & S. H. McDaniel (Eds.), *Integrating family therapy: Handbook of family psychology and systems theory* (pp. 481–495). Washington, DC: American Psychological Association.

Fine, M. J., & Holt, P. (1983). Intervening with school problems: A family systems perspective. *Psychology in the Schools, 20,* 59–66.

Gerler, E. R., Jr. (1986). Skills for adolescence: A new program for young teenagers. *Phi Delta Kappan, 67,* 436–439.

Ginott, H. (1969). *Between parent and teenager.* New York: Macmillan.

Goldstein, A. P., Sprafkin, R. P., Gershaw, N. J., & Klein, P. (1980). *Skill-streaming the adolescent.* Champaign, IL: Research Press.

Gordon, T. (1975). *P.E.T.: Parent effectiveness training.* New York: New American Library.

Gordon, T. (1989). *Teaching children discipline at home and at school.* New York: Random House

Green, B. J. (1985). Systems intervention in the schools. In M. P. Mirkin & S. L. Koman (Eds.), *Handbook of adolescent and family therapy* (pp. 193–206). New York: Gardner Press.

Grob, M. C., Klein, A. A., & Eisen, S. V. (1983). The role of the high school professional in identifying and managing adolescent suicidal behavior. *Journal of Youth and Adolescence, 12,* 163–173.

Hughes, F. P., & Noppe, L. D. (1991). *Human development across the life span.* New York: Macmillan.

Jacobs, J. (1980). *Adolescent suicide.* New York: Irvington.

Jones, V. F. (1980). *Adolescents with behavior problems.* Boston: Allyn & Bacon.

Kidwell, J., Fischer, J. L., Dunham, R. M., & Baranowski, M. (1983). Parents and adolescents: Push and pull of change. In H. 1. McCubbin & C. R. Figley (Eds.), *Stress and the family: Vol. 1. Coping with normal change* (pp. 74–89). New York: Brunner/Mazel.

Leigh, G. K., & Peterson, G. W. (1986). *Adolescents in families*. Cincinnati, OH: South-Western Publishing.

Metcalf, L. (1996). *Parenting toward solutions: How parents can use skills they already have to raise responsible, loving kids*. Upper Saddle River, NJ: Prentice Hall.

Nitz, K. (1999). Adolescent pregnancy prevention: A review of interventions and programs. *Clinical Psychology Review, 19*, 457–471.

Ollendick, T. H., & Hersen, M. (1979). Social skills training for juvenile delinquents. *Behavior Research and Therapy, 17*, 547–554.

Pitcher, G. D., & Poland, S. (1992). *Crisis intervention in the schools*. New York: Guilford Press.

Popkin, M. (1983). *Active parenting: A video-based program*. Atlanta: Active Parenting.

Preto, N. G., & Travis, N. (1985). The adolescent phase of the family life cycle. In M. P. Mirkin & S. L. Koman (Eds.), *Handbook of adolescent and family therapy* (pp. 21–38). New York: Gardner Press.

Robin, A. L., & Foster, S. L. (1989). *Negotiating parent-adolescent conflict: A behavioral-family systems approach*. New York: Guilford Press.

Sarason, I. G., & Sarason, B. R. (1981). Teaching cognitive and social skills to high school students. *Journal of Counseling and Clinical Psychology, 49*, 908–918.

Spivack, G., Platt, J. J., & Shure, M. B. (1976). *The problem-solving approach to adjustment*. San Francisco: Jossey-Bass.

Spivack, G., & Shure, M. (1974). *Social adjustment of young children: A cognitive approach to solving real-life problems*. San Francisco: Jossey-Bass.

Spivack, G., & Shure, M. B. (1989). Interpersonal Cognitive Problem Solving (ICPS): A competence-building primary prevention program. *Prevention in Human Services, 6*, 151–178.

Steele, W., & Raider, M. (1991). *Working with families in crisis: School-based intervention*. New York: Guilford Press.

Szasz, T. (1961). *The myth of mental illness: Foundations of a theory of personal conduct*. New York: Hoeber-Harper.

Todd, T. (2000). Solution focused strategic parenting of challenging teens: A class for parents. *Family Relations, 49*, 165–168.

Trower, P. (1978). Skills training for adolescent social problems: A viable treatment alternative. *Journal of Adolescence, 1*, 319–329.

Youniss, J., & Smollar, J. (1985). *Adolescent relations with mothers, fathers, and friends*. Chicago: University of Chicago Press.

CHAPTER

# 17

# Rape and Sexual Assault

Virginia L. Schiefelbein
University of California, Davis

Often termed "The Silent Epidemic," rape is an unfortunately common occurrence in contemporary America (Ullman & Knight, 1993). It is estimated that 7% to 16% of children and adolescents experience forced sexual intercourse before age 18 (Miller, Monson, & Norton, 1995); moreover, 332,000 to 812,000 U.S. women are raped each year (Ledray, 1986). Rape, as well as other forms of sexual assault, is clearly a major problem in this society and others (Choquet, Darves-Bornoz, Ledoux, Manfredi, & Hassler, 1997), but there is no clear consensus on its causes, the best way to prevent it, or even how to define it. Nevertheless, in this chapter I present our current state of understanding about this crime and the crisis it creates for young victims.

For the purposes of this chapter, I focus on nonconsensual sexual contact between people of similar age; because of differences in legal, causal, and prevention issues, I do not address sexual contact between adults and children nor between members of the same family (incest). In addition, most of this chapter refers to a heterosexual context in which the male is the offender and the female is the victim, although male rape and same-sex assaults do occur.

In order to be consistent with the majority of writing on this topic, I use the term *victim* in this chapter regardless of whether the assaulted person survived. A few authors use the more empowering term *survivor* for those who are not killed during the assault and *victim* only for those who are murdered.

This chapter first addresses some background information about sexual assault, including prevalence, terms, and a review of risk factors and protective factors for both potential victims and potential rapists. The second part of the chapter discusses postassault counseling; reactions to sexual assault; counseling responses; and approaches to use with individuals, groups, victims from specific populations, and the victim's significant others. The third section covers sexual assault prevention; first comes a discussion of a number of theories of the causes of sexual assault, and then the following section addresses sexual assault prevention strategies, including theoretical implications, research findings, and general classes of prevention programs.

## BACKGROUND INFORMATION

### Defining the Problem: Prevalence, Definitions, and Costs

The actual prevalence of rape and other sexual assaults is difficult to measure. Different researchers report very different statistics on the prevalence of rape and sexual assault. Some of this difference derives from variations in definition; another issue is how the prevalence is measured. In a prospective study in rural Appalachia of 112 adolescent girls from age 12 to 27, 8% had experienced stranger or older family friend rape or incest, 23% reported being victims of unwanted sexual abuse by dates/boyfriends, and 10% reported experiencing some other form of sexual assault (Vicary, Klingaman, & Harkness, 1995) In France for Grades 8–12 estimates for rape were 9% for girls and .6% for boys (Choquet et al., 1997). Although statistics on sexual assault of males are harder to come by, men and boys can also be victims of sexual assault. In one Memphis-area study, 9% of sexual assault victims seeking help at a rape crisis center were male (Muram, Hostetler, Jones, & Speck, 1995).

Another commonly studied variable is men's self-reported willingness to sexually assault if they would not be caught. More than 20% in one study reported some future likelihood of raping (Denmare, Briere, & Lips, 1988), whereas in another study 60% indicated a willingness to "force a female to do something she didn't really want to do" and/or "rape" (Briere & Malamuth, 1983). Some of this variation depends on the exact question asked.

The legal definition of rape would be a convenient standard, but different law enforcement agencies operate under different definitions of "rape." A definition used by the FBI is "carnal knowledge of a female forcibly and against her will" (Koss, 1983, p. 89). The broader definition used by the state of Ohio includes "vaginal intercourse between male and female, and anal intercourse, fellatio, and cunnilingus between persons regardless of sex . . ." via force, threat of force, or administering drugs or intoxicants to prevent resistance (Harney & Muehlenhard, 1991, p. 3). Although many of the acts in Ohio's law are also illegal elsewhere, they are not always legally defined as rape. Most researchers define rape as some variation of: sexual intercourse, against one's will, which involves force or threat of force. Some researchers also specify the use of Ohio's definition of sexual intercourse: "[p]enetration, however slight" (e.g., Koss & Dinero, 1988, p. 138).

The term *sexual assault* includes rape, but also includes other nonconsensual sexual activities and is thus a more general term. The acts included may range from rape and attempted rape to "sexual behavior such as fondling or kissing . . . after the use of menacing verbal pressure, the misuse of authority, threats of harm, or actual physical force" (Hanson & Gidycz, 1993, pp. 1047–1048).

*Sexual harassment* is a closely related term which overlaps with the definition of sexual assault. There are many definitions of sexual harassment, but a basic definition is "deliberate and/or repeated sexual or sex-based behavior that is not welcome, not asked for, and not returned" (Webb, 1995, p. 12). At one end of the spectrum, sexual harassment can include such behaviors as leering, the display of offensive photographs or cartoons, and sexual jokes or remarks (Webb, 1995, p. 14); it ranges up through "nasty, personalized graffiti on bathroom walls; . . . bras snapped and body parts groped; and outright physical assault and attempted rape" (Stein, 1995, p. 21). The boundary between sexual assault and sexual harassment is hazy but physical contact, however minor, generally makes the distinction of when harassment also becomes sexual assault. Both are crimes under the law.

Other common terms in the sexual assault literature refer to a distinction based on the previous relationship between the rapist and victim. "Stranger rape" unambiguously refers to the lack of any prior relationship. "Acquaintance rape" has various meanings, but generally the term *acquaintance* refers to "an individual known to the victim in some capacity: they could be friends, dates, lovers, former lovers or spouses, coworkers, neighbors, and so forth" (Lonsway, 1996, p. 230), although the term generally does not include incest, assaults by persons in authority, marital rape, or child abuse (Warshaw, 1988).

Stranger rape, contrary to the common stereotype, is generally considered to be much less common than acquaintance rape. According to a 1990 study, 75% of victims knew their attackers (Calhoun & Atkeson, 1991); a high-end estimate is that acquaintance rapes constitute 80% to 90% of all rapes (Warshaw, 1988). At least one study contradicted this finding and found that less than half of all the sexual assault victims—but 64% of adolescent victims—seeking help at a Memphis-area rape crisis center were attacked by a "date/acquaintance" (Muram et al., 1995).

Prevalence estimates are affected not only by varying definitions and what type of rape (stranger vs. acquaintance) is discussed, but also by the method used to obtain reports. Using rapes reported to police, for example, would give a much lower estimate than using anonymous surveys; according to Calhoun and Atkeson (1991), "the majority of sexual assaults are never reported. A large-scale national probability survey, for instance, found that 84% of sexual assaults had not been reported" (p. 2). Using police reports to compare states would also be problematic; since the definition of "rape" varies between states, the number of acts meeting the legal definition will also vary even if actual occurrences were identical.

Because it is difficult to determine the exact prevalence of rape, it is difficult to quantify its social costs. For those rapes that are reported to police, there are obvious financial costs in the legal and (sometimes) correctional systems. The victim's family bears other financial costs; medical exams, legal fees, and counseling are examples. However, rape also has emotional costs for victims and for society as a whole. Some of the impacts on rape victims include anxiety, depression, poor social adjustment, sexual dysfunction, somatic symptoms, blame, and humiliation (Harney & Muehlenhard, 1991). In addition to the victim's suffering, Harney and Muehlenhard point out that "All women who live in a society with a high prevalence of rape are affected by it" (p. 14). Often, women restrict their activities in an attempt to avoid becoming a victim (Gordon & Riger, 1989).

## RISK FACTORS AND PROTECTIVE FACTORS

This section discusses factors correlated with increased or decreased probability of becoming a victim or perpetrator of sexual assault. Although correlation does not equal causation, some of these factors would logically serve as causes or as prevention.

### Potential Victims

Several risk factors are associated with a higher probability of being a victim, and a few protective factors have been noted. One of the most commonly known risk factors is gender—specifically, being female. As mentioned previously, only a small fraction of sexual assault victims are male.

Age is another risk factor. Although "[r]apes have been reported of infants a few months old and of elderly women in nursing homes" (Calhoun & Atkeson, 1991, p. 2), preadolescence through early adulthood is a time of particularly high risk. In a Memphis-area study, 33% of sexual assault victims seen at a rape crisis center were 13- to 18-year-old rape victims (Muram et al., 1995). A national survey by Smith, Letourneau, Saunders, Kilpatrick, Resnick, and Best (2000), similarly, found that victims' ages at the time they were raped broke down as follows: 25% were under 10; 37% were 11 to 17, 25% were 18 to 24; and the remainder were 25 or older. Thus, age appears to be a rather potent risk factor.

Although age and gender are important risk factors, changing them is not a feasible prevention strategy. One preventable risk factor is alcohol consumption. Norris (1994) cited several findings relating alcohol to sexual assault, including that: drinking women are "considered more sexually disinhibited and available by both men and women," more likely to be victims of completed (as opposed to attempted) rape, and less able to "make judgments about sexual assault" compared with sober women (p. 200). This is fairly intuitive; a woman who has been drinking may have impaired judgment, appear to be an easy mark, or be less able to physically resist an assault. Muram and colleagues (1995) warned that substance use is a particular concern for female adolescents who tend "to be more often . . . under the influence of alcohol or drugs at the time of assault" relative to adult women (p. 375).

Finally, Scott, Lefley, and Hicks (1993) reviewed several "factors [which] may increase the vulnerability of some women to sexual assault," including a history of psychiatric treatment, mental retardation, mental illness, prior sexual assault, being a tourist or visitor, and being homeless (pp. 133–134). Some of these factors, such as being homeless or unfamiliar with the area, seem to be more related to stranger rape than to the more common acquaintance rape. Others, such as mental illness or mental retardation, might make a woman appear vulnerable to either a stranger or acquaintance. Most of these factors, however, are difficult to target for prevention. As a final caveat, only 49% of victims who were studied displayed one or more of the above risk factors (Scott et al., 1993).

The converse of the foregoing risk factors (e.g., being male, being outside the age ranges discussed, abstaining from alcohol, and so forth) probably serve as protective factors. Ullman and Knight (1993) found that forceful resistance methods, "such as fighting, screaming, and fleeing/pushing the offender away," also serve a protective function, at least in reducing the severity of sexual abuse once an attack has begun (p. 35). This effectiveness holds regardless of the relationship between the offender and victim (i.e., strangers or acquaintances) and whether a weapon is present, "[a]lthough women who fought back forcefully when a weapon was present experienced more physical injury" (Ullman & Knight, p. 35). Bloom (1996), after reviewing a similar study by Zoucha-Jensen and Coyne (1993), also concluded "persons threatened with rape would probably be well advised to use physical resistance, forceful verbal resistance, or fleeing" (p. 142).

### Potential Rapists

Other research focuses on potential rapists. For lack of a better criterion, many of these studies use gender (male) as the screening variable. One of the most commonly cited risk factors for sexual aggression is holding beliefs or attitudes that are "rape supportive." Briere and Malamuth (1983), for example, found that men who admitted they might rape or "force a female to do something she didn't really want to do" scored significantly higher than other men in the following belief and attitude categories: "(1) Victims are responsible for their rapes, (2) Rape reports are manipulations, (3) Male dominance is justified, (4) Adversarial sexual beliefs, (5) Women enjoy sexual violence, and (6) Acceptance of domestic violence" (pp. 318–319). Similarly, Koss and Dinero (1988) showed that college men who reported perpetrating sexually aggressive acts on women "were more likely than less sexually aggressive men to believe that force and coercion are legitimate ways to gain compliance in sexual relationships" (p. 144). This risk factor certainly makes sense; feeling that sexual assault is justified correlates with committing such acts.

Psychological variables also yield logical results. Langevin et al. (1988) mentioned that an antisocial personality is one of the "clinically important features common to sadists and other sexually aggressive men" (p. 164). Similarly, Koss and Dinero (1988) reported that "highly sexually aggressive men were typified by greater hostility toward women" (p. 144). Again, these factors are logical; an antisocial or hostile person is more likely to commit aggressive acts.

The potential perpetrator's sexual experience is a less intuitive risk factor. Briere and Malamuth (1983) found that men indicating willingness to rape or use force gave higher self-ratings of "perceptions of relative sexual experience" but did not differ from other men on "sex life rating, importance of sex, relationships with women, . . . or sexual inhibitions" (p. 321). In other words, the men who claimed that they would be willing to use force in a sexual context also claimed to be more experienced, on average, than men who were not willing to use force. Koss and Dinero's (1988) results concurred, finding that highly sexually aggressive men "were more likely to have become sexually active at an earlier age and to report more childhood sexual experiences both forced and voluntary" (p. 144).

Several other characteristics may serve as risk factors for becoming a rapist. Some of the "clinically important features common to sadists and other sexually aggressive men" listed by Langevin et al. (1988) include alcoholism, illegal drug use, a criminal record, and aggressive and alcoholic parents (p. 164). Another factor identified by Koss and Dinero (1988) was the use of "violent and degrading pornography" (p. 144); however, Briere and Malamuth (1983) did not find that the "use of pornography" held any predictive value for their sample.

Few protective factors have been noted in the literature. It seems reasonable to assume that the converse of the risk factors (e.g., being female, not holding rape-supportive attitudes, less sexual experience, and so forth) serve a protective function in making an individual less prone to raping.

## POSTASSAULT CRISIS COUNSELING

### Crisis Reactions of Victims

It is important that care providers recognize that sexual assault is a crisis situation. After a sexual assault, the victim commonly experiences a set of reactions referred to as the rape trauma syndrome. The first stage, and thus the one we are most concerned with in crisis counseling in schools, is the acute or disorganization phase; it may last several weeks after the assault (Ellis, 1983). There are both physical and emotional components to this acute phase.

Physical reactions in the acute phase include the direct physical results of the assault, such as injury, as well as somatic manifestations of emotional trauma. Examples of physical reactions include: soreness and bruising; reproductive disorders such as infection, pain, discharge, or sexually transmitted diseases (STDs); reactions to medication administered to prevent pregnancy; stomachache, headache, and muscle tension; fatigue or exhaustion; changes in appetite or in how food tastes; and sleep disturbances (deAlcorn, 1984).

Emotionally, the acute stage of rape trauma syndrome includes "overwhelming fear and a sense of helplessness, shame, guilt or self-blame, and lack of control" (Weinstein & Rosen, 1988, p. 205). Other emotional reactions may include anger, humiliation, revenge, hysteria, a lack of affect, and lowered self-esteem (deAlcorn, 1984), as well as nightmares and flashbacks. Note that both extremes—hysteria and a complete lack of affect—are possible. This relates to two general styles the victim may exhibit, described by Burgess and Holmstrom (1974); the "expressed style" means that the victim appears upset and visibly emotional, whereas the "controlled style" means that the victim appears calm or controlled but is actually in denial. It is important for care providers to remember that calmness does not necessarily mean there is no underlying trauma.

### Goals of Crisis Counseling

Because crisis counseling is generally short term, it has a narrower set of goals than long-term counseling does. In crisis counseling with a sexual assault victim, "the therapist works to reduce the victim's emotional distress, enhance her coping strategies, and prevent the development of more serious psychopathology" (Calhoun & Atkeson, 1991, p. 39). It is also important to believe the victim. Believing the victim goes beyond simply acknowledging that she was assaulted (i.e., not making up her story). The counselor must believe "her story, that she did her best to prevent the assault and that she utilised all her resources" (Ben-Zvi & Horsfall, 1985, p. 351).

In addition, crisis counseling in a medical setting, such as an emergency room, should include giving the victim information about medical procedures (Weinstein & Rosen, 1988, pp. 208–209). Two areas on which to focus in crisis counseling are restoring the victim's sense of control and dealing with concerns about pregnancy and disease.

***Restoring Sense of Control.*** Recall that many of the emotional components of Rape Trauma Syndrome relate to a lack of a feeling of control. Lack of control is itself a symptom, but other symptoms, such as fearfulness and helplessness, are obviously related to this feeling. For many, if not all, victims of sexual assault, control is a central issue. Thus, "the immediate goal of counseling clients who have experienced sexual assault is to help them reestablish a sense of control over themselves and their environment" (Weinstein & Rosen, 1988, p. 207).

> One of the most important implications of the victim's need for control is that the crisis . . . counselor needs to refrain from taking over decision making or performing tasks of which the client is capable. Such actions can foster dependence and increase feelings of lack of control. . . . Small tasks such as finding the money for and making [a] telephone call themselves reenforce the feeling of regaining of control. (Weintein & Rosen, 1988, p. 209)

In giving the victim these tasks, the counselor must consider the victim's current emotional state; different victims will be capable of different tasks, but it is important to give the victim as much control and choice as she is capable of handling. It is also important, however, not to go to the opposite extreme and expect the victim to immediately resume normal functioning. As Weinstein and Rosen pointed out, victims of sexual assault "need permission to feel disoriented and to give themselves time to regain their sense of control" (p. 208).

The victim's control over her own body may be an especially important facet of regaining control. Some victims will want physical contact–to be hugged or have their hand held–but others will wish to avoid such contact, so it is a good idea to ask before touching her and to follow her lead; this is also a good plan for the victim's friends and family. If the victim undergoes a pelvic examination, the doctor should allow her to be in control of it as much as possible (Kaplan & Holmes, 1999).

***Concerns About Pregnancy and Disease.*** One of the most immediate concerns is the possibility of pregnancy. Rape results in pregnancy about 2% to 3% of the time (MacDonald, 1971; McDermott, 1979). Therefore, the crisis counselor must discuss testing and response options with the victim.

Sexually transmitted diseases are another concern requiring medical intervention and must be dealt with promptly. When discussing these issues, victims "can be expected to be very anxious and apprehensive" (Weinstein & Rosen, 1988, p. 210). A crisis counselor should not dismiss these concerns, but should provide support for the victim in dealing with them.

## Components of Crisis Counseling

***Setting.*** Many of the components of crisis counseling do not change across settings. However, there are a few points to bear in mind for particular settings.

If a victim telephones immediately after a sexual assault, the first priority is to determine whether she is still in danger or needs urgent medical care and to remedy these situations. Weinstein and Rosen (1988) also suggested speaking clearly, precisely, and calmly; offering reassurances that help is available; giving the victim simple tasks to do; remaining on the line until help arrives, if possible; and "inform[ing] the victim that washing, brushing one's teeth, drinking, or eating destroys necessary evidence" (p. 208). This warning can even extend to washing one's hands, because blood or other tissue may be on them or under the fingernails. If there is any possibility that the victim may want to later prosecute her assailant, time is of the essence in obtaining medical care; useful physical evidence can only be recovered for 48 to 72 hours after the assault (Kaplan & Holmes, 1999).

A victim may also have advocacy needs if the police are present, either at a crime scene or in a medical setting. In particular, "the dynamics of the interview, the criminal process, and the person's choices about it should be clearly explained" (Weinstein & Rosen, 1988, p. 211). Some of the jargon commonly used by police, such as "alleged rape," may suggest to the victim that she is not being believed; this language should be avoided (Weinstein & Rosen, 1988).

Some special concerns apply to schools. In particular, the victim should be informed of any limits to confidentiality due to mandatory reporting laws for school personnel. Privacy can also be a concern in a school setting, but sensitive topics such as sexual assault demand that as much privacy as possible be available to the victim.

***Information on the Physical Examination.*** Counseling sexual assault victims often involves providing them with information on medical procedures, but the counselor may or may not be familiar with medical procedures. Lehmann (1991) provided a detailed account of what occurs, from the collection of forensic evidence to the evaluation and photography of visible trauma.

With the exception of pregnancy testing, the medical procedures performed on sexual assault victims "are essentially the same for males as for females" (Weinstein & Rosen, 1988, p. 220). For most male victims, "this is [their] first such invasive physical examination . . . and is therefore likely to add to their trauma" (Weinstein & Rosen, p. 220). This is a point for medical personnel, counselors, and caretakers to keep in mind.

***General Guidelines for Sexual Assault Crisis Counseling.*** This section is not intended to be a comprehensive discussion of crisis counseling techniques, but rather a summary of the basics of crisis counseling with victims of sexual assault. There are several models available, based on various counseling approaches. What follows is a synthesis of several works, mainly Burgess and Holstrom (1979a, 1979b), Burgess, Groth, Holmstrom, and Sgroi (1978), and Calhoun and Atkeson's (1991) excellent discussion of crisis intervention with sexual assault victims.

The first step in crisis counseling, as in all counseling, is to connect with the client; in this case, the sexual assault victim. As Weinstein and Rosen (1988) stated, "the development of a supportive and trusting counselor/client relationship is essential" (p. 209). Establishing trust and a secure, supportive atmosphere with someone who is in crisis may not be easy, but it is necessary. Calhoun and Atkeson (1991) gave an excellent summary of the important points:

> Both verbal and nonverbal strategies must be used to convey understanding and acceptance of the victim's recent experiences. It is important to listen attentively to the victim and show sensitivity and respect for her as a person. Emotional support should include realistic reassurance and a sense of optimism or expectation for recovery in relation to the assault and its impact on the victim. (p. 40)

The general idea is to convey empathy and support for the victim so that she can feel secure enough to talk about her feelings, concerns, and problems. The building of a therapeutic relationship will—or should—continue throughout the counseling session(s), but it is important to establish at least some initial rapport. Although establishing rapport is important, time pressures also place priority on medical attention. Many rape victims have injuries that must be attended promptly.

Once these issues are dealt with, several sources (e.g., Burgess et al., 1978, Calhoun & Atkeson, 1991, Weinstein & Rosen, 1988) referred to assisting the victim in obtaining or "mobilizing" social support. Victims can use the support of their friends, their families, and other community resources to build self-confidence and begin returning to a normal lifestyle (Burgess et al., 1978). Crisis counseling should include preparing the victim to enlist these resources. With friends and family, how the victim confides in them can determine whether their response is supportive; crisis counseling may involve anything from discussing different approaches with the victim to actual notification on her behalf. In addition, friends and family members need to be given "information on what reactions to expect in the victim and themselves and ways in which they can facilitate recovery," such as expressing positive regard for the victim, encouraging emotional expression, validating the victim's feelings, and providing reassurance (Calhoun & Atkeson, pp. 42–43).

Beyond these basic steps, different victims will have different issues come up. Many victims will need help dealing with fears or phobias related to the assault (Burgess et al., 1978). Some other possible issues mentioned by Calhoun and Atkeson (1991) include encouraging the victim to express her emotions and talk about her experience; exploring whether and how she might decrease her daily responsibilities for a short while; exploring ways for her to increase her feelings of personal security and safety; and discussing potential problems with intimacy and sexual functioning (pp. 40–43).

Because crisis counseling tends to be short in duration, it focuses on the days and weeks to come. As part of this, the sexual assault victim should be given information, preferably written, on common reactions to sexual assault (i.e., Rape Trauma Syndrome) so that she knows what to expect (Calhoun & Atkeson, 1991). In addition to knowing what to expect, she needs to have coping strategies ready to deal with her difficulties. Helping her "anticipate and prepare to cope successfully with [likely] problematic situations . . . increas[es] her own self-confidence and feelings of control"; examples of coping strategies to review include deep breathing, muscle relaxation, and breaking down difficult situations and tasks into smaller steps (Calhoun & Atkeson, 1991, p. 41).

***Follow-Up and Referral.*** The last step in crisis counseling is to arrange for some sort of follow-up, either with the person providing the crisis counseling or with another person or agency. Relatively few rape victims, however, actually keep follow-up appointments; therefore, Calhoun and Atkeson (1991) recommended getting permission to later telephone the victim and giving her the counselor's name and phone number (p. 44). If the victim refuses follow-up contact, it is permissible to gently encourage her to continue counseling, but her wishes must be respected. At the very least, however, she should be given the phone number(s) of a local rape crisis center or other community counseling agencies so that she can seek follow-up care herself if and when she chooses to do so.

In referring a sexual assault victim to another counselor or agency, it is important to be sure that she does not feel she is being abandoned.

## Long-Term Reactions

Although the focus of this book is on crisis counseling, the long-term reactions to sexual assault are still relevant. This is partly so that the counselor can explain to the victim what to expect and can make informed decisions regarding referral. Long-term reactions to sexual assault depend on individual factors, such as age and development, coping skills, and circumstances of the assault, even more than crisis reactions do (Weinstein & Rosen, 1988). Bearing this in mind, some reactions are relatively common among sexual assault victims. These reactions—physical, emotional, behavioral, and economic—constitute the long-term or reorganization phase of Rape Trauma Syndrome and may last months or years after the assault (Burgess & Holmstrom, 1979a).

Long-term physical reactions include pregnancy or STDs resulting from the assault; sleeping disturbances, such as a need for frequent sleep, difficulty falling asleep, and nightmares; and changes in eating patterns, particularly overeating or inability to eat (deAlcorn, 1984). Other physical reactions include various symptoms of stress, such as digestive difficulties, headaches, and heart palpitations (Weinstein & Rosen, 1988).

Emotional reactions comprise some of the most common difficulties victims face after sexual assault. Many female victims have trouble with trust in male–female relationships (Weinstein & Rosen, 1988, p. 206). Fear and anxiety are also common. Victims may have sexual fears or various phobias, including fear of being alone, of going outside, of men who have some resemblance to the assailant, or global fear (deAlcorn, 1984). Depression, another common reaction, affected 72% of rape victims in a study by Nadelson, Notman, Zackson, and Gornick (1982). Other emotional reactions include difficulty in relating positively to men; a loss of privacy; and distrust of one's judgment, particularly in regard to safety (Weinstein & Rosen, p. 206).

Victims of sexual assault also often exhibit behavioral reactions, many of which are related to the emotional reactions. These reactions include "changes in lifestyle" and "general upset in normal living patterns" (deAlcorn, 1984). Specific examples include: absenteeism or withdrawl from school; sexual acting out, such as promiscuity or prostitution; suicidal tendencies; and drug and alcohol use.

## Counseling: Individual or Group?

There is quite a bit of debate in the research literature about whether individual or group therapy is generally more appropriate in counseling victims of sexual assault. Both types of therapy have advantages and drawbacks. It seems sensible to let the victim's preference and particular issues serve as a guide. Victims who want to share their story with many people or who want validation from others who have "been there" may do better in a group; those who want more privacy may do better with individual counseling, at least at first. In addition, logistical factors may preclude, or at least hinder, group therapy; many existing support groups are restricted by age or to females only. Finally, some victims may benefit from both types of therapy.

***Individual Approaches.*** Individual counseling may be the best approach for victims who want more personalized attention, who do not feel they can face a group, or who do not have access to support groups for some reason. Some cultures attach a strong feeling of shame to sexual assault, and victims from these cultures may also prefer to speak to a counselor one-on-one.

Many sexual assault victims exhibit symptoms of depression. If the victim has severely reduced her activity level, it may help her to first increase her activity level and then increase specific activities in which she finds pleasure or a sense of mastery (Calhoun & Atkeson, 1991). Other strategies for treatment discussed by Calhoun and Atkeson include: Frank and Stewart's (1983) adaptation of Beck's (1972) cognitive behavior therapy program; biofeedback with anxiety-related symptoms (Weinstein & Rosen, 1988); systematic desensitization; flooding, also referred to as exposure or implosion; Stress Inoculation Training (Cormier & Cormier, 1998); and assertion training.

The counselor plays different roles for victims with different needs. Burgess and Holmstrom (1974) studied how rape victims "wished to utilize the supportive role of the counselor" (p. 200) during follow-up counseling. They categorized the primary requests of those victims who accepted telephone counseling as: confirmation of concern, ventilation, clarification, and advice. Victims in the "confirmation of concern" category, mostly children and adolescents, tended to be rather guarded and volunteered little information. In response the counselor might ask questions and comment on positive steps the victim took. Victims who want ventilation, on the other hand, feel burdened and generally talk spontaneously about their experience and their feelings. The counselor's role with these victims is to give the victim freedom to speak, let her know it is all right to talk about her fears, and provide perspective as needed. Victims seeking clarification also spoke freely, but wanted help in "sort[ing] out the conflicting thoughts and feelings and to actively work on settling the crisis"; with these victims, the counselor followed the victim's verbal lead (Burgess & Holmstrom, p. 201). Finally, the fourth group of victims wanted advice on questions such as legal issues, whom to confide in, family conflicts surrounding the assault, and sexuality issues. Here the counselor's role is to give "direction and guidance in terms of information and alternative from which to choose . . . so the victim could make a decision" (Burgess & Holmstrom, p. 201).

***Group Approaches.*** Group therapy is not appropriate for all victims of sexual assault, but it may be useful for many. Some groups restrict membership by age, gender, and type of assault (incest, childhood sexual abuse, rape, and so on), so one must find or create a group with an appropriate makeup and a convenient meeting time. A member of a therapy group must also be willing to share at least some information about her experience with others.

Group therapy is generally considered effective for sexual assault survivors. "Various group interventions have been found to be effective in decreasing symptoms, especially phobic and anxiety responses of assault survivors who do not have a major personality disorder or other psychopathology" (Weinstein & Rosen, 1988, p. 212). Particular benefits of group therapy include being able to tell one's story to others who are likely to be sympathetic and validation from others who have "been there." As Weinstein and Rosen pointed out, "the sharing of the assault incident with others who have had similar experiences and feelings is often therapeutic" in and of itself (p. 212). Being a member of a group can also give the sexual assault victim a feeling of belonging. "Children and young adolescents who have experienced sexual assault feel somewhat isolated from their peers. . . . [and a therapy] group provides a place of almost guaranteed acceptance and understanding" (Weinstein & Rosen, p. 214). Groups may be especially appropriate for adolescents because adolescence "involves a shift from reliance on family to self-reliance and increased peer orientation" (Berliner & MacQuivey, 1983, p. 106), but sexual assault or abuse can isolate an adolescent from her usual peer group.

Berliner and MacQuivey (1983) summed up the whole idea of group therapy quite well in an introduction given to members of a therapy group for adolescent female victims of incest:

> The group is here to provide you with a safe and supportive place, free of blame, to talk about your sexual-assault experiences, to answer questions, to explore options, and to help you get in touch with your own power and strength. It is a place to meet others who have shared your sexual-assault experience, make new friends, and have fun. Our goal is for you to be able to say, "I'm not feeling so alone, so depressed, suicidal, or guilty. . . . I can feel my feelings and share them with others." (p. 112)

Although written for a very specific demographic, these goals could apply to almost any group for sexual assault victims.

## Counseling Concerns With Specific Populations

***Children and Young Adolescents.*** Many of the reactions to sexual assault discussed earlier are typical of children and young adolescents as well as adults. However, there are some special concerns to be aware of with these victims.

As Weinstein and Rosen (1988) observed, "very young children are not likely to really understand what happened to them" (p. 213). The counselor needs to help answer a young victim's questions in a manner appropriate to the child's age and sexual knowledge. It can be difficult, however, to encourage the child to discuss the assault. Children "often complain of 'bellyaches' or pain 'down there,' rather than describing the specific acts ... [and] find it very frightening just to remember the incident" (Weinstein & Rosen, pp. 213–214). In order to help a child describe what happened and her feelings about it, Weinstein and Rosen suggested using play therapy, particularly dolls and drawing (p. 214).

Another concern with young children is that they may exhibit separation anxiety (Weinstein & Rosen, 1988, p. 214). This is understandable, but may hamper the child's recovery and development if it is prolonged. One way to deal with separation anxiety is to discuss it with the parents and make sure that they are not reinforcing the behavior by supervising their child overly closely or severely restricting the child's activities (p. 214).

A few additional concerns apply to both children and adolescents. One is medical intervention (Weinstein & Rosen, 1988, p. 214). The importance of preparation and support during the medical examination was discussed earlier in reference to sexual assault victims in general; one would expect it to be even more important for a child. "With the sexually inactive child or adolescent the entire medical intervention needs special preparation if it is not to become another frightening assault" (p. 214). The counselor may help the child know what to expect and may help the parents understand how to prepare, support, and advocate for their child; the counselor can also help the child deal with her feelings after the medical examination.

The other concern that applies to both children and adolescents is that the victim may refuse to return to school (Weinstein & Rosen, 1988). This, like separation anxiety, is understandable for a short period, but can create further difficulties if it is prolonged. If it continues for more than a week, Burgess and Holmstrom (1974a, 1974b) suggested that it may be symptomatic of a phobic reaction. The return to school is sometimes eased if the counselor, with approval from the child's parents, encourages the child's teacher(s) and close friends to visit or telephone and helps them communicate acceptance and understanding to the child (Weinstein & Rosen, 1988).

***Racial and Ethnic Considerations.*** In addition to the usual need for cultural sensitivity in any counseling, working with sexual assault victims from diverse cultures involves an awareness of how each victim's culture and family view sexual assault issues. Unfortunately, there is little information available for the counselor to go on. Calhoun and Atkeson (1991) summarized some of the relevant research:

> Comparisons between White and Black victims show no difference in severity of reactions (Frank & Stewart, 1983; Kilpatrick, Veronen, & Best, 1985) or recov-

> ery rate (Morelli, 1981). However, Ruch and Chandler (1983) found that Asian victims suffered greater trauma than Caucasian victims. Ethical and/or cultural beliefs and values may interact with other assault variables such as social support and victim attributions to exacerbate or delay victim recovery. (p. 28)

One would also expect that victims who have recently moved to the area, whose primary language is not locally common, or who feel they "stand out" in terms of race, ethnicity, or religion are likely to feel particularly isolated and may have additional difficulties in dealing with the assault. In addition, Ben-Zvi and Horsfall (1985) pointed out that some "traditional" cultures highly value virginity and that this can add to the distress of a victim from these cultures (p. 346). The same may be true of some devoutly religious families.

The difficulty the counselor faces in dealing with these cultural issues is to try to reassure the victim of her worth without discounting her culture and belief system—a fine line to walk. In some cases, it may be useful to consult with community members with a background similar to the victim's or to help an individual victim find a support group which has other members who share her beliefs or experiences. Finally, keep in mind that some victims may be helped by participating in healing ceremonies from their religion or culture; if the victim expresses an interest in these, the counselor could help her locate community resources.

***Male Victims.*** Although there are some differences, male victims' reactions to sexual assault are similar in many ways to those of female victims. According to Calhoun and Atkeson (1991), "Goyer and Eddleman (1984) identified posttraumatic stress symptoms in 13 male sexual assault victims . . . [including] fear, generalized anxiety, depression, suicidal ideation, sleep disturbances, nightmares, anger, and sexual dysfunctions" (p. 114). These are all common reactions among female sexual assault victims as well, as discussed earlier. Weinstein and Rosen (1988), similarly, cited Burgess and Holmstrom (1974) in pointing out that the symptoms, fears, and emotions male victims experience as counseling progresses are the same as those of female victims (pp. 219–220). Also recall that male victims, like female victims, often find the medical examination traumatic (Weinstein & Rosen, p. 220).

One of the major differences with male victims is that they have usually been assaulted by an assailant of the same sex (Calhoun & Atkeson, 1991). Thus, male victims "frequently worry about the implications . . . for their sexual identity or that others may view a rape as predisposing them to homosexuality" (Calhoun & Atkson, p. 114), and their families may have the same worries (Weinstein & Rosen, 1988). These worries contribute to male victims' sense of shame and unwillingness to report the assault. Weinstein and Rosen recommend reassuring the male victim that these are myths. In the case of a young child, the counselor would need to reassure the parents, as well.

Other difficulties for male victims derive from societal pressures. Men feel they are expected to be able to defend themselves, which is one reason male victims hesitate to report sexual assaults (Weinstein & Rosen, 1988). They also feel that they are expected to appear masculine, and hence may worry that they were selected as a victim because they appeared "feminine." Finally, men in our society tend to expect themselves to be strong and in control. Many male victims "react badly to the loss of control and sense of helplessness experienced during sexual assault . . . [and therefore] may tend to withdraw, deny the experience, avoid reminders of it, or even become amnesic" (Calhoun & Atkeson, 1991, p. 114). Counseling a male sexual assault victim could include discussing gender roles and stereotypes in American society and in his family and helping him assess how realistic they are. As with any sexual assault victim, another part of his recovery is to help the male victim reduce his self-blame and place the responsibility for the assault on the perpetrator.

***Victims With Disabilities.*** Part of the trouble sexual assault victims with disabilities face is simply in trying to get the help they need. For example, local rape crisis centers may lack TTYs, making it impossible for deaf or hearing-impaired victims to call them, and there is also a general lack of sexual assault information available in Braille or audio formats for blind victims to access. In addition, a deaf adolescent may fear that if she tells another deaf person that word of the assault will spread through the generally tightly knit deaf community. Victims who have difficulty with mobility may also be reluctant to report an assault because of "previous negative experiences with hospitals and social service agencies which were not accessible or sensitive to their needs" (Ryerson, 1984, p. B19). Therefore, the first step to assisting victims with disabilities is to make sure that information and resources are available.

Adolescent victims with disabilities often face another set of difficulties, which has to with sexuality and sex education. Disabled teens "often do not receive adequate information about their sexuality at home or in school" (Ryerson, 1984, p. B19), and thus may not have clear knowledge about consent and sexual assault. This lack of knowledge makes them more vulnerable to sexual assault, and probably also heightens their level of crisis and confusion after an assault. These adolescents may need additional help with sexuality issues and self-blame in postassault counseling (Andrews & Veronen, 1993).

Weinstein and Rosen (1988) summed up the other concerns specific to disabled sexual assault victims as follows:

> Those with disabilities who have created a relatively independent life-style may have major setbacks because of the fear reactions common to post-assault victims (especially fears of being alone). Significant others or caretakers may feel highly responsible for not being effective. Society often identifies people with physical disabilities as childlike and may foster dependency behaviors after this crisis. Those with disabilities are often thought of as not being sexual. Thus, counselors may neglect the negative sexual outcomes of the rape trauma. These problems and any special medical difficulties may be exacerbated by the sexual assault and are important for counselors to consider. (p. 219)

Counselors should be alert for these problems when dealing with victims who have disabilities and be prepared to help the victims regain her independence and deal with issues of sexuality and sexual dysfunction.

***Victims Who Are Homosexual.*** Although there is little available information on counseling homosexual victims of sexual assault, a few concerns can be noted. One is that in a study by Waterman, Dawson, and Bologna (1989), both lesbians and gay men "who were victims of forced sex believed that it would be significantly more difficult to get counseling than did those who were not sexually victimized . . . [but] individuals who were not victims of forced sex did not view counseling as particularly easy to get" (p. 123). One reason for this is that programs that assist rape victims may not recognize a need to serve the gay community or may not publicize their services for homosexuals (Waterman et al., p. 123). Another point to consider is that many homosexual victims may not feel comfortable in counseling groups primarily made up of heterosexuals. Lesbians dealing with relationship violence may feel isolated if the rest of the group members are focusing on issues regarding men; perhaps even more isolating would be for a gay man to be in a group of heterosexual male victims, because (as noted earlier) the other group members are likely to be worried about their own sexual identity/orientation and may therefore come across as homophobic.

## Approaches With Significant Others

Although most of the services offered after a sexual assault focus on the victim—and rightly so—other people in the victim's life may also need assistance. Parents and friends may have difficulty dealing with the assault and the with the victim's healing process. Particular issues must be considered in counseling each of these groups.

***Victim's Parents.*** Burgess and Holmstrom (1974a, 1974b) found that parents whose adolescent was sexually assaulted went through an acute disorganization phase and a long-term phase of reorganization in reaction to their son's or daughter's experience. The victim's parents experience their child's assault as a crisis, albeit a qualitatively different crisis than the victim experiences.

Mann (1981) interviewed teenage sexual assault victims and their parents and found many qualitative differences in parents' and victims' concerns and reactions. Half of the parents, particularly those whose child had been physically injured, had continued fears for the safety of their child. Seventy percent expressed anger at the assailant and sought some form of revenge. Surprisingly, 41% of the parents directly blamed their child for the rape, especially if conflict was present in the family prior to the assault. The majority of parents were concerned about future emotional and sexual adjustment and about pregnancy and STDs.

In contrast, teenagers complained about increasing communication difficulties with parents following the rape. Their concerns were about parental overprotectiveness, restrictiveness, and anger. They were also concerned about rejection by their parents. In addition, adolescents had worries related to body image and peer reactions to the rape.

Counseling can help parents deal with their reactions to their child's sexual assault. Simply allowing them to express their feelings may be of some assistance. Schmidt (1981) found that families who ask questions and express their feelings at the emergency room feel more comfortable later with the victim at home. One could speculate answering parents' questions and letting the parents express their feelings later, in counseling, might have a similar benefit. Counselors may also need to teach some parents anger management and communication skills to help them express their emotions and needs in a more productive manner.

Another facet of counseling parents is to help them understand the myths and realities of sexual assault. Schmidt (1981) suggested that parents tend to blame the victim at first because of the parents' perception of rape as a sexual, rather than a violent, crime. Helping them understand rape as a violent, power-based crime may help parents to reduce their focus on the sexual aspects of the assault and to decrease the blame they assign their child; this could help them reopen communication with their child.

Mann (1981) developed several guidelines for counselors working with adolescent sexual assault victims and their families. Two of these are: to use separate interviews in identifying the victim's and parents' concerns; and to assist parents to accept and support the victim's separate feelings and needs. One way to assist parents in dealing with the victim's reactions is to educate them about typical reactions to sexual assault, Rape Trauma Syndrome, and so forth. If the parents know what to expect, they may have an easier time understanding and supporting the victim's behavior.

Finally, counselors should be ready to explain to parents what to expect from the victim's therapy and recovery. Logistical considerations, the victim's use of her assertiveness training in parent–child arguments, new expressions of anger, and the social aspects of therapy groups may all discourage parents from continuing their child's counseling (Berliner & MacQuivey, 1983). Counselors can warn parents that these problems may arise. "If some of the likely reactions or problems can be anticipated, parents can be helped to see the rationale for allowing the girls the time and place to work out all the different feelings that go with being victimized" (Berliner & MacQuivey, p. 115). Encouraging the parents to give their child the time and professional assistance she needs would benefit the child—and thus, indirectly, the parents—in the long run.

***Victim's Boyfriend or Girlfriend.*** Sexual assault, not surprisingly, strongly impacts the victim's boyfriend or girlfriend. Calhoun and Atkeson (1991) summarized the partner's experience:

> Not only must the partner cope with the victim's psychological distress and emotional needs, but he must also deal with his own reactions to the assault. Although reactions are variable, descriptive studies have found partners to exhibit shock, rage, self-blame, concern for the victim, and emotional distress immediately following sexual assault (Holmstrom & Burgess, 1979). Longitudinal studies of partner reaction indicate that the psychological distress (e.g., fear, anxiety, and depression) experienced by partners may be long term in nature and last for at least 1 year following sexual assault. (Veronen, Saunders, & Resnick, 1988, pp. 117–118)

While experiencing his own emotional distress, the victim's partner may also feel torn in trying to balance his emotional needs with those of the victim. The victim and her partner may be unable to provide sufficient support for each other, and couples often avoid even discussing the sexual assault or its effects (Calhoun & Atkeson, 1991, p. 118).

***Victim's Friends.*** Little information is available that specifically addresses counseling the friends of sexual assault victims, although they are often the first to learn of an assault (Hanson, Resnick, Saunders, Kilpatrick, & Best, 1999). Friends of victims may not typically seek out counseling, but those who serve as primary supports for the victim may need some assistance in dealing with their own reactions.

It is likely that very close friends of a sexual assault victim experience many of the same emotional impacts as victims' partners, including shock, rage, concern, and long-term depression, anxiety, and fear (see earlier passage from Calhoun & Atkeson). Female friends in particular may fear for their own safety.

Whereas some victims and their friends may wish to speak to a counselor together, a victim's friends will most likely seek help individually. It may be useful to give them written information on sexual assault and its effects so that they better understand what the victim is going through. Friends who fear for their own safety can probably benefit from attending self-defense or assertiveness-training classes, possibly with the victim. Some friends may also need assistance in setting boundaries with the victim so that the friend does not become overwhelmed.

## SEXUAL ASSAULT PREVENTION: THEORY AND PRACTICE

### Theories of Causation

In order to address how to prevent sexual assault, it is first necessary to consider its causes. There are several broad classes of theories.

***Victim Theories.*** A review of the available literature reveals no academic theories focusing mainly on the victim as the cause of rape. However, this view may be more common among the general population than among researchers. Recall that in 41% of the cases of adolescent sexual assault in Mann's (1981) study, parents of the victim directly blamed their child for the rape. Victim blame is also common among young people. Several studies have found that adolescents tend to blame the sexual assault victim for the assault. For example, Goodchilds and Zellman (1984) reported that, "across a number of vignettes presented to adolescents, one third of the responsibility for coercive sex was attributed to the nonconsenting girl" (Cowan & Campbell, 1995, p. 145). In Cowan and Campbell's (1995) survey of 453 high school students on the causes of rape, boys gave the highest mean responses to "female precipitation" items (pp. 147–148). These results are particularly disconcerting given the potency of rape-supportive attitudes as a risk factor for becoming a rapist. A study by Hall (1987) is an exception, finding that only 3% of adolescent boys and 13% of adolescent girls spontaneously explained rape with victim-blame statements.

***Rapist Theories.*** Several theories focus mainly on the individual rapist as the cause of rape. Evolutionary theory, as the name suggests, postulates "some genetic underpinnings, although these underpinnings could be quite indirect" for male behaviors resulting in rape (Ellis, 1989, p. 43). Without going into the details of natural selection, the basic idea is that "rape may have a selective advantage because, when it leads to procreation, the rapist's genes are propagated" (Renfrew, 1997, p. 207).

Psychopathology models focus on problems with rapists' neurological development. For example, Hucker, Langevin, Dickey, and Handy (1988) showed that the Luria Nebraska Neuropsychological Test Battery finds a relatively high level of impairment in sexually aggressive men and moderate levels in sadists as compared to controls. Langevin et al. (1988) concluded that "the right temporal lobe is somehow more implicated in sexual aggression than are other areas of the brain" (p. 170).

Social learning theory, on the other hand, suggests that certain men rape because they learned to do so by observing models—either in person or via media such as pornography. Evidence for this theory includes Koss and Dinero's (1988) finding that severe forms of sexual aggression correlate with "involvement in peer groups that reinforce highly sexualized views of women" (p. 144). Additionally, some of the risk factors discussed previously, such as having aggressive parents and (learned) rape-supportive attitudes, are consistent with social learning theory.

***Context Theories.*** Context theories are those that emphasize the influence of the societal context. Although they focus on the rapist to some extent, they emphasize society as a whole rather than interactions between individuals. The two theories I address here are feminist theory and cultural spillover theory.

Feminist theory "considers rape to be the result of long and deep-rooted social traditions in which males have dominated nearly all important political and economic activities" (Ellis, 1989, p. 10). In other words, feminist theory says that rape is the result of long-standing inequality between the sexes. Some cross-cultural evidence from studies of tribal societies supports this theory. For example, the Yanomamo are considered a "rape-prone" society, and the men "exert all the political power [while] women essentially function as the profits of fights and wars ... [in contrast] Ashanti society is characterized by sexual equality and a respect for the value of women, and Rattray (1923) could find no evidence of rape among these people" (Marshall & Barbaree, 1990, p. 266).

The other context theory, cultural spillover theory, focuses on a different aspect of society. According to this theory,

> cultural support for rape may not be limited to beliefs and attitudes that directly condone rape ... [but says that] the more a society tends to endorse the use of physical force to attain socially approved ends ..., the greater the likelihood that this legitimation of force will be generalized to other spheres of life where force is less socially approved, such as the family and relations between the sexes. (Baron & Straus, 1989, p. 147)

***Integrated Theories.*** Although many of the theories described earlier seem to be at complete odds with each other, a few integrative theories either combine elements of the others or are consistent with such combinations. Two of these theories are Marshall and Barbaree's (1990) theory of etiology and Russell's (1984) four criteria.

Marshall and Barbaree (1990) described an "integrated theory of the etiology of sexual offending" (p. 257). They consider four types of factors: biological influences; childhood experiences; sociocultural context; and transitory situational factors. Many individual risk factors are examined within each of these domains; this level of interaction is summarized in Fig. 17.1. Additionally, Marshall and Barbaree explain how these factors interact with each other to produce rape:

> Biological inheritance confers upon males a ready capacity to sexually aggress which must be overcome by appropriate training to instill social inhibitions toward such behavior. Variations in hormonal functioning may make this task more or less difficult. Poor parenting . . . typically fails to instill these constraints and may even serve to facilitate the fusion of sex and aggression rather than separate these two tendencies. Sociocultural attitudes may negatively interact with poor parenting to enhance the likelihood of sexual offending, if these cultural beliefs express traditional patriarchal views. The young male whose childhood experiences have ill-prepared him for a prosocial life may readily accept these views to bolster his sense of masculinity. If such a male gets intoxicated or angry or feels stressed, and he finds himself in circumstances where he is not known or thinks he can get away with offending, then such a male is likely to sexually offend depending upon whether he is aroused at the time or not. (pp. 270–271)

Finally, we come to Russell's (1984) adaptation of Finkelhor's (1984) multicausal theory. Finkelhor developed a multicausal theory to explain the occurrence of child sexual abuse, under which four conditions must be met for abuse to occur: the desire to sexually abuse a child; undermining of the perpetrator's internal inhibitions; undermining of the perpetrator's social inhibitions (such as the fear of punishment); and the ability of the perpetrator to "undermine or overcome his or her chosen victim's capacity to avoid or resist." Russell (1984) theorized that these are also preconditions for the sexual assault of women and suggested factors that could predispose men to want to sexually assault: biological influences, childhood sexual abuse, gender role socialization, mass media influence, and pornography.

The factors examined by Marshall and Barbaree could interact to produce each of the four conditions set forth by Russell; this is shown in Fig. 17.2. The drawback of this hybrid is taking two very broad theories and producing an even an even broader theory, making it difficult to choose a specific target for prevention. However, sexual assault may be caused by a wide array of factors working together. The availability of many targets for preventive programs, although it increases the difficulty of choosing a fo-

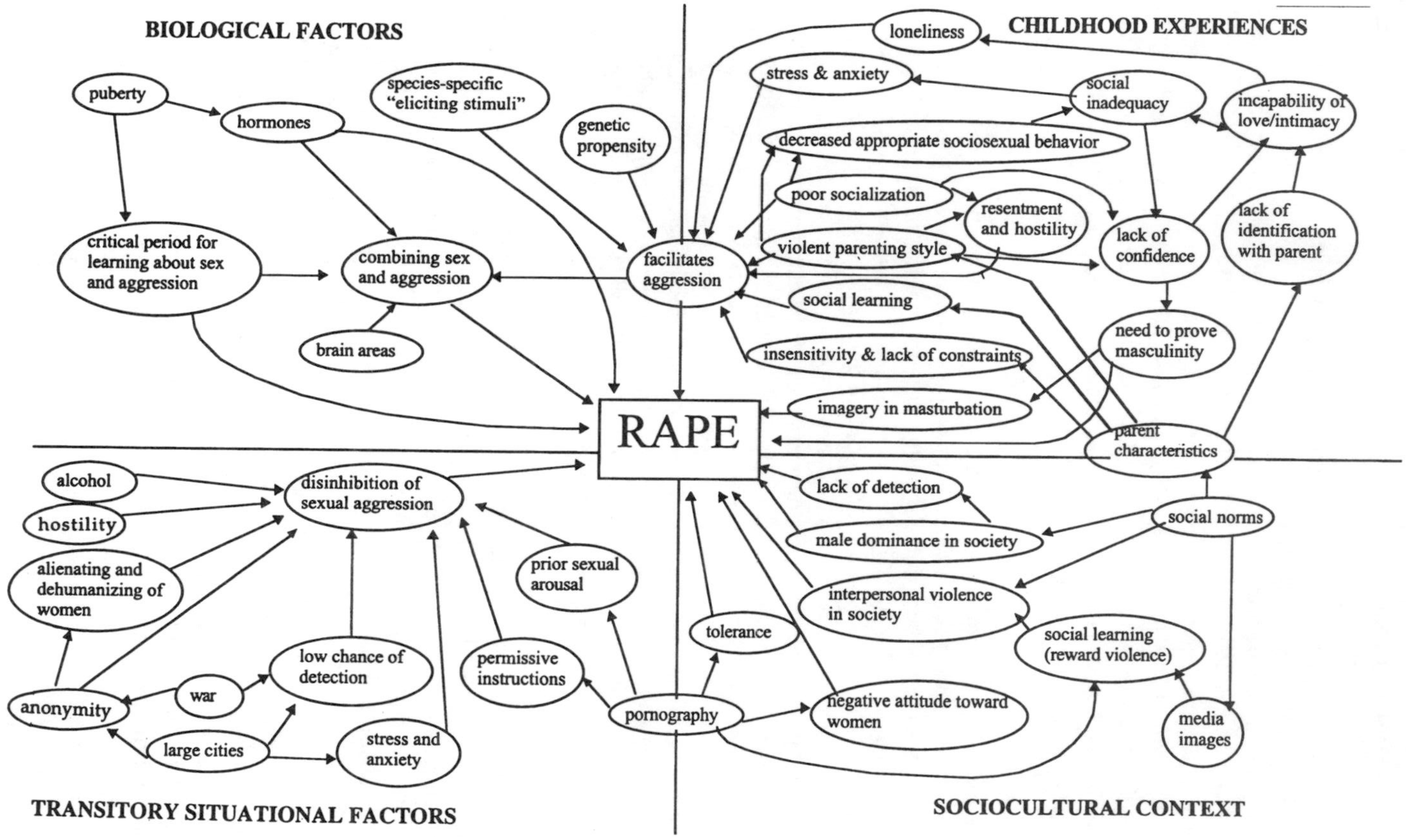


FIG. 17.1. Summary of Marshall and Barbaree (1990).

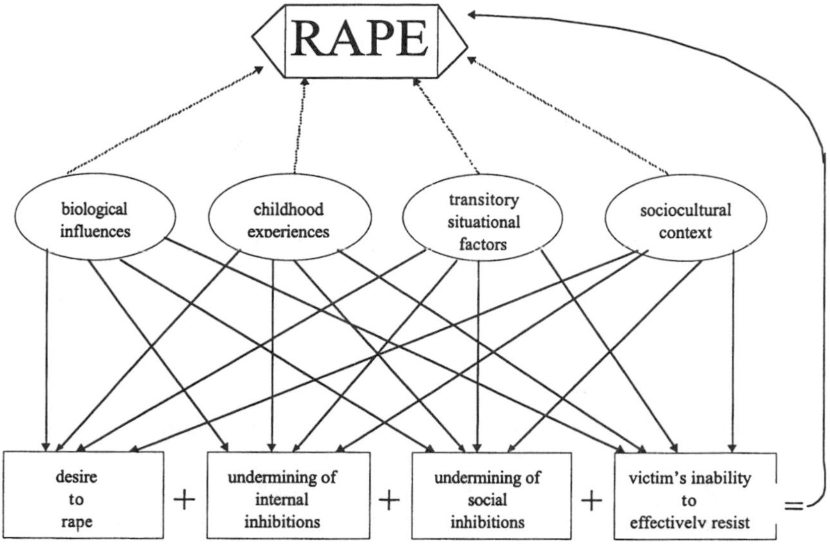


FIG. 17.2. Hybrid of Marshall and Barbaree (1990) and Russell (1984).

cus, may actually be a benefit which allows communities to tailor programs to their resources and needs.

## Prevention of Sexual Assault

***Implications of the Theories.*** Although no true victim-focused theories were available in the literature, the implications of this approach seem obvious. This type of program would target female audiences of high-school to college age and focus on how to avoid becoming a victim. For example, given that alcohol consumption is a risk factor, such programs might recommend against consuming alcohol in "unsafe" situations. Self-defense programs could also fall into this category, inasmuch as resistance prevents the completion of attempted rape.

Rapist-focused theories suggest a very different audience and content. It is difficult to see evolutionary or psychopathology models recommending much in the way of primary prevention; they would more likely focus on screenings to find men likely to commit sexual assault and creating secondary prevention programs for them. Social learning theory, on the other hand, would suggest changing how sexual relationships are presented in the media, eliminating at least violent pornography, and providing nonviolent models of relationships by focusing primary prevention efforts on parents and teachers.

Context theories would suggest changing the sociocultural context. Feminist theory focuses on creating equality between men and women in all spheres of life, including political and economic. Cultural spillover theory emphasizes the need to decrease legitimized violence, by, for example, limiting media portrayal of violence, outlawing corporal punishment, and abolishing the death penalty. Programs based on these two theories would consist largely of convincing the general population to believe the theory and to work on social and legal change.

The integrated theories have less clear implications for prevention programming. Marshall and Barbaree (1990), in particular, presented such a complex suite of interacting factors that prevention programs would have to target multiple areas; for example, community parenting classes to decrease the number of boys exposed to poor parenting, and legal or other changes to decrease violence, and feminist programming to improve the status of women, and so on. Russell (1984) presented more of a chain of events; this implies that only one link of the chain needs to be broken. Although it might be difficult to address men's desire to sexually assault, programs could focus on strengthening moral values (i.e., increase internal inhibitions) or making reporting easier and punishments harsher (i.e., increase social inhibitions) or creating self-defense classes and other safety education (i.e., increasing the probability of effective resistance).

Many possible rape prevention strategies are available; Fischhoff, Furby, and Morgan (1987) documented 1,140 possibilities. However, each of the most common strategies involving education and self-defense, when consistently used, was estimated by groups of men, women, and self-defense experts to reduce the risk of sexual assault by half (Furby, Fischhoff, & Morgan, 1989).

***Classes of Programs.*** Rape prevention programs can be divided into four broad classes. These are environmental control, victim control, self-empowerment, and social change strategies. In practice, not all programs fit neatly into these categories, but these classes describe the emphases of most programs.

The first type of program is what I refer to as environmental control. Lonsway (1996) referred to this as what "rape prevention has historically involved" and listed possible components: "shearing bushes, installing lights and alarm systems, or teaching women self-defense" (p. 230). For example, a project on one college campus involved improving campus lighting and installing signs to notify pedestrians and bicyclists of pathways with good lighting. These programs increase feelings of safety, and it is probably one of the strategies with the lowest financial cost over the long term. The problem with this approach is that it targets stranger rape, which is much less common than acquaintance rape. Thus, the feelings of safety it generates might be a false sense of security. Additionally, the benefits of these measures, with the exception of self-defense training, only affect safety in the immediate area. Although there is no objection to such measures as part of a larger program, I fear that some communities and campuses might provide this type of environmental control without providing anything to address acquaintance rape.

Victim control programs are those in which "the cause of rape is simply attributed to a . . . set of 'risky' behaviors" (Corcoran, 1992, p. 134). This type of program is based on the victim-focused theory described earlier (recall that there is little or no research supporting this theory). These programs warn potential victims of risky behavior such as drinking, walking alone at night, and acting hesitant. Victim control has the same main benefit as environmental control: feelings of safety (at least as long as one avoids "risky" behavior). However, Corcoran points out the high costs of such an approach, including victim blame, further restriction of women's activities, and a lack of effectiveness in decreasing sexual assaults.

Self-empowerment, on the other hand, attempts "to provide women with more options and to strengthen their ability to resist and avoid rape" by providing information, self-defense training, assertiveness and communication training, and so on (Corcoran, 1992, p. 135). One of the strengths of this type of program is that the effects are mobile; women can carry these skills with them. It is also much less restrictive than victim control. Problems with this strategy include victim blame, the lack of 100% effectiveness of resistance, and the possible danger of displacing sexual assaults onto more vulnerable women as rapists seek out new targets (Corcoran, p. 136).

Social change, the final class of programs, parallels the context theories described earlier. One example is set of school reforms recommended by Enke and Sudderth (1991). They urge schools to address peer relationships in current programs on sexual coercion; to encourage egalitarianism; to teach communication and body awareness; to avoid rewarding gender-stereotyped behavior; to encourage cooperation and participation rather than competition; and to teach a more holistic conception of sexuality. Feminist approaches would also fall into this change category. The advantages of social change include possible effectiveness (e.g., the success of gender role discussions; see the section on program evaluation) and applicability to a wide audience. The drawbacks include the amount of time needed to change society and the difficulty of eliciting action after the program is over. Also, this perspective "does not provide specific rape avoidance or self-protection strategies" for individuals (Corcoran, 1992, p. 136).

***Designing Rape Prevention Programs.*** The design of a rape prevention program will, of course, depend on the philosophy or theory behind it. Because I believe that rape is caused by numerous factors and their interactions and multiple levels, I also favor prevention programs with multiple components. Another advantage to multifaceted programs is that different components are likely to appeal to—and affect—different people, so having multiple components increases the potential audience.

I view the causes of sexual assault via a hybrid of Marshall and Barbaree's (1990) and Russell's (1984) theories, as shown in Fig. 17.2. It is difficult for primary prevention efforts to target biological factors or childhood experiences, although childhood experiences could be influenced by providing parenting classes and by directing efforts at the prevention of child abuse (a topic found in other chapters). Situational factors are also difficult to control in practice, although some educational efforts can be directed there. For example, alcohol consumption is a potent enough risk factor that women should be made aware of its effects on sexual assault risks; however, care must be taken to avoid blaming victims who consume alcohol or excusing the behavior of offenders who consume alcohol or attempt to intoxicate their victims. Sociocultural factors, then, are probably the most logical targets for prevention, although this does not mean that they are the easiest to change.

There are four levels on which to examine sociocultural factors: perpetrator desire, perpetrator internal inhibitions, social inhibitions, and victim resistance. It is difficult to address perpetrator desire except as how the media and pornography portray sex and aggression as connected with love and enjoyment; this might be more effectively addressed by legislation or short-term publicity campaigns than by ongoing programs. Programs can successfully address internal inhibitions on a sociocultural level by discussing rape myths; interactive drama is generally considered effective, but videotapes are also commonly used. Social inhibitions are generally addressed governmentally (i.e., via the courts and correctional system), but can also be addressed by increasing a potential perpetrator's fear of being caught in the first place. One way is to provide victim support services and to make it as easy as possible for victims to report sexual assault and get legal help. Finally, victims' ability to resist can be increased by commonly used means such as self-defense training.

Although crisis and advocacy services are not really primary prevention, they are important elements in a comprehensive program. First, one hopes that they mitigate whatever impacts sexual assault may have. Providing support for victims of sexual assault also creates an environment in which rape is not accepted and victims are not blamed or stigmatized—a possible model under social learning theory. Providing these services may not always be feasible in a school-based program, but students can be made aware of community resources which do provide them.

An additional consideration is that programs may cause distress in participants who are victims or friends of victims. Therefore, I recommend against making such programs and rape-education presentations mandatory. Although making them completely voluntary would probably result in a rather small audience, there should at least be some unobtrusive option available for students who wish to opt out. One could argue that the students who most need the program are also likely to excuse themselves, but I believe it is more important to have an escape available for victims who need it. I also agree with Heppner, Humphrey, Hillenbrand-Gunn, and DeBord (1995) decision to have counselors available at rape prevention presentations. Peer counselors would suffice as long as low-cost professional resources were also publicized to participants.

## Program Evaluation

Program evaluation research indicates that rape prevention programs aimed at men work, to at least some extent. Gilbert, Heesacker, and Gannon (1991) found that a 1-hour "psychoeducational" program presented to college men produced statistically significant attitude change and higher willingness to listen to and comment positively on a telephone appeal regarding a women's safety project, but no more willingness to volunteer time on the project compared to a control group. Schewe and O'Donohue (1996), using two types of 1-hour presentations, were able to produce "statistically and even clinically significant changes [in rape-supportive attitudes] in males who are judged to be at high risk for raping" (p. 467). This study also found that a presentation based on rape myths was more effective in changing rape-supportive attitudes than a victim empathy program (Schewe & O'Donohue, 1996). Thus, educational programs alone seem to be able to influence males' attitudes—a first step toward influencing their behavior.

Positive results have also been found for programs aimed at women. Hanson and Gidycz (1993) examined a program for college students which included statistics, a worksheet on rape myths, discussion of a videotaped date rape scenario and a video on "possible protective behaviors," information on resources, and a question-and-answer session. Their results for women with no prior history of sexual assault included increased knowledge on a posttest, changes in dating behavior to avoid risky situations (but no change in self-perceived clarity of sexual communication), and, perhaps most impressively, a lower rate of sexual victimization (6%, compared to a control group's rate of 14%) over an academic quarter.

At least one study, however, has not found entirely positive results. Heppner et al. (1995) used two types of programs (an interactive drama and a didactic video) with mixed-gender audiences and found mixed results. They found no immediate change in rape-supportive attitudes, except for men in the didactic video program, and found a rebound effect (i.e., scores returning to the same or worse as pretest scores) for both types of programs over 5 months. However, there were increases in knowledge scores, especially for the interactive drama program but also for the video program, and these did not rebound. Finally, Heppner and colleagues found that subjects in the interactive drama program were more likely than the other two groups to volunteer time for a rape prevention project, but found no difference between the groups in willingness to accept a fee increase to support rape prevention programming.

A meta-analysis by Lonsway (1996) examined the effectiveness of several components commonly found in rape prevention programs. Her findings included that addressing rape myths "is one of the most widely used techniques . . . and it is the strategy most commonly associated with desirable attitude change" (pp. 246–247), but warns that this outcome is confounded by the use of rape myths to measure participants' attitudes. Explicit discussions of sex roles and gender inequality is also fairly successful. Lonsway additionally reported mixed results on interactive participation (e.g., discussion) and empathy induction. Finally, confrontational presentation styles actually decrease success. She noted that "although educational programs challenging rape culture *do* require confrontation of established ideologies, such interventions *do not necessitate a style of personal confrontation*" (p. 250).

The success of a rape prevention program probably depends on the quality of its materials and presenters as well as its philosophy and aims. Although Hanson and Gidycz (1993) did not have perfect success, their reduction in the rates of sexual assault over one academic quarter was impressive enough that their materials could serve as a model.

There are several cautions, however, in trying to evaluate a rape prevention model. Although attitude change is a common criterion, Heppner et al. (1995) showed that it may rebound after the program; thus, either programs must be repeated frequently or another measure should be used. Behavioral outcomes are, of course, ideal, and Hanson and Gidycz's (1993) use of actual sexual assault rates is again a model for other programs; where participants cannot be followed, however, attitude change immediately after a presentation may be the only short-term measure available. A decrease in the rates of sexual assault is the ultimate goal, but this can be seen only over the long term; ideally, it should be measured by methods such as retrospective questionnaires, as police reports represent only a fraction of sexual assaults. An additional evaluation consideration is that an increase in reports to police agencies and support services may represent an increased willingness for victims to seek assistance rather than an increase in the number of victims.

Finally, rape prevention educators should be alert for unintended effects. Some of these may be positive; for example, self-defense training can provide a good form of exercise and might increase physical health measures, or attitude change to decrease rape-supportive attitudes could conceivably impact attitudes on and reporting of domestic violence. Some impacts, however, may not be positive. For example, victim control programs may lead women to restrict their activities. Programs may lead to increased levels of fear, although including self-empowerment components may ameliorate this concern. In addition, programs may cause distress in participants who are victims or friends of victims; this has already been discussed.

## CONCLUSIONS

Sexual assault is a crime that is far too common in the United States at present. When sexual assaults occur, it is important that counseling be available to the victim, her parents, her romantic partner, and her friends. Specific concerns and various modes and strategies for counseling and prevention have been discussed, and the schools are a place where efforts should be launched.

There does not seem to be any one simple cause of sexual assault. There are many causal influences described by many theories. However, there is good evidence that sexual assault can be prevented through the use of various programs. Program evaluations offer some consensus on what components should be included, particularly discussion of rape myths and gender roles. The most important components of a comprehensive program are victim support services, education that facilitates internal and social inhibitions for potential rapists, and resistance (i.e., self-defense) training for potential victims. With effort the silent epidemic of rape and sexual assault can be quelled.

## REFERENCES

Andrews, A. B., & Veronen, L. J. (1993). Sexual assault and people with disabilities. *Journal of Social Work & Human Sexuality, 8*, 137–159.

Baron, L., & Straus, M. A. (1989). *Four theories of rape in American society: A state-level analysis.* New Haven, CT: Yale University Press.

Beck, A. T. (1972). *Depression: Causes and treatment.* Philadelphia: University of Pennsylvania Press.

Ben-Zvi, R., & Horsfall, E. (1985). Adolescent rape: The role of rape crisis counseling. *International Journal of Adolescent Medicine and Health, 1*, 343–356.

Berliner, L., & MacQuivey, K. (1983). A therapy group for female adolescent victims of sexual abuse. In M. Rosenbaum (Ed)., *Handbook of short-term therapy groups* (pp. 101–116). New York: McGraw-Hill.

Bloom, M. (1996). *Primary prevention practices.* Thousand Oaks, CA: Sage.

Briere, J., & Malamuth, N. M. (1983). Self-reported likelihood of sexually aggressive behavior: Attitudinal versus sexual explanations. *Journal of Research in Personality, 17*(3), 315–323.

Burgess, A. W., Groth, A. N., Holmstrom, L. L., & Sgroi, S. M. (1978). *Sexual assault of children and adolescents*. Lexington, MA: Lexington.

Burgess, A. W., & Holmstrom, L. L. (1974). Crisis and counseling requests of rape victims. *Nursing Research, 23*(3), 196–202.

Burgess, A. W., & Holmstrom, L. L. (1979a). *Rape: Crisis and recovery*. Bowie, MD: Brady.

Burgess, A. W., & Holmstrom, L. L. (1979b). Rape: Sexual disruption and recovery. *American Journal of Orthopsychiatry, 49*, 648–657.

Calhoun, K. S., & Atkeson, B. M. (1991). *Treatment of rape victims: Facilitating psychosocial adjustment*. New York: Pergamon Press.

Choquet, M., Darves-Bornoz, J. M., Ledoux, S., Manfredi, R., & Hassler, C. (1997). Self-reported health and behavioral problems among adolescent victims of rape in France: Results of a cross-sectional survey. *Child Abuse & Neglect, 21*, 823–832.

Corcoran, C. B. (1992). From victim control to social change: A feminist perspective on campus rape prevention programs. In J. C. Chrisler & D. Howard (Eds.), *New directions in feminist psychology: Practice, theory, and research* (pp. 130–140). New York: Springer.

Cormier, S., & Cormier, B. (1998). *Interviewing strategies for helpers: Fundamental skills and cognitive behavioral interventions*. Pacific Grove, CA: Brooks/Cole.

Cowan, G., & Campbell, R. R. (1995). Rape causal attitudes among adolescents. *The Journal of Sex Research, 32*, 145–153.

deAlcorn, S. (1984). *Victim reactions to rape*. In Alternatives to fear (Ed.), *This is it!: Teen acquaintance rape information and prevention activities for groups*. Seattle, WA: Author.

Denmare, D., Briere, J., & Lips, H. M. (1988). Violent pornography and self-reported likelihood of sexual aggression. *Journal of Research in Personality, 22*, 140–153.

Ellis, E. M. (1983). A review of empirical rape research: Victim reactions and response to treatment. *Clinical Psychology Review, 3*, 473–490.

Ellis, L. (1989). *Theories of rape: Inquiries into the causes of sexual aggression*. New York: Hemisphere.

Enke, L. E., & Sudderth, L. K. (1991). Educational reforms. In E. Grauerholz & M. A. Koralewski (Eds.), *Sexual coercion: A sourcebook on its nature, causes, and prevention* (pp. 149–159). Lexington, MA: Lexington Books.

Finkelhor, D. (1984). *Child sexual abuse: New theory and research*. New York: The Free Press.

Fischhoff, B., Furby, L., & Morgan, M. (1987). Rape prevention: A typology of strategies. *Journal of Interpersonal Violence, 2*, 292–308.

Frank, E., & Stewart, B. D. (1983). Treatment of depressed rape victims: An approach to stress-induced symptomatology. In P. J. Clayton & J. E. Barrett (Eds.), *Treatment of depression: Old controversies and new approaches* (pp. 307–330). New York: Raven Press.

Furby, L., Ficshhoff, B., & Morgan, M. (1989). Judged effectiveness of common rape prevention and self-defense strategies. *Journal of Interpersonal Violence, 4*, 44–64.

Gilbert, B. J., Heesacker, M., & Gannon, L. J. (1991). Changing the sexual aggression-supportive attitudes of men: A psychoeducational approach. *Journal of Counseling Psychology, 38*(2), 197–203.

Goodchilds, J. D., & Zellman, G. L. (1984). Sexual signaling and sexual aggression in adolescent relationships. In N. M. Malamuth & E. Donnerstein (Eds.), *Pornography and sexual aggression* (pp. 233–243). New York: Academic Press.

Gordon, M. T., & Riger, S. (1989). *The female fear*. New York: The Free Press.

Goyer, P., & Eddleman, H. (1984). Same sex rape of nonincarcerated men. *American Journal of Psychiatry, 141*, 576–579.

Hall, E. R. (1987). Adolescents' perceptions of sexual assault. *Journal of Sex Education & Therapy, 13*, 37–42.

Hanson, K. A., & Gidycz, C. A. (1993). Evaluation of a sexual assault prevention program. *Journal of Counseling and Clinical Psychology, 61*, 1046–1052.

Hanson, R. F., Resnick, H. S., Saunders, B. E., Kilpatrick, D. G., & Best, C. (1999). Factors related to the reporting of childhood rape. *Child Abuse & Neglect, 23*, 559–569.

Harney, P. A., & Muehlenhard, C. L. (1991). Rape. In E. Grauerholz & M. A. Koralewski (Eds.), *Sexual coercion: A sourcebook on its nature, causes, and prevention* (pp. 3–15). Lexington, MA: Lexington Books.

Heppner, M. J., Humphrey, C. F., Hillenbrand-Gunn, T. L., & DeBord, K. A. (1995). The differential effects of rape prevention programming on attitudes, behavior, and knowledge. *Journal of Counseling Psychology, 42*, 508–518.

Holmstrom, L. L., & Burgess, A. W. (1979). Rape: The husband's and boyfriend's initial reactions. *The Family Coordinator, 28*, 321–330.

Hucker, S., Langevin, R., Dickey, R., & Handy, L. (1988). Cerebral damage and dysfunction in sexually aggressive men. *Annals of Sex Research, 1*, 33–47.

Kaplan, D., & Holmes, M. M. (1999). Clinical management of rape in adolescent girls. *Patient Care, 33*, 42–56.

Kilpatrick, D. G., Veronen, L. J., & Best, C. L. (1985). Factors predicting psychological distress among rape victims. In C. R. Figley (Ed.), *Trauma and its wake* (pp. 113–141). New York: Brunner/Mazel.

Koss, M. P. (1983). The scope of rape: Implications for the clinical treatment of victims. *Clinical Psychologist, 36*, 88–91.

Koss, M. P., & Dinero, T. E. (1988). Predictors of sexual aggression among a national sample of male college students. In R. A. Prentky & V. L. Quinsey (Eds.), *Human sexual aggression: Current perspectives* (pp. 133–147). New York: *Annals of the New York Academy of Sciences*. Vol. 528.

Langevin, R., Bain, J., Wortzman, G., Hucker, S., Dickey, R., & Wright, P. (1988). Sexual sadism: Brain, blood, and behavior. In R. A. Prentky & V. L. Quinsey (Eds.), *Human sexual aggression: Current perspectives* (pp. 163–171). New York: *Annals of the New York Academy of Sciences*. Vol. 528

Ledray, L. E. (1986). *Recovering from rape*. New York: Henry Hill.

Lehmann, D. (1991). Sexual assault. In M. L. Pernoll (Ed.), *Current obstetric & gynecologic diagnosis & treatment* (pp. 1142–1147, 7th ed.). Norwalk, CT: Appleton & Lange.

Lonsway, K. A. (1996). Preventing acquaintance rape through education: What do we know? *Psychology of Women Quarterly, 20*(2), 229–265.

MacDonald, J. M. (1971). *Rape offenders and their victims*. Springfield, IL: Thomas.

Mann, E. M. (1981). Self-reported stresses of adolescent rape victims. *Journal of Adolescent Health Care, 2*, 29–33.

Marshall, W. L., & Barbaree, H. E. (1990). An integrated theory of the etiology of sexual offending. In W. L. Marshall, D. R. Laws, & H. E. Barbaree (Eds.), *Handbook of sexual assault: Issues, theories, and treatment of the offender* (pp. 257–275). New York: Plenum Press.

McDermott, M. J. (1979). *Rape victimization in 26 American cities*. Washington, DC: U.S. Department of Justice, Law Enforcement Assistance Administration, National Criminal Justice Information Statistics Service.

Miller, B. C., Monson, B. H., & Norton, M. C. (1995). The effects of forced sexual intercourse on white female adolescents. *Child Abuse & Neglect, 19*(10), 1289–1310.

Morelli, P. H. (1981, March). *Comparison of the psychological recovery of black and white victims of rape*. Paper resented at the meeting of the Association for Women in Psychology, Boston, MA.

Muram, D., Hostetler, B. R., Jones, C. E., & Speck, P. M. (1995). Adolescent victims of sexual assault. *Journal of Adolescent Health, 17*(6), 372–375.

Nadelson, C. C., Notman, M. T., Zackson, H., & Gornick, J. (1982). A follow-up study of rape victims. *American Journal of Psychiatry, 139*, 1266–1270.

Norris, J. (1994). Alcohol and female sexuality: A look at expectancies and risks. *Alcohol Health and Research World, 18*(3), 197–201.

Rattray, R. S. (1923). *Ashanti.* Oxford, England: Clarendon.

Renfrew, J. W. (1997). *Aggression and its causes: A biopsychological approach.* New York: Oxford University Press.

Ruch, L. O., & Chandler, S. M. (1983). Sexual assault trauma during the acute phase: An exploratory model and multivariate analysis. *Journal of Health and Social Behavior, 24,* 174–185.

Russell, D. E. (1984). *Sexual exploitation.* Beverly Hills, CA: Sage.

Ryerson, E. (1984). Adolescents with disabilities and acquaintance rape. In Alternatives to fear (Ed.), *This is it!: Teen acquaintance rape information and prevention activities for groups.* Seattle, WA: Author.

Schewe, P. A., & O'Donohue, W. (1996). Rape prevention with high-risk males: Short-term outcome of two interventions. *Archives of Sexual Behavior, 25,* 455–471.

Schmidt, A. M. (1981). Adolescent female rape victims: Special considerations. *Psychosocial Nursing and Mental Health Services, 19,* 17–19.

Scott, C. S., Lefley, H. P., & Hicks, D. (1993). Potential risk factors for rape in three ethnic groups. *Community Mental Health Journal, 29*(2), 133–141.

Smith, D. W., Letourneau, E. J., Saunders, B. E., Kilpatrick, D. G., Resnick, H. S., & Best, C. L. (2000). Delay in disclosure of childhood rape: Results from a national survey. *Child Abuse & Neglect, 24,* 273–287.

Stein, N. (1995). The definition of sexual harassment applies to schools. In K. L. Swisher (Ed.), *What is sexual harassment?* (pp. 19–24). San Diego, CA: Greenhaven Press.

Ullman, S. E., & Knight, R. A. (1993). The efficacy of women's resistance strategies in rape situations. *Psychology of Women Quarterly, 17,* 23–38.

Veronen, L. J., Saunders, B. E., & Resnick, H. S. (1988, November). *Partner reactions to rape.* Paper presented at the meeting of the Association for the Advancement of Behavioral Therapy, New York.

Vicary, J. R., Klingaman, L. R., & Harkness, W. L. (1995). Risk factors associated with date rape and sexual assault of adolescent girls. *Journal of Adolescence, 18,* 289–306.

Warshaw, R. (1988). *I never called it rape.* New York: Harper & Row.

Waterman, C. K., Dawson, L. J., & Bologna, M. J. (1989). Sexual coercion in gay male and lesbian relationships: Predictors and implications for support services. *The Journal of Sex Research, 26*(1), 118–124.

Webb, S. L. (1995). Sexual harassment should be defined broadly. In K. L. Swisher (Ed.), *What is sexual harassment?* (pp. 10–18). San Diego: Greenhaven Press.

Weinstein, E., & Rosen, E. (1988). *Sexuality counseling: Issues and implications.* Pacific Grove, CA: Brooks/Cole.

Zoucha-Jensen, J. M., & Coyne, A. (1993). The effects of resistance strategies on rape. *American Journal of Public Health, 83,* 1633–1634.

CHAPTER

# 18

# Helping Children With Eating Disorders: Quintessential Research on Etiology, Prevention, Assessment, and Treatment

Shane R. Jimerson
Renee Pavelski
Micah Orliss
University of California, Santa Barbara

Increasingly, educational professionals have recognized the influence of socioemotional health on both classroom adjustment and achievement. However, it seems that relatively few professionals working in the schools are adequately prepared to consider the potential implications of eating disorders on subsequent school adjustment and achievement, and provide support for these students. This avoidance has been due in part to the belief that eating disorders are medical disabilities separate from educational concerns. However, eating disorders pose particular problems in the educational setting for numerous reasons. First, the age range of eating disorders now extends to early elementary school (age 7 years), with increasing prevalence in children and adolescents (Bryant-Waugh & Lask, 1995; Phelps & Bajorek, 1991). Second, recent research suggests that the incidence of eating disorders has risen dramatically over the past two decades with no evidence of abatement (Lucas, Beard, O'Fallon, & Kurland, 1991; Steiner & Lock, 1998). The prevalence of anorexia nervosa and bulimia nervosa among girls between the ages of 10 and 19 (approximately 2% and 4%, respectively) places eating disorders among the most common chronic illnesses of adolescent girls (Lucas et al., 1991; Stice & Agras, 1998). With this increased scope and significance, eating disorders can no longer be overlooked in our schools.

Broadly, eating disorders include rumination, pica, obesity, anorexia, and bulimia. Of particular concern for our students are both anorexia nervosa and bulimia nervosa. The *Diagnostic and Statistical Manual of Mental*

*Disorders*–Text Revised (DSM–IV–TR) (American Psychiatric Association, 2000) definition of anorexia includes symptoms of low body weight, fear of gaining weight, distorted body image, and the absence of menstruation in females (see Table 18.1). DSM–IV–TR symptoms of bulimia nervosa include recurrent episodes of binge eating, inappropriate compensatory behavior (purging), and a self-evaluation unduly influenced by body weight (see Table 18.2). A primary difference between the disorders is that anorexics are significantly underweight, while bulimics generally are within normal weight ranges or only slightly underweight.

This chapter provides important information regarding the etiology, prevention, assessment, and treatment of eating disorders. A review of the recent research and relevant literature is summarized reflecting the current knowledge regarding anorexia nervosa and bulimia nervosa during childhood and adolescence. In addition, several web sites are included for professionals who use the Internet as a resource (see Table 18.3). Within this

TABLE 18.1
*DSM–IV–TR* Criteria for Anorexia Nervosa

**The diagnostic criteria according to the *DSM–IV–TR* (APA, 2000) for Anorexia Nervosa;**

a) Refusal to maintain body weight at or above a minimally normal weight for age and height (e.g., weight loss leading to maintenance of body weight less than 85% of that expected; or failure to make expected weight gain during period of growth, leading to body weight less than 85% of that expected).
b) Intense fear of gaining weight or becoming fat, even though underweight.
c) Disturbance in the way in which one's body weight or shape is experienced, undue influence of body weight or shape on self-evaluation, or denial of the seriousness of the current low body weight.
d) In postmenarcheal females, amenorrhea, i.e., the absence of at least three consecutive menstrual cycles. (A woman is considered to have amenorrhea if her periods occur only following hormone, e.g., estrogen).

**Specify types:**

Restricting Type: during the current episode of Anorexia Nervosa, the person has not regularly engaged in binge- eating or purging behavior (i.e., self-induced vomiting or the misuse of laxatives, diuretics, or enemas).

Binge-Eating/Purging Type: during the current episode of Anorexia Nervosa, the person has regularly engaged in binge-eating or behavior (i.e., self-induced vomiting or the misuse of laxatives, diuretics, or enemas).

Reprinted with permission from the *Diagnostic and Statistical Manual of Mental Disorders, Fourth Edition, Text Revision.* Copyright 2000 American Psychiatric Association.

TABLE 18.2

*DSM–IV–TR* Criteria for Bulimia Nervosa

---

**The diagnostic criteria according to the DSM-IV-TR (APA, 2000) for Bulimia Nervosa;**

a) Recurrent episodes of binge eating. An episode of binge eating is characterized by both of the following:

   1. eating, in a discrete period of time (e.g., within any 2-hour period), an amount of food that is definitely larger than most people would eat during a similar period of time and under similar circumstances
   2. a sense of lack of control over eating during the episode (e.g., a feeling that one cannot stop eating or control what or how much one is eating)

b) Recurrent inappropriate compensatory behavior in order to prevent weight gain, such as self-induced vomiting; misuse of laxatives, diuretics, enemas, or other medications; fasting; or excessive exercise.

c) The binge eating and inappropriate compensatory behaviors both occur, on average, at least twice a week for 3 months.

d) Self-evaluation is unduly influenced by body shape and weight.

e) The disturbance does not occur exclusively during episodes of Anorexia Nervosa.

**Specify types:**

Purging type: during the current episode of bulimia nervosa, the person has regularly engaged in self-induced vomiting or the misuse of laxatives, diuretics, or enemas.

Nonpurging type: during the current episode of bulimia nervosa, the person has used other inappropriate compensatory behaviors, such as fasting or excessive exercise, but has not regularly engaged in self-induced vomiting or the misuse of laxatives, diuretics, or enemas.

---

Reprinted with permission from the *Diagnostic and Statistical Manual of Mental Disorders Fourth Edition, Text Revision.* Copyright 2000 American Psychiatric Association.

TABLE 18.3

Selected World Wide Web Sites Related to Eating Disorders

---

Anorexia—Information and Guidance for Patients, Family, and Friends - http://users.neca.com/cwildes/index.htm

Eating Disorders Shared Awareness - http://www.mirror-mirror.org/eatdis.htm

American Dietetic Association - http://www.eatright.org/aanorexiainter.html

American Anorexia Bulimia Association - http://www.aabainc.org

National Eating Disorders Organization (NEDO) - http://www.kidsource.com/nedo/index.html

Nidus Information System - http://noah.cuny.edu/wellconn/eatdisorders.html

Internet Mental Health - http://www.mentalhealth.com/dis/p20-et01.html

Mental Health Resources - http://www.mentalhealth.com/dis/p20-et02.html

---

chapter there is an emphasis on the importance of understanding the multidimensional nature of eating disorders. A developmental perspective explores how these conditions emerge, considering sociocultural, biogenetic, personality, family, emotional, cognitive, and behavioral domains. With the increased scope and significance of eating disorders, educational professionals are in a critical position to facilitate the academic achievement and healthy development of individuals who are suffering with anorexia or bulimia. This chapter provides professionals with essential information that is needed to be the most effective advocates and collaborators for students and families facing the challenges of eating disorders.

## Understanding the Etiology of Eating Disorders

Biological models of eating disorders look at the genetic predisposition to the diseases (e.g., twin studies; Brooks-Gunn & Reiter, 1990; Ericsson, Poston, & Foreyt, 1996; Sullivan, Bulik, & Kendler, 1998; Walters & Kendler, 1995; Young, 1991). Psychological models of anorexia have focused on the importance of family interactions (e.g., individuation–separation difficulties) and the patient's view of self (e.g., intrapsychic paranoia) as important factors (Altman & Lock, 1997). Psychological theories of bulimia point to binge eating as a coping mechanism for those suffering from mood disorders (Stice & Agras, 1998). Additionally, the association between dieting and binge eating has been emphasized (Lowe, Gleaves, & Murphy-Eberenz, 1998; Walsh & Devlin, 1998). In recent years, researchers and practitioners have begun to view the etiology of anorexia and bulimia as multifactorial rather than resulting from a single cause (Szmukler, Dare, & Treasure, 1995; Wren & Lask, 1993). Accordingly, etiology is being viewed in terms of the interactions between various risk factors, and there is a growing consensus that biological vulnerability, psychological predisposition, family situation, and social climate all contribute to the risk of developing an eating disorder (Stoylen & Laberg, 1990).

## The Developmental Perspective

The developmental perspective provides a conceptual framework for understanding disordered behavior in relation to the course of normal development. This framework also considers multiple factors that contribute to adaptive success as well as the origins and developmental course of disordered behavior (Smolak, Levine, & Striefel-Moore, 1996; Wicks-Nelson & Israel, 1997). With regard to eating disorders, the developmental perspective considers how these conditions arise out of sociocultural, biogenetic, personality, family, and behavioral domains. This paradigm also emphasizes the interaction between these different factors (Attie & Brooks-Gunn, 1995).

Researchers have not reached a consensus about which single factor is most responsible for eating disorders. Thus, in recent years, professionals in the field have increasingly looked to a developmental perspective for understanding the etiology of eating disorders. In addition, developmental psychopathology provides a means for conceptualizing how pathways of risk may lead to anorexia as opposed to other pathology or how pathways of resilience may prevent the onset of this illness.

Experts are now beginning to explore the incorporation of developmental ideas into their treatment plans (e.g., multidimensional and family therapies). To better understand these ideas, treatments should be tailored to developmental stage, something that has been done infrequently to date. However, educators have a wealth of knowledge to lend to this perspective. By becoming more familiar with the issues surrounding eating disorders, professionals working in the schools can provide integral developmental information to teachers, staff, students, and families. The following information provides educational professionals with an overview of the etiological factors related to eating disorders.

## Sociocultural

Modell and Goodman (1990) provided a compelling historical perspective on adolescent development and eating disorders from the early 19th century through the 1990s. One common thread tying this developmental perspective through time is the powerful influence of society on disordered eating.

Stoylen and Laberg (1990) also provided a historical introduction to eating disorders, from a sociocultural perspective. The authors point out that none of the common theories of etiology are complete on their own and that the question is not which of these factors is the cause but rather which of these factors is primary. According to this article, the current social norms that emphasize unrealistic slimness have more to do with the etiology of eating disorders than any other single factor. Thus, this article approaches etiological issues from a developmental, multifactorial perspective.

## Biological

Brooks-Gunn and Reiter (1990) provided a thorough review of the role of the pubertal process in development and the association with eating disorders. Specific focus is given to how hormonal changes influence growth. Specifically, the authors review how levels of hormonal secretions are suppressed when women experience a considerable loss of weight. This results in lack of menstrual cycles in which fertility is impaired.

Young (1991) examined how levels of estrogen contribute to anorexic symptoms. Young discusses evidence that estrogen contributes to the symptoms seen in anorexia and suggests that estrogen may underlie sex differences in the incidence rate. The author posits that an abnormal response to estrogen may be implicated in the manifestation of anorexia and suggests that progesterone, which blocks estrogen, may be a promising treatment in the future. Biological factors associated with eating disorders warrant further investigation.

### Psychological

Altman and Lock (1997) reviewed psychological and behavioral factors associated with eating disorders. Specifically, they discuss how children's feeding difficulties at very young ages are associated with later eating problems. The authors also discuss how certain personality traits, such as being compliant, perfectionistic, goal oriented, shy, and obsessive, can sometimes be associated with patients with anorexia. Additionally, children who are depressed and who have been exposed to a greater number of stressful life events than is normal are also more likely to develop eating disorders. Finally, insecure attachment styles are also discussed as recognized characteristics in individuals with eating disorders.

### General

Keel, Fulkerson, and Leon (1997) completed an empirical study of the precursors of eating disorders, including both males and females in the sample. The researchers assessed fifth- and sixth-grade boys and girls in terms of depression, body image, self-esteem, eating behaviors and attitudes, weight, height, and pubertal development over 2 years. For girls, Year 1 body mass index and pubertal development predicted Year 2 disordered eating, whereas for boys, Year 2 disordered eating was predicted by poor body image in Year 1. This is a carefully conducted study that provides a thorough background of the problem as well as a discussion of the implications of the findings.

Wren and Lask (1993) emphasized the importance of viewing eating disorders as multifactored syndromes and of understanding how various factors interact and develop over time to produce the eating disorder. This is an excellent overview of etiology that discusses biological factors, psychodynamic models, adverse sexual experiences, family models, and cultural explanations. The authors conclude with a discussion of how these theories of etiology may be integrated.

In examining the research and literature on the etiology of eating disorders, it appears that psychological, sociocultural, and biological theories all play some role in contributing to the onset of this condition and that no single factor alone can explain the development of this disorder. Accordingly, it is critical that future research and literature acknowledges and explores multifactorial explanations for the onset of anorexia and bulimia. Utilizing an etiological model, it is recommended that prevention efforts be directed toward female and male young adolescents with an orientation toward increasing factors which attenuate risk status while reducing elements that place teens in jeopardy.

## PREVENTION

Just as educational professionals are in unique positions to help students with eating disorders, they are also crucial in its prevention. Concern regarding the significant health consequences and multidimensional etiology of eating disorders is obvious and well documented (Rosenvinge & Borresen, 1999). Given the increasing prevalence and severity of eating disorders, there has been growing interest in developing school-based prevention programs in this area (Rosenvinge & Borresen, 1999; Stewart, 1998). Three subcategories exist within the realm of prevention programming: (a) primary prevention—aimed at preventing the disorder from developing in the general populations without an identified risk status; (b) secondary prevention—early identification and selective programming targeted to meet the needs of individuals or subgroups who are at significantly higher risk than the general population; and (c) tertiary prevention—specific procedures intended for high-risk persons who have minimal but, nonetheless, detectable symptoms of the disorder (Phelps, Sapia, Nathanson, & Nelson, 2000; Striegel-Moore & Steiner-Adair, 1998).

There have been many attempts at the prevention of eating disorders; however, little success has been achieved (O'Dea & Abraham, 2000; Rosenvinge & Borresen, 1999). Researchers have indicated that most prevention programs are targeting youth too late, as behaviors and beliefs are already ingrained in adolescents and these behaviors and beliefs become extremely difficult to change (Smolak et al., 1996). By identifying children at risk of developing eating disorders at a younger age, primary prevention programs may be more successful in reducing the likelihood of developing of an eating disorder (Lask & Bryant-Waugh, 1992; Phelps et al., 2000). Although some claim that prevention programs are effective, others argue they are not effective.

Results of several studies show that primary prevention programs are effective in that they eliminate or decrease the incidence of later problems (Phelps, Johnston, & Augustyniak, 1999; Stewart, 1998). Specifically, schools have been a popular arena for primary prevention work because they provide access to the majority of children and adolescents effected by this disorder (O'Dea & Abraham, 2000; Rosenvinge & Borresen, 1999). Because the myriad of psychological, physical, and social effects of eating disorders can interfere with students' learning, educational professionals have a vested interest in its prevention (Stipke, de la Sota, & Weishaupt, 1999). Research suggests that over the past 10 years, school-based prevention programs have converged around activities like lecturing about health consequences of eating disorder symptoms, identifying and coping with pressures towards thinness, improving nutritional habits, and lecturing about physical and psychological pubertal changes (Piran, 1999). In general, a didactic, general population strategy has been the emphasis of prevention activities in the schools (O'Dea & Abraham, 2000).

Rosenvinge and Borresen (1999) asserted that the majority of primary prevention programs that fail to effect change suffer from a reliance on the wrong model. They note that prevention programs have a greater chance of being successful if they focus on changing both individuals and society, thereby operating from a biopsychosocial and health promotion model of causation rather than a medical or disease prevention one. The traditional medical model assumes that disease can be explained entirely by biological variables with a focus on individual characteristics, whereas the broader biopsychosocial perspective asserts that biological, psychological, social, and cultural factors may all be important contributors to illness. This health promotion paradigm focuses on protective factors (e.g., self esteem, personal competence, family support) for understanding and preventing eating disorders.

Research indicates a number of general suggestions that are important to consider in conducting eating disorder prevention programs in the schools. First, educational professionals need to recognize that eating disorders are serious and complex problems. Their expression, causes, and treatments typically have physical, personal, and social (i.e., familial) dimensions. Consequently, one should avoid thinking of them in simplistic terms like "anorexia is just a plea for attention" or "bulimia is just an addiction to food." With these complexities in mind, it is also critical to recognize that programs should be tailored to the specific needs of the youth in a particular school (Shisslak, Crago, Estes, & Gray, 1996; Striegel-Moore & Steiner-Adair, 1998).

Second, prevention programs should not be considered "just a women's problem" or "something for the girls." Males who are preoccupied with shape and weight may also develop disordered eating patterns as well as dangerous shape control practices such as steroid use. Moreover, both males and females should understand that objectification and other forms of mistreatment of women by men contribute directly to two underlying features of an eating disorder: obsession with appearance and shame about one's body (Keel et al., 1997).

Third, prevention efforts will fail, or worse, inadvertently encourage disordered eating, if they concentrate solely on warning parents and children about the signs, symptoms, and dangers of eating disorders. For instance, distribution of information delineating signs and symptoms of eating disorders may provide youth with innovative ideas to alter their physical appearance (e.g., purging or using diet pills to lose weight), thus resulting in an increase in disordered eating. Therefore, any attempt to prevent eating disorders must also address: (a) our cultural obsession with slenderness as a physical, psychological, and moral issue; (b) the distorted meaning of both femininity and masculinity in today's society; and (c) the development of people's self-esteem and self-respect (Rosenvinge & Borresen, 1999).

Finally, if at all possible, prevention programs for schools should be coordinated with opportunities for individuals to speak confidentially with a trained professional and, where appropriate, to receive referrals to sources of competent, specialized care (O'Dea & Abraham, 2000; Phelps et al., 1999; Phelps et al., 2000).

Additional factors outlined in the research as central to the success of school-based primary prevention programs include: identifying variables that are predictive of body dissatisfaction as this construct is the single strongest predictor of eating disorder symptomatology; and increasing self-esteem, and feelings of personal competence (Phelps et al., 1999; Phelps et al., 2000). However, to gain long-term benefits from these school-based programs, research suggests that this information must be reinforced by teachers and family (O'Dea & Abraham, 2000). These individuals are an important influence on the generalization of knowledge and in sustaining the effects.

Although it is imperative to recognize these basic factors in the implementation of primary prevention programs, Shisslak et al. (1996) asserted that most of these programs have not emphasized the importance of developmental factors in relation to eating disorders. These authors review prevention strategies specific to each developmental period. For prepubertal children, strategies include: educating parents about children's eating patterns and how their own eating can affect their children; teaching day-care workers to detect feeding problems; alerting parents and teacher to the possibility that a child may develop eating problems in response to family conflict; and teaching children healthy eating and exercise habits, helping them to accept a wide range of body shapes, and encouraging them to develop interests that will lead to personal fulfillment not based on appearance.

Shisslak and colleagues (1996) also discussed specific prevention strategies for early, middle, and late adolescents. For early adolescents, these authors suggest six strategies: disseminating information regarding the changes that occur with puberty; educating parents and their children about normal adolescent development; incorporating peer groups into all efforts; providing behavioral training in assertiveness and relaxation to facilitate healthy emotional regulation; teaching problem solving and time management skills to cope with academic and social pressures; and educating youth about realistic body weights.

For middle adolescents, four strategies are noted: teaching cognitive–behavioral techniques for dealing with emotions; discussing and questioning personal values, self-worth, and achievement; providing a forum for the discussion of peer and family conflicts; and building on factual information regarding nutrition and weight to explore the abstract issues of body image.

Prevention strategies for late adolescents include three components: preparing youth for another series of transitions (e.g., to college or to the workforce); recognizing society's values and expectations for men and women and exploring their own conceptualization of these issues; and continuing to questions the associations between society's ideal body image, happiness, self-esteem, and success.

## Prevention in Student Athletes

There are conflicting models of how athletic participation might be related to eating problems among girls and women (Smolak, Murnen, & Ruble, 2000). On the one hand, athletic participation might actually serve to protect against the development of eating problems. Specifically, being an athlete might give a girl a sense of pride that is separate from appearance and may help her to invest in what her body can do rather than in how it looks (Butcher, 1989). In contrast, it has been shown that early and frequent exercise induces eating problems (Sundgot-Borgen, 1994). Understanding research related to this dispute is important. Since Title IX was instituted in 1972, the rate of female participation in both high school and college sports has skyrocketed (Smolak et al., 2000). Helping to ensure that such participation is a positive and healthy experience is imperative.

Smolak et al. (2000) analyzed data from 34 studies and concluded that athletes are slightly more at risk for eating problems than nonathletes. This was especially true of dancers. Significant effects did not emerge for gymnasts. Elite athletes (i.e., those competing at a national, international, or professional level), especially those in sports emphasizing thinness (e.g., ballet, cheerleading), were at increased risk. Nonelite athletes, especially in high school, had reduced risk of eating problems compared to controls. Body dissatisfaction was lower in athletes than nonathletes. Therefore, these authors suggest that there appear to be circumstances under which sports participation by women constitutes a risk factor for certain elements of eating problems. In other situations, athletic participation may be protective against eating problems.

Shisslak and colleagues (1996) offered prevention strategies for athletes including: presenting information regarding high-risk behaviors and the contagion effect of dieting and binge eating; desensitizing individuals to personal comments about body size; and providing information about emotional health and stress management. In addition, consultation and training for coaches and other professionals involved in the lives of athletes is also essential in these efforts.

In sum, it is important to recognize both the general and specific developmental factors in the creation of primary prevention programs for eating disorders. Research suggests that educational professionals may play an important role in ensuring the success of these programs. By focusing on resiliency-based, health promotion models of prevention and incorporating the strategies listed earlier, primary prevention efforts targeting individuals at risk of developing eating disorders may facilitate the healthy development and educational success of many students.

## ASSESSMENT

Assessing eating disorders remains a complex area of clinical activity because they present with a range of disturbances in multiple domains. Anorexia and bulimia can be expressed in many dimensions, such as cultural, social, behavioral, familial, and physical. Therefore, diagnostic assessment materials must address each of these levels. During the typical assessment process, individuals are asked to complete a series of questionnaires. Selecting appropriate instruments facilitates treatment recommendations, and creates a database that allows for the evaluation of treatment effectiveness across time. School professionals can be of particular help in assessing eating disorders. Structured and semistructured interviews, clinical and self-reports, and physiological measures are all utilized in this process.

### Interviews

Numerous semistructured interviews for eating disorders have been described in the research literature: Eating Disorder Examination (EDE), Interview for Diagnosis of Eating Disorders (IDED), the Schedule for Affective Disorders and Schizophrenia for School-Age Children-Present and Lifetime version (K–SADS–PL), and Clinical Eating Disorder Rating Instrument (CEDRI).

Bryant-Waugh, Cooper, Taylor, and Lask (1996) reported the results of a recent study using a slightly modified EDE. The two main modifications to the EDE were: the inclusion of a sort task to assess overvalued ideas about weight and shape, and the reformulation of certain items to assess intent rather than actual behavior. Results indicate that it may be a useful assessment tool for not only adolescents and adults, but also for children (aged

7–14 years). However, only 16 subjects were utilized in this study, thus, results should be interpreted with caution.

Fichter, Herpertz, Quadflieg, and Herpertz-Dahlmann (1998) provided a review of the recently revised Structured Interview for Anorexic and Bulimic Disorders (SIAB–EX) including a discussion of the validity of the SIAB–EX. Specifically, a five-factor solution was shown to have good internal consistency and interrater reliability. Additionally, DSM–IV diagnoses for eating disorders can be derived directly or by using a computer algorithm from the SIAB-EX.

Kauffman, Birmaher, Brent, and Rao (1997) presented reliability and validity data regarding a general interview for psychiatric diagnosis, the Schedule for Affective Disorders and Schizophrenia for School-Age Children-Present and Lifetime version (K–SADS–PL). This measure includes sections for the assessment of eating disorders and all other DSM–IV childhood diagnoses and may therefore be especially useful if comorbidity is a concern. It has been found to have adequate reliability and validity.

Kutlesic and colleagues (1998) tested the most recent version of the IDED (IDED–IV) for the purpose of differential diagnosis of eating disorders. Evidence for internal consistency was found for symptom ratings relevant to bulimia nervosa, anorexia nervosa, and binge eating disorder. Additionally, support was found for the content, concurrent and discriminant validity of the IDED-IV. Interrater reliability for differential diagnosis of eating disorders was also high. Therefore, it can be concluded that the IDED–IV yields sufficiently valid and reliable data.

Palmer, Robertson, Cain, and Black (1996) outlined the many uses of the Clinical Eating Disorders Rating Instrument (CEDRI) in assessing many of the behaviors associated with clinical eating disorders. A recent study confirmed the pattern of results that provides evidence for the validity and reliability of this instrument. Specifically, the ability of the CEDRI to discriminate between a weight concerned comparison group and a sample of subjects with clinical eating disorders could be seen as a particularly exacting test of validity.

## Clinical and Self-Report Assessments

An assortment of clinical and self-report measures related to eating disorders are outlined in the literature. What follows is a summary of the most highly utilized assessments.

Garner, Olmsted, Bohr, and Garfinkel (1982) described the Eating Attitudes Test (EAT) which is commonly used as a measure of attitudes regarding eating and weight. A factor analysis conducted with the EAT identified three factors including: Dieting, Bulimia and Food Preoccupation, and Oral Control. The EAT has been found to yield reliable and valid data.

Keel et al. (1997) provided information on the Self-Image Questionnaire for Young Adolescents (SIQYA), which asks adolescents to rate how much they like and are comfortable with their bodies. This article suggests that the psychometric properties of this measure are strong.

Kutlesic and colleagues (1998) also reported information about the Eating Disorders Inventory–2 (EDI–2). The authors suggest that it has been found to yield data with moderate-to-high levels of internal consistency, test–retest reliability, and convergent and discriminant validity. The entire EDI–2 has 11 subscales that measure cognitive and behavioral dimensions of both anorexia and bulimia nervosa.

Sunday, Halmi, and Einhorn (1995) described the Yale–Brown–Cornell Eating Disorder Scale (YBC–EDS) which can be used to assess the preoccupation with rituals associated with eating disorders. This article suggests that results confirm the reliability and validity of the YBC–EDS. Additionally, the authors state that this measure characterizes and quantifies preoccupations and rituals associated with eating disorders. It is useful both for research and clinical purposes.

Williamson, Davis, Bennerr, and Goreczny (1989) provided an overview of the Body Image Assessment procedure (BIA) which may be used to examine body image disturbances. The BIA measures perceived current body size, preferred body size, and the discrepancy between these two. Evidence for adequate test–retest reliability, and construct validity has been reported in this article.

Thelan, Farmer, Wonderlich, and Smith (1991) described the development of the revised Bulimia Test (BULIT–R). The BULIT–R is based on DSM–III–R criteria for bulimia, but has been shown to be accurate in its diagnoses even when using DSM–IV criteria (Hohlstein, Smith, & Atlas, 1998). The test itself is a 32-item, Likert-type scale that classifies individuals not only as bulimic or nonbulimic, but also provides information as to the degree of their symptomatology. The authors present high sensitivity and specificity scores for the BULIT–R.

Mintz, O'Halloran, Mulholland, and Schneider (1997) described the development of the Q–EDD. This is a very promising new eating disorder assessment tool that claims to have improved on other existing questionnaires. One of its greatest benefits is its recent development, a fact that allows it to make use of the current DSM–IV diagnostic criteria as well as the current understanding of the disorder. The Q–EDD has the ability to diagnose an individual into numerous categories, the most broad being eating disordered or non-eating-disordered. Available reliability and validity data support the use of the Q–EDD. However, due to its recent development, there has not been a great deal of research that has conclusively demonstrated its validity.

### Physiological Measures

Casper (1998) suggested that physical exams should include weight and height measurements, body mass index, a record of menstrual cyclicity and regularity, and an endocrine profile. However, it should be noted that there are no biological measures with proven specificity for anorexia nervosa or bulimia nervosa.

Assessing eating disorders requires a multifactored approach. One must take the many cultural, societal, behavioral, familial, and biological factors into consideration. Interviews, clinical and self-reports, and physiological measures are all important in this process. Utilizing a developmental model is most useful in gaining a full picture of these various factors and how they interact. Ideally, an assessment should include a full physical exam, a general diagnostic interview, and a specific interview that goes into more detail regarding symptoms. It is crucial that this specific interview is based on the most recent changes in diagnostic criteria.

## TREATMENT

Individuals with eating disorders rarely seek treatment voluntarily. Most enter treatment under duress from alarmed relatives, friends, or school professionals who have cajoled them into the therapist's office. The few true volunteers are typically seeking relief from food preoccupation, depression, or anxiety rather than eating disorder symptoms. Often, the first job of the counselor is to help the patient overcome their resistance to change. The goals of treatment for anorexics and bulimics apply to the medical, nutritional, psychological, and familial aspects of their lives. Specifically, there must be adequate weight gain and return to physical health, a resumption of nutritionally balanced eating habits, resolution of distorted cognitions, body image problems, self-image and comorbid conditions, and a focus on individuation, family relationships, and parent–child conflict issues (Robin, Gilroy, & Dennis, 1998).

Considering the multiple goals, a variety of different therapies have been proposed. However, research has not determined one treatment of choice for eating disorders. Additionally, no well-controlled psychopharmacological studies of patients with eating disorders have been performed (Gillberg & Rastam, 1998). Individual psychotherapy, group therapy, family therapy, cognitive behavioral therapy, and multidimensional approaches have all been acknowledged as acceptable forms of treatment. However, there is no conclusive research that specifies the efficacy rates of these various forms of therapy.

### Individual Psychotherapy

Robin and colleagues (1998) reviewed the treatment of eating disorders in children and adolescents. The authors state that long-term psychodynamic therapies are probably the most frequently utilized outpatient treatment for anorexia nervosa in the United States. They point to evidence that suggests an ego-oriented, self psychology approach has proven clinically useful. This approach has been subjected to rigorous evaluation in a randomly assigned, controlled comparison to Behavioral Family Systems Therapy. Additionally, individual therapy was found to be superior to family therapy on weight gain (but not psychosexual functioning or nutritional status) for those who became anorexic at age 19 or later.

Crisp (1997) provided a detailed rationale for seeing anorexia as a "flight from growth." He then offers specific and detailed suggestions for working with patients, including psychotherapy and dietary advice. Although Crisp focuses on individual therapy, he also provides some information about family and group therapies.

Eisler and colleagues (1997) conducted a 5-year follow-up study on anorexics that participated in a previous trial of family and individual therapy. Results suggest that individual supportive therapy works best for patients with late-onset anorexia nervosa as compared to early onset. Although it was possible to detect long-term benefits of individual psychotherapy, some of these improvements can be attributed to the natural outcome of the illness.

### Family Therapy

Eisler and colleagues (1997) also suggested that family therapy is most effective with a particular group of individuals with anorexia nervosa: those with early onset and short history. Sargent, Liebman, and Silver (1985) described the rationale for family therapy for anorexics. The authors provide specific treatment steps and addresses special problems that might arise (e.g., lack of progress, single parent families). This chapter is part of a classic text on anorexia and is an important resource even though it is somewhat dated.

Robin et al. (1998) reported that Dare and Szmukler's (1991) approach to family therapy for adolescents with anorexia nervosa emphasizes the family as a resource that has to be mobilized to help the starving youngster. The therapist refrains from expressing views about the etiology of the condition, but suggests that the family is presented with a problem of unknown origin which is not their fault, but that will require all of their resources to overcome. When this therapy was compared to a supportive individual therapy, family therapy had a more favorable outcome for the early onset (before aged 18), short duration (less than 3 years) type of anorexia (similar to the results found in the Eisler et al. [1997] article). In general, their research supports the effectiveness of family-oriented treatments. The authors suggest a number of important issues to remember: use nonblaming terms, direct parents to take charge of their child's eating routines, maintain a structured behavioral weight gain program, after weight gain give gradual control of eating back to the child, and once the patient begins to gain weight, focus treatment on broader topics such as autonomy, parent–child conflicts and family interactions.

### Group Therapy

Garfinkel and Garner (1982) provided a thorough overview of the multidimensional aspects of anorexia nervosa. They suggest that group therapy be instituted when the starvation symptoms have begun to be reduced. Their research has found that assertive training groups are beneficial to patients because they allow them to display a more direct expression of appropriate affect in a controlled setting. They state that the purpose of these groups is to provide a setting in which patients may discuss their feelings connected with the disorder and how it has affected them, in a setting where they can be accepted and understood. Additionally, the group should provide support, models of coping, peer feedback, and education. The authors also note the benefits of group therapy for parents.

### Cognitive–Behavioral Therapy

Robin et al. (1998) stated that in the cognitive–behavioral approach to the treatment of anorexia nervosa (Garner, 1986), the therapist should focus on using cognitive restructuring to modify distorted beliefs and attitudes about the meaning of weight, shape, and appearance, which are believed to underlie dieting and fear of weight gain. The authors state that little empirical work has been done with cognitive–behavioral approaches to anorexia nervosa, and that none of this work has been done with children or adolescents. They report the results from a study that found no significant differences between cognitive–behavioral therapy, behavior therapy, or a no-treatment control group with patients presenting with anorexia. Given the perfectionistic characteristics of the majority of individuals with anorexia, the use of cognitive–behavioral treatment would appear to have promise with this population. However, issues have been raised about the minimum age and level of cognitive development necessary for implementing this type of treatment.

Wilfley and Cohen (1997) described a typical example of cognitive behavioral treatment for bulimia nervosa. They divide treatment into three phases. The first phase consists of behavioral interventions designed to interrupt the bingeing–purging cycle. Next, cognitive strategies are used to challenge the disordered thought patterns that influence the disordered eating. Distorted body image is an example of something that might be targeted in this stage. Treatment concludes with relapse prevention techniques that help ensure the patient will not resume his or her old thoughts and behaviors. Cognitive behavioral therapy is generally considered the therapeutic treatment of choice for bulimia nervosa.

Schmidt (1998) outlined that even though cognitive–behavioral therapy is the gold standard treatment for bulimia nervosa, the evidence supporting its usefulness with anorexic patients is much more mixed. The authors suggest that basic cognitive–behavior therapy may need to be supplemented with other measures to achieve better outcomes for individuals with anorexia.

Johnson, Tsoh, and Varnado (1996) reviewed the efficacy of pharmacological and psychological interventions with eating disorders. This article provides valuable information about and a comparison of two types of treatment: medication versus cognitive–behavioral. For example, the authors discuss different types of medication and give an overview of the different components of cognitive behavior therapy. These authors conclude that medications are often helpful in the management of the psychopathology associated with anorexia nervosa; however, no pharmacological compound has been shown to reliably assist weight gain or alter other core features of eating disorders. Antidepressants were found to reduce bingeing and purging in bulimia nervosa and binge eating disorder, although this action appeared to be independent of any antidepressant effect. Contingency management and other behavior therapy procedures were found to be effective in promoting weight gain in anorexics. The limited effectiveness of cognitive interventions for anorexia nervosa was postulated to be a result of the complex physical symptoms associated with low body weight. Additionally, cognitive–behavioral interventions also reduce bingeing and purging. Comparisons of cognitive–behavioral therapy and medication–pharmacological interventions indicate that psychotherapy alone is more effective than medication alone. Moreover, changes produced by cognitive–behavioral interventions endure longer than medication where higher relapse rates are common. Finally, most studies also revealed no advantage of medication over cognitive–behavioral therapy alone in the reduction of bulimic symptoms.

### Multidimensional Approach

Mantero, Giovanni, Raffaele, and Gaetano (1998) outlined the importance of utilizing an integrated treatment of anorexia. This effective treatment entails some guidelines for cooperation among specialists involved in the management of such patients. The authors outline the importance of utilizing a problem-solving approach in this type of treatment.

Shekter-Wolfson, Woodside, and Lackstrom (1997) provided a brief and comprehensive overview of both anorexia and bulimia. This article discusses issues related to etiology, assessment, and treatment options. The authors advocate a multidisciplinary, multidimensional approach to treating anorexia, including psychoeducation, medication, cognitive–behavior therapy, individual, and family therapy. This is a good resource in providing practitioners with different treatment options but does not provide enough detailed information with regard to specific treatment plans.

Golder and Birmingham (1994) focused not on a specific type of treatment but instead, on a set of primary treatment components (e.g., medical stabilization, establishment of therapeutic alliance, weight restoration). The authors allude to different types of treatment, such as cognitive behavioral, family, and psychodynamic therapies. Rather than endorsing one type of treatment, this chapter acknowledges the validity of multiple types of therapies and emphasizes the need to focus on key components of treatment.

Eating disorders can be seen as a process. There are continuous interactions between the individual and his or her external world, the symptoms and his/her attempts to deal with the symptoms, that result in an elaboration of the disorder in a variety of forms for each person. Because the development of eating disorders is influenced by these different factors for each individual, a multidimensional approach is recommended as the treatment of choice. This type of therapy allows the practitioners to tailor the treatment to the individual patient. In addition, the multidimensional approach recognizes that treatment must address biological, familial, sociocultural, and psychological components of the individual's recovery. Individuals with anorexia nervosa and bulimia nervosa may come to treatment at various stages in the course of their disorder. Some may require immediate medical attention whereas others may be in a condition to benefit more from insight-oriented therapy. Thus, depending on the individual (including age) and the stage of their disorder, the multidimensional treatment allows for a focus on whichever aspects are most salient at that time.

Optimal treatment within this multidimensional framework should include a clinical team of different professionals including school psychologists and other educational professionals. This allows the patient to receive specific interventions from individuals with the most training and knowledge of the issues at hand. It is in this type of environment where the patient and his or her family can be fully understood.

Because eating disorders, especially in its childhood-onset form, are known to be an extremely difficult disorder to treat, many different kinds of therapies should be considered. There are no controlled studies of any interventions for eating disorders in children, so treatment recommendations must be based on uncontrolled studies, clinical case reports, and extrapolation downward from controlled studies with adolescents and adults. A multidimensional approach offers the most flexibility and options for the practitioner or team of health care providers. Most importantly, it provides the most specific and personalized type of treatment to individuals and families suffering from an eating disorder.

## SUMMARY

Eating disorders have many deleterious, morbid, and even mortal consequences. More than three decades of research on anorexia and bulimia has clearly underscored its public health importance. However, the most basic questions in the field, those concerned with the problem's prevalence and incident, have not yet been unequivocally answered. With the increased significance and scope of eating disorders, professionals in the schools are in a pivotal position to better understand and assist youth who are suffering with anorexia or bulimia.

It is necessary to account for the normal development of many factors in multiple domains and their interaction within this developmental model. Considering the cumulative nature of development and acknowledging that early events impact subsequent adjustment, it is essential that efforts target prevention, early identification, and treatment for children and adolescents. The school environment is a critical, but often overlooked, domain to consider.

Thus, researchers and practitioners are encouraged to approach eating disorders and their treatment from a developmental and multidimensional perspective. Further research should include the critical perspective of educational professionals, and investigate the efficacy of integrated approaches as opposed to traditional treatments.

## ACKNOWLEDGMENT

Portions of this chapter were adapted from an article previously published in The California School Psychologist, Jimerson, S. R., & Pavelski, R. (2000). *The School Psychologists primer on anorexia nervosa: A review of research re-*

*garding epidemiology, etiology, assessment, and treatment, 5*, 65–77. Copyright 2000 California Association of School Psychologists.

## REFERENCES

Altman, T. M., & Lock, J. (1997). Eating disorders. In H. Steiner (Ed.), *Treating school-age children* (pp. 215–242). San Francisco, CA: Jossey-Bass.

American Psychiatric Association. (2000). *Diagnostic and statistical manual of mental disorder, Fourth edition, Text revision*. Washington, DC: Author.

Attie, I., & Brooks-Gunn, J. (1995). The development of eating regulation across the life span. In D. Cicchetti & D. Cohen (Eds.), *Developmental psychopathology—Vol. 2: Risk, disorder, and adaptation* (pp. 332–368). New York: Wiley.

Brooks-Gunn, J., & Reiter, E. O. (1990). The role of pubertal processes. In S. S. Feldman & G. R. Elliott (Eds.), *At the threshold: The developing adolescent* (pp. 16–53). Cambridge, MA: Harvard University Press.

Bryant-Waugh, R., & Lask, B. (1995). Annotation: Eating disorders in children. *Journal of Child Psychology and Psychiatry, 36*, 431–437.

Bryant-Waugh, R. J., Cooper, P. J., Taylor, C. L., & Lask, B. D. (1996). The use of the Eating Disorder Examination with children: A pilot study. *International Journal of Eating Disorders, 19*(4), 391–397.

Butcher, J. (1989). Adolescent girls' sex role development: Relationship with sports participation, self-esteem, and age at menarche. *Sex Roles, 20*, 575–593.

Casper, R. C. (1998). Recognizing eating disorders in women. *Psychopharmacology Bulletin, 34*, 267–269.

Crisp, A. H. (1997). Anorexia nervosa as flight from growth: Assessment and treatment based on the model. In D. M. Garner & P. E. Garfinkel (Eds.), *Handbook of treatment for eating disorders* (pp. 248–277). New York: Guilford Press.

Dare, C., & Szmukler, G. (1991). Family therapy of early-onset, short-history anorexia nervosa. In D. B. Woodside & L. Shekter-Wolfson (Eds.), *Family approaches in treatment of eating disorders* (pp. 23–47). Washington, DC: American Psychological Association.

Eisler, I., Dare, C., Russell, G. F., Szmukler, G., Grange, D., & Dodge, E. (1997). Family and individual therapy in anorexia nervosa. A 5-year follow-up. *Archives of General Psychiatry, 54*, 1025–1030.

Ericsson, M., Poston, W. S. C., & Foreyt, J. P. (1996). Common biological pathways in eating disorders and obesity. *Addictive Behaviors, 21*(6), 733–743.

Fichter, M. M., Herpertz, S., Quadflieg, N., & Herpertz-Dahlmann, B. (1998). Structured interview for anorexic and bulimic disorders for DSM-IV and ICD-10: Updated (3rd) revision. *International Journal of Eating Disorders, 24*(3), 227–249.

Garfinkel, P. E., & Garner, D. M. (1982). *Anorexia nervosa: A multidimensional perspective*. New York: Brunner/Mazel.

Garner, D. M. (1986). Cognitive therapy for anorexia nervosa. In K. D. Brownell & J. P. Foreyt (Eds.), *Handbook of eating disorders: Physiology, psychology, and treatment of obesity, anorexia, and bulimia* (pp. 301–327). New York: Basic Books.

Garner, D. M., Olmsted, M. P., Bohr, Y., & Garfinkel, P. E. (1982). The Eating Attitudes Test: Psychometric features and clinical correlates. *Psychological Medicine, 12*(4), 871–878.

Gillberg, C., & Rastam, M. (1998). Do drugs have a place in the treatment of eating disorders in adolescence? *International Journal of Psychiatry in Clinical Practice, 2*, 79–82.

Golder, E. M., & Birmingham, C. L. (1994). Anorexia nervosa: Methods of treatment. In L. Alexander-Mott & D. B. Lumsden (Eds.), *Understanding eating disorders: Anorexia nervosa, bulimia nervosa, and obesity* (pp. 135–157). Washington, DC: Taylor & Francis.

Hohlstein, L. A., Smith, G. T., & Atlas, J. G. (1998). An application of expectancy theory to eating disorders: Development and validation of measures of eating and dieting expectancies. *Psychological Assessment, 10*, 49–58.

Johnson, W. G., Tsoh, J. Y., & Varnado, P. J. (1996). Eating disorders: Efficacy of pharmacological and psychological interventions. *Clinical Psychology Review, 16*(6), 457–478.

Kauffman, J., Birmaher, B., Brent, D., & Rao, U. (1997). Schedule for Affective Disorders and Schizophrenia for School-Age Children-Present and Lifetime version (K-SADS-PL): Initial reliability and validity data. *Journal of the American Academy of Child & Adolescent Psychiatry, 36*(7), 980–988.

Keel, P. K., Fulkerson, J. A., & Leon, G. R. (1997). Disordered eating precursors in pre- and early adolescent girls and boys. *Journal of Youth and Adolescence, 26*(2), 203–216.

Kutlesic, V., Williamson, D. A., Gleaves, D. H., Barbin, J. M., & Murphy-Eberenz, K. P. (1998). The Interview for the Diagnosis of Eating Disorders-IV: Application to DSM-IV diagnostic criteria. *Psychological Assessment, 10*(1), 41–48.

Lask, B., & Bryant-Waugh, R. (1992). Early-onset Anorexia Nervosa and related eating disorders. *Journal of Child Psychology and Psychiatry, 33*(1), 281–300.

Lowe, M. R., Gleaves, D. H., & Murphy-Eberenz, K. P. (1998). On the relation of dieting and bingeing in bulimia nervosa. *Journal of Abnormal Psychology, 107*, 263–271.

Lucas, A. R., Beard, C. M., O'Fallon, W. M., & Kurland, L. T. (1991). 50-year trends in the incidence of anorexia nervosa in Rochester, MN: A population-based study. *American Journal of Psychiatry, 148*(7), 917–922.

Mantero, M., Giovanni, R., Raffaele, P., & Gaetano, P. (1998). Integrated treatment for eating disorders. In P. Bria & A. Ciocca (Eds.), *Psychotherapeutic issues on eating disorders: Models, methods, and results* (pp. 162–184). New York: Plenum.

Mintz, L. B., O'Halloran, M. S., Mulholland, A. M., & Schneider, P. A. (1997). Questionnaire for Eating Disorder Diagnosis: Reliability and validity of operationalizing DSM-IV criteria into a self-report format. *Journal of Counseling Psychology, 44*, 63–79.

Modell, J., & Goodman, M. (1990). Historical perspectives. In S. S. Feldman & G. R. Elliott (Eds.), *At the threshold: The developing adolescent* (pp. 93–122). Cambridge, MA: Harvard University Press.

O'Dea, J. A., & Abraham, S. (2000). Improving the body image, eating attitudes, and behaviors of young male and female adolescents: A new educational approach that focuses on self-esteem. *International Journal of Eating Disorders, 28*(1), 43–57.

Palmer, R., Robertson, D., Cain, M., & Black, S. (1996). The clinical eating disorders rating instrument (CEDRI): A validation study. *European Eating Disorders Review, 4*(3), 149–156.

Phelps, L., & Bajorek, E. (1991). Eating disorders of the adolescent: Current issues in etiology, assessment, and treatment. *School Psychology Review, 20*(1), 9–22.

Phelps, L., Johnston, L. S., & Augustyniak, K. (1999). Prevention of eating disorders: Identification of predictor variables. *Eating Disorders: The Journal of Treatment & Prevention, 7*(2), 99–108.

Phelps, L., Sapia, J., Nathanson, D., & Nelson, L. (2000). An empirically supported eating disorder prevention program. *Psychology in the Schools, 37*(5), 443–452.

Piran, N. (1999). Eating disorders: A trial of prevention in a high risk school setting. *Journal of Primary Prevention, 20*(1), 75–90.

Robin, A. L., Gilroy, M., & Dennis, A. B. (1998). Treatment of eating disorders in children and adolescents. *Clinical Psychology Review, 18*(4), 421–446.

Rosenvinge, J. H., & Borresen, R. (1999). Preventing eating disorders—Time to change programmes or paradigms? Current update and further recommendations. *European Eating Disorders Reviews, 7*(1), 5–16.

Sargent, J., Liebman, R., & Silver, M. (1985). Family therapy for anorexia nervosa. In D. M. Garner & P. E. Garfinkel (Eds.), *Handbook of psychotherapy for anorexia nervosa and bulimia* (pp. 257–279). New York: Guilford Press.

Schmidt, U. (1998). Cognitive-behaviour therapy for children and families. In P. J. Graham (Ed.), *Eating disorders and obesity* (pp. 292–304). New York: Cambridge University Press.

Shekter-Wolfson, L. F., Woodside, D. B., & Lackstrom, J. (1997). Social work treatment of anorexia and bulimia: Guidelines for practice. *Research on Social Work Practice, 7*(1), 5–31.

Shisslak, C. M., Crago, M., Estes, L. S., & Gray, N. (1996). Content and method of developmentally appropriate prevention programs. In L. Smolak, M. P. Levine & R. Striegel-Moore (Eds.), *The developmental psychopathology of eating disorders: Implications for research, prevention, and treatment* (pp. 341–363). Mahwah, NJ: Lawrence Erlbaum Associates.

Smolak, L., Levine, M., & Striefel-Moore, R. (1996). *The Developmental psychopathology of eating disorders: Implications for research, prevention, and treatment.* Mahwah, NJ: Lawrence Erlbaum Associates.

Smolak, L., Murnen, S. K., Ruble, A. E. (2000). Female athletes and eating problems: A meta-analysis. *International Journal of Eating Disorders, 27*(4), 371–380.

Steiner, H., & Lock, L. (1998). Anorexia nervosa and bulimia nervosa in children and adolescents: A review of the past 10 years. *Journal of the American Academy of Child and Adolescent Psychiatry, 37*(4), 352–359.

Stewart, A. (1998). Experience with a school-based eating disorders prevention programme. In W. Vandereycken & G. Noordenbos (Eds.), *The prevention of eating disorders* (pp. 99–136). New York: New York University Press.

Stice, E., & Agras, W. S. (1998). Predicting onset and cessation of bulimic behaviors during adolescence: A longitudinal grouping analysis. *Behavior Therapy, 29*, 257–276.

Stipke, D., de la Sota, A., & Weishaupt, L. (1999). Life lessons: An embedded classroom approach to preventing high-risk behaviors among preadolescents. *Elementary School Journal, 99*(5), 433–451.

Stoylen, I. J., & Laberg, J. C. (1990). Anorexia nervosa and bulimia nervosa: Perspectives on etiology and cognitive behavior therapy. *Acta Psychiatrica Scandinavica, 82*(361), 52–58.

Striegel-Moore, R. H., & Steiner-Adair, C. (1998). Primary prevention of eating disorders: Further considerations from a feminist perspective. In W. Vandereycken & G. Noordenbos (Eds.), *The prevention of eating disorders* (pp. 1–22). New York: New York University Press.

Sullivan, P. F., Bulik, C. M., & Kendler, K. S. (1998). Genetic epidemiology of binging and vomiting. *British Journal of Psychiatry, 173*, 75–79.

Sunday, S. R., Halmi, K. A., & Einhorn, A. (1995). The Yale-Brown-Cornell Eating Disorder Scale: A new scale to assess eating disorders symptomatology. *International Journal of Eating Disorders, 18*(3), 237–245.

Sundgot-Borgen, J. (1994). Eating disorders in female athletes. *Sports Medicine, 17*, 176–188.

Szmukler, G., Dare, C., & Treasure, J. (1995). *Handbook of eating disorders: Theory, treatment and research.* London: Wiley.

Thelan, M. H., Farmer, J., Wonderlich, S., & Smith, M. (1991). A revision of the Bulimia Test: The BULIT-R. *Psychological Assessment, 3*, 119–124.

Walsh, B. T., & Devlin, M. J. (1998). Eating disorders: Progress and problems. *Science, 280*, 1387–1390.

Walters, E. E., & Kendler, K. S. (1995). Anorexia nervosa and anorexia-like syndromes in a population-based female twin sample. *American Journal of Psychiatry, 152*(1), 64–71.

Wicks-Nelson, R., & Israel, A. C. (1997). *Behavior disorders of childhood.* Upper Saddle River, NJ: Prentice-Hall.

Wifley, D. E., & Cohen, L. R. (1997). Psychological treatment of bulimia nervosa and binge eating disorder. *Psychopharmacology Bulletin, 33*, 437–454.

Williamson, D. A., Davis, D. J., Bennerr, S. M, & Goreczny, A. J. (1989). Development of a simple procedure for assessing body image disturbances. *Behavioral Assessment, 11*(4), 433–446.

Wren, B., & Lask, B. (1993). Etiology. In B. Lask, & R. Bryant-Waugh, (Eds.), *Childhood onset anorexia nervosa and related eating disorders* (pp. 69–89). Hillsdale, NJ: Lawrence Erlbaum Associates.

Young, J. K. (1991). Estrogen and the etiology of anorexia nervosa. *Neuroscience & Biobehavioral Reviews, 15*(3), 327–331.

# Author Index

Q



R

S

T

# Subject Index

R



S